13.99 ✓

The Longman Companion to

The Tudor Age

Longman Companions to History
General Editors: Chris Cook and John Stevenson

THE LONGMAN COMPANION TO THE TUDOR AGE
Rosemary O'Day

Now available

THE LONGMAN COMPANION TO NAPOLEONIC EUROPE
Clive Emsley

THE LONGMAN COMPANION TO EUROPEAN NATIONALISM,
1789–1920
Raymond Pearson

THE LONGMAN COMPANION TO THE MIDDLE EAST SINCE 1914
Ritchie Ovendale

THE LONGMAN COMPANION TO BRITAIN IN THE ERA OF THE
TWO WORLD WARS, 1914–45
Andrew Thorpe

THE LONGMAN COMPANION TO NAZI GERMANY
Tim Kirk

THE LONGMAN COMPANION TO COLD WAR AND DETENTE,
1914–91
John W. Young

The Longman Companion to

The Tudor Age

Rosemary O'Day

Longman
London and New York

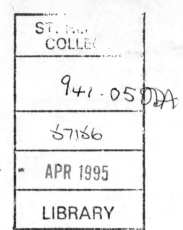
Longman Group Limited,
Longman House, Burnt Mill,
Harlow, Essex CM20 2JE, England
and Associated Companies throughout the world.

*Published in the United States of America
by Longman Publishing, New York*

First published 1995

ISBN 0 582 06725 1 CSD
ISBN 0 582 06724 3 PPR

British Library Cataloguing-in-Publication Data

A catalogue record for this book is
available from the British Library

Library of Congress Cataloging-in-Publication Data
O'Day, Rosemary.
  The Longman companion to the Tudor age / Rosemary O'Day.
    p. cm. – (Longman companions to history)
  Includes biographical references and index.
  ISBN 0–582–06725–1 (cased). – ISBN 0–582–06724–3 (paper)
    1. Great Britain–History–Tudors, 1485–1693–Handbooks, manuals,
  etc. 2. Great Britain–History–Tudors, 1485–1603–Chronology.
  I. Title. II. Series.
  DA315.O33 1995
  942.05–dc20   94–9970
                                                    CIP

Set by 15LL in 9½/11 pt New Baskerville
Produced by Longman Singapore Publishers (Pte) Ltd.
Printed in Singapore

Contents

Preface

You would think that it would be easy to establish the date of a battle, a birth or a book. Not a bit of it. My head is spinning after writing this book. I have been kept steadfast by the hope that students of the Tudor period will find this to be a true companion. I recall all too well the puzzlement engendered by historians' blithe references to 'transubstantiation', 'the court of Chancery', 'tillage', 'the Treaty of Blois', 'Francis Knollys' and the like. Although no book can pretend to be comprehensive, I hope that this companion will solve most such problems.

Needless to say, I have relied upon an enormous number of authorities for the information contained in this book. Accuracy is of great importance in a companion, but it is not always easy to achieve. Where there has been some doubt concerning precise dates or particular facts, I have had to use my discretion. The Royal Historical Society's *Handbook of British Chronology* (3rd edition, 1986) and *Handbook of Dates* (1961) have proved indispensable. When there has been a conflict about a particular date or name or title I have normally elected to use those cited in these works. I have found especially reliable A.G. Dickens' *The English Reformation* (1989), Patrick Collinson's *The Elizabethan Puritan Movement* (1967), G.E.R. Elton's *England Under The Tudors* (1962 edition) and *The Tudor Constitution* (1960), John Guy's *Tudor England* (1988) and *The Oxford Dictionary of the Christian Church* (1988) and have preferred the dates cited in these works where there is room for doubt.

I have tried to write a companion which contains the categories of information most needed by the student of the period. So, for example, the biographies section does not contain the complete life story of each individual included but rather the salient points of that life. A degree of cross referencing is provided in the text. Comprehensive cross referencing occurs in the index. Students who turn to this book to provide them with a pithy explanation of the various institutions of government will find especially useful the printer's highlighting of key points about the development of the institution. This is achieved in the following way:

- **Up to and including Wolsey, the Lord Chancellor or Keeper was normally a high ranking cleric. Mary I reverted to this policy with the appointment of Gardiner.**
- **Under Thomas Cromwell's Secretaryship (1533–40)**

I would like to thank, in particular, my son Daniel Englander for his assistance with the complicated index for this book and the rest of my family, David and Matthew, for their patience as I wrestled with countless works of reference. I am grateful to John Stevenson for asking me to write the Companion and to Longman for their expert and congenial co-operation in producing it.

Last, but certainly not least, I thank the people, some of them now dead, who have taught me Tudor history over the years – Professor S.T. Bindoff, Professor Claire Cross, Professor Patrick Collinson, Professor A.G. Dickens, Professor Jack Fisher, Professor Joel Hurstfield and Professor James Cargill Thompson – who made me want to understand more of that fascinating period.

Rosemary O'Day
The Open University
24 March 1994

I dedicate this book to my son
Daniel Englander
who,
at the time that it was written,
was a young student of Tudor history.

SECTION I

General Chronological Commentary: 1485–1603

This chronology is designed to provide students with a year-by-year, month-by-month chronicle of major events. I have not subdivided it because it is helpful to be able to see events in very diverse areas of life juxtaposed. There are more detailed subject chronologies later in the book: religious developments; the world of learning; and Ireland. Terms which are covered in Section XIV (Glossary) appear in bold.

1483

9 Apr. d. of Edward IV; protectorate of Richard III; sons of Edward IV declared illegitimate; 26 June: Richard accepts Crown by proclamation; 6 Jul.: coronation of Richard III; Edward V and Richard Duke of York confined to Tower; Queen Elizabeth Woodville in sanctuary with daughters at Westminster Abbey; execution of Hastings; Margaret Beaufort negotiates with Richard III and proposes m. between Elizabeth of York and Henry Tudor, July: failed attempt to reinstate Edward V; princes never seen again; autumn plot by Woodvilles and Margaret Beaufort to place Henry VII and Elizabeth of York on throne; Thomas Grey, Marquis of Dorset joined Henry VII in exile after failure of plot.

1484

Margaret Beaufort spared attainder by loyalty of Thomas Stanley to Richard; Thomas Stanley made Steward of Household and Constable of England; body of Henry VI moved to Windsor.

The Reign of Henry VII

1485

Battle of Bosworth. 22 Aug.: Henry VII proclaimed King by Sir William Stanley, 7 Sept. Henry VII entered London; remained with Queen Mother at Woking; grant of Coldharbour House to Margaret Beaufort; accommodation at Coldharbour provided for Elizabeth of York, bride-to-be of Henry VII (she was brought from imprisonment at Sheriff Hutton), Edward Stafford, child Duke of Buckingham, the Crown's most valuable wardship, and ten year-old Edward Plantagenet, Earl of Warwick, son of George, Duke of Clarence, the greatest threat to Henry's position; Margaret arranged m. between Thomas Grey (son of Marquis of Dorset) and Eleanor St John (one of her kin); Margaret takes custody of royal ward, Ralph, son of Earl of Westmorland; Princess

3

Cecily of York heiress-apparent of house of York, placed in Margaret's household; 30 Oct.: coronation of Henry by Cardinal Bourchier, Archbishop of Canterbury; 7 Nov.: parl. assembled; stressed bloodlink through Margaret Beaufort, the King's mother, between Henry VI and Henry VII by re-enacting 1397 statute declaring the Beauforts legitimate and omitting clause of 1407 which barred them from succession; but Henry VII justifies his succession by *verum Dei Judicum*; nobles who had suffered at hands of Richard III recompensed; Thomas Grey was restored as Marquis of Dorset and John de Vere as Earl of Oxford. Thomas Rotherham, Archbishop of York, Lord Chancellor, was replaced by John Alcock, Bishop of Worcester. Dr Richard Fox was made Secretary of State; John Welles, half-brother of Queen Mother, restored to barony of Welles; Margaret Beaufort declared *femme sole*.

1486

18 Jan.: Henry Tudor m. Elizabeth Plantagenet, eldest daughter of Edward IV, to consolidate claim to throne. Mar.: Henry begins progress through kingdom, both as a public relations exercise and to quash potential rebellion. 27 Mar.: Pope Innocent VIII issues a bull declaring excommunicate anyone who challenges the validity of Henry's m. to Elizabeth of York (they were both descendants of John of Gaunt) or his claim to throne. Apr.: risings against Henry at Middleham (led by Francis Lord Lovell) and in the West Midlands (by the Stafford brothers). Lovell captured; he later escapes to France. 20 Apr.: Henry VII visits York, once Yorkist stronghold and potential focus of rebellion to assert control and win support; triumphal entry. May: the Staffords flee to **sanctuary** at Culham and are dragged out. During the trial of Humphrey Stafford the King attacks the privilege of sanctuary, declaring that only the King could grant sanctuary for treason. Later Pope Innocent VIII issues a bull withdrawing the right of sanctuary for second offenders. July: execution of Humphrey Stafford. 20 Sept.: b. of Prince Arthur, Duke of Cornwall at Winchester, capital of ancient Britain. Anglo-Scottish truce operative. Marriage of Cecily of York and Ralph Scrope dissolved. Sweating sickness grips the kingdom.

1487

The so-called 'Star Chamber' act vested the Privy Council with considerable power to act against sedition and corruption. 24 May: Lambert Simnel, aged 10, was crowned Edward VI at Christ Church, Dublin. 2,000 German troops arrive in Ireland to assist Simnel in invasion of England, headed by John de la Pole, Earl of Lincoln. 4 June: Simnel's forces landed at Furness Lancashire. 16 June: Battle of Stoke near Newark, last battle of Wars of Roses, at which Simnel was defeated and captured.[1] He had the support of the Queen Mother, Elizabeth Woodville, and of the

---

[1] Both the *DNB* and *Chronicle of Britain* incorrectly give this as Stoke-on-Trent.

Earl of Lincoln. Henry was so relieved that he sent the royal standard to Walsingham (centre of pilgrimage). Execution of Earl of Lincoln. Nov.: coronation of Elizabeth of York, accompanied by river pageants; m. between Cecily of York and John Viscount Welles, half-brother of Lady Margaret Beaufort, solemnised.

1488

11 June: d. of King James III of Scotland at Battle of Sauchieburn, near Stirling, tackling rebels claiming to fight under the orders of his son, James, Duke of Rothesay, aged 15; Dec.: ceremonial reburial of Edmund Beaufort, last Duke of Somerset (d. 1471) and his brother John at Tewkesbury Abbey marks culmination of rehabilitation of King Henry's maternal family; King's mother begins rebuilding of Corfe Castle, residence of the Beaufort family; Margaret Beaufort and Queen Elizabeth jointly admitted to Order of Garter, wearing identical gowns.

1489

14 Feb.: Treaty of Redon between Brittany and England provides for defence against France; 17 Mar.: Treaty of Medina Del Campo between England and Spain agrees m. between Prince Arthur Tudor and Catherine of Aragon: 29 Nov.: b. of Princess Margaret Tudor; Arthur proclaimed Prince of Wales and Earl of Chester.

1490

11 Aug.: Sea-battle between Scots privateer, Sir Andrew Wood, and English squadron under Stephen Bull in Firth of Forth. Bull captured. One of a number of such incidents despite official truce since 1486.

1491

Henry VII levied a benevolence. Mar.: d. of Queen's uncle, Richard Earl Rivers. 28 June: b. of Prince Henry at Greenwich. Nov.: in Cork, Perkin Warbeck (who had the support of Margaret of Burgundy, Edward IV's sister) claimed to be Richard, Duke of York, escaped from the Tower.

1492

Expedition to France supported considerably by Margaret Beaufort; 3 Nov.: Treaty of Etaples between Charles VIII of France and Henry VII of England compensated England for involvement in campaign and ensured that French would not support Warbeck or other pretenders to the English throne.

1493

Kildare pardoned; Dec.: Warbeck in Vienna with the Emperor Maximilian, who supported his claim to the English throne; Henry VII retaliated by banning English trade with Antwerp and Low Countries.

1494

Conspiracies involving King's Chamberlain, Sir William Stanley; Oct.: Prince Henry created Duke of York; declaration via this ceremony that Richard, Duke of York was dead and Perkin Warbeck was an impostor.

1495

Feb.: execution of Sir William Stanley. 25 June: negotiations begin for m. between Princess Margaret and James IV of Scotland. 3 July: Warbeck's invasion failed at Deal, Kent; Warbeck flees to Scotland. Morality Play, *Everyman*, performed for the first time in England. It is already popular in Europe. 20 Nov.: Warbeck accepted as Richard IV of England by Scots court. Warbeck m. Catherine Gordon, King of Scotland's cousin.

1496

Feb.: *Magnum Intercursus*, an Anglo-Burgundian trade treaty, denies Warbeck sanctuary in his native Flanders. 18 Mar.: b. of Princess Mary Rose: May: John Cabot sets out on voyage of exploration and colonisation to the Americas, partially financed by Henry VII. June: act of parliament in Scotland requires barons to send eldest sons to grammar schools. 30 July: King makes progress to Corfe Castle. 17 Sept.: Earl of Kildare returns to Ireland as Deputy. 26 Sept.: James IV of Scotland withdraws from English invasion in support of Warbeck; King begins to build Lady Chapel at Windsor to house his own tomb and that of Henry VI. (Henry emphasising close links between his family and that of Henry VI.)

1497

Syphilis reaches Scotland via Warbeck's Neapolitan mercenaries, garrisoned at Aberdeen. Jan.: foundation of Jesus College, Cambridge, the project of Bishop John Alcock of Ely; 17 July: Cornish rebels crushed at Blackheath. 26 July: Warbeck's troops arrive in Cork City to enlist support. 6 Aug.: Genoese explorer, John Cabot, returns to Bristol after discovering Nova Scotia. 7 Sept.: Warbeck lands at Land's End. 30 Sept.: Anglo-Scottish truce. 5 Oct.: Warbeck captured. Henry seems to accept Warbeck's confession that he is not Richard, Duke of York and to accept him at court. Christmas: royal palace of Sheen destroyed by fire.

1498

Escape of Warbeck; 9 June: Warbeck recaptured and imprisoned in Tower; July: King agrees to remove Henry VI to chapel in Westminster Abbey – this never happens; King, Queen and Queen Mother visit Cambridge.

1499

21 or 22 Feb.: b. of Prince Edmund; Mar.: first Irish parliament to be held under Poyning's Law opens; May: confirmation of *Magnum Intercursus* (1496); July: Treaty of Peace and Alliance between England and Scotland; Lady Margaret Beaufort, Countess of Derby takes vow of chastity

despite her marriage to Thomas Stanley; unprecedented move during life of a husband; Lady Margaret Beaufort's council at Collyweston near Stamford is used as unofficial Council of the Midlands; 23 Nov.: hanging of Perkin Warbeck; 28 Nov.: Edward, Earl of Warwick beheaded for treason.

1500

19 Feb.: Flemish engineer, Matthew Hake, contracted by Crown to build dam and sluice on river Witham at Boston to stop serious fen flooding which is adversely affecting the properties of Queen Mother, Margaret Beaufort, in the area. 19 June: d. of Prince Edmund, Duke of Somerset. King begins building of Richmond Palace, near Sheen.

1501

Henry VII makes Baynard's Castle his principal London residence; Richmond Palace is completed. 2 Oct.: Catherine of Aragon landed at Plymouth; 14 Nov.: Prince Arthur m. Catherine of Aragon, daughter of Ferdinand V of Spain at St Paul's after ten years of negotiations; a month of pageants and celebrations.

1502

24 Jan.: Treaty of Perpetual Peace between Scotland and England, m. between James IV of Scotland and Princess Margaret Tudor agreed. 15 Feb.: d. of Henry Deane, Archbishop of Canterbury. 2 Apr.: d. of Prince Arthur at Ludlow Castle, Shropshire; Prince Henry declared Duke of Cornwall. 6 May: execution of Sir James Tyrell, Commander of Guines near Calais, for plotting v. King with other Yorkist sympathisers including Edmund and William de la Pole, sons of one of Edward IV's sisters; Margaret Beaufort's ambitious building programme at Collyweston for royal visit of Princess Margaret. 26 Dec.: Edmund de la Pole, Earl of Suffolk proclaimed an outlaw; widowed Cecily of York banished from court for marrying a mere esquire without royal permission; foundation of Lady Margaret Lectureships in theology at Oxford and Cambridge.

1503

Appointment of Sir John Hussey as first Master of the King's Wards in newly created Court of Wards and Liveries (*see* Section VI). Edinburgh High School founded. 11 Feb.: d. of Queen Elizabeth in childbirth with Princess Katherine. 23 June: betrothal of Prince Henry to Catherine of Aragon; July: great progress of Princess Margaret to Collyweston. 16 July: politically conciliatory marriage at Collyweston between Elizabeth Zouche (kinswoman of Margaret Beaufort) and Gerald, the hostage heir to Kildare. 8 Aug.: Princess Margaret m. James IV of Scotland. 8 Nov.: Sir Thomas Lovell (Chancellor of the Exchequer) elected Speaker of House of Commons. 29 Nov.: William Warham given papal approval to become Archbishop of Canterbury; Thomas Marowe discusses, with reference to Lady Margaret Beaufort's council at Collyweston, the view

that a *femme sole* could be made a justice by royal commission; Margaret
as president of the Collyweston council arbitrates successfully between
town and gown in Cambridge.

1504
18 Feb.: Prince Henry declared Prince of Wales and Earl of Chester. 9
Mar.: William Warham enthroned Archbishop of Canterbury. Henry
VII appoints royal printer. Apr.: parliament (led by Thomas More)
opposes royal financial plans and reduces grant by two-thirds. 30 Oct.:
Lady Margaret Preachership founded at Cambridge.

1505
27 June: Prince Henry protests against proposed m. with Catherine of
Aragon despite Papal Dispensation. 1505: John Fisher elected President of
Queens' College, Cambridge at Margaret Beaufort's behest. Re-founda-
tion of God's House as Christ's College, Cambridge by Margaret Beaufort.

1506
Early in the year Henry VII received Philip of Hapsburg, King of Castile
and his Queen Joanna at court at great expense; Mar.: Philip agreed to
surrender surviving Yorkist claimant, Edmund de la Pole, Earl of Suffolk.
30 Apr.: trade and mutual defence treaty with Burgundy; Emperor
Maximilian proposes marriage between Mary Tudor and his grandson
Charles; Henry VII named Protector of Order of St John at Rhodes after
he and his mother had financially supported their crusade.

1507
Royal printing press founded in Edinburgh. June: Prince Henry displays
prowess at tournament; Aug.: Chancellor John Fisher delivers oration at
Cambridge to Henry VII and his mother; 24 Dec.: George Neville, Lord
Abergavenny heavily fined for raising a large private army and instigating
a riot in Kent in 1503.

1508
Mar.: Henry VII so seriously ill that his mother, with her servants,
moved into Richmond to watch over him; 17 Dec.: Princess Mary
betrothed to Prince Charles, son of Duke of Burgundy and grandson of
Emperor Maximilian.

The Reign of Henry VIII

1509
Mar.: Margaret Beaufort travels between Coldharbour and Richmond to
attend Henry VII in last illness; 21 Apr.: d. of Henry VII at Richmond;
on deathbed Henry made Margaret chief executrix of will; kept secret

until 23 Apr.: the council which arranged burial was headed by 'the moder of the said late king'; 24 Apr.: imprisonment of Edmund Dudley and Sir Richard Empson, two of Henry VII's most unpopular ministers, for plotting v. Henry's accession; 11 May: Lady Margaret Beaufort accorded precedence over all other royal women at funeral; 11 June: King Henry VIII m. Catherine of Aragon at Greenwich, having overcome (temporarily) his earlier reservations about marrying his brother's widow; 24 June: splendid coronation of Henry and Catherine at Westminster Abbey; 29 June: d. of Queen Mother; 9 July: burial of Margaret Beaufort in Westminster Abbey; Nov.: Henry VIII promotes Thomas Wolsey, Dean of Lincoln, to position of Almoner.

1510

31 Jan.: Queen Catherine bears stillborn daughter. June: Wolsey joins the Council; 8 Nov.: Earl of Kildare confirmed Deputy of Ireland.

1511

1 Jan.: Prince Henry, Duke of Cornwall b. at Richmond. 22 Feb.: Prince Henry d. at Richmond. Aug.: Desiderius Erasmus, aged 45, made first Professor of Greek and divinity at Cambridge. 17 Nov.: England joins Holy League with Pope Julius II, the Venetian Republic and Ferdinand of Aragon, v. King Louis XII of France. Henry founds royal armoury at Greenwich.

1512

Completion of chapel of Henry VII at Westminster, notable for its elaborate Gothic style and beautiful fan vaulting; Pietro Torrigiano, Florentine sculptor, still working on the tomb of Henry VII and his Queen. Mar.: James IV of Scotland renews 1492 alliance with France and refuses to join Holy League. 10 Apr.: b. of Prince James of Scotland. Henry VIII declares war on France. May: foundation of St Leonard's College, St Andrew's. 15 June: John Colet asks Mercers to run new foundation of St Paul's School, London.

1513

Mar.: Nicholas West, Dean of Windsor, asks James IV of Scotland to stay neutral in French war. 25 Apr.: Emp, Maximilian joins Holy League. 4 May: execution of Earl of Suffolk without trial. 8 May: King Louis of France promises to pay James IV for equipping and manning a Scottish navy. 30 June: 35,000 strong English army, led by Henry VIII, lands at Calais. 16 Aug.: Battle of the Spurs at Therouanne; 22 Aug.: Therouanne surrendered to Henry VIII. 3 Sept.: Earl of Kildare succeeded by son, Gerald. 9 Sept.: Scots defeated at Battle of Flodden Field, near Berwick. Death of James IV in battle. 21 Sept.: infant successor crowned James V; Council of Regency under Queen Margaret, sister of Henry VIII, who is herself only 24. 23 Sept.: Tournai surrenders to Holy League.

1514

2 Feb.: Thomas Howard created Duke of Norfolk, his son Thomas Howard created Earl of Surrey, Charles Brandon created Duke of Suffolk, and Charles Somerset made Earl of Worcester. 13 June: Henry launches *Henri Grace à Dieu*, world's largest warship. 6 Aug.: Queen Mother Margaret of Scotland m. Archibald Douglas, Earl of Angus. 7 Aug.: Anglo-French peace treaty signed at St Germaine-en-Laye; 52 year-old King Louis is to marry Princess Mary Rose, aged 18, the King's sister. Tournai ceded to England, Wolsey becomes Bishop of Tournai and given French pension. 15 Sept.: Wolsey consecrated Archbp of York. 14 Dec.: Richard Hunne, London merchant tailor, found hanged in bp's prison at St Paul's. John Fisher made Chancellor of Cambridge for life.

1515

Pietro Torrigiano completes tomb of Henry VII and Elizabeth of York in Westminster Abbey. Feb.: widowed Queen Mary of France (Mary Tudor) secretly m. Charles Brandon, Duke of Suffolk, in Paris. 12 July: Duke of Albany replaces Queen Mother Margaret as Regent of Scotland. Sept.: Cardinal's hat conferred on Thomas Wolsey. Nov.: judges give permission to King to make new law with Lords and Commons and to exclude the bps in certain circumstances. 24 Dec.: Thomas Wolsey is made Lord Chancellor.

1516

18 Feb.: b. of Princess Mary at Greenwich. May: Hampton Court Palace completed. 2 May: Wolsey announces intention to reform Star Chamber (see Section IX) as instrument for impartial enforcement of law against the highest in the land. Dec.: publication of More's *Utopia* in Louvain.

1517

30 Apr.: London mob attacks French, Italian and Dutch immigrants in riot instigated by John Lincoln, a broker, and Dr Bele, a preacher. 26 Aug.: new Franco-Scottish alliance. Plague in London drives court out. Royal Commission of Inquiry into Enclosures established.

1518

May: Henry VIII sides with humanists at Cambridge in dispute between 'Greeks' (humanists) and 'Trojans' (those who opposed teaching of Greek on humanist lines). 17 May: Wolsey made Papal Legate. 23 Sept.: Royal College of Physicians founded in London by Charter. 5 Oct.: Treaty of London makes peace between France, England, Empire, Papacy, Spain, Burgundy and the Netherlands. Separate peace between England and France results in betrothal of 2 year-old Dauphin to Princess Mary, the cession of Tournai to England, and an annual pension to Wolsey in return for his relinquishment of the see of Tournai. 8 Nov.: case brought v. Nicholas Vaux for enclosing land and destroying houses at Stantonbury, Bucks. This was one among many cases arising out of the inquiry.

1519
Birth of Henry Fitzroy to Henry VIII's mistress, Elizabeth Blount. Henry VIII orders suppression of brothels. 28 June: Charles, grandson of Emperor Maximilian, made Emperor Charles V. July: Wolsey leads midnight raid on brothels in City of London.

1520
10 Mar.: Thomas Howard, Earl of Surrey leads English army v. Irish rebels. 7 June: meeting of King Henry VIII and King Francis I at 'Field of Cloth of Gold' at Guines, France, contrived by Wolsey to bring about detente with France. Meeting with Emp. Charles V balances this action.

1521
John Longland, Bishop of Lincoln, launches campaign to extirpate Lollardy from around Amersham in Bucks. Feb.: Duke of Buckingham applied for licence to visit his Welsh lordships, accompanied by a retinue of 400 armed men. Interpreted, probably correctly, as threatening to the régime. 12 May: burning of Luther's writings in St Paul's churchyard in presence of Wolsey, a huge crowd and the papal nuncio. 17 May: execution of Edward Stafford, Duke of Buckingham, for treason. 12 July: Henry VIII publishes *The Assertion of the Seven Sacraments*, which contains a condemnation of Luther. 25 Aug.: secret Anglo-Imperial Treaty of Bruges arranges alliance in event of war with France. 11 Oct.: Pope bestows title *Fidei Defensor* (Defender of the Faith) upon Henry VIII after receiving copy of Henry's book. Oct.: Henry confers English knighthood on Conn O'Neill. 21 Dec.: Thomas Howard resigns post as Lieutenant of Ireland.

1522
Jan.: Wolsey fails in attempt to be elected Pope. Mar.: Wolsey orders national survey of England's financial and military strength in preparation for war with France in spring 1523. 13 June: Franco-Scottish Treaty of Rouen (signed 1517) ratified. 19 June: Treaty of Windsor between England and Empire. July 1522: Scottish nobles, under Duke of Albany's command, refuse to attack England without French help. 17 Sept.: Anglo-Scottish truce agreed. Sept.: English patrol Irish sea after hearing of negotiations between Earl of Desmond and France. 15 Oct.: Earl of Surrey leads unsuccessful expedition to Picardy and returns. 25 Oct.: Duke of Albany visits France to solicit support against the English.

1523
1 Jan.: Kildare returns to Ireland after 4 years' detention in England. Lord Henry Percy's suit for hand of Anne Boleyn forbidden by Wolsey.

June: English troops burn Kelso Abbey on border raid: 6 July: parliament grants half of required subsidy for war with France. 24 Sept.: Earl of Surrey burns Jedburgh Abbey on raid. 3 Nov.: relief of Wark Castle, Northumberland, by Earl of Surrey. Dec. 1523: Tyrconnell tries to enlist Scottish support v. England. 15 Dec.: Duke of Suffolk's march on Paris ends in retreat after Constable of France fails to give promised support to overthrow Francis I.

1524
21 Jan.: Wolsey made Papal Legate for life. 20 May: Duke of Albany sails to France to negotiate m. between James V and a French princess. 26 July: Queen Mother Margaret (who is pro-English) becomes Regent during palace coup in Albany's absence. July: earls of Kildare and Ormond form alliance. 16 Nov.: Duke of Albany fails to reclaim power. Wolsey exacts Amicable Grant, a non-parliamentary tax, to help refill the royal coffers following the costly war with France.

1525
Wolsey makes gift of Hampton Court to King. 25 Feb.: Emp. Charles V defeats and captures Francis I of France at Pavia. 11 May: East Anglian rebellion in agricultural and clothing communities, against the Amicable Grant, is crushed. 13 May: Amicable Grant withdrawn. June: Wolsey suppresses religious houses in Oxford to fund new college and school. 18 June: Henry Fitzroy (aged 6) made Duke of Richmond. June: Emp. Charles V repudiates terms of Treaty of Windsor, by refusing to marry Princess Mary. Aug.: Fitzroy made Warden of the Northern Marches and Lieutenant-General in the north of England, based at Sheriff Hutton; Princess Mary (aged 9) to rule Wales and the Welsh Marches through a council. 30 Aug.: Anglo-French Treaty of the More. Tyndale's English Bible is being printed in Cologne.

1526
26 Jan.: three Hanse merchants arrested for smuggling heretical books into England. Mar.: Margaret of Scotland m. Henry Stewart, Treasurer and Lord Chancellor of Scotland, although she is not divorced from Earl of Angus. Mar.: 6,000 copies of Tyndale's English Bible seized in London and later burnt. May: England joins League of Cognac with France, Milan, Florence and Venice against the Empire. Aug.: Anne Boleyn publicly favoured by the King. Hans Holbein welcomed to court. Wolsey's recoinage.

1527
Thomas Bilney arrested at Ipswich and sent to Tower for Lutheran heresy. Jan.: John Fisher, Bishop of Rochester, publishes *De veritate corporis et sanguinis Christi in Eucharista*. 30 Apr.: Treaty of Westminster between England and France v. Emperor Charles V. 22 June: King

announces to Catherine of Aragon his intention to seek divorce. Sends envoys to Rome to seek papal support.

1528

23 Feb.: Piers Ruadh Butler, Earl of Ormond, made Earl of Ossory and title of Earl of Ormond conferred upon Sir Thomas Boleyn, 29 Feb.: Patrick Hamilton, teacher at University, is first Scottish Protestant martyr at St Andrews. 6 July: 16 year-old James V enters Edinburgh to assert right to rule as King. 4 Aug.: Earl of Ossory made Deputy of Ireland. 20,000 Irish (on the side of the Earl of Kildare) emigrate to Pembrokeshire, Wales.

1529

22 June: Henry Fitzroy, Duke of Richmond, appointed Lieutenant of Ireland. 4 Aug.: Dublin Council sacks Earl of Ossory as Deputy of Ireland. 18 Oct.: Wolsey surrenders Great Seal, 25 Oct.: Sir Thomas More made Lord Chancellor. Thomas Cranmer appointed Royal Chaplain and Archdeacon of Taunton. Dec.: parliament begins to support church reform. 3 Nov.: parliament assembles. 16 Dec.: parliament prorogued.

1530

Mar.: Sir Thomas Boleyn visits Pope to ask for royal divorce. 8 Apr.: univs of Oxford and Cambridge declare in favour of royal divorce. 2 June: Sir William Skeffington replaces Ossory as Deputy of Ireland. July: Pope revokes legatine powers of Blackfriars court hearing King's divorce appeal. Nov.: arrest of Wolsey for treason. 24 Nov.: d. of Wolsey at Leicester Abbey, en route from York to Tower. Henry VIII takes possession of Hampton Court Palace given him by Wolsey in 1525. Thomas Cromwell joins the King's Council.

1531

5 Jan.: Pope Clement VII orders Henry VIII not to remarry. Thomas Cranmer and Edward Fox propose to King that if the univs and canon-law experts declare in favour of the divorce, there will be no need for further approaches to Rome. 'Reformation Parliament' reassembles. 11 Feb.: Convocation reluctantly agrees to a royal tax demanded by the King as 'supreme head of the English Church and clergy'. 14 July: Henry VIII moves into Woodstock Palace with mistress Anne Boleyn. Thomas Bilney executed as heretic in Norwich. Dec.: Thomas Cromwell promoted to King's inner council.

1532

Thomas Cromwell prominent as King's Councillor. 25 Jan.: Pope threatens Henry VIII with excommunication. Mar.: Act of Annates; Commons' Supplication against the Ordinaries. 15 May: Submission of the Clergy to royal authority. 16 May: Sir Thomas More resigned Lord Chancellorship. 5 July: Earl of Kildare appointed Deputy of Ireland. 28 Aug.: d. of William Warham, Archbishop of Canterbury. 1 Sept.: Anne Boleyn created Marchioness of Pembroke. 20 Oct.: meeting of Henry VIII and French King at Calais in effort to gain support for divorce.

1533
25 Jan.: secret m. of Henry and Anne Boleyn at Whitehall. Mar.: Act in Restraint of Appeals. Apr.: Thomas Cromwell made Chancellor of Exchequer. 9 Apr.: Catherine of Aragon told she is no longer Queen. 10 Apr.: Ambassador advises Catherine's nephew, Emp. Charles V to wage war on England. 23 May: Archbp Cranmer annuls King's marriage to Catherine of Aragon. 1 June: coronation of Anne Boleyn. Sept.: Earl of Kildare ordered to London to answer charges of maladministration in Ireland. 7 Sept.: Princess Elizabeth b. at Greenwich; 23 Nov.: imprisonment of Elizabeth Barton, 'Holy Maid of Kent' or 'Nun of Kent', in Tower for treason.

1534
23 Mar.: Pope declares m. with Catherine of Aragon valid. 26 Mar.: Act of Succession. 30 Mar.: Act forbidding flocks of more than 2,000 sheep. 17 Apr.: Thomas More sent to Tower for refusing oath of succession. 20 Apr.: Elizabeth Barton, Dr Edward Bocking and two others hanged at Tyburn. 21 Apr.: John Fisher, Bp of Rochester, sent to Tower for refusing both Acts. Apr.: Thomas Cromwell appointed Principal Secretary and Master of the Jewels. May: Catherine of Aragon placed under house arrest in Cambridgeshire. Rowland Lee, Bp of Coventry and Lichfield, made President of Council of Marches and Wales. 11 May: Anglo-Scots Peace Treaty signed. 29 June: Kildare sent to the Tower. 28 July: John Alen, Archbishop of Dublin, murdered by supporters of Kildare's son, Lord Offaly. 30 July: Sir William Skeffington replaces Kildare as Lord Deputy. 2 Sept.: d. of Kildare. Offaly succeeds him as Earl and besieges Dublin. 24 Oct.: arrival of Sir William Skeffington, Lord Deputy, to quash Kildare's rebellion. 17 Nov.: Act of Supremacy. 19 Dec.: truce between English and Kildare.

1535
Apr.: Cromwell orders imprisonment of clergy preaching Papal supremacy. 23 Mar.: Kildare crushed at Maynooth Castle, County Kildare. 20 May: Cardinal's hat conferred on John Fisher, Bp of Rochester, who is in the Tower. 22 June: execution of John Fisher. 6 July: Sir Thomas More beheaded. Aug.: Kildare surrenders to Skeffington. 31 Dec.: d. of Skeffington.

1536
Privy Council replaces King's Council. 7 Jan.: d. of Catherine of Aragon at Kimbolton, Cambs. 29 Jan.: Queen Anne miscarries male child. 18

Mar.: Act of Suppression. 14 Apr.: royal assent to bill uniting Wales and England. 1 May: beginning of reformation of Church in Ireland. 2 May: Anne Boleyn imprisoned in Tower. 10 May: Anne Boleyn indicted for High Treason. 19 May: Anne Boleyn beheaded. 30 May: Henry m. Jane Seymour. 11 July: Ten Articles. 22 July: d. of Henry Fitzroy. July: Act of Succession declares Mary and Elizabeth illegitimate. Oct.: beginnings of Pilgrimage of Grace. 6 Oct.: execution of William Tyndale in the Low Countries. 8 Dec.: northern rebels accept general pardon from Duke of Norfolk. Poor Law enacted.

1537

1 Jan.: James V of Scotland m. Princess Madeleine of France. Jan.: minor riots connected with the northern rebellion. 3 Feb.: execution of 'Silken Thomas', Earl of Kildare and his five uncles for treason. Feb. and Mar.: executions of 'pilgrimage' rebels. June: Carthusian House, the London Charterhouse, finally surrenders to King. 30 June: d. of Henry Percy, Earl of Northumberland, who leaves all lands to Crown. July: Robert Aske, leader of Pilgrimage of Grace, executed at York. 7 July: d. of Queen Madeleine of Scotland. Sept.: Council of North reorganised. 12 Oct.: b. of Prince Edward at Hampton Court. 18 Oct.: Edward Seymour, the Queen's brother, is made Earl of Hertford. 24 Oct.: d. of Queen Jane. 12 Nov.: burial of Queen Jane.

1538

Hans Holbein visits European Courts making portraits of suitable candidates for position as Henry's fourth wife. May: Henry VIII seriously ill at Hampton Court. 4 May: m. of James V of Scotland and Mary of Guise by proxy. 10 June: Mary of Guise arrives in Scotland. 18 June: France and Empire sign Treaty of Nice. June: remnants of Kildare faction plan uprising to place Gerald Fitzgerald, the heir, on throne of Ireland. Aug.: arrest of Geoffrey Pole; Lord Montague; Henry Courtenay, Marquess of Exeter; Sir Edward Neville and the Countess of Salisbury. Sept.: Royal Injunctions issued ordering cessation of superstitious worship and rituals. Destruction of shrines. 17 Dec.: Henry excommunicated by Pope Paul III. 19 Dec.: Henry exchanges Lincolnshire Church lands with Charles Brandon's East Anglian holdings and bases Brandon, Earl of Suffolk, in Lincolnshire to keep the peace. 27 Dec.: Cardinal Pole sets out to rally French and Spanish support v. Henry. Execution of the Pole brothers and the Marques of Exeter and Sir Edward Neville.

1539

28 Apr.: parliament meets. 16 June: Act of Six Articles. 1 July: bps of Salisbury and Worcester resign. July: Archbishop of Canterbury sends wife to Germany. Lord Leonard Grey, Deputy, defeats the Kildare faction of O'Donnell and O'Neill at Bellahoe. Act of Proclamations passed.

1540

6 Jan.: Henry m. Anne of Cleves. 21 Mar.: Gerald FitzGerald escapes to St Malo. Apr.: Thomas Cromwell made Earl of Essex and Lord Great Chamberlain. 19 June: Thomas Cromwell accused of treason in House of Lords. June: King takes Catherine Howard as mistress. Imprisonment of Lord Grey, Deputy of Ireland.: July: **Statute of Wills**. 12 July: annulment of m. to Anne of Cleves. 28 July: King m. Catherine Howard at Oatlands. Thomas Cromwell beheaded. English Bible ordered in every parish church. 12 Aug.: Sir Anthony St Leger made Deputy.

1541

Jan.: Arrest and imprisonment of Cromwell's most prominent supporters, Sir Ralph Sadler and Thomas Wyatt. Spring: d. of both sons of James V of Scotland and Mary of Guise. Jun. – Sept.: royal progress to York. 18 June: Dublin parliament passed act declaring Henry VIII King of Ireland as well as England. 28 July: execution of Lord Leonard Grey for treason. 6 Aug.: Tyrconnell submits to Sir Anthony St Leger. 18 Oct.: d. of Margaret Tudor of Scotland. 14 Nov.: Catherine Howard under house arrest at Syon House for adultery. 28 Dec.: Conn O'Neill submits to St Leger. 10 Dec.: execution of Francis Dereham and Thomas Culpeper, alleged lovers of Catherine Howard.

1542

Creation of sees of Bristol and Oxford. 13 Feb.: Catherine Howard executed. 1 Oct.: Conn O'Neill created Earl of Tyrone. 24 Nov.: English defeat Scots at Battle of Solway Moss. 8 Dec.: b. of Princess Mary to Mary of Guise. 14 Dec.: d. of James V of Scotland. 29 Dec.: Henry frees Scots nobles captured at Solway Moss in return for their support for a m. between Prince Edward Tudor and infant Queen Mary of Scotland.

1543

Act of parl. extends all English law to Wales. 3 Jan.: James Hamilton, Earl of Arran, formerly heir to the throne, is Regent of Scotland. 11 Feb.: Anglo-Imperial alliance against France. Apr.: plot against Cranmer foiled. May: *King's Book* published. 1 July: Anglo-Scots Treaty of Greenwich provides for the marriage of Queen Mary to Prince Edward once she reaches 10 years of age. 12 July: Henry m. Catherine Parr. 9 Sept.: Mary crowned Queen of Scots. 11 Dec.: Scots parliament rejects Treaty of Greenwich.

1544

3 May: Earl of Hertford burns Edinburgh. 10 June: attempted coup by Mary of Guise. 11 June: Henry VIII orders use of English liturgy. 14 July: Henry VIII joins troops in Calais. 18 Sept.: Henry VIII besieges and takes Boulogne. His ally, Emperor Charles V, makes peace with the French at Crépy. 7 Nov.: troops of Mary of Guise and Earl of Arran

stand together against the English in Lothian. Debasement of the coinage begins.

1545

27 Feb.: English defeated by Scots at Battle of Ancrum Moor. 15 July: French fleet attempts invasion of England to divert English from Boulogne. 20 July: *Mary Rose* sinks in Solent. 22 Aug.: d. of Charles Brandon, Duke of Suffolk. 9 Sept.: Earl of Hertford launches counter-offensive on Scottish Borders. Sept.: John Dudley, Lord Admiral, raids the French coast. 24 Dec.: King calls for religious unity in speech marking end of parliamentary session.

1546

Jan.: defeat of Henry Howard, Earl of Surrey and Governor of Boulogne, and his army as they attempt to ward off French army besieging Boulogne. 21 Mar.: Earl of Hertford and Viscount Lisle take command of English army in France from Surrey. Apr.: Henry orders closure of London brothels. 1 Apr.: Henry summons Earl of Ormond and St Leger to London to settle feud. 7 June: Anglo-French peace treaty of Camp, near Ardres, gives England control of Boulogne for 8 years. 16 July: Anne Askew burnt at Smithfield for heresy. Sept.: King ill. Orders English troops to destroy French fort near Boulogne. Oct.: Sir Anthony Denny, ally of Hertford, made Chief Gentleman of King's Privy Chamber. 2 Dec.: Bp Stephen Gardiner refuses to exchange lands with Crown. 12 Dec.: Earl of Surrey sentenced to death for treason. 26 Dec.: Hertford, Lisle and Denny witness changes to King's will, by which Bp Gardiner is removed from Regency Council. 31 Dec.: James Butler, Earl of Ormond and Ossory, poisoned to death.

The Reign of Edward VI

1547

21 Jan.: execution of Henry Howard, Earl of Surrey. 28 Jan.: d. of Henry VIII. Will signed by stamp. Regency Council. 31 Jan.: Council appoints Edward Seymour, Earl of Hertford, Lord Protector. 16 Feb.: Edward Seymour created Duke of Somerset. 19 Feb.: coronation procession of Edward VI. 20 February: coronation of Edward VI at Westminster. May: Catherine Parr m. Thomas Seymour. Bp Gardiner attempts to suppress extreme Protestants in Winchester diocese. 31 July: *Book of Homilies* published. 10 Sept.: Scots defeated at Battle of Pinkie by Somerset's army. 11 Sept.: Mary of Scotland sent to Inchmahome. 25 Sept.: Bp Gardiner impr. in Fleet for opposing *Book of Homilies*. Dec.: act passed dissolving Chantries.

1548

20 Feb.: Bp Gardiner freed. 7 Mar.: Hugh Latimer invited to preach

before Edward VI. 21 May: Sir Edward Bellingham made Deputy of Ireland. 29 June: Bp Gardiner imprisoned in Tower. June: French troops augment Scots army to prevent England gaining control of Lowlands. 1 June: commission of inquiry into enclosures. 7 Aug.: Mary of Scotland flees to France. 7 Sept.: d. of Catherine Parr in childbirth. 17 Dec.: beginning of parliamentary debate on Act of Uniformity.

1549

15 Jan.: House of Lords passed Act of Uniformity prescribing use of the new prayer book. 20 Mar.: Thomas Seymour executed for high treason. May: revolts against enclosure begin. 2 July: siege of Exeter by 'Prayer-Book rebels'. 23 July: Kett's rebels besiege Norwich. 18 Aug.: Lord John Russell quells Western Rebels at Battle of Sampford Courtenay, near Okehampton. Aug.: state censorship reintroduced by proclamation. Dearth of corn throughout country. 13 Oct.: Protectorate dissolved. 14 Oct.: Somerset and family sent to Tower. Imprisonment shared with William Cecil for a while.

1550

21 Feb.: John Dudley, Earl of Warwick, appointed Lord President of the Council and Master of the King's Household. Feb.: French conspire with Tyrconnell in Ireland. 24 Mar.: Anglo-French Treaty of Boulogne – England abandons Boulogne and withdraws from Scotland. 5 Sept.: William Cecil made Secretary of State and Privy Councillor. 10 Sept.: St Leger reappointed Deputy and ordered to enforce Protestant forms of worship. Dearth of corn throughout country. 23 Nov.: Bp Ridley orders replacement of altars by communion tables in London diocese. 25 Dec.: Princess Mary rebuked by King Edward for her continued Catholicism.

1551

Feb.: Northumberland founds strong palace guard. 3 Mar.: Privy Council orders removal of plate from churches. 18 Mar.: Princess Mary rejects new liturgy and continues to hold Mass in her home. 10 June: Anglo-Scots Peace Treaty. 19 July: m. arranged between King Edward and daughter of Henri II of France. 11 Oct.: Warwick created Duke of Northumberland. Dearth of corn throughout land. 1 Dec.: Somerset sentenced to death.

1552

22 Jan.: Somerset executed. Spring: Royal Commission investigates royal finances and revenue courts. 15 Apr.: Act. v. Usury. 24 Sept.: Anglo-Scottish treaty settles border issue. Oct.: Northumberland disbands palace guard. 1 Nov.: 2nd Edwardine Prayer Book published. Dec.: Royal Commission recommends streamlining of revenue courts.

The Reign of Mary I

1553

Jan.: commissioners augment government finances by stripping churches of wealth. 2 Feb.: consecration of Protestant John Bale as Bishop of Ossory, Ireland. 12 June: Edward VI changes will to name Lady Jane Grey as successor. 21 June: Princesses Mary and Elizabeth declared illegitimate by royal patent. 6 July: Edward d. at Greenwich. 10 July: Lady Jane Grey (Dudley) proclaimed Queen at Tower. 3 Aug.: Mary Tudor acclaimed Queen in London. Lady Jane imprisoned in Tower. 22 Aug.: Northumberland executed for treason. John Bale. Bishop of Ossory, flees Ireland after Catholic protest. 14 Sept.: Cranmer to be arrested. 1 Oct.: coronation of Mary I. Proxy m. to Philip of Spain. 16 Nov.: Mary informs Commons delegation that she will marry Philip of Spain. 5 Dec.: Mary dissolves parliament after passing act restoring her legitimacy. She relinquishes title of 'Supreme Head of the English Church'.

1554

Jan.: Sir Thomas Wyatt's Kentish plot to prevent Mary's m. to Philip. 7 Feb.: Wyatt arrested. 12 Feb.: Jane Grey executed. Princess Elizabeth imprisoned in Tower. 6 Mar.: Mary formally betrothed to Philip. 11 Apr.: Thomas Wyatt executed. 12 Apr.: Mary of Guise Regent of Scotland. 14 Apr.: Pope orders Archbishop of Armagh to deprive married clergy. 22 May: Elizabeth freed. 25 July: Mary m. Philip of Spain. 28 Nov.: Cardinal Pole reunites English and Roman Churches with parl.'s assent.

1555

Richard Chancellor's Muscovy Company obtains English and Russian royal charters to open trade between the two countries. 13 May: Gerald FitzGerald is restored to earldom of Kildare. Sept.: John Knox returns to Scotland from exile. General dearth of corn. 16 Oct.: Bps Latimer and Ridley burnt at stake before Balliol College, Oxford 25 Oct.: Philip becomes ruler of Netherlands. Nov.: death of Stephen Gardiner, Bishop of Winchester. 13 Nov.: Thomas Cranmer deprived of Archbpric. Dec.: Cardinal Pole made Archbishop of Canterbury.

1556

16 Jan.: Charles V abdicates and Philip II, his son, becomes King of Spain and the Netherlands. His uncle, Ferdinand, becomes Emp. 18 Mar.: Mary orders arrest of Sir Henry Dudley and others after plot to place Elizabeth on throne. 21 Mar.: Cranmer burnt on stake at Balliol College, Oxford. 22 Mar.: Pole consecrated Archb. 28 Apr.: English plan extension of Pale in Ireland by plantation of Co. Laois and Co. Offaly. 26 May: St Leger replaced as Deputy by Thomas Radcliff(e), Lord Fitzwalter. July: Fitzwalter campaigns v. Scots in Ulster. Sept.:

Philip II's war against Papacy puts English relations with Pope in jeopardy. General dearth of corn. Worst harvest of century. Stationers' Company given printing monopoly in England. Refoundation of Benedictine Westminster Abbey.

1557

17 Feb.: Fitzwalter created Earl of Sussex. 20 Mar.: Philip II returns to England for financial assistance in war. June: Dublin parliament renames Co. Laois 'Queen's County' and Co. Offaly 'King's County'. Cardinal Pole recalled to Rome to face heresy charges but Mary refuses to allow him to go. 2 July: Dublin parliament ends with repeal of all Reformation legislation. 10 July: Sussex campaigns v. the O'Connors in Co. Offaly. Widespread dearth and sickness in England. 27 Oct.: Sussex destroys Armagh City in campaign v. O'Neill. 3 Dec.: a few Scots nobles sign Covenant in favour of Protestant religion.

1558

7 Jan.: Calais surrendered to French. 24 Apr.: Mary of Scotland m. dauphin Francis in Paris. 3 Mar.: act reforming militia. 30 Mar.: Mary I alters will to exclude all but her own children from succession. 1 Sept.: Protestant riots in Edinburgh. 15 Sept.: beginning of Sussex's campaign against the Scots in the Isles. Dearth widespread and severe. Accompanied by sickness, including devastating influenza epidemic. 8 Nov.: Sussex returns triumphant to Dublin. 11 Nov.: Scots parliament offers dauphin Francis the Crown Matrimonial in the event of Mary's death. 17 Nov.: d. of Mary Tudor and of Cardinal Pole. Elizabeth, at Hatfield, succeeds. Reorganises royal household and reappoints William Cecil as Chief Secretary of State. 28 Nov.: Elizabeth I enters London in triumph. 14 Dec.: burial of Mary I at Westminster. Dec.: influenza epidemic. In Scotland, John Knox is urging rebellion against regency of Mary of Guise.

The Reign of Elizabeth I

1559

10 Jan.: Philip II proposes m. to Elizabeth. 15 Jan.: Elizabeth I crowned at Westminster Abbey. 25 Jan.: parliament assembles. 10 Feb.: Elizabeth announces to parliament that she has no plans to marry. 2 Apr.: Anglo-French Treaty of Cateau-Cambresis gives France control over Calais for eight years. 29 Apr.: Acts of Uniformity and Supremacy passed, renouncing papal authority in England. 11 May: John Knox preaches inflammatory sermon at Perth. 5 June: Elizabeth rejects proposal of marriage from Charles, Archduke of Austria and son of the Emperor Ferdinand. 30 June: Henri II of France d. and is succeeded by Francis and Mary of Scotland. 7 July: Scottish Protestants occupy Edinburgh. 17 July: d. of

Conn O'Neill; son Shane succeeds to earldom of Tyrone. 24 July: truce between Mary of Guise and Protestant Lords of the Congregation. 30 Aug.: Sussex re-appointed Lord Deputy of Ireland. 24 Sept.: Scottish Protestants appeal to England for help. 17 Oct.: Protestant Lords of the Congregation depose Mary of Guise as regent. Nov.: Scots Protestants fail to take garrison at Leith. 6 Nov.: Mary of Guise reintroduces the Mass. Dec.: Protestant army of the Congregation forced to flee from Stirling by French troops. 17 Dec.: Matthew Parker enthroned as Archbishop of Canterbury.

1560

12 Jan.: Dublin parliament assembles to pass Act of Uniformity. 23 Jan.: French troops abandon Fife in face of English fleet. 22 Feb.: Treaty of Berwick between Scottish Protestants and England. 6 May: Sussex made Lord Lieutenant of Ireland. June: d. of Mary of Guise. 6 July: Treaty of Edinburgh provides for French and English withdrawal from Scotland, Mary of Scotland's recognition of Elizabeth as rightful Queen of England and a Protestant provisional government. 24 Aug.: Scotland turns Protestant. 5 Dec.: d. of Francis II; Queen Mother, Catherine de Medici, assumes regency. 20 Dec.: First General Assembly of Church of Scotland.

1561

27 Jan.: *First Book of Discipline* introduced by Church of Scotland. 8 June: Sussex proclaims Tyrone traitor. 13 July: Elizabeth refuses Mary Queen of Scots safe passage en route to Scotland because she has refused to ratify Treaty of Edinburgh. Aug.: Lady Catherine Grey, sister of Lady Jane, imprisoned, in Tower. 26 Dec.: Ambrose Dudley created Earl of Warwick.

1562

24 Aug.: total recoinage restores European confidence in English money. 20 Sept.: treaty secures English help for French Protestants in exchange for English possession of Le Havre. Oct.: Queen Elizabeth ill with smallpox at Hampton Court; Robert Dudley named Protector. 28 Oct.: Mary Queen of Scots' victory over Earl of Huntly, 'cock o' the north', at Corrichie in Aberdeenshire. Huntly d. of heart attack. 2 Nov.: execution of Huntly's son. Nov.: Shane O'Neill plundering Co. Fermanagh. Dec.: Shane O'Neill campaigning to take Ulster. In this year John Hawkins begins slaving expeditions to Africa.

1563

12 Jan.: new parliament assembles. Attempt to debate succession is stymied. Feb.: 39 Articles of faith agreed upon by Convocation. Mar.: worsening civil war between Catholics and Protestants in France. Apr.: Statute of Artificers regulates wages and conditions of employment. parl. orders Welsh translation of Prayer Book. Sussex leads campaign v.

O'Neill in Ireland. 28 July: Earl of Warwick surrenders his troops to the French at the Havre, under terms of Treaty of Amboise. 11 Sept.: O'Neill submits to Earl of Sussex. Plague epidemic is severe.

1564

Winter: deep freeze in the Highlands, following upon dearth and inflation, said to depopulate whole valleys. Mar.: Elizabeth offers Robert Dudley as husband for Mary of Scotland. 11 Apr.: Anglo-French Treaty of Troyes hands Calais to the French. 25 May: Earl of Sussex recalled from Ireland. 28 Sept.: Robert Dudley created Earl of Leicester. Oct.: Court of High Commission established in Ireland to enforce religious conformity. Riots against English plantation of Co. Offaly and Co. Laois, now called Queen's County and King's County.

1565

22 Feb.: Queen places Archbishop of Armagh in Tower. 2 May: O'Neill defeats MacDonnells at Glenshesk, Co. Antrim. 29 July: Mary of Scotland m. Henry Stuart, Lord Darnley, great grandson of Henry VII, at Holyrood. Summer: Queen visits Coventry. Aug.: Lady Mary Grey imprisoned for secretly marrying Thomas Keys. 6 Oct.: anglophiles in the Borders, led by James, Earl of Moray, defeated by Mary Queen of Scots. Oct.: Sir Henry Sidney takes up post as Lord Deputy of Ireland.

1566

Mar.: London clergy suspended for refusing to wear vestments. 9 Mar.: Darnley involved in coup that results in murder of David Rizzio. Mary arrested. 20 Mar.: Mary of Scotland resumes control in Edinburgh. 16 June: b. of Prince James Stuart. 29 June: Monopoly of Stationers' Company confirmed. Aug. and Sept.: Elizabeth I's summer progress to Stamford, Woodstock and Oxford. 3 Aug.: Shane O'Neill proclaimed traitor after he burns Armagh Cathedral. Autumn and winter campaign of Sir Henry Sidney against O'Neill. 25 Oct.: Mary of Scotland seriously ill at Roxburgh. 24 Dec.: royal pardon for Rizzio's murderers. Wrangles in parliament touching the succession and religion.

1567

20 Jan.: Mary of Scotland persuades syphilitic Darnley to return with her to Edinburgh. 10 Feb.: Darnley murdered at Kirk O'Field, Edinburgh. 24 Apr.: Bothwell abducts and impr. Mary at Dunbar Castle. 15 May: Mary m. James Hepburn, Earl of Bothwell. 2 June: d. of Shane O'Neill in brawl. 15 June: Scots nobles' victory at Carberry Hill, near Edinburgh; Bothwell flees. 20 June: Mary imprisoned for complicity in Darnley's murder. 2 July: Papacy severs links with Mary of Scotland. 24 July: Mary abdicates in favour of year-old son. 29 July: Prince James proclaimed King James VI. 22 Aug.: Earl of Moray proclaimed Regent. 9 Oct.: Sir Henry Sidney recalled to England for talks about Ireland.

1568

22 Jan.: Lady Catherine Grey d. at Yoxford, Suffolk. 1 Mar.: Hugh O'Neill made Baron of Dungannon. 2 May: Queen Mary escapes from Lochleven and joins supporters in southern Scotland. 13 May: Moray defeats Mary at Langside, near Glasgow. 16 May: Mary flees to Workington, Cumbria. 21 Sept.: Anglo-Spanish clash off coast of Mexico when John Hawkins attacks treasure ships. Hawkins routed at San Juan de Ulloa. 20 Oct.: Sidney returns to Ireland to implement government reforms. Dec.: Cecil orders seizure of Spanish bullion on ships at Plymouth and Southampton. Oct. – Jan.: Commissioners at York and, later, at Westminister, hear the case for and against Mary of Scotland. The 'Casket Letters' are produced against Mary.

1569

Feb.: fierce plague in Edinburgh. Feb.: James FitzMaurice FitzGerald proposes asking Spain for assistance v. England. June: Munster and south Leinster rebellion v. English rule is crushed by Sidney. Sept.: Duke of Norfolk plotting against Elizabeth. Nov.: Rebellion of the Northern Earls (Thomas Percy, Earl of Northumberland, and Charles Neville, Earl of Westmoreland), in favour of Mary Queen of Scots, then held at Sheffield Castle. Earls flee to Liddesdale, Scotland. 1 Nov.: Thomas Howard, 4th Duke of Norfolk, arrested.

1570

Jan.: 450 participants in rebellion of the earls executed. 23 Jan.: Regent Moray shot dead in Linthingow. Feb.: Ormond's brother surrender to Sidney; Thomond's rebellion. Pope Pius V issues *Regnans in Excelsis*, excommunicating Elizabeth. June: local unrest against Huguenot workers quashed in Norwich. 8 July: Pope finally excommunicates Elizabeth I. 3 Aug.: Duke of Norfolk released into house arrest. Sept.: Elizabeth considering m. either with Archduke Charles or Henri, duc d'Anjou. 21 Dec.: Earl of Thomond surrenders and receives pardon.

1571

25 Feb.: William Cecil created Lord Burghley. 27 Feb.: Sir John Perrot(t), President of Munster, arrives in Waterford. 25 Mar.: Sidney recalled in disgrace. Mar.: Kilmallock burnt by FitzGerald. Apr.: Matthew Stewart, Earl of Lennox and Regent of Scotland, sends men to take Dumbarton Castle. They hang John Hamilton, Archbishop of St Andrews. 3 Sept.: Duke of Norfolk arrested for complicity in Ridolfi Plot and put in Tower. Mary Queen of Scots' supporters kill Earl of Lennox. Dec.: Sir John Perrot(t) begins anglicisation programme in Munster by enforcing clothing regulation. In this year every cathedral and collegiate church in England is ordered to obtain and display Foxe's *Book of Martyrs*.

1572

16 Jan.: Norfolk found guilty of treason. 21 Jan.: Queen defers Norfolk's execution. 1 Mar.: Elizabeth sees off the 'sea-beggars', Dutch refugees, who then seize Brill in the Netherlands. 21 Apr.: Anglo-French Treaty of Blois provides for mutual assistance in case of attack and a joint effort to pacify Scotland. 2 June: execution of Duke of Norfolk. 13 June: Poor Law passed. June: Elizabeth's name linked to duc d'Alençon and parliament presses for heir. Summer: Queen visits Warwick. 24 Aug.: **St Bartholemew's Day Massacre**. 27 Aug.: Huguenots seek asylum at Rye, East Sussex. 29 Aug.: Sir Francis Drake seizes Spanish treasure in West Indies. 28 Oct.: Earl of Mar, Regent of Scotland, dies and is succeeded by Earl of Morton. 24 Nov.: d. of John Knox.

1573

23 Feb.: agreement between Morton and Mary ends resistance to James VI with the single exception of Edinburgh. Feb.: James FitzMaurice FitzGerald, rebel leader, submits to Sir John Perrot(t), President of Munster. Mar.: Earl of Desmond returns to Ireland from prison in England. Re-arrested almost immediately. 28 May: Edinburgh garrison surrenders to Morton. July: Perrot(t) leaves for England for health reasons. 9 July: Queen awards Earl of Essex colonisation rights over Co. Antrim. 9 Aug.: Drake brings enormous treaure to Plymouth. Queen sees this as threat to improved relations with Spain. Oct.: Essex and Hugh O'Neill of Dungannon clash with Bryan O'Neill of Clandeboye. 11 Nov.: Desmond escapes from Dublin Castle. Dec.: Sir Francis Walsingham, radical Protestant, made a Secretary of State along with Sir Thomas Smith.

1574

7 May: Elizabeth renews Treaty of Blois but lends some money to the French Huguenots. 8 May: Brian O'Neill submits to Earl of Essex. Summer: Queen visits Bristol. 2 Sept.: Earl of Desmond submits to Fitzwilliam(s), Vice-Deputy of Ireland. Nov.: Essex orders execution of Brian O'Neill and sparks off rebellion.

1575

Mar.: James Fitzmaurice FitzGerald sails for France to seek assistance against Elizabeth. 17 May: Archbishop Parker dies. 22 May: Queen withdraws support for Essex's plans to colonise Ulster. July: Queen progresses to Kenilworth. Visits Worcester, Lichfield, Reading, Woodstock and Windsor. 7 July: Anglo-Scots border row in response to arrest of English warden. 26 July: Essex's army massacres inhabitants of Rathlin Island, Co. Antrim. 18 Sept.: Sir Henry Sidney sworn in as Lord Deputy of Ireland.

1576

8 Feb.: Peter Wentworth, Puritan M.P. for Barnstaple, claims that freedom of speech should prevail in parliament. 9 Mar.: Earl of Essex

made Marshal of Ireland. 15 Mar.: Peter Wentworth, M.P., imprisoned in Tower. 22 Sept.: Brian O'Neill's supporters fatally poison Earl of Essex. 20 Dec.: Edmund Grindal challenges Queen's authority to suppress the 'prophesyings'.

1577

24 Mar.: John Aylmer appointed Bishop of London. May: Archbishop Grindal placed under house arrest. 23 Sept.: John Whitgift, Dean of Lincoln, appointed Bishop of Worcester. 11 Nov.: Christopher Hatton knighted and made Vice-Chamberlain of Privy Council. 13 Dec.: Drake sets out in *Pelican* on circumnavigatory voyage.

1578

4 Mar.: eleven-year-old James VI dismisses Regent Morton and assumes reins of government. 4 Apr.: Morton regains control of James VI at Stirling. Bothwell dies in dungeon at Dragsholm, Denmark. June: Elizabeth reconsiders proposals for m. to duc d'Alençon. Aug.: Queen progresses to Norwich and takes plague to the town. 12 Sept.: Sir Henry Sidney resigns as lord Deputy. In this year the General Assembly in Scotland approved *The Second Book of Discipline*.

1579

18 July: James FitzMaurice FitzGerald builds fortress at Smerwick, Co. Kerry. 24 July: Sir Humphrey Gilbert attacks FitzMaurice and Munster rebels at Smerwick. Aug.: Francis, Duke of Alençon, woos Elizabeth 1 Aug.: brothers of the Earl of Desmond murder the English negotiator as he sleeps. 16 Aug.: Sir John Perrot(t) made Admiral of English fleet to prevent aid reaching FitzMaurice. 18 Aug.: FitzMaurice d. in fight in Co. Limerick. 2 Nov.: Earl of Desmond pronounced traitor. 3 Nov.: Elizabeth has John Stubbs executed for objecting to proposed m. with Alençon.

1580

6 Apr.: St Paul's Cathedral damaged by earthquake. June: Jesuit missionaries, Edmund Campion and Robert Parsons, arrive at Dover. 15 July: Arthur, Lord Grey de Wilton appointed Lord Deputy of Ireland. 25 Aug.: Grey's troops defeated by Munster rebels at Glemalure, Co. Wicklow. James FitzMaurice FitzJames killed in skirmish. His cousin, Earl of Desmond, joins in revolt. Sept.: Drake completes circumnavigation. 10 Nov.: Grey crushes Irish rebellion and massacres occupants of FitzMaurice's fort at Smerwick. 31 Dec.: Earl of Morton arrested for treason in Edinburgh.

1581

18 Mar.: parl. dissolved after passing law making it treasonable offence to convert anyone to Catholicism. Mar.: widespread rebellion in province of

Munster. 4 Apr.: Drake knighted onboard *Golden Hind*. 2 June: Earl of Morton beheaded in Edinburgh. 17 July: Edmund Campion, Jesuit missionary, arrested in Berkshire and accused of treason. 5 Aug.: Esme Stuart, Earl of Lennox, created Duke of Lennox. 2 Nov.: Francis, duc d'Alençon and Dauphin of France, arrives in London to finalise m. negotiations with Elizabeth. 1 Dec.: execution of Campion.

1582

Feb.: Alençon leaves England after failure of m. negotiations. English aid promised against the Dutch. Aug.: Protestant Earls (Gower, Mar and Angus) and Lord Lindsay capture James VI at Ruthven Castle, near Perth. 31 Aug.: Lord Grey de Wilton, Lord Deputy, recalled from Ireland because of savagely repressive policies.

1583

6 July: d. of Archbp Grindal under house arrest at Lambeth. July: execution of 3 separatists at Bury St Edmunds for implying that the Queen is 'jezebel'. Sept.: mob destroys Mortlake, Surrey house of John Dee, astrologer and mathematician. 23 Sept.: John Whitgift, Bishop of Worcester, consecrated Archbishop of Canterbury. Nov.: Francis Throckmorton, under torture, confesses to Catholic plot to place Mary of Scotland on English throne. 11 Nov.: Earl of Desmond killed when in hiding in Co. Kerry. End of the Munster rebellion.

1584

Jan.: expulsion of Spanish ambassador, Bernadino de Mendoza, for complicity in Throckmorton plot. 7 Jan.: John Perrot(t) made lord Deputy of Ireland. Apr.: coup attempts to unseat government of James Stewart, Earl of Arran, in Stirling. 2 May: William Ruthven, Earl of Gowrie, executed for part in plot against Arran. May: Scottish parliament declares James VI 'head of the church' and ends Presbyterian system. 10 June: d. of duc d'Alençon. Protestant Henri of Navarre is the heir to the French throne. Assassination of William of Orange at Delft. 10 July: Francis Throckmorton executed. Oct.: Burghley and Walsingham draft proposal for 'Bond of Association' which people will sign to pledge themselves to protect Elizabeth and overthrow her enemies. Nov.: Perrot(t) reveals proposal for plantation of Ulster.

1585

Jan.: Mary Queen of Scots moved to Tutbury Castle; Feb.: Act of Parliament banishes Catholic priests and recalls Englishmen who have entered seminaries abroad. Noncompliance will be judged treasonable. 'Bond of Association' to protect the Queen given legal force. 9 Apr.: Sir Richard Grenville sets sail to colonise New World. May: Anglo-Spanish relations deteriorate when Philip II orders seizure of English ships in Atlantic ports. 27 July: Elizabeth infuriated when Scots kill Sir Francis

Russell. She plots against Arran government. 10 Aug.: Anglo-Dutch Treaty of Alliance at Nonsuch Palace. England pledges assistance, in the form of 7,000 soldiers led by Earl of Leicester, to the Dutch Protestant cause against Spanish rule. 7 Sept.: Drake sets sail for Spanish America. 18 Oct.: Grenville returns with news of the colonisation of Roanoke Island, Virginia. 2 Nov.: Arran government at Stirling collapses after English-backed coup. Dec.: Mary of Scotland is moved to Chartley Manor.

1586

June: Sir Francis Drake evacuates English from Roanoke Colony. June: Philip of Spain amassing armada. 7 July: Anglo-Scots Treaty of mutual defence. Parl. ratifies 'Bond of Association'. 20 Sept.: execution of Anthony Babington and six others. Severe famine after failure of harvest. 11 Oct.: trial of Mary of Scotland at Fotheringay Castle, Northamptonshire. 14 Oct.: Mary declared guilty of treason. 17 Oct.: Sir Philip Sidney killed during battle against Spanish at Zutphen, Flanders. Oct.: Hawkins returns from scouting trip to Spain with reports of planned Spanish invasion of England.

1587

1 Feb.: Elizabeth reluctantly signs death warrant of Mary of Scotland, her cousin. Feb.: Leicester's troops forced to surrender to Duke of Parma in Low Countries. 8 Feb.: execution of Mary Queen of Scots at Fotheringay Castle. 14 Feb.: Elizabeth in mourning for Mary; imprisons her secretary, William Davison, for drawing up death warrant. 27 Feb.: Anthony Cope, Puritan, introduces bill into parl. to abolish Church of England and replace it with Presbyterian system. Queen forbids debate. 23 Mar.: Wentworth and Cope protest against attempt to silence the debate about religious reform in parl. and are imprisoned. Bill dropped. Apr.: Sir Christopher Hatton appointed Lord Chancellor. 2 Apr.: Drake leaves Plymouth to destroy Spanish fleet and hinder invasion. 21 Apr.: Drake singes King of Spain's beard by destroying much of fleet. 8 May: Sir Walter Raleigh sets out to found New World colony. 2 July: Drake sets off for Azores to attack Spanish fleet. Oct.: Spanish fleet in need of repair. 24 Dec.: Peregrine Bertie, Lord Willoughby replaces Earl of Leicester as commander of troops in Low Countries.

1588

17 Feb.: Sir John Perrot(t) recalled from Ireland. Sir William Fitzwilliam(s) made Lord Deputy. 27 Feb.: Spain enters into peace talks with England at Ostend. 20 May: Spanish **Armada** sets sail under Duke of Medina Sidonia for England from Lisbon. 30 June: Fitzwilliam sworn in as Lord Deputy. June: James VI quells Catholic rebellion in Dumfreys. 26 June: preparations for defence of England and especially London in case of invasion. 19 July: Spanish **Armada** sighted off Scilly Isles. 25 July:

collapse of Anglo-Spanish peace talks at Bourbourg in the Low Countries. 28 July: destruction of much of Armada by English fire ships at Calais. **Armada** forced to flee. 29 July: Battle of Gravelines. 9 Aug.: renewed fears of Spanish invasion spur Elizabeth to rally troops at Tilbury. 4 Sept.: d. of Leicester at Cornbury, Oxon. 11 Sept.: storm off Ireland destroys at least 25 Spanish ships. Oct.: 'Marprelate tracts' in circulation in London. 24 Nov.: royal thanksgiving service for salvation from Armada at St Paul's Cathedral.

1589

Feb.: Richard Bancroft's St Paul's sermon declares that bishops rule church by divine right. 8 Apr.: Drake and Sir John Norris sail from Plymouth to harass Spanish and place Don Antonio on throne of Portugal. 17 Apr.: James VI suppresses Catholic rebellion near Aberdeen. July: Drake returned after disastrous voyage. 22 July: murder of Catholic Henry III of France; Henri of Navarre proclaimed King by troops. Sept.: England gives support to Henri of Navarre. 'Marprelate' printing press discovered in transit in Lancashire. 23 Dec.: Fitzwilliam(s) begins campaign to restore order in Connacht. Dec.: Sir Francis Vere's troops achieve significant victory over Spanish in Netherlands.

1590

Jan.: Lord Willoughby's troops leave France. 14 Mar.: Fitzwilliam(s) campaigns against Brian O'Rourke, Lord of Leitrim. 6 Apr.: d of Sir Francis Walsingham. 1 May: James VI brings his wife, Anne, from Denmark to Edinburgh.

1591

Mar.: Sir Roger Williams leads small force to assist Henri IV. 13 May: charge of sedition brought in Star Chamber against Puritans associated with 'Marprelate' tracts. 20 May: Robert Cecil knighted. May: Lord Howard and Grenville set off from Plymouth to seize Spanish treasure ships in Azores. 3 Aug.: Earl of Essex lands at Dieppe with large army to assist Henri IV. Aug.: Sir Robert Cecil made a Privy Councillor. 23 Sept.: royal progress to Earl of Hertford's home in Hampshire marks return to favour of Edward Seymour. Sept.: chastened Howard returns with fleet to Plymouth. Story of Grenville and the *Revenge* recounted. 7 Oct.: Stephen Trefulack, gentleman, indicted at Sessions in London for exercising 'certain wicked, detestable and diabolical arts called witchcrafts, enchantments, charms and sorceries' to cause George Southcott to unlawfully love Eleanor Thursbye. 1 Nov.: capture of father Edmund Jennings, S[ociety] of J[esus] in Holborn by Richard Topcliffe. 3 Nov.: Brian O'Rourke executed at Tyburn. 5 Nov.: proclamation against vagrant soldiers who are to be treated as vagabonds unless they substantiate their service claims. 20 Nov.: d. of Sir Christopher Hatton, Lord Chancellor. 21 Nov.: proclamation against Jesuits, dated 18 Oct., published. 10 Dec.: execution of 7 Catholics, including 4 Jesuits. 26 Dec.: Hugh Roe O'Donnell, son and heir of Hugh O'Donnell, lord of Tyrconnell, escapes from imprisonment in Dublin Castle.

1592

Jan.: recall of Earl of Essex from command of English forces at Rouen. Feb.: reinforcement of garrison at Rouen. 7 Feb.: murder of James Stewart, Earl of Moray, by Catholic Earl of Huntly in Edinburgh. 21 Feb.: execution of Thomas Pormort, seminary priest. 25 Feb.: Lord Mayor's petition to Archbishop of Canterbury concerning corrupting influences of plays and playhouses on apprentices and servants. 27 Apr.: trial of Sir John Perrott on charges of attempting rebellion against Queen when Lord Deputy in Ireland, 1587/8. 3 May: Hugh Roe O'Donnell made Lord of Tyrconnell on resignation of his father Hugh. 12 June: riots in Southwark amongst feltmakers' apprentices and masterless men. 23 June: measures taken against further rioting. 28 June: Francis, Earl of Bothwell, fails in attempt to capture James VI. 7 Aug.: Sir Walter Raleigh imprisoned after seducing Bess Throckmorton, lady in waiting to Queen. Masterless Irishmen ordered to be deported to repopulate Ireland. 15 Aug.: Robert Parsons' (alias Andreas Philopater) pamphlet answering the proclamation against Jesuits discovered. 1 Sept.: large Spanish invasion feared on south coast. 17 Sept.: Thame Fair postponed for fear of plague spreading. 23–8 Sept.: Queen at Oxford. Sept.: Raleigh set free to recapture Spanish treasure. 28 Sept.: Queen's progress to Oxford University; 21 Oct.: plague having little abated, sessions of the central courts moved to Hertford. Dec.: Synod of Catholic bishops held in Tyrconnell.

1593

1 Jan.: Spanish Catholic plot v. James VI uncovered. 21 Jan.: plays and games banned because of plague. 24 Feb.: Sir Peter Wentworth and Sir Henry Bromley petition Lord Keeper desiring House of Lords to join with Commons in pleading with Queen to entail the succession. 25 Feb.: Robert Devereux, Earl of Essex, made Privy Councillor. Wentworth and Bromley brought before the Council and imprisoned. 26 Feb.: bill against the Bishops disallowed by the Queen. 27 Feb.: Gilbert Laton, recusant, confesses Jesuit plot to kill Queen. 22 Mar.: arraignment and condemnation of Barrow and Greenwood. 6 Apr.: radical Protestants Henry Barrow and John Greenwood hanged for sedition. 7 Apr.: execution at Huntingdon of Alice and John Samuel and their daughter Agnes for bewitching to death Lady Cromwell, wife of Sir Henry, and bewitching daughters of Robert Throckmorton. 11 Apr.: Lords Lieutenant ordered to relieve maimed soldiers to tune of 2s a week. Apr.: Tyrconnell negotiates with Spain. 28 May: Stratford Bow Goose fair forbidden, to prevent disorder. 30 May: Christopher Marlowe stabbed to death in tavern brawl. 31 May: John Penry hanged for role in Marprelate tracts. 5 June: Londoners forbidden to enter Windsor in attempt to keep it clear of

plague for Queen's visit. 29 June: city feasts curtailed because of plague. July: King Henry IV converts to Catholicism. 1 July: London fairs abandoned because of plague. 19 July: Surrey Assizes held in a tent in St George's Field because of plague. 24 July: Bothwell stages coup and controls James VI's court at Holyrood. Spares King when James agrees to withdraw witchcraft charges.

1594

6 Jan.: Twelfth Night revels at Court: Earl of Essex at Queen's side. 2 Feb.: English capture Enniskillen, Co. Fermanagh. 19 Feb.: b. of Prince Henry of Scotland. 26 Mar.: Queen refuses to promote Francis Bacon to Solicitor-Generalship and falls out with Essex over it. 28 Feb.: torture and arraignment of Queen's physician, Roderigo Lopez, at Essex's instigation. 3 Apr.: Bothwell fails to capture Edinburgh. 16 May: Sir William Russell appointed Lord Deputy. June: Maguire and Tyrconnell besiege Enniskillen. 3 June: d. of Bp John Aylmer of London. 7 June: execution of Lopez at Tyburn. 26 July: execution of John Boste, S.J. for high treason. 20 Aug.: discovery of Spanish assisted plot by Father Holt, Sir William Stanley and Captain Edmund Yorke to kill Queen. 30 Aug.: English led by Russell raise siege of Enniskillen. 3 Oct.: Huntly and Catholic rebels defeat King's Lieutenant, Earl of Argyll, at Glenlivet. 17 Nov.: Queen gives banquet to celebrate thirty years on throne. 30 Nov.: Lord Mayor calls conference to discuss suppression of rogues in capital. 8 Dec.: d. of Cardinal Allen reported. 24 Dec.: pamphlet, *A Conference about the next succession to the Crown of England*, (dedicated to Earl of Essex and supposedly by a Jesuit writing abroad) is circulating in England.

1595

25 Jan.: Tyrone's rebellion in Ireland. 31 Jan.: reported that Jesuits held in Wisbeach Castle are grown dangerous through overmuch liberty. 6 Feb.: Sir Walter Raleigh sails to find 'El Dorado'. 20 Feb.: trial of Robert Southwell, S.J. at King's Bench. 22 Feb.: execution of Southwell at Tyburn. Last English troops leave France. Apr.: Earl of Bothwell escapes to France. 15 May: Tyrconnell and Hugh Maguire recapture Enniskillen. 13–16 June: apprentices and masterless men riot in London. 23 June: apprentices and servants involved in disorder in Southwark. 29 June: unruly youths in riot on Tower Hill. 4 July: proclamation against unlawful assemblies prompted by disorders. 18 July: Provost Marshal appointed to oversee order in London. 24 July: youths involved in Tower Hill riot hanged and disembowelled on Tower Hill. Aug.: Raleigh returns empty handed. 7 Aug.: fear of new Spanish Armada. 23 Aug.: Tyrconnell and Tyrone invite Archduke Albert, Governor of the Low Countries, to be King of Ireland. 28 Aug.: Drake and Hawkins sail for West Indies. 15 Sept.: great fire at Woburn, Beds, consumes much of town. 18 Oct.: Dublin government makes peace with Tyrone and Tyrconnell. Oct.: Spanish fleet intending to invade Ireland is lost at sea. 6 Nov.: Essex' loss

of favour signalled by Queen's refusal to make Francis Bacon Solicitor General. Dec.: Elizabeth forbids publication of Whitgift's **Lambeth Articles**. 14 Dec.: Henry Hastings, Earl of Huntingdon, 'the puritan earl', Lord President of the Council of the North, dies at York.

1596

29 Jan.: Drake d. at sea off Panama. 23 Feb.: Middlesex justices ordered to suppress building of 'base tenements and disorderly houses' erected in the suburbs of London which have attracted beggars and unemployed people and encouraged the spread of sickness, thievery and sedition. 17 Mar.: Spanish raid near Plymouth. 12 May: Tyrone receives royal pardon. 6 July: Tyrone in Munster incites rebellion. 20 June: Earl of Essex's English and Dutch army takes Cadiz by surprise. 4 July: Essex leaves Cadiz. 5 July: Sir Robert Cecil made principal royal secretary. One of the worst harvests of the century. Food riots in Kent. 11 July: order of Council that blackamoors brought in as servants be deported. 22 July: plays forbidden in City because of plague. 18 Aug.: touching for the Queen's Evil. 18 Oct.: wreck, off Finisterre, of Spanish fleet bound for invasion of Ireland. 28 Oct.: fear of large Spanish invasion. 31 Oct.: proclamation against dearth forbids export of grain etc. Nov.: Oxfordshire protests against enclosure and food prices at Enslow Hill.

1597

Jan.: Anglo-Scottish border commission created. Sir Robert Cecil in great favour with the Queen. 6 Feb.: trade between Ireland and Spain banned. 5 Mar.: Russell replaced as Lord Deputy by Thomas, Lord Burgh. 14 Mar.: male witch hanged at Lancaster. May: grain riots in Kent, Sussex and Norfolk. 23 May: Insolent behaviour of Lady Mary Howard, lady in waiting to Queen. July: Burgh marches v. Tyrone. 29 July: reports of devastation on Scots border. Oct.: Spanish fleet bound for Ireland wrecked in Bay of Biscay. 13 Oct.: d. of Burgh from typhus at Newry. 26 Oct.: Earl of Essex returned empty handed from expedition v. Spanish treasure fleet. 27 Oct.: mustering in southern counties for defence against expected Spanish invasion. 29 Oct.: Earl of Ormond made Lieutenant-General of Queen's army in Ireland. 22 Dec.: chastened Tyrone submits to Ormond. Dec.: Earl of Essex made **Earl Marshal**.

1598

1 Jan.: Tyrone submits. 9 Feb.: legislation passed restoring recently enclosed land to tillage and rebuilding of houses destroyed in process of enclosure. 30 May: town v. gown fray at Oxford. 25 June: Ormond campaigns v. Tyrone at Leinster. 4 Aug.: Lord Burghley d. at house in Strand. 14 Aug.: Tyrone, Tyrconnell and Fermanagh defeat English at Battle of the Yellow Ford in Ulster. 9 Sept.: lawlessness near London to be put down by J.P.s and a provost marshal. 22 Sept.: Ben Jonson wounded. Oct.: Essex apologises to Elizabeth for row in 1596. Back at

court. Nov.: Tyrone and others lead raids on Dublin. 5 Nov.: Lincs., Northants., Hunts., Isle of Ely, Sussex and Surrey are devastated by floods. 9 Nov.: arraignment of Edward Squire for conspiracy to kill Queen. 5 Dec.: Queen seeks and obtains loan from City to finance army in Ireland.

1599

Feb.: Earl of Essex prepares army for Ireland; crazed by delays. 12 Mar.: Essex made Lord Lieutenant. 27 Mar.: Essex leaves for Ireland. 15 Apr. Essex arrives in Dublin. 29 May: Essex defeated at Deputy's Pass, Co. Wicklow. May.: Robert Cecil appointed Master of Court of Wards (*see* Section VI). 14 July: witch hanged at St Edmondsbury, Suffolk. Aug.: Spanish fleet sent to invade Ireland is defeated off Brittany. Spanish alarms. 8 Sept.: Essex and Tyrone discuss a truce in Ulster. 24 Sept.: Essex returns to England without royal permission. 28 Sept.: Essex ordered by Queen to keep to his apartment. 2 Oct.: Essex put under close arrest in house of Lord Keeper. 4–20 Nov.: English nunnery opened in Brussels. 28 Nov.: Star Chamber (*see* Section IX) hears Essex case. 2 Dec.: Essex's household dismissed. 4 Dec.: Anne Kerke hanged as witch at Tyburn. 15 Dec.: Earl of Essex desperately ill.

1600

Jan.: Queen refuses Essex's **New Year Gift**. Feb. and Mar.: the clown Will Kemp wagers to dance from London to Norwich and does so. 21 Mar.: Essex returns home under house arrest. Apr.: Earl of Ormond captured by O'Mores. 23 Apr.: township of Gamlingay, Camb., destroyed by fire. 25 May: Queen orders collection to relieve Gamlingay. May: Charles Blount, Lord Mountjoy, new Lord Deputy, arrives in Ireland. May: George Carew, President of Munster, wastes province in campaign v. Tyrone's rebels. 6 June: Essex tried before private commission on five counts: desertion of post; failure in Ireland; conferring of knighthoods and appointment of Southampton as general of horse despite Elizabeth's orders; tone of his letters; and his meeting with Tyrone. He threw himself on Elizabeth's mercy. 5 June: Queen partly pardons Essex but he is deprived of most of his offices and placed under house arrest in Essex House on the Strand. 13 June: Ormond escapes. 18 June: Somerset grain riots. 21 Aug.: execution of 2 seminary priests at York. 26 Aug.: Essex released but barred from court. Sept.: Essex petitions Queen for forgiveness. 25 Sept.: licensing of restricted number of rag and bone collectors in City. 5 Oct.: James VI survives Gowrie Plot, Perth. Oct.: Mountjoy enters Tyrone's lands in Ulster. 30 Oct.: Essex deprived of main source of income, duties on sweet wines. 1 Dec.: Essex reported to be resentful and rebellious. 22 Dec.: Essex returns to London and keeps open house at Essex House, where public sermons attract much attention.

1601

2 Jan.: preachers at Essex House opine that the superior magistrates of the realm have power to restrain kings themselves. 7 Feb.: performance of *Richard II* at the Globe at the specific request of some of Essex's followers. 8 Feb.: Essex captures privy councillors sent to bring him before the council for conspiracy. Dismal failure of Essex's attempt to raise the city on his behalf. 15 Feb.: royal proclamation orders non Londoners and those without business there out of London. 19 Feb.: Essex and Southampton on trial. 21 Feb.: Essex confesses. 25 Feb.: Essex privately executed at Tower. 27 Feb.: Father Barkworth, priest, executed at Tyburn along with a Jesuit and a lay recusant woman. 1 Mar.: Dr Barlow preaches sermon against Essex at Paul's Cross. 5 Mar.: arraignment of Essex's collaborators. 13 Mar.: execution of Merrick and Cuffe, two of the conspirators. 15 Mar.: execution of Sir Christopher Blount and Sir Charles Danvers, more of the conspirators. Apr. to June: Cecil conducts secret correspondence with James VI. 25 May: commission inquiring into preservation of wealth of the realm. July: Anglo-Dutch forces defend Ostend against Spanish invasion. 2 Aug.: fear of Spanish invasion. 22 Aug.: Walton, Leics, destoyed by fire. Sept.: Spanish fleet lands at Kinsale to lend assistance to Tyrconnell and Tyrone against England. 26 Oct.: Mountjoy arrives at Kinsale with 10,000 men. 7 Nov.: Carew joins Mountjoy in siege of Kinsale. 20 Nov.: bill concerning abuse of monopolies (a matter for the royal prerogative) introduced into parliament. 30 Nov.: Elizabeth soothes fears of parliamentary delegates concerning abuse of monopolies. 24 Dec.: Mountjoy's resounding defeat of Tyrone at Kinsale. 27 Dec.: Tyrone withdraws to Ulster and Tyrconnell escapes to Spain.

1602

2 Jan.: Spanish commander surrenders to Mountjoy. 22 June: Proclamation seeks to restrict building of new buildings in London which draw in impoverished people. 30 July: Earl of Lincoln accused of disrespectful speeches about relationshiop between Queen and Essex. 2–3 Aug.: Queen visits Lord Keeper at Harefield. 21 Oct.: Tyrone submits to Queen. 5 Nov.: proclamation advocating removal of Jesuits and secular priests. 6 Dec.: Queen entertained by Robert Cecil at Strand. 27 Dec.: Queen noted to be infirm.

1603

31 Jan.: secular priests join to assure fidelity to Queen. 17 Feb.: Elizabeth authorises Mountjoy to pardon Tyrone if he surrenders. 9 Mar.: court alive with talk of Queen's imminent death and question of succession. 17 Mar.: council consults with nobility. Rogues pressed and sent to Netherlands. Recusants committed. 24 Mar.: d. of Elizabeth I at Richmond. She names James VI as successor with dying breath. Couriers ride to Scotland to inform James. 30 Mar.: Tyrone submitted in exchange for generous pardon.

1604

Jan.: Hampton Court Conference. King receives 'Millenary Petition' from Puritans but calms fears of the bps. Apr.: Commissioners appointed to discuss King's title, union of parliaments, laws and economies. Aug.: Anglo-Spanish Peace Treaty ends war after summer of negotiations. 20 Oct.: James VI adopts title 'King of Great Britain, France and Ireland'.

Ireland

Chronology

Ireland had been conquered by the Normans in the twelfth century and a feudal ruling class had been imposed. The Kings of England claimed to be lords of Ireland but ruled little of it. The area which was ruled by the English – the Pale – was little more than a stretch of coast reaching 50 miles north from Dublin. Anglo-Irish families like the FitzGeralds (Geraldines) and Butlers had become as Irish as the Irish themselves. Ireland in Tudor times was made up of the Pale under English rule (stretching from Dundalk to Dublin and beyond) and four provinces, each under the control of tribal chiefs. As Map 2 indicates, the extent of the Pale was increased under Mary (by the inclusion of King's County and Queen's County) and Elizabeth. The term Geraldine is applied to the followers of both Kildare and Desmond.

LEINSTER – Earl of Kildare (FitzGerald); Earl of Ormond.

MUNSTER – FitzGeralds of Desmond; O'Briens of Thomond.

CONNAUGHT (also CONNACHT) – wild.

ULSTER – O'Donnell of Tyrconnell; O'Neil of Tyrone, Fermanagh, Monaghan and Armagh. Clandeboy in Antrim was under the control of the Macdonalds, a Scottish clan from the Western Isles.

The Reign of Henry VII

When Henry VII ascended the throne the Irish chiefs were using the English dynastic struggle as a vehicle for their own fight for independence. Kildare and Desmond espoused the Yorkist cause while their enemies, the Butlers under the Earl of Ormond, supported the Lancastrians. Ireland was a springboard for pretenders to the English throne. Kildare gave assistance to Lambert Simnel (1487) and, despite Henry VII's forbearance after this, proceeded to aid Warbeck (1491). Henry finally deprived Kildare of the Deputyship and put in his own men.

1493 Henry pardons Kildare after personal submission.

1494 Sir Edward Poynings is made Deputy (the nominal governor of

Ireland is Prince Henry). Poynings plans to conquer Ulster and impose English constitution.

1494   Poynings fails to take Ulster.

1494   December: Irish parliament at Drogheda enacts Poynings' Law which destroys legislative independence of Irish parliament; attainder of Kildare – sent to Tower.

1496   Henry VII effectively gives up on problem of imposing English rule in Ireland. Recall of Poynings; Kildare made Lord Deputy.

1497   26 July: Warbeck lands at Cork.

The Reign of Henry VIII
1521   Surrey recalled from Ireland. Ireland effectively ruled by Sir Piers Butler and Gerald, Earl of Kildare, in succession.

1526   Kildare imprisoned in Tower. Skeffington rules Ireland.

1529   return of Kildare.

1532   Kildare made Lord Deputy. Disorder.

1534   Kildare dies in the Tower. His son besieges Dublin. Skeffington and Brereton lead relief of Dublin.

1536   Lord Leonard Grey replaces Skeffington as Lord Deputy.

1537   'Silken Thomas' FitzGerald, Earl of Kildare, and others executed in London. Geraldine power finally crushed.

1540   Sir Anthony St Leger made Lord Deputy.

1541   June: Henry assumes title of King of Ireland and Head of the Irish Church.

1542   First Jesuit mission to Ireland lands.

The Reign of Edward VI
1548   Sir Edward Bellingham replaces St Leger.

1549   Bellingham suppresses rebellions in King's and Queen's Counties.

1550   St Leger returns as Lord Deputy.

1550   St Leger recalled for alleged Catholicism.

1552   Privy Council acquits St Leger.

The Reign of Mary I
1553   St Leger again Lord Deputy.

1556 St Leger charged with embezzlement and recalled; died; Earl of Sussex is made Lord Deputy; Shane O'Neill supreme in Ireland.

The Reign of Elizabeth I

1560 Elizabeth orders crushing of O'Neill.

1561 defeat of Sussex in Ireland.

1562 Shane O'Neill submits to Queen in London.

1563 Failure of Sussex's attempts to restore order.

1564 Sussex recalled.

1566 Henry Sidney appointed Lord Deputy.

1567 Shane O'Neill's death.

1568 Devon Adventurers attempt to colonise Munster.

1569 Revolt of the Desmonds (FitzGerald) led by James FitzMaurice FitzGerald. Elizabeth's second Irish parl. meets.

1573 Desmond crushed. Plantation of Ulster attempted.

1576 Henry Sidney returns as Lord Deputy.

1579 Desmond revolt under Gerald FitzGerald, Earl of Desmond. Destruction of Munster. July: Spanish troops arrive to aid revolt.

1580 Lord Grey de Wilton made Lord Deputy.

1582 Famine in Munster.

1583 Death of Gerald FitzMaurice FitzGerald, 14th Earl of Desmond. Plantation of Munster initiated.

1584 John Perrot(t) made Lord Deputy.

1585 April: Elizabeth's third parl. meets.

1588 when Perrot(t) is replaced by Fitzwilliam, Ireland is at peace.

1589 commission set up to assess progress of plantation of Munster.

1591 Royal foundation of Trinity College, Dublin. Sir Henry Bagnal appointed Chief Commissioner for Government of Ulster.

1594 Earl of Tyrone (Hugh O'Neill) leads Ulster revolt and appeals to Spain for help.

1595 Sir John Norreys, commander of the English forces, fails to crush the Ulster revolt.

1597 Lord Burgh is made Lord Deputy but dies in October 1597.

1597–June 1598 Truce.

1598 Aug: at Battle of the Yellow Ford the English army under Bagnal is defeated. Hugh O'Neill supreme in Ireland.

1599 Essex made Lord Lieutenant. 15 April: Essex reaches Dublin. 8 September: Essex treats with Tyrone and gives him a breathing space to await Spanish assistance. English army wasting away with disease. 24 September: Essex leaves Ireland. 28 September: Essex in London.

1600 January: Tyrone invades Munster. Mountjoy is made Lord Deputy. July–August: order restored in English Pale. September–October: Tyrone forced to go north. November: Earl of Desmond captured.

1601 Spanish occupy port of Kinsale. Mountjoy and Carew occupy Kinsale. Battle of Kinsale with Irish troops. Tyrone and Tyrconnel(l) (Hugh Roe O'Donnell) routed.

1603 March: Tyrone surrenders.

Governors of Ireland

LJ = Lord Justice
KL = King's Lieutenant
LD = Lord Deputy
LL = Lord Lieutenant
D = Deputy

21 Aug. 1484   John de la Pole, Earl of Lincoln, KL.

The Reign of Henry VII
11 Mar. 1486   Jasper Tudor, Duke of Bedford, KL.

24 May-Oct. 1487   Gerald, 8th Earl of Kildare, KL.

11 Sept. 1494   Prince Henry, KL (There were a series of Deputies. Most important was Sir Edward Poynings, D from Sept. 1494 to Dec. 1495.).

The Reign of Henry VIII
8 June 1509-d. 3 Sept. 1513   Gerald, 8th Earl of Kildare, LJ and LD.

4 Sept. 1513–26 Nov. 1515   Gerald, 9th Earl of Kildare, LJ and LD.

13 Apr. 1515   William Preston, Viscount Gormanston, LJ.

Before Sept. 1515 – Sept. 1519   Gerald, 9th Earl of Kildare, LD.

After Sept. 1519 – Mar. 1520   Maurice FitzGerald of Lackagh, LJ.

10 Mar. 1520–6 Mar. 1522   Thomas Howard, Earl of Surrey, LL.

6 Mar. 1522–13 May 1524   Piers Butler, pretended 8th Earl of Ormond, LD.

13 May 1524 – Nov. 1526   Gerald, 9th Earl of Kildare, LD (appointment secret until 4 August).

1527–15 May 1528   Richard Nugent, Baron Devlin, LJ.

15 May 1528–4 Aug. 1528   Thomas FitzGerald, LJ.

4 Aug. 1528–22 June 1529   Piers Butler, 1st Earl of Ossory, LD.

22 June 1529 – d. 22 July 1536   Henry FitzRoy, Duke of Richmond, LL. (**22 June 1530–5 July 1532**   William Skeffington was D; **5 July 1532 – Feb. 1534**   Gerald, 9th Earl of Kildare, was D; **Feb. – June 1534**   Thomas, Lord Offaly, was D.).

June – Aug. 1534   Richard Nugent, acting D.

23 July 1534 – d. 31 Dec. 1535   William Skeffington, LD.

23 Feb. 1536–1 Apr. 1540   Leonard, Lord Grey, LD.

1 Apr. 1540–7 July 1540   Sir William Brereton, LJ.

7 July 1540–22 Apr. 1548   Anthony St Leger, LD. (**12 Oct. 1543–1 Dec. 1546**   William Brabazon was LJ and D.).

The Reign of Edward VI
22 Apr. 1548–27 Dec. 1549   Edward Bellingham, LD.

27 Dec. 1549–2 Feb. 1550   Francis Bryan, LJ.

2 Feb.–4 Aug. 1550 William Brabazon, LJ.

4 Aug. 1550–29 Apr. 1551   Anthony St Leger, LD.

29 Apr. 1551–6 Dec. 1552   Thomas Cusack and Gerald Aylmer, LJs.

The Reign of Mary I
Oct. 1553–27 Apr. 1556   Anthony St Leger, LD.

27 Apr. 1556–Dec. 1558   Thomas Radcliff, Lord Fitzwalter (1557: Earl of Sussex), LD. (**January-December 1558**: Henry Sidney, LJ, was D.).

The Reign of Elizabeth I
12 Dec. 1558–3 Jul. 1559   Henry Sidney, LJ.

3 July 1559–13 Oct. 1565   Thomas Radcliff, Earl of Sussex, LD and then LL. (During this period there was a D. **18 January 1560–2 May 1564**: William Fitzwilliams was LJ and D; **2 May 1564–9 October 1567**: Nicholas Arnold was LJ and D.).

13 Oct. 1565–1 Apr. 1571   Henry Sidney, LD. (**9 October 1567**: Robert Weston and William Fitzwilliams were appointed Ds when Sidney was recalled to London to discuss Irish programme.).

1 Apr. 1571–5 Aug. 1575   William Fitzwilliams, LJ and then LD.

5 Aug. 1575–12 Sept. 1578 resigned   Henry Sidney, LD.

27 Apr. 1578–11 Oct. 1579   William Drury, LJ.

11 Oct. 1579–15 July 1580   William Pelham, LJ.

15 July 1580–25 Aug. 1582   Arthur, Lord Grey de Wilton, LD.

25 Aug. 1582–7 Jan. 1584   Adam Loftus, Archbishop of Dublin, and Henry Wallop, LJs.

7 Jan. 1584–17 Feb. 1588   John Perrot(t), LD.

17 Feb. 1588–16 May 1594   William Fitzwilliam(s), LD.

16 May 1594–5 Mar. 1597   William Russell, LD.

5 Mar. 1597–29 Oct. 1597   Thomas, Lord Burgh, LD. (**29 October 1597**: Thomas, 10th Earl of Ormond, appointed in charge of military affairs.).

29 Oct 1597–15 Nov. 1597   Thomas Norreys, LJ.

15 Nov. 1597–12 Mar. 1599   Adam Loftus, Archbishop of Dublin, and Richard Gardiner, LJs.

12 Mar. 1599–24 Sept. 1599   Robert Devereux, 2nd Earl of Essex, LL.

24 Sept. 1599–21 Jan. 1600   Adam Loftus, Archbishop of Dublin, and George Cary, LJs.

21 Jan. 1600–30 May 1603   Charles Blount, Lord Mountjoy, LD, LJ, LD and LL.

30 May 1603–1 Feb. 1605   Sir George Cary, LD.

Rebellions Against the Tudors: Chronologies

Terms which are covered in Section XIV (Glossary) appear in **bold**

Yorkist Risings Against Henry VII, 1486–87 March 1486: Francis Lord Lovell attempted unsuccessfully to raise North Yorkshire v. Henry.

March 1486: Thomas and Humphrey Stafford failed to raise the West Country v. Henry. The Staffords claimed sanctuary at Culham, Oxon. but were removed. July: Humphrey Stafford executed.

16 June 1487: Lambert Simnel defeated at Battle of Stoke near Newark. Supported by Earl of Lincoln. Execution of Lincoln.

The Yorkshire Rebellion, 1489 Earl of Northumberland murdered while collecting parliamentary subsidy for the war in Brittany. Rioting led by Sir John Egremont. Earl of Surrey suppressed riot.

The Cornish Rebellion, 1497 15,000 Cornish rebels marched against London in protest against taxes for a war on Scotland. The leaders were Lord Audley, Michael Joseph (a blacksmith) and Thomas Flamank (a lawyer). 16 June 1497: camped on Blackheath. 17 June 1497: numbers reduced by half through desertion; defeated by royal troops; leaders executed; rebels fined heavily.

Resistance to the Amicable Grant, 1525 Widespread resistance, especially in Suffolk, to Wolsey's **Amicable Grant** to finance French war. Henry VIII got the point, relinquished the grant and gave up the idea of war.

The Pilgrimage of Grace, 1536 1 October: Rising at Louth, Lincolnshire – it collapsed within a fortnight; Duke of Suffolk's threat of armed intervention effective.

Spreads to Yorkshire.

16 October: Robert Aske and Yorkshire pilgrims defeated at York.

Duke of Norfolk forced to parley with rebels at Doncaster in face of 30,000 strong rebel force. 6 December: Aske delivers demands to Norfolk who persuades rebels to disperse with promise of royal pardon and summoning a free parliament.

January and February 1537: fresh northern risings.

Henry revokes pardon. 216 executions of rebels. July 1537: Robert Aske hanged.

Much debate amongst historians concerning the motivation for the pilgrimage and the rebels' membership. Their demands showed general hostility towards Cromwell's regime and the religious innovations in particular, but also concern about the regional economy.

The Western Rebellion, 1549   June 1549: Rising in West of England against Prayer Book and Edward VI's religious programme in general.
6 August 1549: Lord Russell aided by Italian mercenaries relieved 6 week siege of Exeter.
17 August 1549: Rebellion finally crushed at Sampford Courtenay.

Kett's Rebellion, 1549   12 July 1549: Robert Kett, Norfolk tanner and landowner, and rebels encamp on Mousehold Heath, near Norwich, in protest against enclosures and exploitation. They also expressed grievances against the clergy but actually adopted the new Prayer Book.
27 August: Rebellion crushed at Battle of Dussindale by Earl of Warwick, using foreign mercenaries.

Wyatt's Rebellion, 1554   January 1554: Sir Thomas Wyatt led 4,000 men from Kent to London. The rebels crossed the Thames at Kingston but were stopped at Ludgate, where Wyatt surrendered on 7 February. Wyatt was executed on 11 April 1554. The rebellion was part of a wider plot to depose Mary I and thus prevent her marriage to Philip II of Spain.

The Rebellion of the Northern Earls, 1569   November 1569: when the Duke of Norfolk was imprisoned in the Tower and the Earls of Northumberland and Westmorland were summoned to court to answer for their part in a conspiracy to marry Norfolk to Mary Stuart, the Earls rebelled. On 14 November the rebels entered Durham and restored Catholic worship in its cathedral. They retreated when the Earl of Sussex raised an army against them.
January 1570: a separate rebellion was staged by Leonard Dacre but he was defeated in battle between Hexham and Carlisle.

The Essex Rebellion, 1601   In late 1599 the Earl of Essex was placed under house arrest for his conduct in Ireland. He hatched a conspiracy and on 8 February 1601 attempted to raise London in his defence. He was executed on 25 February 1601.

Ecclesiastical and Religious Developments

Chronology

Terms which are covered in Section XIV (Glossary) appear in **bold**

The Reign of Henry VII

1487 Those charged with high treason denied right of **sanctuary**

1489 further attacks on clerical privileges. Guilty felons who claim **benefit of clergy** are to be branded on the thumb. Proof of holy orders required if they commit a second indictable offence and demand right of clergy.

1496 John Colet, humanist scholar, lectures at Oxford on St Paul's *Epistle to the Romans*. He sets the epistle in its historical context and compares the late fifteenth-century church unfavourably.

1497 those charged with petty treason denied right of **sanctuary**.

1498 Henry VII founded Franciscan Observant Houses.

1499 English Province of the Observants established. New convents were founded at Newcastle-upon-Tyne and Canterbury.

1500 House of Observants founded at Richmond.

1503 William Warham appointed Archbishop of Canterbury.

The Reign of Henry VIII

1509 Death of Henry VII. Erasmus arrives in England for an extended period. He is given a position at Cambridge.

1511–14 Erasmus working on his Latin translation of the Greek New Testament.

1512 Act of Parliament consolidates Henry VII's legislative attacks on **benefit of clergy** in the case of serious crimes.

1514 Thomas Wolsey, Bishop of Lincoln, made Archbishop of York. May: **Pope** declares that no layman may have authority over a cleric. Richard Hunne was sued in the Consistory Court (*see* Section *IX*) for non-payment of a **mortuary.** The priest won and Hunne was imprisoned.

Hunne retaliated by suing the priest, Thomas Dryffeld, in the Court of King's Bench under the statutes of **praemunire**. December: Richard Hunne found dead in his cell. Murder is suspected.

1515 parliament debates bills to abolish mortuary fees and to limit **benefit of clergy**. In connection with Hunne's case, Dr Richard Kidderminster, Abbot of Winchcombe, and Dr Henry Standish, the Crown's appointee, debated the right of the secular courts to try clergy and, therefore, the independence of the church and its servants from state jurisdiction. **Convocation** summons Standish to answer for his criticisms of the church but the King secures his release and later rewards him with the See of St Asaph. A compromise, which included the suppression of all anti-clerical bills and the exaction of fines from the guilty parties in the Hunne case, is worked out. December: Thomas Wolsey made Lord Chancellor and Cardinal.

1518 June: Wolsey appointed **Papal Legate** *a latere* in England.

1520 regular meetings of Hugh Latimer, Thomas Cranmer, Miles Coverdale, Robert Barnes and John Frith and others at the White Horse tavern, Cambridge. This discussion group was characterised by a broadly sympathetic attitude to church reform.

1521 Wolsey acts against importation of Lutheran books. May: solemn public burning of Lutheran books before Wolsey in London. Persecution of heretics in London diocese; many heretics burnt. Henry VIII published his anti-Lutheran work, *Assertio Septem Sacramentorum*, and in May presented a copy to Pope Leo X. Pope Leo X confers title of *Fidei Defensor* (Defender of the Faith) upon Henry.

1522 Martin Luther publishes his German translation of the New Testament which is based on Erasmus's text.

1523 28 year-old scholar, William Tyndale, seeks but does not receive support from Bishop Tunstall of London for English translation of Bible.

1524 Tyndale visits Hamburg, Wittenberg and Cologne. He bases his English translation of the New Testament on Erasmus and Luther.

1525 Thomas Wolsey suppresses 29 religious houses and transfers their financial resources to Cardinal College, Oxford. Robert Barnes, a friar in the Austen House at Cambridge, attacks ceremonies in religion. Printing of Tyndale's English New Testament begins at Cologne but, because of intervention by church authorities, has to be transferred to and completed at Worms.

1526 April: copies of Tyndale's New Testament on sale in England. Bishop of London forbids its dissemination or possession in his diocese and a copy burned at Paul's Cross. New edition printed by Christopher Endhoven at Antwerp.

1527 Henry has doubts about the legality of his marriage to Catherine of Aragon (against which he had originally protested). May: Wolsey cites Henry VIII before a court on charges of illicit cohabitation. June: Sack of Rome. Catherine of Aragon's nephew, Emperor Charles V, now controls the Papacy and any hopes of papal approval for a divorce have been dashed. Beginnings of persecution of **Lollards,** especially in Essex and Buckinghamshire.

1528 Cardinal Wolsey prosecutes some, including Thomas Garrett of Oxford, for distributing Tyndale's New Testament.

1529 October: Thomas More becomes Lord Chancellor but does not disguise his disapproval of the divorce. Wolsey resigns most ecclesiastical offices and retires to York. November: First meeting of the so-called Reformation Parliament, which opens with renewed calls for ecclesiastical reform. Acts passed to regulate burial and probate fees; to remove **Benefit of Clergy** from those charged with murder or robbery; to limit **pluralism**; to limit clerical involvement in trade and commerce; to remove possibility of papal dispensations. Commons draws up a Supplication directed against the bishops.

1530 Hoochstraten of Antwerp publishes Tyndale's English version of the Pentateuch (first five books of the Old Testament). Endhoven publishes a new edition of his New Testament. Henry VIII sets up **commission** of inquiry into need for English Bible which reports back favourably. George Joye publishes *Psalms* in English. The Pope is petitioned by 22 abbots to approve a divorce between Henry VIII and Catherine of Aragon. Henry VIII's agents toured the major universities of Europe soliciting academic support for the divorce. **Praemunire** charges brought against leading churchmen who had had financial dealings with Wolsey. November: d. of Wolsey at Leicester as he travels south to meet charges.

1531 January: Pope orders Henry VIII not to remarry until divorce issue is settled. Whole clergy charged with **praemunire**. Act for the Pardon of the Clergy passed in exchange for the levy of an enormous fine. This amounted to £19,000 from the **Convocation** of York and £100,000 from the **Convocation** of Canterbury. March: Thomas Bilney, Lutheran preacher, arrested. Bilney burnt as heretic at Norwich.

1532 January: Pope threatens Henry VIII with **excommunication**. March: Archbp Warham excommunicates Hugh Latimer. Cromwell promotes act restricting payment of annates (yearly taxes) to **Papacy** by the bps to 5 per cent of income. Henceforward the King and not the Papacy would provide the necessary authority for consecration of new bps. This act will not come into force for a year. Thomas Cromwell revives the Supplication Against the Ordinaries (*see* 1529) which objects to the number of **Holy Days**, the unrepresentative nature of **Convocation**, the oppressions and exactions of the church courts and of the priesthood. 18 March: Supplication handed to King; **Convocation** replies with Answer of the Ordinaries, penned by Bishop Stephen Gardiner of Winchester. May: King suspends legislative business of **Convocation** and orders inquiry into **Canon Law**. 15 May: Warham and seven other bps sign the Submission of the Clergy. Thomas More resigns as Lord Chancellor. August: d. of Archbp Warham. September: publication, with Henry's consent, of *A Glass of the Truth*, supporting the divorce.

1533 January: private m. of Henry and Anne Boleyn, by Thomas Cranmer. February: Act in Restraint of Appeals to Rome. March: Thomas Cranmer consecrated Archbishop of Canterbury. (Papal **Bull** secured.) 23 May: Archbp Cranmer declares marriage with Catherine void and that with Anne valid. September: Papal **excommunication** of Henry VIII.

1534 German Bible published at Wittenberg. New edition of Tyndale's New Testament published at Antwerp. Miles Coverdale starts work on his English Bible at Antwerp. January–March: important legislation – Act in Restraint of Annates; Dispensations Act; Act for Submission of the Clergy; Act of Succession. April: Elizabeth Barton, 'Holy Maid of Kent', Dr Bocking and other hanged at Tyburn, for speaking out against the divorce. November–December: important legislation – Act of Supremacy; Treason Act; Acts concerning First Fruits and Tenths. The Oath of Supremacy is administered to all religious houses. The Observant Houses are closed. All houses of friars are visited. December: **Convocation** petitions King for English Bible. Cranmer organises modification of Tyndale's New Testament but the project is unsuccessful. In this year Cromwell and others discuss financial nationalisation of the English Church, but discard the plan.

1535 Thomas Cromwell appointed **vice-gerent** and **Vicar-General** in spiritual matters to the Supreme Head of the Church. *Valor Ecclesiasticus* completed within a matter of months. Carthusian monks, including Prior Houghton, are executed for denying that succession lies with heirs of Henry and Anne. A **visitation** of all religious houses begins. Suppression envisaged. May: imprisonment of Tyndale near Brussels. 22 June: Cardinal John Fisher beheaded for treason after refusing the Oath of Supremacy. 6 July: Thomas More beheaded for treason. Hugh Latimer consecrated Bishop of Worcester. James Nicholson seeks and receives royal permission to print Coverdale's English Bible in London. Henry however, withholds approval.

1536 Cromwell's plan to order the placement of the English Bible in all churches had to be dropped when Anne Boleyn falls from grace. The visitation of religious houses continues. Act for the Dissolution of the Lesser Monasteries passed (27 Henry VIII, cap. 28) May: Cranmer dissolved m. with Anne Boleyn. 19 May: Anne beheaded. 30 May: Henry

m. Jane Seymour. 11 July: Henry promulgates the **Ten Articles** which are perceived to be pro-Lutheran. Cromwell issues the first Royal **Injunctions**, by which the clergy are ordered to preach quarterly sermons, to provide religious instruction in English for the young, to sustain the poor and to discourage what is seen as the superstitious devotion to **shrines** and images. August: Tyndale condemned for obstinate heresy. October: Tyndale executed at Vilvorde Castle, near Brussels. 1–12 October: Lincolnshire rising. 9 October: outbreak of revolt in Yorkshire, Lancashire and the north, known to posterity as the Pilgrimage of Grace. 8 December: leaders of the Pilgrimage offered pardon by Duke of Norfolk.

1537 Nicholson publishes two editions of Coverdale's Bible. The second claims to have royal approval January: second Yorkshire rising under Sir Francis Bigod. June: more Carthusian monks executed and the London Charterhouse submits. July: publication of *The Institution of a Christian Man or Bishops Book* by a committee of bps led by Cranmer and appointed by the King. August: Thomas Mathew (alias John Rogers, a friend of Tyndale) publishes the 'Mathew Bible', based on Tyndale and more Protestant than Coverdale's translation, with the King's permission. December: Henry VIII amends the so-called *Bishops' Book* in an unpredicted fashion. He excludes astrology from the list of prohibitions and alters the wording of the First Commandment to read that Christians must pray only to Christ, not God the Father. During this year many **religious** voluntarily withdrew from their orders, some taking pension, others not.

1538 Friars surrender to the Crown. The larger monasteries begin to surrender under official pressure. Summer: Coverdale supervises production in Paris of a new, official English Bible based on a toned down 'Mathew Bible'. The French authorities intervene and the press moved to London to complete the work. September: Cromwell issues 2nd set of Royal Injunctions which are very radical. The English Bible is to be placed in every church and bps are to supervise this. The shrine of Thomas à Becket at Canterbury is broken up at Cromwell's instigation as part of a widespread campaign against **shrines** and images. The Crown takes the spoils. 3 December: Abbot of Rievaulx, North Yorkshire, signs deed of surrender. 17 December: Pope Paul III excommunicates Henry VIII.

1539 April: Publication of the Great Bible. 16 June: Act of Six Articles restores conservative religious belief supported by draconian penalties. 1 July: Hugh Latimer, Bishop of Worcester, and Nicholas Shaxton, Bishop of Salisbury resign in aftermath of Act. More large monasteries surrender. Cranmer sends wife to Germany, because Act denies priests right to marry. Miles Coverdale leaves England. Act for the Dissolution of the Greater Monasteries (31 Henry VIII, cap.13) leads to the closure of those still extant. Three abbots, Thomas Beche of Colchester, Richard

Whiting of Glastonbury and Hugh Cook of Reading, are executed for treason.

1540 January: King m. Anne of Cleves, whom he detests. Cromwell, who was responsible, is eclipsed by Stephen Gardiner. April: 2nd edition of Great Bible, with preface by Cranmer, published. Berthelet publishes a cheap edition. A young London layman, John Porter, is arrested by the Bp of London for reading aloud and commenting upon the Bible in St Paul's. June: Cromwell charged with treason. July: enforcement of injunction ordering all parish churches to own and display an English Bible. July: Cromwell executed. Robert Barnes, William Jerome and Thomas Garrett burned for heresy. King balances repression of radical Protestantism with execution of three Catholics for treason. King pardoned all heresy before July 1540. Creation of See of Westminster.

1541 Great Bible goes into 5th edition. Creation of Sees of Chester, Gloucester, Peterborough. July: Abolition of many ancient customs connected with Holy Days. October: Abolition of all **shrines** ordered. Catholic plot discovered in Yorkshire. Order reinforces instruction that Great Bible must be set up in all parish churches.

1542 Creation of Sees of Oxford and Bristol. Conservatives in **Convocation** secure agreement that Great Bible will be revised in a more conservative fashion in the light of the Vulgate translation. Cranmer initiates this but the project is transferred by Henry to the universities and it never bears fruit. The Great Bible is still available.

1543 King permits Cranmer to proceed with plans for liturgical reform of a radical nature. April: He guards Cranmer against attack. But no radical reform of the liturgy is approved by **Convocation**. Cranmer's vernacular *Book of Homilies* and the conservative *Rationale of Ceremonial* alike are rejected. July: King allies himself with moderate Protestantism by marrying Catherine Parr. July: Gardiner executes Protestants. Act of Advancement of True Religion forbids the lower sort and all women below the rank of gentlewoman from reading the Scriptures. Conservative Bps Salcot, Heath and Thirlby, are ordered by the King to revise the Bishops' Book of 1537. They produce *The Necessary Doctrine and Erudition of a Christian Man*, which defends the doctrines of **transubstantiation** and salvation by works.

1544 May: English **liturgy** introduced into churches, with much decreased emphasis on the saints. July: Protestant humanist scholar, Sir John Cheke, appointed tutor to Prince Edward (aged 6).

1545 24 December: Henry VIII calls for religious unity in passionate closing speech to parliament.

1546 *King's Prymer*, probably authored by Cranmer, replaces earlier

Catholic devotional primers. **Chantries** Act passed to allow Crown dissolution of these institutions. It was never enforced. July: Protestant gentlewoman, Anne Askew, burned for heresy. Attempts to implicate Catherine Parr fail. King nominates heavily Protestant Council of Regency for his heir.

The Reign of Edward VI

1547   Act for the Dissolution of the Chantries. King's Lynn and Coventry exempted from its provisions. 28 January: d. of Henry VIII. 31 July: Vernacular *Book of Homilies* published. 22 September: City of London orders survey of churches to curtail wanton destruction of church statues and stained glass. 25 September: Bp Gardiner imprisoned in Fleet for opposing *Book of Homilies*.

1548   January: Cranmer issued vernacular *Order of the Communion*. 20 February: Gardiner freed after pledging obedience. 22 February: orders from Privy Council for destruction of all religious images and statues and abolition of various ceremonies, including the use of holy water. 7 March: Hugh Latimer preaches before Edward VI. 29 June: Gardiner imprisoned in Tower after preaching before Edward VI and making clear his implacable opposition to protestantising policies. **Convocation** debates Cranmer's English **Prayer Book**. Several bps, including Bonner of London and Tunstall of Durham, oppose it. December: foreign Protestants granted permission to establish congregation in London. 17 December: House of Lords begins debate on the new English Prayer Book.

1549   January: House of Lords passes, first Act of Uniformity by huge majority. This makes the **Book of Common Prayer** the prescribed **liturgy**. Penalties imposed on those using other forms of service. February: clerical marriage sanctioned by parliament. 10 September: bp Edmund Bonner of London deprived of see for opposing Prayer Book. June: riots v. the Prayer Book start in Devon and Cornwall. 2 July: Exeter besieged by rebels. 18 August: John, Lord Russell finally routed the rebels at Sampford Courtenay, near Okehampton. Return of John Hooper from exile; he becomes Somerset's Chaplain.

1550   John Hooper a prominent preacher at **court**. March: introduction of English **Ordinal** and abolition of **minor orders**. 1 April: Nicholas Ridley made Bishop of London (incorporating Henrician See of Westminster). June: bp Nicholas Heath imprisoned and Gardiner tried. Bps (including Ridley and Hooper) issue Visitation **Injunctions** ordering the removal of altars and screens from parish churches. 29 June: John Ponet consecrated Bishop of Rochester in Ridley's place. July: John Hooper named as Bishop of Gloucester. Hooper refuses to wear vestments for consecration. (*See* **Vestiarian Controversy**). The government tries to put a brake on radical Protestantism. Burning of Joan Bocher and other **Anabaptists** in London. Act for the Abolition of Divers Books and

Images orders destruction of all statues and images, including rood screens. November: Council orders removal of altars and replacement by tables. 25 December: Edward rebukes the Princess Mary for her Catholicism.

1551 Bps discuss a draft of a new, more Protestant, Prayer Book. February: Gardiner deprived of See of Winchester and replaced by radical Protestant, John Ponet. 3 March: Privy Council orders removal of plate from parish churches. 18 March: Princess Mary rejects the Book of Common Prayer and **mass** continues to be said in her Essex home. October: Nicholas Heath deprived of See of Worcester. December: Edward orders his sister Mary to renounce her Catholicism. She remains defiant. Hooper's vigorous episcopate.

1552 April: Second Act of Uniformity. This ordered the use of a revised **Book of Common Prayer** as from November. Continental influence evident. May: Hooper named as Bishop of both Gloucester and Worcester dioceses. 1 November: publication of *Second Book of Common Prayer*, including the **Black Rubric** and the **Ornament Rubric**. Henceforth the **Mass** is totally abolished. Prayers for the dead and private confession follow suit. The government plans to issue a set of articles and holds talks with divines, including John Knox.

The Reign of Mary I

1553 January: commission of Sir Richard Cotton to seize church plate and vestments. 12 June: issue of the **Forty-Two Articles**. These define the **Eucharist** in a Zwinglian sense and argue that **Justification** before God is by faith alone. Works play no part in salvation and **purgatory** is denied. They are directed against the threat from **Anabaptism**. July: d. of King Edward. 6–14 July: reign of Queen Jane. 19 July: Mary proclaimed Queen. Rapid ecclesiastical about-turn. September: Bp Bale of Ossory flees. Bps Ponet, Scory and Coverdale are deprived and eventually go overseas. Bp Barlow resigns and follows suit in spring, 1554. Release of Gardiner and Bonner. September: Mary orders arrest of Archbp Cranmer. Latimer, Hooper, Ridley and others imprisoned. Autumn: parliament meets and refuses to repeal Act of Supremacy. Parliament passes Act of Repeal which effectively undoes the Edwardian reformation and revives the **Mass**, ritual worship and clerical **celibacy**. December: Mary relinquishes title of Supreme Head.

1554 January: mass exodus of Protestants to Germany and Switzerland, predating official persecution of married clergy. March: Mary issues Royal **Injunctions** ordering bps to suppress heresy, remove married clergy, divorce ex-religious, ordain clergy who had been ordained under English **Ordinal**, and restore **Holy Days**, processions and ceremonies. Bp Gardiner begins deprivation of married priests. Eventually between 10 per cent and 25 per cent of parish clergy are deprived for marriage. Some reinstated when they conformed. April–Mary: parliament initially rejects reintroduction of heresy laws but agrees when a promise is exacted that monastic lands will not be restored. September: John Bale in exile in Frankfurt. November: Cardinal Pole returns and sentence of **excommunication** is lifted off England. November: parliament passes 2nd Act of Repeal which undoes all anti-papal legislation since 1529 and the Henrician Reformation.

1555 Mary I appoints a **commission** to consider refoundation of some religious houses. 4 February: John Rogers Biblical translater and the first Protestant martyr of the reign, is burned under the restored heresy laws. 16 October: Bps Ridley and Latimer burnt for heresy at stake outside Balliol College, Oxford, after 18 months' impr. 12 November: d. of Stephen Gardiner. 13 November: Cranmer depr. of See of Canterbury. December: Reginald Cardinal Pole named Archbishop of Canterbury.

1556 Refoundation of Benedictine House at Westminster under Abbot John Feckenham, Dean of St Paul's. Many more burnings for heresy during continued persecution of Protestants. 21 March: Cranmer recants all retractions and is burnt at stake in front of Balliol College, Oxford. Cardinal Pole argues with Pope Paul IV and is deprived of position as Legate. 22 March: Pole consecrated Archbishop of Canterbury.

1557 A number of refoundations of small religious houses. June: Pole recalled to Rome to answer charges of heresy. Mary I refuses to allow him to go and rejects Friar William Peto the papal appointment as Pole's replacement as Legate.

1558 10 November: 5 Protestants burnt at stake at Canterbury. In all about 300 were executed during Mary's reign. Popular nickname: 'Bloody Mary'. Thomas Bentham, a returned exile, is ministering to the Protestants of London. 17 November: Queen Mary and Reginald Pole d.; Elizabeth I acclaimed. 25 December: Elizabeth commanded Bp Oglethorpe to omit **elevation of the host** from the **mass** in the royal chapel; she left the chapel when he declined to obey.

The Reign of Elizabeth I
1559 January: first parliament of the reign assembles. 15 January: at her coronation, Elizabeth again displays her displeasure at **elevation of the host**. 31 March-3 April: conference between Protestant and Catholic divines at Westminster. 29 April: Acts of Supremacy and Uniformity approve a new religious settlement, by declaring that Elizabeth is Supreme Governor of the Church of England with power of visitation, by reviving all the legislation which Mary's parliaments had repealed, by revoking the heresy acts and the Papal supremacy, by enforcing conformity to the Prayer-Book **liturgy**. The **Prayer Book** provided 'a remarkable latitude of Eucharistic belief', omitted the **Black Rubric** of 1552 and

amended the **Ornaments Rubric** of 1552. Royal **Injunctions** reinforce the new settlement.

1560 21 January: John Jewel consecrated Bishop of Salisbury. 24 March: Thomas Bentham consecrated Bishop of Coventry and Lichfield. 1 September: John Parkhurst consecrated Bishop of Norwich. Publication of William Whittingham's English translation of the *Geneva Bible*, with strongly Calvinist notes. The bible, with its oddly-worded translation of Genesis III, v.7 as 'They sewed fig-leaves together and made themselves breeches', has led to it being nicknamed 'The Breeches Bible'. It was destined to become the most popular Elizabethan text of the Bible.

1561 English translation of Genevan *Forme of Prayer* is published in Geneva. An English translation of John Calvin's *Institutes of the Christian Religion* also appears, (**see Calvinism**).

1562 Publication of John Jewel's *Apology of the Church of England* as a defence of the Elizabethan settlement against Catholicism.

1563 John Day publishes John Foxe's *Acts and Monuments*, which becomes immensely popular. January: Act of Parliament obliges graduates, schoolmasters and M.P,s to take Oath of Supremacy. In **Convocation** Protestant attempts to reform the **Prayer Book** in a more radical direction are narrowly defeated. The reforms would have abolished **Holy Days**, the use of the sign of the cross, the compulsory wearing of the **surplice**, the practice of kneeling for the sacrament and also the use of organs in churches. Passage through **Convocation** of the **Thirty-Nine Articles**, a somewhat indeterminate definition of the church of England's doctrine which serves to infuriate the Puritan wing. The Queen declines to give them statutory form until 1571.

1564 Many clergy deprived for refusing to wear the **surplice**.

1565 Activities of a group of Puritan hardliners, centred on St John's College, Cambridge, causes unease at **court** and makes the Queen and Archbp Parker yet more determined to protect *status quo*. Thomas Sampson, Dean of Christ Church, Oxford, and Laurence Humphrey, President of Magdalen College, Oxford, are both suspended for their Protestant nonconformity regarding vestments and ritual. At the same time, persecution of Catholics at Oxford sends William Allen into exile.

1566 March: 37 London clergy deprived for refusing to wear vestments (surplice). March: Archbp Parker and a group of bps draw up Royal Injunctions. Queen refuses to give these official sanction and Archbp Parker issues them unofficially as his *Book of Advertisements* which lays down rules for the examining and licensing of preachers; the control of ordination; conduct of services and apparel of officiators; clerical discipline. In response the Puritans engage in lively debate which has come to be called the **Vestiarian Controversy**. Robert

Crowley, vicar of St Giles, Cripplegate, London, publishes his *Briefe Discourse against the Outwarde Apparell and Ministering Garmentes of the Popishe Church*. Puritans begin to transfer campaign to parliament. When parliament began to debate bills to curb **simony**, non-residence and **pluralism**, Elizabeth responded by forbidding debate of religious issues, a royal **prerogative**.

1567 Continental reformers, Theodore Beza and Heinrich Bullinger (appealed to in the matter of vestments) counsel submission to the Elizabethan Settlement. Residue of bitterness against the bps. A **separatist** congregation is discovered in London. Welsh translations of *The Book of Common Prayer* and the *New Testament* are published.

1568 William Allen founds College at Douai, Flanders, to train English Catholic priests.

1569 Puritan Thomas Cartwright appointed Lady Margaret Professor of Divinity at Cambridge. October-November: anti-Protestant revolt of the Northern Earls. December: Catholic Earls flee.

1570 February: Pope Pius V issues **Bull** *Regnans in Excelsis*, excommunicating Elizabeth and calling on Catholics to bring about her deposition. August: execution of John Felton for displaying copy of **Bull**. Most English Catholics loyal to Queen but placed in a dilemma. Thomas Cartwright, Lady Margaret Professor of Divinity at Cambridge, lectures on the early church and compares it favourably with the Elizabethan. He criticises the latter for it structure, especially as regards episcopacy. He is deprived of his Chair.

1571 John Foxe's *Book of Martyrs* to be set up in every cathedral and collegiate church in England. Parliament assembles. Puritan M.P.s introduce campaign for legislative church reform. William Strickland tables a bill for the amendment of the Prayer Book and the abolition of the ring in marriage, the **surplice** and kneeling for communion. The Privy Council quashes the bill. Strickland barred from the House. There are unsuccessful attempts to revive bills against non-residence, **pluralism, simony** and other abuses and to improve preaching provision. Parliament passes Subscription Act, ordering that all clergy ordained under Henry VIII or Mary I, and any new ordinand or appointee to a benefice, should swear obedience to the **Thirty-Nine-Articles**. **Convocation,** in bid to answer Puritan criticisms, introduces Canons curtailing pluralism, simony and abuses in the Courts Christian. Summer: deprivations of Puritan ministers, including John Field. Parliament's enthusiasm for repressive anti-Catholic legislation stamped on by the Queen. Nevertheless, three important acts – Treasons Act, Act against Papal Bulls, and Act against fugitives over the sea – were passed. The discovery of the Ridolfi Plot to kill Elizabeth intensifies anti-Catholic feeling.

1572 Matthew Parker publishes *De Antiquitate Britannicae Ecclesiae*, a history of his archiepiscopal ancestors. Thomas Cartwright, John Field and Walter Travers engage in Puritan campaign preparatory to assembly of Parliament. May: Puritans attempt to introduce a bill into Parliament which would permit individual congregations to amend the **Book of Common Prayer** as they see fit and which would enforce the Act of Uniformity only against Catholics. The Crown insisted on its withdrawal. June: Thomas Wilcox publishes *First Admonition to the Parliament* which asks parliament to introduce a Genevan form of church organisation. Wilcox and John Field impr. briefly. This leads to a spirited debate with John Whitgift and other defenders of the *status quo*. 24 August: **Massacre of St Bartholemew's Eve**, Paris. 27 August: Huguenot refugees arrive in England.

1573 John Whitgift replies to Puritans with *Answer to the Admonition*. Thomas Cartwright goes into exile.

1574 Walter Travers, in exile, publishes *Full and Plain Declaration of Ecclesiastical Discipline*, which outlines a system of church government by elders, deacons and ministers. Several Catholics are released from prison as anti-Catholic feeling diminishes. First Catholic missionary priests arrive from Douai and Rheims and establish contact with Catholic families.

1575 17 May: d. of Archbp Parker. Archbp Edmund Grindal of York named as his successor.

1576 Peter Wentworth leads Puritan attacks in Parliament on clerical abuses. 15 March: Peter Wentworth sent to Tower. **Convocation** passes new Canons (*see* **Canon Law**) to curb abuses. Preaching exercises or **prophesyings** among the clergy meet with Grindal's approval. Queen alarmed. December: Queen orders Grindal to suppress **prophesyings**. Grindal refuses and denies her authority in spiritual matters. 'I choose rather to offend your earthly majesty than to offend the heavenly majesty of God.'

1577 John Aylmer named Bishop of London. May: Archbp Grindal placed under house arrest at Lambeth Palace. Aylmer appointed Chairperson of an **Ecclesiastical Commission** to suppress nonconformity. Under the protection of powerful lay and ecclesiastical patrons, many **prophesyings** continue. The government orders a return of recusants in the dioceses (*see* **Recusancy**) Seminary priests hounded. November: execution of Cuthbert Mayne, a seminary priest, at Launceston, Cornwall.

1578 February: John Nelson, seminary priest from Douai, hanged at Tyburn. Hanging of Thomas Sherwood, a Catholic layman, a few days later. Archbp Edwin Sandys of York introduces Quarterly Synods in an attempt to improve standards of clerical education in his diocese.

1579 English College founded at Rome under the supervision of the Jesuit Order.

1580   Robert Parsons, Edmund Campion and a lay-brother Ralph Emerson, all **Jesuits**, arrive in England. Parsons and Campion conduct a mission to Catholic families.

1581   Fiercely anti-Catholic mood in Parliament produces proposal of draconian penalties: death sentences for priests found saying **Mass** and heavy fines for recusants. Elizabeth manages to modify the penalties but two acts ensue: Act to Retain the Queen's Majesty's Subjects in their True Obedience; Act against Seditious Words and Rumours. December: execution of Edmund Campion, S.J. and two Douai priests. Alexander Bryant and Ralph Sherwin. Parsons, condemned to death *in absentia*, having fled to France. Queen rejects Peter Wentworth's move in parliament for a public fast on the grounds that this is infringement of royal **prerogative**. Commons petition to the Crown for church reform is considered by the bps and rejected. John Field and Walter Travers are appointed to lectureships in London, thus raising the profile of the Puritans in the capital.

1582   Presbyterian classes begin to meet in East Anglia.

1583   Robert Parsons and other **Jesuits** deeply implicated in the French Throckmorton Plot. July: execution of 3 **separatists**, at Bury St Edmunds for villifying the Queen as 'Jezebel'. 6 July: d. of Edmund Grindal. August: John Whitgift, Bishop of Worcester, named Archbishop of Canterbury. September: Whitgift consecrated Archbp. Whitgift issues anti-Catholic and anti-Puritan articles and draws up a list of questions to be administered to suspect nonconformist ministers by his new High Commission. Between 300 and 400 ministers refused to subscribe. Philip Stubbes' controversial Puritanical denunciation of the times, *The Anatomy of Abuses*, is published.

1584   Whitgift issues revised articles and secures the subscription of most clergy who had refused to sign previously. November: Complaints in parliament about Whitgift's policies and petitions from Essex, Warwickshire and Lincolnshire about his curtailment of preaching under the articles. Elizabeth continues strong support for Whitgift and his policies. Peter Turner proposes bill to introduce Presbyterian order with Genevan **liturgy** – known as 'The Bill and Book' – but it is denied a reading. Sir Walter Mildmay founds Emmanuel College, Cambridge, for the training of Puritan ministers.

1585   Whitgift campaigns to prevent Puritans being elected to parliament. February: Legal force given to Bond of Association to protect Queen's person. In the Lords, the Queen orders bps to suppress the Puritans. In the Commons, parliament defies royal displeasure to discuss bill concerning clerical recruitment. In **Convocation**, Whitgift pursues reforms relating to the educational standards of recruits and the residence of **benefice** holders. Parliament passes Act against **Jesuits**, seminary priests and other suchlike disobedient persons. Thomas Cartwright returns from eleven-year exile to employ with the Earl of Leicester.

1586 Twelve Catholic priests and three lay-persons executed. Margaret Clitheroe killed in York for giving refuge to priests. June: Decree of Star Chamber tightens press censorship. October: parliament presses for and secures heavier **recusancy** fines of £20 a month. Peter Wentworth to the forefront in unsuccessful attempt in parliament to replace *Book of Common Prayer* with Genevan *Forme of Prayer*.

1587 Anthony Cope moves to reintroduce 'Bill and Book' in Parliament. Peter Wentworth argues M.P.s' right to debate religious matters in Parliament. Infuriated Queen orders imprisonment of Wentworth, Cope and Edward Lewknor and government dissuades M.P.s from debating the bill further. Puritans outside Parliament discuss Travers' *Disciplina Ecclesiae*. October: Imprisonment of Henry Barrow and John Greenwood, London **separatist** leaders.

1588 Government determination to crush Catholicism leads to execution of 31 priests. March: d. of John Field, prominent Puritan. October: Puritan anti-episcopal propaganda from secret press is issued under pseudonym of Martin Marprelate (*see* Section XI).

1589 Sir Christopher Hatton opens Parliament with speech denouncing both Catholics and Puritans. Appearance of more Marprelate tracts motivates royal **proclamation** against printers of seditious works. Summer: arrest of Marprelate printers but John Penry escapes to Scotland. Robert Parsons founds third English Catholic seminary at Valladolid, Spain. Richard Bancroft denounces Puritan sedition in sermon at **St Paul's Cross**.

1590 Thomas Cartwright and others brought before Court of High Commission. John Udall, minister at Kingston-on-Thames, d. in prison after being arrested for printing seditious books.

1591 Star Chamber accuses Thomas Cartwright and others of participating in Presbyterian organisations and slandering the bps. Royal **Proclamation** against priests, **Jesuits** and seminaries. This links Catholicism with the Spanish threat. Commissioners are appointed in every county to investigate.

1592 Robert Parsons established a further seminary in Seville, seeming to underline the message of the Royal **Proclamation**. The Jesuit poet Robert Southwell publishes a defence of Catholic loyalty to the Queen, *An Humble Supplication to her Majestie*.

1593 John Penry executed for part in Marprelate pamphleteering. Henry Barrow and John Greenwood also executed. February: parliament meets. Government sought to introduce severe measures against Catholics (£10 monthly fines; removal of Catholic children over the age of seven from their homes; exclusion of Catholics from office). The Commons resists and passes legislation effectively identifying Catholics in the population. It is directed against those Catholics who are demonstrably 'seditious sectaries and disloyal persons' (The Act against popish recusants and The Act to retain the Queen's subjects in obedience). The extreme Protestants were in a weak position. Penry, Barrow and Greenwood's execution are meant to show that not only Catholic but Protestant activity can be defined as seditious. It frightened many. Peter Wentworth raised the issue of the succession in the Commons, is imprisoned and dies in gaol. Publication of Richard Hooker's, *On the Laws of Ecclesiastical Polity*, which defends a moderate Protestant position. Richard Bancroft further attacks the Presbyterian position with his *A Surveye of the Pretended Holy Discipline* and *Dangerous Positions and Proceedings*.

1594 Death of William, Cardinal Allen. Robert Parsons, S.J., publishes *A conference about the next succession* [to] *the Crowne of England* in support of the claims of the Spanish Infanta. This enrages many English Catholics who become opposed to the **Jesuits** as a result. Arguments in Wisbech Castle, the official prison for Catholics, between Jesuits and other priests underline the breach.

1595 University of Cambridge riven by controversy over predestination (*see* **Calvinism**). The University forces William Barrett, a chaplain who had argued against the doctrine, to recant. John Whitgift enters the debate by agreeing to a set of articles, known as the **Lambeth Articles**, which restate Calvinist opinions. Elizabeth intervenes to prevent further debate.

1596 The debate at Cambridge persists, with Peter Baro taking up the gauntlet against the predestinarians.

1597 Extreme Protestant bills against ecclesiastical fees and subscription to the articles of religion have to be withdrawn because of the weakness of the group in parliament. **Convocation** approves a set of constitutions drawn up by Whitgift to tackle various abuses within the church.

1598 George Blackwell made **archpriest** of England by **Papacy**. **Jesuits** excluded from his jurisdiction. English Catholics enraged; their attempt to petition the Pope was quashed when Parsons ordered their return from Rome.

1599 Some anti-Jesuit priests negotiate with Bishop Bancroft. The bps are eager to exploit divisions within Catholicism.

1602 Royal **proclamation** v. priests discriminates in favour of non-Jesuits. **Jesuits** to leave England immediately and actively to be sought out. Other priests given until 1603 to leave but encouraged to submit and promised favourable treatment if they did.

1603 Thirteen secular priests do submit to the authorities.

List of Dioceses

Names and dates of bishops of those Sees marked with * appear in Section XIII.

Province of Canterbury
Bangor, Bath and Wells, Bristol, Canterbury*, Chester, Chichester, Coventry and Lichfield*, Ely, Exeter, Gloucester, Hereford, Lincoln*, Llandaff, London*, Norwich, Oxford, Peterborough, Rochester, Salisbury, Sodor and Man, St Asaph, St David's, Westminster, (existed only briefly between 1540 and 1550), Winchester* , Worcester*.

Province of York
Carlisle, Durham, York*.

The World of Learning

Universities

In the middle ages the Universities of Oxford and Cambridge had been small, although variable in number of students (in 1500 each admitted about 150 men), and almost exclusively concerned with the education of a pool of clergy from whom would be drawn the Church's leadership and the King's chief servants. During the Tudor period the universities grew in size and altered in character. By 1600 they admitted between 400 and 500 men each per annum. The colleges developed as institutions for the tuition, residence and supervision of undergraduate students. Prior to this most teaching was done by the university and students lived in halls or town lodgings. These undergraduate students now included large numbers of well-born students who had no intention of pursuing a career in the church, as well as men from humbler backgrounds who eventually took holy orders and much more often than not entered the church in humble positions. Corpus Christi College, Oxford, and Emmanuel College, Cambridge, for instance, were both established with the training of ministers uppermost in the minds of their founders. University education was not open to all: it was expensive and it was seen as appropriate only to some vocations. The universities educated distinct groups of students for different roles in society. They combined the roles of fashionable colleges for young gentlemen, who frequently completed their education at the Inns of Court in London, and secular seminaries for determined professional recruits. The type of curriculum and teaching offered was influenced by the student composition of the colleges.

Chronology

1481 Building of Duke Humphrey Library, Oxford.

1483 John Russell, Bishop of Lincoln, made Chancellor of Oxford.

1485 Thomas Rotherham, Archbishop of York, made Chancellor of Cambridge.

1490 Thomas Cosyn made Chancellor of Cambridge.

1494 John Blythe, Bishop of Salisbury, made Chancellor of Cambridge. John Morton, Archbishop of Canterbury, made Chancellor of Oxford.

1496 John Alcock, Bishop of Ely, founded Jesus College, Cambridge.

1497 Readerships in Divinity at Oxford and Cambridge founded by Lady Margaret Beaufort, mother of Henry VII. George Fitzhugh made Chancellor of Cambridge.

1499 A humanist, John Dogget, appointed Provost of King's College, Cambridge. Thomas Rotherham made Chancellor of Cambridge.

1500 William Grocyn began to lecture on Greek at Oxford. Richard Fox, Bishop of Durham, made Chancellor of Cambridge. William Smyth, Bishop of Lincoln, made Chancellor of Oxford.

1501 John Fisher appointed Vice Chancellor of Cambridge. He was Chaplain to Lady Margaret Beaufort.

1502 George Fitzhugh made Chancellor of Cambridge.

1503 Thomas Ruthall made Chancellor of Cambridge. He later became Bishop of Durham. Richard Mayew, Bishop of Hereford, made Chancellor of Oxford.

1504 John Fisher made Bishop of Rochester and Chancellor of Cambridge.

1505 John Fisher made Provost of Queens' College, Cambridge. Refoundation of God's House, Cambridge, as Christ's College; statutes stipulate college lectures.

1506 William Warham appointed Chancellor of Oxford. Erasmus visited Fisher.

1509 Foundation of Brasenose College, Oxford.

1511 Lady Margaret Beaufort founded St John's College, Cambridge and stipulated college lectures in statutes. Erasmus returned to lecture in Greek at Cambridge. Appointed as Lady Margaret Professor of Divinity.

1514 Erasmus left Cambridge.

1517 Corpus Christi College, Oxford, founded by Richard Fox, Bishop of Winchester; inaugurates lectures in Greek, Latin and Divinity. Wolsey appointed several other lecturers at Oxford. A printing press was established in Oxford.

1518 Richard Croke lectured in Greek and lectureships in Logic, Philosophy and Rhetoric endowed at Cambridge by Sir Robert Reade.

1520 Beginnings of printing at Cambridge.

1524 Medical lectures established at Oxford by Thomas Linacre.

1525 Attempt to eradicate Lutheranism at Cambridge following Robert Barnes' sermon attack on Wolsey.

1526 Thomas Wolsey founded Cardinal College, Oxford.

1530 Universities debated Royal Divorce. Examination of dangerous books by special committees.

1532 John Longland, Bishop of Lincoln, made Chancellor of Oxford. Henry VIII refounded Cardinal College, Oxford, as King's College.

1535 Reform of the University Statutes following Royal Visitation of the Universities. Thomas Cromwell appointed Chancellor of Cambridge.

1536 End of monastic colleges.

1540 Foundation of Regius Professorships in Divinity, Law, Hebrew, Greek and Medicine. Stephen Gardiner became Chancellor of Cambridge.

1542 Thomas, Lord Audley founded Magdalene College, Cambridge.

1546 Foundation of Trinity College, Cambridge, by Henry VIII; college lectures stipulated in statutes. Refoundation of King's College, Oxford, as Christ Church.

1547 Chantry Act exempts colleges of the universities from its terms. Somerset made Chancellor of Cambridge. Richard Cox, Dean of Christ Church, made Chancellor of Oxford.

1549 Reform of University statutes following Royal Visitation. Destruction of images and 'popish' books. Martin Bucer and other foreign reformers arrived in England.

1551 College lectures in Logic and Sophistry at Clare College, Cambridge.

1552 John Dudley, Duke of Northumberland, made Chancellor of Cambridge. Sir John Mason made Chancellor of Oxford.

1553 Order that all members of the universities subscribe to the new articles of religion not carried out because of death of Edward VI. Marian government orders graduates to declare Catholic faith and deprives many college heads.

1554–55 Foundation of Trinity College, Oxford, by Sir Thomas Pope, Treasurer of Court of Augmentations. Sir Thomas White, Alderman of London, founded St John's College, Oxford.

1556–57 Reginald Pole made Chancellor of Oxford. His Visitations of the University enforce Catholic worship and creed.

1557 John Caius refounded Gonville Hall as Gonville and Caius College, Cambridge.

1559 Henry Fitzalan, Lord Arundel, made Chancellor of Oxford. Sir John Mason made Elizabeth's first Chancellor of Oxford and William Cecil her first Chancellor of Cambridge. Royal Visitations result in removal of Catholic heads of many colleges at Oxford. Revival of the Edwardian Statutes.

1564 Queen's visit to Cambridge. Robert Dudley, Earl of Leicester made Chancellor of Oxford.

1565 Oxford receives new statutes. Oxford Arts course lasts seven years; B.A. after 4 years' study of Grammar, Rhetoric, Dialectics or Logic; M.A. after 3 years' study of Greek, Geometry, Natural, Moral and Metaphysical Philosophy. Gentlemen may graduate B.A. after three years, presumably because they knew sufficient Latin grammar before they started to be exempt from this part of the course. Cambridge academics protest against Matthew Parker's plans for imposing orthodoxy.

1566 Elizabeth visits Oxford.

1569 Thomas Cartwright, the new Lady Margaret Professor of Divinity at Cambridge, demands church reform from the pulpit.

1570 John Whitgift, Vice-Chancellor of Cambridge, deprived Thomas Cartwright of Chair. New Statutes received at Cambridge. Cambridge Arts course to cover 7 years; B.A. after 4 years' study of Rhetoric, Logic and Philosophy; followed by M.A. after further 3 years' study of Natural, Moral and Metaphysical Philosophy, Astronomy, Drawing and Greek.

1571 Dr Hugh Price, Chancellor of St David's Diocese, founded Jesus College, Oxford. Strong and continuing Welsh links.

1574 Peter Baro, opponent of Calvinism, appointed Lady Margaret Professor of Divinity, Cambridge.

1576 Ordered that all graduands subscribe to 39 Articles of Religion.

1580 Ordered that all graduands take Supremacy Oath.

1581 All those at Oxford to take oath of subscription.

1584 Sir Walter Mildmay, Chancellor of the Exchequer, founded Emmanuel College, Cambridge. Dudley Fenner published translation of Pierre de la Ramée's work which substituted scriptural for classical examples.

1585 Cambridge University Press founded. Sir Thomas Bromley deputises for Leicester as Chancellor of Oxford.

1588 Sir Christopher Hatton appointed Chancellor of Oxford.

1589 Two fellows of Christ's College, Cambridge, imprisoned for sedition.

1591 Thomas Sackville, Lord Buckhurst made Chancellor of Oxford.

1592 Elizabeth visited Oxford.

1595 John Whitgift silenced William Barrett's attack on Calvinism at Cambridge.

1596 Peter Baro silenced and left Cambridge. Lady Frances Sidney, Dowager Countess of Sussex, founded Sidney Sussex College, Cambridge.

1598 Robert Devereux, Earl of Essex, made Chancellor of Cambridge.

1601 Robert Cecil, Earl of Salisbury, made Chancellor of Cambridge.

1602 Thomas Bodley re-established University Library with 2,000 volumes. Not a lending library and restricted to graduates.

Education

Sixteenth-century England was not a schooled society like our own and we must avoid the temptation to identify an 'educational system' as such. The bringing up of most children was still firmly rooted in the family, the Church, and the workshop. For centuries academic learning had been the preserve of the clergy and potential clergy because only they needed advanced literacy for their work. There did, however, emerge a movement for the schooling of society. Renaissance scholars saw in education on classical lines a way to improve society: the school was thought to counteract the evil influences of family and society upon the young. Out of this belief grew the grammar schools endowed in large numbers in our period. But the town grammar schools owed a good deal also to demand among tradesmen and craftsmen for basic vernacular literacy. It was common for the grammar schools, therefore, to combine a classical side (with a curriculum of Latin Grammar, Logic and Rhetoric) with a vernacular side (offering Writing, Arithmetic and more 'modern' subjects) and for boys within them to be thus 'streamed'. Alongside the grammar schools existed a plethora of more ephemeral establishments' ranging from ABC or 'dame' schools, which taught little more than reading and basic numeracy, to the classical education offered by the local clergyman or freelance schoolmaster to groups of boys. Wealthier homes employed private tutors to teach their sons and daughters. Important though these developments were, we should resist the belief that the majority of children attended school.

Chronology
Single placenames indicate foundation or refoundation of a school at that date.

1487   Stockport.

1490s   First editions of Erasmus' *Adagia* (Adages).

1502   Macclesfield.

1509   St Paul's School, London.

1512   Publication of Erasmus' *De Copia*. Giggleswick, Yorkshire.

1513   Nottingham.

1515   Wolverhampton, Staffordshire; Manchester.

1519   First publication of Erasmus' *Colloquies*. Pocklington, Yorkshire; King's, Bruton, Somerset.

1520   Cranbrook, Kent.

1522   King's College, Taunton, Somerset.

1524   Bolton.

1525   Sedburgh, Yorkshire.

1529   Bingley, Yorkshire.

1532   Bristol.

1536   Royal Injunctions ordered clergy to teach the young in their care. Wealthier clergymen were to provide scholarships to finance able boys either at grammar school or university.

1538   Royal Injunctions ordered the provision of an English Bible in every parish church. The clergy were to expound this to their parishioners.

1539   Crypt, Gloucester; Colchester, Essex.

1540–42   Official Latin Grammar issued. Known as Lily's Latin Grammar although only based on an earlier work by William Lily.

1541   Berkhamstead, Hertfordshire; Canterbury, Kent; Northampton; Christ's College, Brecon; King's, Worcester; King's, Chester.

1542   King's, Rochester, Kent.

1543   Devizes, Wiltshire; King's, Ely.
Access to vernacular Bible denied to all but gentlemen.

1545   Newcastle.

1547   Royal Injunctions restore access to vernacular Bible. Priests ordered to buy Erasmus' *Paraphrases* on the Gospels to improve their scriptural understanding. Chantry priests ordered to teach young to read and write and bring them up in good manners.
Chantry Act surrenders to Crown all chantry and college endowments with the exception of those belonging to colleges of Oxford and Cambridge, Winchester and Eton.

1548   Survey of educational institutions, most of which are accorded stipend for continuance. Some schools protected by Act of Parliament.

1549   Maidstone, Kent; Wellingborough, Northants (refoundation); Ilminster (refoundation).

Publication of a new royal Latin grammar.

1550 Bury St Edmund's, Suffolk; Sherborne, Dorset; Bruton; Stafford; Stourbridge, Worcestershire; Marlborough.
Many of the former chantry schools receive new endowments from the Chancellor of the Court of Augmentations.

1551 High Wycombe, Bucks; King Edward's, Chelmsford, Essex; Louth; Great Yarmouth; Leeds; Spilsby; Sedburgh, Yorkshire (refoundation).

1552 Christ's Hospital, London; King Edward's, Poole; King Edward's, Birmingham; Leeds; Bedford (refounded 1566); Shrewsbury; East Retford; Macclesfield; Ludlow, Shropshire (refoundation); Bath (refoundation); Abingdon; Beverley, Yorkshire; Stratford-upon-Avon; Morpeth (refoundation); Nuneaton, Warwickshire.

1553 Tonbridge, Kent (refoundation); Stratford-on-Avon, Warwickshire (re-endowment); St Alban's; Guildford; Totnes; Tavistock; Christ's College, Giggleswick (refoundation); Bradford; Ripon.
Publication of official catechism by John Ponet; Thomas Wilson, *Art of Rhetoric*.

1554 Queen Mary's, Walsall; Gresham's, Holt, Norfolk; Leominster, Herefordshire (refoundation).

1555 Derby; Boston, Lincs.

1556 Oundle, Northamptonshire.

1557 Brentwood, Essex; Repton, Derbyshire.
All new schoolmasters to be licensed by bishop of diocese in which they intend to work.

1559 Act provides for statutory foundation of schools left incomplete at Mary's accession.
Act dissolves Marian chantry and monastic foundations but preserves educational establishments attached to them.

1561 Merchant Taylors', London.

1562 High Wycombe, Buckinghamshire (refoundation).

1563 Elizabeth College, Buxton, Derbyshire; Sir Roger Manwood's School, Sandwich, Kent.

1564 Felsted, Essex; Wyggeston, Leicestershire.

1565 Rochdale, Lancashire; Highgate, Middlesex.

1567 Blackburn, Lancashire; Rugby, Warwickshire.

1569 Publication of John Harte, *Orthography*.
Dorchester, Dorset.

1570 Derby (refoundation).
Publication of Roger Ascham, *The Scholemaster*, John Harte, *Method*.

1571 Andover, Hampshire; St Olave's, London; Harrow, Middlesex.
All teachers ordered by Convocation to subscribe to 39 Articles of
Religion and the Prayer Book. Those who refuse are deprived.
Catechism by Alexander Nowell prescribed for general use.

1572 Queen Elizabeth's, Barnet.

1574 Norwich.

1580 Wrexham, Wales.

1581 Publication of Richard Mulcaster, *Positions . . . The Training up of
Children*

1582 Publication of Richard Mulcaster, *The First Part of the Elementarie.*

1584 Oakham, Rutland; Uppingham, Rutland.

1585 The practice of sending Catholics abroad for their education is
declared illegal and offenders are fined £100.

1588 Publication of William Kempe, *Education of Children in Learning.*

1590 Wallasey, Cheshire.

1591 Wakefield, Yorkshire.

1595 Wellingborough, Northamptonshire refoundation.

1596 Publication of Edmund Coote, *The English Schoolmaster.*

1597 Alleyn's, London; Aldenham, Herts.

1598 Aylesbury Grammar School, Bucks.

1599 Blundell's, Tiverton, Somerset.

Books of the Tudor Period

A select bibliography of important contemporary works by title
This is a brief list of works often referred to by title rather than author in student texts and monographs. See Authors listing (below) for additional works of importance.

Acts and Monuments (*see* Book of Martyrs)

Adages (*see* Desiderius Erasmus)

Admonition to the people of England: against Martin Marprelate, An (1589)   The Bishop of Winchester's defence of the bishops and attack on the writings of Martin Marprelate.

Admonition to the Parliament, An (1572)   Important Puritan manifesto. Edited by W.H. Frere and C.E. Douglas, *Puritan Manifestoes, 1954.*
John Field and Thomas Wilcox. 'Polemic of the highest order, measured and serious, but with shafts of infectious satire' directed against episcopal government and arguing for full reformation. Thomas Wilcox responsible for solemn Admonition proper and John Field for 'vituperative and journalistic' attack on 'popish abuses yet remaining in the English church'. Autumn 1572: Authors sentenced to a year's imprisonment.

Admonition to the Parliament, A Second (1572)   Sometimes attributed, apparently erroneously, to Thomas Cartwright.

Anglica Historica (1485–1537)   Polydore Vergil. A prime source for the events of the reign of Henry VII. Printed by Denys Hay in Camden Society, 3rd series, LXXIV, 1950.

Annales Rerum Anglicarum et Hibernicarum, Regnante Elizabetha (1615)   William Camden. Fed the myth of Elizabeth as the second Deborah.

Apology of the Church of England (1562)   John Jewel, Bishop of Salisbury. Written from the point of view that the monarchy was the bulwark v. threat of restored Catholicism. Believed that the church would be protected by the Crown, which would leave it free to perform its spiritual functions without interference.

Assertio Septem Sacramentorum (1521)   Henry VIII. Important treatise. English translation printed with Latin original, by L. O'Donovan, New York, 1908.

Autobiography of an Elizabethan (manuscript in circulation)   William Weston. Superior of the Jesuit mission in England, 1584. A persecuted Catholic priest during the reign of Elizabeth. Translation by Philip Caraman, published 1955.

Autobiography of John Gerard (manuscript in circulation from early 17th century)   A persecuted Jesuit priest in Elizabeth I's reign. Translation 1951.

Boke named the Governour, The (1531)   Sir Thomas Elyot. Treats the education of the aristocracy.

Book of Martyrs (see Dialogi Sex, Confutation)   John Foxe's seminal history of the Christian church. Latin text published in 1559. Much revised English version published in 1563 by John Day during the succession crisis. It provided a vivid account of events leading up to Elizabeth I's accession, concentrating upon the edifying lives and deaths of the martyrs of the Reformation, and it supplied a history of the Reformation within the context of providential history. There was a struggle between Christ and Antichrist and Elizabeth was a second Deborah sent to rescue the nation from Antichrist and restore the rule of Christ. The Church of England was not revolutionary and innovatory: it instead represented a return to the primitive and pristine early Christian church. The book had a wider circulation than any other English book apart from the Bible.

Catechism, The (reign of King Edward VI)   Thomas Becon. Important Protestant teaching from reign of Edward VI. Edited by John Ayre for The Parker Society, Cambridge, 1844.

Chronicles of England (1580)   John Stowe. Presented in chronicle form the legend of England as a people chosen by God for His own purposes.

Chronicles of England, Scotland and Ireland, The (1578, revised 1587)   Raphael Holinshed 1587 version, based on Stow's *Chronicles*, is useful for reign of Elizabeth down to 1586.

Collectanea Satis Copiosa (1530)   Collaborative index, sponsored by Edward Foxe and Thomas Cromwell, of over two hundred citations from Scripture, the early Fathers and medieval works addressing the questions of royal and ecclesiastical jurisdiction and power. The work supported the idea of a royal supremacy in spiritual matters but also propounded the view that each province of the church had its own jurisdictional independence.

Colloquies (*see* **Desiderius Erasmus**)

Confutation (1565) (*see* **Book of Martyrs**) Thomas Harding. Attacked Foxe's account and conclusions in *Book of Martyrs*.

De Antiquitate Britannicae Ecclesiae (1572) Matthew Parker, Archbishop of Canterbury. Aimed to trace the apostolic origins of the English church.

De Copia (*see* **Desiderius Erasmus**)

De Vera Obedentia (1535) Bp Stephen Gardiner's influential work which saw church and commonwealth as a unitary body politic, comprehensive of all the people, and ruled over by a single person, head of the church and King of the commonwealth, to whom God ordered obedience.

Dialogue between Reginald Pole and Thomas Lupset, A (1535) Thomas Starkey. Major humanist political treatise. Presented in fashionable dialogue form a programme of reforms for the public good. Attacked growing individualism and lack of concern for commonweal.

Dialogi Sex (1566) (*see* **Book of Martyrs**) Nicholas Harpsfield under the alias Alan Cope. Refutation of Foxe's *Book of Martyrs*.

Discourse of the Common Weal of this Realm of England. (c1549, unpublished until 1581) Variously attributed to John Hales and Sir Thomas Smith. Current opinion favours Smith. Sophisticated survey of contemporary politics and economy from the perspective of one who urges action for the good of the commonweal.

Discourse on Usury (Elizabethan) Thomas Wilson. Important treatise. Edited by R.H. Tawney, New York, 1925.

Elementarie, The First Parte of the (1582) (*see* **Richard Mulcaster**)

First and Chiefe Grounds of Architecture, The (no date but Elizabethan) John Shute. This is the principal Elizabethan work on architecture.

Harborowe for Faithful and True Subjectes, An (April 1559) John Aylmer, later Bishop of London. Presents Elizabeth as having been saved from martyrdom only by divine intervention (death of Mary I), so that the English nation was committed to her preservation. Conspiracies v. Elizabeth were conspiracies against the true church.

How superior powers ought to be obeyd (1558 edn) Christopher Goodman. Tract by Marian exile on obedience due to secular powers.

If you know not me you know nobody; or the Troubles of Queen Elizabeth (1603) Thomas Heywood. Protestant historiographical propaganda presenting Elizabeth as second Deborah.

Laws of Ecclesiastical Polity, The (1593) Richard Hooker. Portrays the monarch as guardian of the Church of England but is implicitly critical of the way in which the Queen was exercising the royal supremacy. This part, Book 8, was published posthumously in 1662.

Lily's Latin Grammar In the late 1530s a royal commission was set up to produce a Latin grammar based on the St Paul's texts of John Colet, William Lily and Desiderius Erasmus, the multiplicity of different grammars having caused confusion. The composite version was known as Lily's Latin Grammar and was prescribed for use in grammar schools until 1604. Ten thousand copies were published annually.

Marchants Aviso, The (Elizabethan) John Browne, Bristol merchant during Elizabeth's reign. A manual for merchants and factors involved in overseas trade. Edited by Patrick McGrath, Boston, 1957.

Obedience of a Christian Man (1528) Williarn Tyndale traced long-drawn-out contest between clergy and the Crown, casting the English monarchs as the dupe of the Roman clergy and only potentially as saviours of the church.

Positions ... The Training up of children (1581) (*see* Richard Mulcaster)

Praise of Folly (*see* Desiderius Erasmus)

Reformatio Legum Ecclesiasticarum (1571) Reprinted in English translation as *The Reformation of the ecclesiastical laws as attempted in the reigns of King Henry VIII, King Edward VI and Queen Elizabeth*, Oxford, 1850.

Scholemaster, The (1570) (*see* Roger Ascham)

Sermon on the Ploughers or Sermon on the Plough (1548) Hugh Latimer. One of a series of four sermons based on Christ's Parable of the Sower. The clergy are the ploughers, who prepare the land (the people) to receive the seed (the Word of God). Much of the sermon is an attack on preachers (or 'prelates' as Latimer calls them) who are failing in their duty. A remarkable sermon characterised by powerful use of language. Some controversy as to Latimer's approach to England's problems in the 1540s. It is now accepted that he was not a member of a 'commonwealth party' (*see* Crowley, Brinkworth, Smith) and, indeed, he rarely mentions the word *commonwealth*. But to see him even primarily as a socio-economic critic or as a champion of the poor is probably a mistake. He regarded the material evils of the day as the by-products of England's failure to follow God's word: in this the poor were as guilty as the rich.

Short Treatise of Politicke Power, A (1556) John Ponet. Marian exile's advocacy of limited monarchy. Published in Strasbourg.

Supplication for the Beggars, A (1529)   Simon Fish described the excesses of the Roman clergy, showed them to be seditious and prescribed a political remedy to be administered by the Crown. F.J. Furnivall and J.M. Cooper (eds), Early English Text Society, extra series, XIII, 1871.

Tree of the Commonwealth, The (1509?)   (*see* **Edmund Dudley**)

Troubles at Frankfurt, A Briefe Discourse of the Troubles at Frankfort, 1554–1558.   Variously attributed to William Whittingham and Thomas Wood. An account of conflicts between the Marian exiles.

Union of the Two Noble and Illustre Famelies of Lancastre and York, The (1548)   Edward Hall. Good example of native writing which assumed that dynamic monarchs caused change.

Utopia (*see* Thomas More)

Valor Ecclesiasticus (1535)   Enormous survey of ecclesiastical benefices commissioned by Thomas Cromwell as vicegerent.

Vitae Romanorum Pontificum (1536)   Robert Barnes demonstrated that the very decline of the Church of Rome was due in large part to the Papacy's usurpation of temporal powers. The King might defend the faith by banishing the clerical estate to its own sphere but it would still be the clergy who would determine the form of religion in accord with Scripture.

Wolsey, The Life and Death of (no date)   George Cavendish. Written by a servant of Wolsey. Printed version in Richard S. Sylvester, Early English Text Society, original series, vol. CCXLIII, 1959.

Authors of the Tudor Period

Included here are some European authors whose work was extremely influential in Tudor England as well as many of the English authors most frequently mentioned in student texts and monographs. Excluded are collections of letters and other manuscript materials, such as diaries and autobiographies, which have since been published.

Agrippa, Henry Cornelius (1486–1535)
His important *De nobilitate et praecellentia feminei sexus* (1534) was translated into English immediately. Women have been forced to give place by male tyranny not by incapacity.
The English translation was: David Clapham, *A Treatise of the Nobilitie and Excellencye of Woman Kynde* (1534, 1542).

Ascham, Roger (1515–68)   *Toxophilus* (1540).   Treatise on archery.
The Scholemaster (1570).   Subtitled 'A plain and perfect way of teaching children to understand, write and speak, the Latin tongue.' 'Teach yourself' manual.

Bale, John (1495–1563)
A Comedy Concerning Three Laws (1532, pub. 1538).   First Protestant morality play in English. Attack on Papacy and monasticism.
A Tragedy of John, King of England (1538).   Good King is duped by Archbp and the Papacy. Use of allegory.
Image of Both Churches (1541).   Detailed run through book of Revelations, casting the Pope as Antichrist.
The Acts of English Votaries (1546).   Scurrilous attack on veneration of saints, via descriptions of sexual exploits of saints, is part of argument justifying the Henrician break with Rome.

Barnes, Robert (1495–1540)
That Men's Constitutions, which are not grounded in Scripture, bind not the conscience of Man (pub. with *Supplication* in 1534).   It is God who institutes political authority and men are bound to obedience by Him. Resistance

is in no circumstances justifiable but there is a distinction between disobedience and resistance.

Becon, Thomas (1512–67)

Thomas Becon. Works, ed. by J. Ayre in 3 vols, Parker Society, Cambridge, 1843–1844. Includes influential *Catechism* and also much of socio-economic as well as religious interest.

Bilson, Thomas (1547–1616)

The Perpetual Government of Christ's Church (1593). Defence of episcopacy.

Brinklow, Henry (d. 1546)

The Complaint of Roderick Mors (1546). Prototype of the so-called 'Commonwealth tracts' which angrily chastised the exploitative activities of nobles and landlords.

Browne, Robert (?1550–?1633)

A treatise of reformation without tarrying for anie (1582). Sets out separatist position on the church and presents separatist attack on Puritans.

Cartwright, Thomas (1533–1603)

A reply to an answere made of M Dr Whitgifte agaynste the Admonition to Parliament (1574).
The second replie of T.C. against Master Doctor Whitgift's second answer, touching the church discipline (1575).
The rest of the second replie . . . (1577). Part of important debate concerning manner of church government (whether by episcopacy or not) sparked off by John Field and Thomas Wilcox's *Admonition to the Parliament* (1572). The latter work is detailed under 'Books of the Tudor Period' above.

Cleaver, Robert (fl.1590s)

Godlie Forme of householde governement: for the ordering of private families, according to the direction of God's Word (1598). This is normally cited in its 1612 edition and attributed to John Dod and Robert Cleaver. A popular marriage conduct book designed for the middle classes. It describes' a way of ordering the famelie aright'.

Coote, Edmund (fl.1590s)

The English Schoolmaster (1596). Most popular manual for teaching of reading. Twenty-six editions between 1596 and 1656; still used in 18th Century. Upper and lower-case alphabets; vowels and consonants; graded syllable-based vocabularies using verses to produce mechanical accuracy but with little attention to comprehension; syllabification; rules of pronunciation; spelling contest; reading practice; rules of behaviour and number.

Cranmer, Thomas (1489–1556)
The Works of Thomas Cranmer, ed. by J.E. Cox in 3 vols, Parker Society, Cambridge, 1844–46.   Important for understanding of religious developments in Henry VIII's and Edward VI's reigns.

Crowley, Robert (?1518–88)
The Way to Wealth (1550).   Angry work of protest against those who undermine the common good by pursuing their own advancement. One of the so-called 'Commonwealth tracts'. See Brinklow, Henry, above.
The Voice of the Last Trumpet (1550).   Versified critique of those merchants and others who pursue their own selfish concerns at the expense of the public good.

Dee, John (1527–1608)
Translation of Euclid's *Elements of Geometry* with important preface, (1570). Preface treats diverse subjects such as music, navigation, and astronomy. Defends translation of learned book for wide audience. Suggests practical applications of mathematical principles.

Dudley, Edmund (1462–1510)
The Tree of the Commonwealth (1510).   Extravagant allegory of the commonwealth as a tree rooted in love of God, justice, fidelity, concord and peace. Portrays 'prince' as defender of these roots, often against clerical encroachment. Marked hostility to the clergy as an estate.

Elyot, Sir Thomas (?1490–1546)
The Boke of the Governour (1531)(also referred to as The Boke Called the Governor; The Boke Named the Governor).   The paramount importance of education for the nobility as a preparation for public life is stressed and an ideal humanist curriculum proposed.
Latin-English Dictionary (1538).   Widely used in grammar schools.

Erasmus, Desiderius (c.1469–1536)
Adagiorum Collectanea. Adages (several editions beginning with 1490s).   A collection of pithy sayings with their meanings compiled by Erasmus as a teaching aid. Adages, according to Erasmus, have four chief uses: to sum up basic philsophies; to assist persuasive argument; to be decorative; to help understanding of classical authors. The collection was relied upon heavily by generations of English and other European schoolboys as part of an attempt to enrich the Latin then in use and to make the language more effective.
Ciceronianus (1527).   Dialogue debating the approach of humanists to the ancient authors. Erasmus does not favour slavish imitation of, for example, Cicero, but rather creative use of ancient forms.

Colloquies (first edition, 1519). Dialogues designed to illustrate forms of speech and address and to familiarise students with Latin as an everyday language. Widely used in grammar schools and universities. Success, and historical significance, ensured by treatment within the dialogues of issues of contemporary importance – for example, the corruptions and abuses apparent in the church; the relationships between men and women, husbands and wives; the nature of true religion. See especially: *A Pilgrimage for Religion's Sake* (1526); *The Exorcism or Apparition; Courtship* (1523); *Marriage* (1523); *The Religious Banquet.*

Conscribendis Epistolis [*On Letter Writing*] (1522). Published as a text book on the fashionable art of letter writing. Immensely successful because of its widespread use in schools and universities. Long lists of sample classical letters from Cicero, Pliny and Horace. Erasmus turned it into a lively book by treating each class of letters to a discrete study and by using vivid contemporary examples containing absorbing subject matter.

De Copia [*De Duplici Verborum ac Rerum*] (1512). Standard work throughout Europe for teaching of Latin rhetoric and composition. Went through 100 editions in sixteenth century alone. Contained extended vocabulary to diversify expression.

Enchiridion Militis Christi (1503); published in English as *The Handsome Weapon of a Christian Knight* Here Erasmus sees the Christian life as a war in which the chief weapons are knowledge and prayer. He pleads for the inwardness of the spiritual life and attacks outward, ritualistic religion. He sees study of the classical world as preparing the Christian to study the Scriptures and receive the revelation of God's Word. Secular learning is therefore a means to a spiritual end. Important work in development of Christian humanism.

The Institution of Christian Marriage (1526). Important work on Christian marriage translated into English and published by Richard Tavernour, *A ryght fruteful Epystle devysed by the most excellent clerke Erasmus, in laude and prayse of matrymony,* 1532.

New Testament (Greek version, Latin translation) (1516). *Paraclesis* or introduction seeks to open up the scriptures to everyone.

The Praise of Folly (*Moriae Encomium*) (1509). Folly defends herself and enumerates her admirers, which include the lawyers, the princes and their courtiers and the Pope and all churchmen. Their position depends upon folly: 'were wisdom to descend on them, how it would inconvenience them!' by depriving them of wealth and honour. The oration concludes with an attack on the corruptions and abuses of the church and the Papacy.

Foxe, Edward (c.1496–1538)

The True Difference between the Regal Power and the Ecclesiastical Power (1534). Part of justification for royal divorce and supremacy.

Foxe, John (1516–87)
Actes and Monuments of these Latter and Perilous Days (1563). *See* 'Books of
the Tudor Period' above.

Froissart, Sir John (?1337–?1410)
Chronicles (c.1400). Translated into English by John Bourchier Berners
(1469–1533). Provided Shakespeare with details for *Richard II*. Froissart
lived in England from 1360 to 1366, partly as clerk to Queen Philippa of
Hainault, wife of Edward III. He revisited England in 1395 when he
met Richard II.

Gardiner, Stephen (1483–1555)
De Vera Obedientia (*The Oration of True Obedience*) (1535). Support for
royal supremacy. Vindication of royal divorce. Markedly Lutheran view
of temporal and spiritual authority. Princes reign by God's authority and
resistance is resistance to God. There are no parallel temporal and
spiritual jurisdictions. Papal and ecclesiastical power is usurped from the
King. There continues to be an area of spiritual activity but not of
separate spiritual jurisdiction.
Discourse on the Coming of the English and Normans to Britain (1555). Advice
book to Philip II thinly disguised as history of early Britain. Advocates
Machiavellian idea that reason of state is a defence for any ruler to
employ 'unvirtuous' strategies to protect the interests of the commonwealth. First northern European humanist to provide defence of
Machiavelli.

Goodman, Christopher (?1520–1603)
How Superior Powers ought to be obeyed of their subjects (1558). Goodman,
Edwardian Lady Margaret Professor of Divinity at Cambridge, wrote
this tract while pastor of English congregation at Geneva. All rulers
under obligation to defend the true faith. Assigned a monarchy limited
by God. Private-law doctrine used to justify forcible resistance: when
'kings and rulers are become altogether blasphemers of God, and oppres-
sors and murderers of their subjects . . . [then] . . . ought they to be
accounted no more for kings or lawful magistrates, but as private men,
and to be examined, accused, condemned and punished by the law of
God, whereunto they are and ought to be subject'.

Grindal, Edmund (?1519–83)
Grindal's Remains, ed. by W. Nicholson, Parker Society, Cambridge, 1843.

Hall, Edward (1498–1547)
The Union of the Two Noble and Illustre Famelies of Lancastre and York (1548).
Chronicle of English history from Henry IV to Henry VIII which

influenced all sixteenth-century historians, including Holinshed and Shakespeare, with its moralistic view of history.

Harte, John (d. 1574)
Orthography (1569) and *Method* (1570). Early printed manuals of instruction for teachers.

Holinshed, Raphael (?1530–?80)
History of England. History of Scotland (translation of Hector Boece). Formed part of *The Chronicles of England, Scotland and Ireland* (1577 and 1587). Second edition of 1587 was principal source for Shakespeare's maturer history plays and, together with Hall, for the earlier cycle from Henry VI to Richard III.

Hooker, Richard (?1554–1600)
Of the lawes of ecclesiasticall politie (Books I–IV, 1594; Book V, 1597; Books VI and VII, 1644; Book VIII, 1662). Authorship of Book VI doubtful; Books VII and VIII constructed from Hooker's rough notes. Defence of Elizabethan Church against Puritan criticism. Extremely important contribution to sixteenth-century political thought.

Hooper, John (d.1555)
Early Writings of John Hooper, ed. by S. Carr in 2 vols, Parker Society, Cambridge, 1843. *Later Writings of John Hooper*, ed. by C. Nevinson in 2 vols, Parker Society, Cambridge, 1852. Crucially important for primitivist Protestant thought – regarding, for example, the nature of the ministry and of worship and the question of adiaphora or 'things indifferent'.

Jewel, John (1522–71)
Works of John Jewel, ed. by J. Ayre in 4 vols, Parker Society, Cambridge, 1840–1850. *Apology* (1562) is included in vol. 3. This was the first important defence of the Elizabethan Church of England.

Kempe, William (d. 1601)
Education of Children in Learning (1588). Treatise which displays influence of Pierre de Ramée, who emphasised the utility of knowledge.

Latimer, Hugh (c.1485–1555)
Sermons by Hugh Latimer, ed by G.E. Corrie, Parker Society, Cambridge, 1844. *Sermons and Remains of Hugh Latimer*, ed. by G.E. Corrie, Parker Society, Cambridge, 1845. Forty-one sermons survive, most preached during the reign of Edward either at court or on preaching tours. These were taken down verbatim by an amanuensis and not revised for publication. They are conveniently collected together in this

nineteenth-century edition. Contain much valuable socio-economic comment. For Sermon on the Ploughers see 'Books of the Tudor Period' above.

Machiavelli, Niccolo (1469–1527)
The Prince (*1532*).   Spirited defence of reason of state as justification for political action. Considerable historical debate as to its influence on English thought.

Marprelate, Martin
Nom de plume of author or authors of tracts against the bishops.

Marshal, William (fl.1530s)
Defender of Peace (1535).   Translation into English of Marsiglio of Padua's *Defensor Pacis*. Commissioned by Thomas Cromwell. Translation omitted passages on the popular origins of political authority. Preface maintained that book proved that Popes have always been usurpers of power.

More, Sir Thomas (1478–1535)
Apology (*see* St German, Christopher).   Counterattack to St German's blast against the legal jurisdiction of the church.
Dialogue concerning Heresies (1529). (*See* Tyndale, William).   Accuses Tyndale of arguing in favour of rebellion. Enters into debate about access to Bible: Church must supervise translation; no indiscriminate access to Bible.
Debellacion between Salem and Bizance (1533). (*See* St German, Christopher).   Rejoinder to St German's dialogue.
Utopia (1516).   'Unquestionably the greatest contribution to the political theory of the northern Renaissance, it also embodies by far the most radical critique of humanism written by a humanist . . . [It] believes that one of the most urgent tasks of social theory is to discover the root causes of injustice and poverty . . . [and believes] that these evils are mainly caused by the misuse of private property' (Skinner, *Foundations of Modern Political Thought*, Vol. I, pp. 256–62.) Use of mythical state of Utopia to explore ideas. Through humanist belief that virtue constitutes the only true nobility, More attacks both hereditary aristocracy and 'comfortable social philosophy' of many fellow humanists such as Elyot. Attacks whole concept of hierarchical society. Denunciation of Italianate preoccupation with the art of war. Latin text.

Morrison, Richard (d.1556)
Apomaxis Calumniarum (1537).   Account of the schism which includes an attack on Thomas More and John Fisher.

Lamentation (1536) and *Remedy for Sedition* (Oct. 1536) showed the consequences of sedition and rebellion in the wake of the Pilgrimage of Grace.
Invective against the great and destestable vice, Treason (1539). The Northern rebellion.
An Exhortation to stir all Englishmen in Defence of their Country (1539). Patriotic view of the reformation settlement, written against the background of reimposition of Clement VII's excommunication of Henry VIII, which released Catholic subjects from allegiance. Extremely influential. Reiterates Lutheran call to non-resistance in all circumstances. Denounces his former patron, 'pestiferous Pole', alongside Catholics in general.

Mulcaster, Richard (?1530–1611)

Positions . . . The Training up of Children (1581) and *The First Part of the Elementarie* (1582). These two books provided Mulcaster with a platform to deal with two fundamental problems facing humanist education programme: ill qualified and uncommitted teachers; poor method that turned pupils away from learning. He recommended a teacher-training college; the direction of the best teachers to the elementary forms; full-time commitment to teaching; a carefully planned and standardised curriculum; standard teaching methodology.

Perkins, William (1558–1602)

The Works of William Perkins. Extremely influential Protestant Cambridge divine during reign of Elizabeth. His works of pastoral theology particularly important. No complete modern edition of his voluminous writings.

Pole, Reginald (1500–58)

Apology to Charles V (1539). Includes attack on Machiavelli's ideas as destructive of the virtues.
A Defence of Ecclesiastical Unity (1536). A Latin tract defending impossibility of royal supremacy. Church is gift of God but kingship is creation of the people themselves who 'spontaneously submit' to an authority set up in their own self-interest. Weakened by vitriolic attack on King as head of church of Satan. Includes attack on Machiavelli's ideas as destructive of the virtues. Contributed to downfall and eventual execution of his brother, Henry, Lord Montague and his mother Margaret, Countess of Salisbury.

Ponet, John (?1514–56)

Short Treatise of Politicke Power (1556). Justification of forcible resistance written during Marian exile in Frankfurt by Edwardian Bishop of Winchester.

Sadoleto, Jacopo (1477–1547)
The Right Education of Boys (1534).

Sampson, Richard (d. 1554) (*See* Foxe, Edward and Gardiner, Stephen)
Oration to teach everyone that they must be obedient to the will of the King (1534).

Shakespeare, William (1564–1616)

Chronology of writing of Shakespeare's Elizabethan plays

1588–94
Titus Andronicus
Henry VI, Part I
The Comedy of Errors
The Two Gentlemen of Verona
Henry VI, Part 2
Henry VI, Part 3
King John
Love's Labour's Lost
Richard III
The Taming of the Shrew

1594–6
Romeo and Juliet
Richard II (published 1597 apart from abdication scene)
A Midsummer Night's Dream
Henry IV, Parts 1 and 2

1596–98
The Merry Wives of Windsor
The Merchant of Venice
Henry V
Much Ado About Nothing

1599–1601
As You Like It
Twelfth Night
Julius Caesar
Hamlet

1602–3
All's Well That Ends Well
Troilus and Cressida

Sidney, Sir Philip (1554–86)   *Arcadia* (1593).   A pastoral romance. Two versions. The first, a straightforward affair, was not published until twentieth century. A second version, incomplete but richer and more complex, was published as *Countess of Pembroke's Arcadia* in 1593

Smith, Henry (?1550–1591)
A Preparative to Marriage (1591).   Contains attack on wet-nursing. Discusses relationship between husbands and wives and nature of woman.

Smith, Sir Thomas (1513–77)
De Republica Anglorum. The Maner of Gouvernement or policie of the Realme of England (1583).   Otherwise known as *The Commonwealth of England*. Description of English constitution and government.
Discourse of the Common Weal (1549, unpublished until 1581).   Disputed authorship. Sometimes attributed to John Hales (d.1571) but currently most commonly attributed to Smith. Sophisticated survey of polity and economy from perspective of commonwealthmen of Edward's reign.

Spenser, Edmund (1552–97)
The Faery Queen (1589–96).   Pastoral poem which combined epic and romance.

Starkey, Thomas (?1499–1538)
A Dialogue Between Reginald Pole and Thomas Lupset (1535).   Major treatise of humanist political thought. A series of reform proposals for the commonwealth presented in fashionable dialogue form. The universities were designed to educate clergy, therefore there was a need for a separate academy in London for the education of the elite.
An Exhortation to the People (1535, published 1536).   Defence of the Reformation settlement inspired by and perhaps revised by Thomas Cromwell. Instructed people to 'unity and obedience'. Stresses the power of statute.

St German, Christopher (c.1460–1540)
Dialogue between a Doctor and a Student (Latin version 1523; English version 1531).   Dialogue about the foundations of law and especially the relationship between the eternal law, the laws of nature and the law of God on the one hand and the laws of England on the other. The conclusion is that the customary laws of England are supreme. The English version included a second dialogue (published separately in 1530) which brought out the anti-clerical aspects of St German's thought on the law.

Treatise (concerning the division between the spirituality and the temporality) (1532). (*See* Thomas More, *Apology* and *Debellacion of Salem and Bizance*. Attack on clerical estate and its claim to legal jurisdiction. Opening salvo in war, in which Thomas More campaigned on the clergy's behalf with the *Apology*.

Dialogue (between Salem and Bizance) (1532). More responded to this with *Debellacion between Salem and Bizance*.

Answer to a Letter (1535). All power is secular. The common law is supreme and legislative authority is vested in the King in Parliament. The King is resuming his headship of the church, which had been delegated by his forbears to the Papacy, and this headship includes even the power to determine doctrine. This provided useful independent support for the government's propaganda in support of the break with Rome.

Tilney, Edmund (d. 1610)

A Briefe and Pleasant Discourse of Duties in Marriage (1568). The author was Master of Revels in the royal household, 1579–1609.

Travers, Walter (?1548–1635)

Ecclesiasticae discipliniae et Anglicanae ecclesiae . . . explicatio (1574). English translation, *A Full and Plain Declaration of Ecclesiastical Discipline*, published in 1574, generally attributed to Thomas Cartwright. Not to be confused with Puritan *Book of Discipline* (Directory which is also often attributed to Travers).

A Directory of Church Government . . . Found in the Study of . . . Cartwright after his decease (1644). Late version of document, *Book of Discipline*, produced by Puritans in the 1580s. Sometimes attributed to Cartwright and sometimes to Travers. Modern scholarship plumps for composite authorship of a document of which Travers was draftsman.

Tyndale, William (c.1494–1536) (*See* 'The Bible and Biblical Scholarship' below.)

The Obedience of a Christian Man (1531). Lutheran emphasis on distinction between disobedience and resistance. Rulers must be obeyed in all things because God has so ordered it. Forcible resistance is never justifiable. The subject enjoined to do evil must desist but must suffer death rather than resist. The church, defined as a purely spiritual body, is not exempt from this obligation. The ruler has a duty to rule the people as God wants for they are God's people. All jurisdiction is secular and, therefore, the Pope and the church have usurped the power of the King.

Answer to Sir Thomas More's Dialogue (1531).

Vives, Jean Luis (sometimes given as Ludovico) (1492–1540)

De Instructione Feminae Christianae (1524) translated by Richard Hyrde as *Instruction of a Christian Woman*. A manual which, while advocating a humanistic education for girls, nevertheless emphasised that a woman's domestic vocation dictated the limits of her educational needs.

De Tradendis Disciplinis (1531). Suggested value of technique of double translation which was, in consequence, widely used in English grammar schools.

Latinae Linguae Exercitatio (1539). Colloquies particularly useful for schoolboys.

Office and Duty of a Husband (1550).

Whitgift, John (?1530–1604) (*See* Cartwright, Thomas; *Admonition*)

An Answere to a certen libel entituled an admonition to the parliament (1572).

The Defense of the aunswere to the admonition, against the replie of T.C. (1574).

Wilson, Thomas (?1525–81)

Rule of Reason (1551). Manual for teaching of logic.

Art of Rhetoric (1553). Manual for teaching of rhetoric, i.e. oral communication.

The Bible and Biblical Scholarship: Chronology

1496/7 John Colet lectured at Oxford on St Paul's Epistle to the Romans. The lectures were unusual because Colet set the text in its historical context. Moreover, Colet employed St Paul's arguments to criticise the contemporary church and to call for a return to primitive Christianity.

1499 Erasmus visited England and was received by John Colet who encouraged Erasmus's dislike of scholasticism and directed him towards scriptural study. Erasmus thought that he did not possess the technical expertise to translate the Old Testament as Colet suggested but vowed to acquire it.

1503 Erasmus published the *Enchiridion Militis Christiani* (The Handbook of the Christian Soldier).

1504 Erasmus wrote to Colet urging him to publish his work on St Paul and the Gospels.

1509 Erasmus returns to England.

1511–14 Erasmus working on translation of Greek New Testament while at Cambridge Univ.

1516 Erasmus published translated *New Testament* and includes *Paraclesis* exhorting people to read the scriptures; Colet begged Erasmus to produce detailed commentaries on his scriptural translations to make entirely clear his interpretation of the 'philosophia Christi'.

1522 publication at Wittenberg of Martin Luther's German New Testament (based on Erasmus' translation).

1523 William Tyndale unsuccessfully sought patronage of Cuthbert Tunstal, Bishop of London for translation of Bible into English. Tyndale associated with Protestants. Publication at Wittenberg of Luther's German translation of the Pentateuch (first five books of the Old Testament).

1524 Humphrey Monmouth, a London merchant, assisted Tyndale to visit Germany. Tyndale visited Cologne, Hamburg and Wittenberg.

1525 Tyndale's English New Testament, based on Luther's and Erasmus's translations, completed. Printing began at Cologne but was interrupted by the church authorities and had to continue at Worms.

1526 April: Tyndale's New Testament on sale in England. The Bishop of London banned its sale and use in his diocese and a copy was burned at St Paul's Cross. Second edition printed by Christopher Endhoven of Antwerp.

1528 Cardinal Wolsey prosecuted several, including Thomas Garrett of Oxford, for circulating Tyndale's New Testament.

1530 Hoochstraten of Antwerp printed Tyndale's translation of the Pentateuch. Endhoven printed 3rd edition of New Testament. Henry VIII set up commission of inquiry into need for English Bible and this reported in favour of an official translation. George Joye translated Psalms into English from Martin Bucer's Latin translation.

1531 George Joye published translation of Book of Isaiah.

1533 Winken de Worde publishes Tyndale's English translation of Erasmus' *Enchiridion* under title *The Manuell of the Christen Knyght*.

1534 Publication of German Bible at Wittenberg. 4th edition of Tyndale's New Testament published at Antwerp. George Joye published Book of Jeremiah. Miles Coverdale began work on English translation of Old Testament at Antwerp. December: Canterbury Convocation petitioned King for English Bible. At Cranmer's request a group of bishops and scholars set to work to amend Tyndale's New Testament but the project bore no fruit.

1535 Arrest and imprisonment of Tyndale at Vilvorde Castle, near Brussels. Coverdale put together Tyndale's translation of the Pentateuch and New Testament and his own translation of the rest of the Old Testament to publish complete English Bible at Cologne; Henry VIII gave the printer James Nicholson permission to print Coverdale's Bible but did not give it official approval.

1536 Execution of Anne Boleyn puts end to Cromwell's plan to make English Bible compulsory in parish churches. Tyndale executed at Vilvorde in October.

1537 Nicholson printed two revised editions of Coverdale's Bible, claiming official sanction. August: John Rogers published 'Mathew Bible', based on Tyndale's, at Antwerp with the permission of the King. It was so called because Rogers used the pseudonym Thomas Mathew.

1538 Coverdale in Paris worked to modify the radical Protestantism of the Mathew Bible; publication was interrupted by the French authorities but moved to London. Cromwell's Injunctions ordered an English Bible to be placed in every church.

1539 Coverdale's Great Bible printed. Richard Taverner, one of Cromwell's protégés, also produced a modified Mathew Bible.

1540 Second edition of Great Bible with preface by Cranmer. Berthelet printed 1st cheap edition of Great Bible. Bishop of London arrested John Porter for reading English Bible aloud in St Paul's and offering commentary.

1541 Fifth edition of Great Bible. Order for English Bible to be placed in every parish church repeated.

1542 Conservative revision of Great Bible (to be based on Vulgate version) demanded. Cranmer appointed panel of 15 bishops to examine New Testament but Henry VIII handed the task to the universities. No revision was forthcoming.

1543 Act for the advancement of true religion passed. Right to read vernacular scriptures restricted.

1551 William Salesbury published Welsh translation of Epistles and Gospels.

1553–8 English Bibles destroyed.

1556 English translation of the Psalms produced at Geneva by William Whittingham and William Kethe.

1557 Whittingham translated New Testament.

1559 Royal Injunctions order English Bible to be set up in every church. Elizabethan Book of Common Prayer (excluding Black Rubric of 1552).

1560 April: William Whittingham, Anthony Gilby and Richard Sampson produced 'Geneva Bible' or 'Breeches Bible'. This Bible was Calvinist, relatively cheap and more accessible to the reader. For example, it was printed in roman type and the text was divided into chapters and verses.

1563 Commission of bishops of Bangor, St David's, St Asaph's, Llandaff and Hereford set up to translate Bible into Welsh.

1566 Edition of Great Bible. Matthew Parker directed amended translation of Bible.

1567 Bible in Welsh published. William Salesbury largely responsible.

1568 Parker's Bible (the Bishops' Bible) published.

1572 Revised version of Bishops' Bible published.

1576 Geneva Bible first published in England.

1578 Work begun on Rheims/Douay Catholic translation of the Bible into English by Gregory Martin. William Allen supervised this translation of the Vulgate.

1582 Martin New Testament published.

1588 William Morgan, Bishop of St Asaph, published 1st Welsh Bible.

1596 Hugh Broughton published English translation of Book of Daniel from the Hebrew.

1611 Authorized Version of Bible published.

Central Government: (1) The Monarchy and the Royal Household

The Monarchy

England was governed by a monarch. Changes to the royal style occurred during Henry VIII's reign. In 1521 Pope Leo X conferred the title of *fidei defensor* (defender of the faith) on Henry VIII. Henry was the first monarch to place a numeral after his or her name (1525). In 1541 Henry was declared King rather than lord of Ireland by statute (33 Henry VIII, c.1). Both Henry and his son Edward maintained the style: *Dei Gratia Angliae, Franciae, et Hiberniae Rex, Fidei Defensor, et in terra Ecclesiae Anglicanae et Hibernicae supremum caput* (by the grace of God king of England, France and Ireland, Defender of the Faith, and Supreme Head of the Church of England and Ireland on earth). 1 & 2 Ph. & Mary repealed the statute of 1541 (35 Henry VIII, c.3) by which it was declared high treason to deprive the monarch of this title and the claim to supremacy was dropped. Philip's titles were added to those of Mary. When Elizabeth succeeded she adopted the style: 'Dei Gratia Angliae, Franciae et Hiberniae regia, fidei defensor . . .'.

Monarchs
Henry VII, b. 28 January 1457-d. 21 April 1509. Ruled 1485–1509.
Henry VIII, b. 28 June 1491-d. 28 January 1547. Ruled 1509–47.
Edward VI, b. 12 October 1537-d. 6 July 1553. Ruled 1547–53.
'Queen Jane Grey', b. October 1537-d. 12 February 1554. 'Ruled' 6–14 July 1553.
Mary I, b. 18 February 1516-d. 17 November 1558. Ruled 1553–58.
Elizabeth I, b. 7 September 1533-d. 24 March 1603. Ruled 1558–1603.

The Tudor dynasty *ruled* England. It did so with the assistance of a council, occasional Great Councils, a parliament and a number of officers of state. The period was one of experiment. Henry VII, for example, carried on medieval experiments with chamber financial administration while under King Henry VIII new courts were created to deal with new sources of revenue. Under Henry VIII and his heirs, the Secretaryship of State became an increasingly important office and the Lord Chancellorship's executive role shrank in relation to its position as chief legal officer of the Crown.

Listings of office holders below are restricted to the major offices of state (Lord Chancellor, Keeper, Keeper of the Privy Seal, Secretaries of State).

The Royal Council

The monarch selected a council of advisers from among the powerful of the realm – lay and ecclesiastical. In medieval times the royal council was large and unwieldy and made up of bishops and magnates who assembled to advise the King during the legal terms only because they had to attend to other business during much of the year. The monarch, of course, needed advice all the time and not just while the law courts were sitting so he habitually consulted those councillors who were always present (often members of his household) and who came to form a more influential and select Privy Council. Thomas Cromwell's reform of the council and establishment of the Privy Council in the 1530s as the supreme executive was a formalisation of an existing tendency in royal government.

Chronology

15th century   Council at its most important.

Henry VII   Large council of 40 to 50 members; some functional divisions make the council more effective by reducing its size in particular circumstances: e.g. Star Chamber; Court of Requests; small group of itinerant councillors who accompany king. Council is managed by the Lord Chancellor, backed by the Chancery.

Henry VIII   also has large council but largely relies on Wolsey for advice and action:

1526   Wolsey proposes in the Eltham Ordinances a smaller council of about 20 members but this comes to nothing when he falls from power.

mid 1530s   Cromwell revives idea of smaller council and establishes a Privy Council of 19 office holders and royal servants sitting under the King's chairmanship by 1536: Thomas Cromwell as Principal Secretary initiates and organises the business of the Privy Council and has much executive power as a result.

1540   Cromwell fell from office and a permanent clerk to the council was appointed who kept the minutes. The administrative and judicial work of the council was thereafter kept strictly separate although the Star Chamber and Court of Requests were staffed by Privy Council members.

Edward VI   Large and ineffective council of about 40 members, riven by faction, which worked by committees. Proposals for reform mooted but impossible to arrive at agreement.

Mary I   Council grew even larger and more unmanageable; Crown relied on a very few advisers such as Cardinal Reginald Pole and this had repercussions for the success of the government.

Elizabeth I   Privy Council drawn from about 58 men and at any one time numbered about a dozen; deliberate return to small Privy Council; extremely effective in managing the government and keeping it in touch with the rest of the nation.

Uses the J.P.s and Lords Lieutenant to implement its acts. Controls and purges membership of local commissions of the peace (e.g. of recusants) to ensure compliance. Works through special agencies of the regional councils (e.g. Council of the North) which receive a stream of orders from the Privy Council and also seek the council's advice. Decline of the Privy Council in the later years of the century because of political factionalism.

- **Thomas Cromwell reduces size and increases efficiency of the Royal Council in the 1530s, thus building on Wolsey's ideas**
- **Reversion to larger and ineffective council under the middle Tudors**
- **Effective partnership between Privy Council and local agencies during Elizabeth's reign**
- **Decline of the Privy Council under Elizabeth as it becomes an arena for the manoeuvrings of Cecil, Essex, Walsingham and Leicester.**

The following listings of the membership of the Privy Council may be used to illustrate its changing size and composition.

Membership of Privy Council, 1526 (Eltham Ordinances), 20 members

Thomas Wolsey, Chancellor; Duke of Norfolk, Treasurer; Cuthbert Tunstall, Bishop of London and Keeper of Privy Seal; Duke of Suffolk, Marshal of England; Marquess of Dorset; Marquess of Exeter, Earl of Shrewsbury, Steward of Household; Earl of Oxford, lord Chamberlain; John Clerk, Bishop of Bath; John Longland, Bishop of Lincoln; Lord Sandys, Chamberlain of the Household; Sir William FitzWilliam, Treasurer of Household; Sir Henry Guilford, Comptroller; Richard Pace, Secretary; Sir Thomas More, Chancellor of Duchy of Lancaster; Richard Sampson, Dean of King's Chapel; Sir Henry Wyatt, Treasurer of king's Chamber, Sir Richard Wingfield, Vice Chamberlain; Sir William Kingston, Captain of the Guard; Doctor Wolman, Almoner.

Membership of the Privy Council, 1540, 19 members

Thomas Cranmer, Archbishop of Canterbury; Thomas, Lord Audley, Chancellor, Thomas, Duke of Norfolk, High Treasurer, Charles Duke of Suffolk, Master of king's Household and President of the Council; William, Earl of Southampton and Lord Privy Seal; Robert, Earl of Sussex and Great Chamberlain; Edward Seymour, Earl of Hertford; John, Lord Russell, Great Admiral; Cuthbert Tunstall, Bishop of Durham; Stephen Gardiner, Bishop of Winchester, William, Lord Sandys, King's Chamberlain; Sir Thomas Cheyney, Lord Warden of the Cinque Ports and Treasurer of Household; Sir Anthony Browne, Master of the King's Horse; Sir William Kingston, Comptroller of Household; Sir Anthony Wingfield, Vice Chamberlain of Household; Sir Thomas Wriothesley, Secretary; Sir Richard Rich, Chancellor of Court of Augmentations; Sir John Baker, Chancellor of Court of First Fruits and Tenths.

Membership of the Privy Council, 1553 (Edward VI), 40 members

Thomas Cranmer, Archbishop of Canterbury; Thomas Goodrich, Bishop of Ely and Lord Chancellor, The Marquess of Winchester, Lord Treasurer; The Duke of Northumberland; Lord John Russell, Lord Privy Seal; The Duke of Suffolk; The Marquess of Northampton; The Earl of Shrewsbury; The Earl of Westmorland; The Earl of Huntingdon; The Earl of Pembroke; The Viscount Hereford; Lord Clinton, Lord Admiral; Lord Darcy, Lord Chamberlain; The Lord Cobham; The Lord Rich; Sir Richard Cotton, Mr Comptroller, Sir Thomas Cheyney, Mr Treasurer; Sir John Gates, Mr Vice Chamberlain; William Petre, Secretary; William Cecil, Secretary; Sir Philip Hoby; Sir Robert Bowes; Sir John Gage; Sir John Mason; Mr Ralph Sadler; Sir John Baker; Judge Bromley; Judge Montague; Mr Wotton; Mr North; Nicholas Ridley, Bishop of London; Thomas Thirlby, Bishop of Norwich; Sir Thomas Wrothe; Sir Richard Cotton; Sir Walter Mildmay; Edward Griffyn, former solicitor; Mr Coke; Mr Lucas.

Membership of Privy Council, 1591, 10 members

John Whitgift, Archbishop of Canterbury; Sir Christopher Hatton, Lord Chancellor; Sir William Cecil, Lord Burghley, Lord High Treasurer; Charles Howard, Baron Effingham, Lord Admiral; Henry Carey, Lord Hunsdon, Lord Chamberlain; Thomas, Lord Buckhurst, Lord High Butler; Sir Francis Knollys, Treasurer of the Queen's Household; Sir Thomas Heneage, Vice Chamberlain to the Queen, Chancellor of the Duchy of Lancaster, Mr John Wolley, Esq., Secretary for the Latin Tongue and Chancellor of the Order of the Garter; Mr John Fortescue, Esq., Master of the Great Wardrobe and Under Treasurer of the Exchequer.

Membership of Privy Council, 1601, 13 members

John Whitgift, Archbishop of Canterbury; Sir Thomas Egerton, Lord Keeper; Sir Thomas Sackville, Lord Buckhurst, Lord High Treasurer; Charles, Earl of Nottingham, Lord High Admiral; Gilbert, Earl of Shrewsbury; Edward, Earl of Worcester, Master of the Horse; Sir George Carey, Lord Hunsdon, Lord Chamberlain; Sir William Knollys, Comptroller of Household; Sir John Stanhope, Vice Chamberlain and Treasurer of the Chamber; Sir Robert Cecil, Principal Secretary and Master of Court of Wards; Sir John Foretscue, Chancellor and Under-Treasurer of the Exchequer; Sir John Popham, Lord Chief Justice; Mr John Herbert, Secretary.

Henry VII also summoned five Great Councils between 1487 and 1502. These occasional assemblies of peers of the realm and councillors (and sometimes burgesses) were called to give advice and provide authority for war and taxation and should not be confused with the King's Council as described above. Rather they demonstrate Henry VII's attempts to govern consensually and his belief that great councils were important to this process whereas parliament had no part in the making of policy.

Government by Ministers

The Seals

Traditionally government was by the seals: the Great Seal of England (held by the Lord Chancellor), the Privy Seal and the Signet. Henry VII and Henry VIII continued this tradition. All the work of the government was handled by the offices of the Keepers of the seals who authorised all decisions by applying the relevant seals. It was the Lord Chancellor who managed the work of the government. But the Tudor period witnessed the decline of government by the seals. There was, for example, no Lord Chancellor between 1558 and 1579 and 1592 and 1596. (The seal was held by a Lord Keeper) The Lord Chancellor, when there was one, was important chiefly as a the principal legal officer of the Crown. The Keepers of the Privy Seal derived their importance not so much from control of the seal as from their simultaneous occupancy of the Secretaryship of State. The mid century saw the development of government by ministers as a replacement for the medieval government by seals.

Lord Chancellors and [Lord] Keepers [of the Great Seal]

1485 Thomas Rotherham, Archbishop of York

1485–7 John Alcock, Bishop of Worcester and then Ely

1487–1500 John Morton, Archbishop of Canterbury

1500–02 Henry Deane, Archbishop of Canterbury (Keeper)

1502–4 William Warham, Bishop of London and then Archbishop of Canterbury (Keeper of the Seal until he became Chancellor in 1504)

1504–15 William Warham, Archbishop of Canterbury

1515–29 Thomas Wolsey, Cardinal Archbishop of York and Papal Legate

1529–32 Sir Thomas More

1532–3   Sir Thomas Audley (Keeper)

1533–44   Sir Thomas Audley (created 1st Lord Audley, 1538)

1544–7   Thomas Wriothesley, 1st Lord Wriothesley (created 1st Earl of Southampton, 1547)

1547   William Paulet, 1st Lord St John (Keeper)

1547–51   Richard Rich, 1st Lord Rich

1551–2   Thomas Goodrich, Bishop of Ely (Keeper of the Seal until he became Lord Chancellor in 1552)

1552–3   Thomas Goodrich, Bishop of Ely

1553–5   Stephen Gardiner, Bishop of Winchester

1556–8   Nicholas Heath, Archbishop of York

1558–79   Sir Nicholas Bacon (Lord Keeper)

1579–87   Sir Thomas Bromley

1587–91   Sir Christopher Hatton

1592–6   Sir John Puckering (Lord Keeper)

1596–1603   Sir Thomas Egerton (Lord Keeper), created 1st Lord Ellesmere, 1603

- **Up to and including Wolsey, the Lord Chancellor or Keeper was normally a highranking cleric. Mary I reverted to this policy with the appointment of Gardiner.**
- **Under Thomas Cromwell's Secretaryship (1533–40) the Lord Chancellor was pushed into a subsidiary role as principal legal officer of the Crown.**

Keepers of the Privy Seal
1485–7   Peter Courtenay, Bishop of Exeter

1487–1516   Richard Fox

1516–23   Thomas Ruthall, Bishop of Durham

1523   Sir Henry Marny, 1st Lord Marny

1523–30   Cuthbert Tunstal, Bishop of London

1530–6   Thomas Boleyn, 1st Earl of Wiltshire and Ormonde

1536–40   Thomas Cromwell, 1st Lord Cromwell (created 1st Earl of Essex, 1540), Secretary of State

1540–2   William FitzWilliam, 1st Earl of Southampton

1542–55   John Russell, 1st Lord Russell (created 1st Earl of Bedford, 1550)

1555   William Paget

1559–72   William Cecil (created 1st Lord Burghley, 1571)

1572–3   William Howard, 1st Lord Howard of Effingham

1573–6   Sir Thomas Smith, Secretary of State

1576–90   Sir Francis Walsingham, Secretary of State

1590–8   Lord Burghley

1598–1603   Robert Cecil

Secretaries and Principal Secretaries of State
Down to the 1530s the Secretary of State was the King's personal secretary and keeper of the signet. He was not on a par with the great officers of state. After Cromwell's fall in 1540 there were normally two secretaries, one of whom assisted the Principal Secretary. Throughout the century the office was poorly defined and tended to rely for its relative importance in the government upon the men who held it. So both Thomas Cromwell and William Cecil made it the principal office of government while, under Sir Thomas Smith, the office achieved little.

Function of the Office
- Provide a link between Crown and council, parliament and people
- Manage the agenda of the council
- Represent the Crown in parliament
- Head the diplomatic service
- Guard the peace of the realm

Secretaries of State
1485   Dr Richard Fox

1487   Dr Owen King

1500   Dr Thomas Ruthall

1516   Dr Richard Pace

1526   Dr William Knight

1528   Dr Stephen Gardiner (from 1531 Bishop of Winchester)

1533   Thomas Cromwell

Principal Secretaries
1540–4   Sir Thomas Wriothesley

1540–3   Sir Ralph Sadler

1543–8   Sir William Paget

1544–57   Sir William Petre

1548–9   Sir Thomas Smith

1549–50   Sir Nicholas Wotton

1550–3   Sir William Cecil

1553   Sir John Cheke

1553–8   Sir John Bourne

1557–8   Sir John Boxall

1558–72   Sir William Cecil

1572–6   Sir Thomas Smith

1573–90   Sir Francis Walsingham

1577–81   Thomas Wilson

1586–7   William Davison

1596–1603   Sir Robert Cecil

1600   John Herbert

The Royal Household

The Exchequer

(The development of the Exchequer is dealt with in further detail on pp. 151–3.) The Exchequer consisted of two sections:

1. Exchequer of Receipt
- For receipt and disbursement of revenue
- Main work is done by the Under-Treasurer and the Chamberlains

2. Upper Exchequer or Exchequer of Account
- For audit
- Chancellor of the Exchequer: a relatively unimportant office

Treasurer
- Honorary position
- Henry VIII bestowed it upon peers of the realm
- 1572–99 William Cecil, Lord Burghley is Treasurer.

- **Free of embezzlement**
- **Most royal revenue anticipated so Exchequer deals in tallies rather than money**
- **Audit is very slow**
- **Medieval monarchs had turned Wardrobe and Chamber into secondary financial institutions which permitted receipt and disbursement**
- **Henry VII seeks to make Chamber centre of administration of his revenues. Treasurer of Chamber to receive all revenues except customs, which remain with Exchequer.**

The Household/The Chamber

In the fifteenth century the household officers of the Crown had had considerable influence in government. The Tudor period saw household government in decline but offices were bestowed as a mark of royal favour and withheld as a mark of equal disapproval. The following are the chief offices within the household. When a household was set up, for example for a young prince or princess, these offices would be duplicated in the new household.

Treasurers of the Household
Comptrollers of the Household
Lords Stewards of the Household
Treasurers of the Chamber
Keepers of the Jewel House
Chief Butlers of England

Royal Financial Administration

Chamber Finance
There was one significant exception to the decline of the household and this lay in the development of the Chamber as a financial department.

Monarchical government was financed from a wide number of sources: receipts from royal lands; customs; sale of wardships; subsidies granted by parliament and Convocation; benevolences; fines; (after the break with Rome) first fruits and tenths; monastic and chantry endowments.

Court of Augmentations
– Established by statute in 1536 (27 Henry VIII c.27) to administer the transfer of the dissolved monasteries' lands to the Crown
– Chief officials were Chancellor and Treasurer and, after 1547, General Surveyor
– 1547: Amalgamated with Court of General Surveyors

Court of General Surveyors of the King's Lands
– Established in 1515 by parliament (6 Henry VIII c.24) from one parliament to the next to administer Crown lands acquired by Henry VII and Wolsey
– Established as permanent office in 1535
– General surveyors
– Amalgamated with Court of Augmentations in 1547.

Court of Wards and Liveries
– Regular Master of the Wards appointed from 1503
– Statute of 1540 (32 Henry VIII c.46) made court responsible for feudal revenues
– Chief officers are: Master of King's or Queen's Wards; Surveyor of Liveries; Receiver-General; Attorney
– Under Elizabeth, used as powerful instrument for control of aristocracy and for raising revenue.

Court of First Fruits and Tenths
- Established in 1540 (32 Henry VIII, c.45)
- Officers are: Chancellor; Attorney; Treasurer; Auditor.

Court of Duchy of Lancaster
- Ancient court administering lands of the duchy.

The Chamber: Chronology
Under Henry VII all revenues (except customs, which continued to go to the Exchequer) were diverted to the Chamber. Disbursement by word of mouth or signet warrant. King audits accounts. Rapid audit.

1491   Henry VII levied benevolence.

1500   Regular committee to collect fines on penal statutes.

1503   Appointment of Master of Wards, with bureaucracy, to secure revenues from feudal wardships owned by the Crown.

1504 and 1508   Temporary commissions of inquiry search for prerogative rights etc.

1508   Office of Surveyor of King's Prerogative established to replace temporary commissions. Very shortlived.

1512   Graduated poll tax experimented with.

1514   Wolsey's first subsidy.

1515   Appointment of two General Surveyors of Crown lands who audit not only the Chamber accounts but also those of other revenue collecting courts. Given temporary statutory authority (6 Henry VIII c.24).

1523   Wolsey offers anticipation discounts to those who pay their subsidy early.

1528   Sir Brian Tuke appointed Treasurer of the Chamber and reorganises the office.

1531   Praemunire fine on clergy raises £118,000.

Cromwell's financial administration reforms
1535   Powers of King's General Surveyors made permanent.

1536   Statute creates Court of Augmentations (27 Henry VIII, c.27).

1540   Statute makes First Fruits and Tenths office a court (32 Henry VIII, v.45). Statute makes Court of Wards and Liveries responsible for feudal revenues (32 Henry VIII, c.46).

1545   Henry VIII levies benevolence.

1547   Augmentations and General Surveyors merge into second Court of Augmentations.

1536–40 Crown seizes monastic endowments. Administered by Court of Augmentations.

1554 New courts absorbed into Exchequer as specialised subdepartments. Court of Wards and Duchy of Lancaster remain independent of Exchequer.

Later 16th century Lord Treasurer becomes minister of finance. Chancellor of Exchequer becomes officer of importance as does the Auditor of the receipt.

- **Henry VII makes Chamber centre of revenue administration but does so on informal basis supervised carefully by himself**
- **Under Henry VIII, Wolsey and, at first, Cromwell continue this policy of Chamber administration but they institutionalise it**
- **New revenue from monastic lands etc. made Cromwell think that more fundamental reforms were required. He broke the links between the Chamber and the Household and created new departments (known as courts) for specific sections of the revenue: Augmentations, First Fruits and Tenths; Exchequer; Duchy of Lancaster; Wards and Liveries; General Surveyors**
- **Too diverse; too many officials. Eventual amalgamation of courts into a reformed Exchequer.**

Central Government: (2) Parliament

Parliament was an established part of the King's government but it was an intermittent part, called for special purposes, usually the granting of money. Originally it had been the King's most important court but by the sixteenth century the function of settling legal problems had devolved to the conciliar courts (see under Central Government and Courts) and parliament was not used for trials. The Reformation Parliament of 1529–1536 signalled enormous changes in the nature and function of parliament both because the monarch chose to implement a revolution through it and also because the legislation it produced incorporated parliament fully into the system of government of church and state.

Parliamentary Officers

The Speaker of the House of Commons.
Clerk of the Parliaments.
Gentleman Usher of the Black Rod.
Clerk of the Crown in Chancery.

The Speaker

Sir Thomas Lovell, M.P. for Northamptonshire (d.1524), elected 8 Nov. 1485.

Sir John Mordaunt, M.P. for Bedfordshire (d.1504), elected 10 Nov. 1487.

Sir Thomas FitzWilliam, M.P. for Yorkshire (d.1495), elected 14 Jan. 1489.

Sir Richard Empson, M.P. for Northamptonshire (d.1510), elected 18 Oct. 1491.

Sir Robert Drury, M.P. for Suffolk (d.1536), elected 15 Oct. 1495.

Sir Thomas Englefield, M.P. for Berkshire (d.1514), elected 19 Jan. 1497.

Edmund Dudley, M.P. for Staffordshire (d.1510), elected 26 Jan. 1504.

Sir Thomas Englefield, M.P. for Berkshire (d.1514), elected 23 Jan. 1510.

Sir Robert Sheffield, M.P. for Lincolnshire (d.1518), elected 5 Feb. 1512.

Sir Thomas Neville, M.P. for Kent (d.1542), elected 6 Feb. 1515.

Sir Thomas More, M.P. for Middlesex (d.1535), elected 16 Apr. 1523.

Sir Thomas Audley, M.P. for Essex (d.1544), elected 5 Nov. 1529.

Sir Humphrey Wingfield, M.P. for Great Yarmouth (d.1545), elected 9 Feb. 1533.

Sir Richard Rich, M.P. for Colchester (d.1567), elected 9 Jan. 1536.
Sir Nicholas Hare, M.P. for Norfolk (d.1557), elected 28 Apr. 1539.
Sir Thomas Moyle, M.P. for Kent (d.1560), elected 19 Jan. 1542.
Sir John Baker, M.P. for Huntingdonshire (d.1558), elected 4 Nov. 1547.
Sir James Dyer, M.P. for Cambridgeshire (d.1582), elected 2 Mar. 1553.
Sir John Pollard, M.P. for Oxfordshire (d.1557), elected 5 Oct. 1553.
Sir Robert Brooke, M.P. for City of London (d.1558), elected 2 Apr. 1554.
Sir Clement Higham, M.P. for West Looe (d.1570), elected 12 Nov. 1554.
Sir John Pollard, M.P. for Chippenham (d.1557), elected 21 Oct. 1555.
Sir William Cordell, M.P. for Suffolk (d.1581), elected 20 Jan. 1558.
Sir Thomas Gargrave, M.P. for Yorkshire (d.1579), elected 25 Jan. 1559.
Thomas Williams, M.P. for Exeter (d.1566), elected 12 Jan. 1563.
Richard Onslow, M.P. for Steyning (d.1571), elected 1 Oct. 1566.
Sir Christopher Wray, M.P. for Lugershall (d.1592), elected 2 Apr. 1571.
Sir Robert Bell, M.P. for Lyme Regis (d.1577), elected 8 May 1572.
Sir John Popham, M.P. for Bristol (d.1607), elected 18 Jan. 1581.
Sir John Puckering, M.P. for Carmarthen (d.1596), elected 23 Nov. 1584.
Sir John Puckering, M.P. for Gatton (d.1596), elected 29 Oct. 1586.
Thomas Snagge, M.P. for Bedford (d.1592), elected 4 Feb. 1589.
Sir Edward Coke, M.P. for Norfolk (d.1634), elected 19 Feb. 1593.
Sir Christopher Yelverton, M.P. for Northamptonshire (d.1612), elected 24 Oct. 1597.
Sir John Croke, M.P. for City of London (d.1620), elected 27 Oct. 1601.

Sessions

Parliament was not in continuous session. Most parliaments were brief. There were often lengthy gaps between parliaments.

Henry VII
7 November 1485-4 March 1486
9 November 1487-18 December 1487
13 January 1489-27 February 1490
17 October 1491-5 March 1492
14 October 1495-21-2 December 1495
16 January 1497-13 March 1497
25 January 1504-c.1 April 1504

Henry VIII
21 January 1510-23 February 1510
4 February 1512-4 March 1514
5 February 1515-22 December 1515

15 April 1523-13 August 1523
3 November 1529-4 April 1536   (The Reformation Parliament)
8 Jun. 1536-18 Jul. 1536.
28 Apr. 1539-24 Jul. 1540.
16 Jan. 1542-28 Mar. 1544.
23 Nov. 1545-31 Jan. 1547.

Edward VI
4 Nov. 1547-15 Apr. 1552.
1 Mar. 1553-31 Mar. 1553.

Mary I
5 Oct. 1553-5 Dec. 1553.
2 April 1554-5 May 1554.
12 Nov. 1554-16 Jan. 1555.
21 Oct. 1555-9 Dec. 1555.
20 Jan. 1558-17 Nov. 1558.

Elizabeth I
23 Jan. 1559-8 May 1559.
11 Jan. 1563-2 Jan. 1567.
2 Apr. 1571-29 May 1571.
8 May 1572-19 Apr. 1583.
23 Nov. 1584-14 Sept. 1585.
15 Oct. 1586-23 Mar. 1587.
4 Feb. 1589-29 Mar. 1589.
19 Feb. 1593-10 Apr. 1593.
24 Oct. 1597-9 Feb. 1598.
27 Oct. 1601-19 Dec. 1601

James I
19 Mar. 1604-9 Feb. 1611

The Franchise

Borough Originally the vote was given to all those called burgesses but by Henry VII's accession was much more restricted so that in some boroughs only a small number of elite burgesses voted. The borough franchise was much more idiosyncratic than the county franchise.

County Vote was restricted to inhabitants of the shire who held freehold land worth at least 40s per annum (8 Henry VI, c.7).

Qualifications Those eligible for election for county seats were to be knights of the county concerned or persons of similar substance 23 Henry VI, c.14.

Development of Parliamentary Privilege and Procedure: Chronology

1513   Strode's Case. Richard Strode, M.P., was imprisoned for proposing bills to regulate the tin-mining industry and thus interfering with the stannary courts. The House of Commons obtained his release. It enacted that members of the Commons could not be sued in a court of law for what they said or did in parliament. Acknowledgement that the House of Commons and its business were privileged as part of the High Court of Parliament against the inferior courts of the realm.

1515   Act of Parliament (*6 Henry VIII, c.16*) gives Speaker power to license absenteeism among M.P.s. This privilege had previously been exercised by the Crown alone.

1523   The Speaker, Thomas More, made the first known request by a Speaker for free speech in parliament.

1534   Thomas Cromwell begins to manage parliamentary elections.

1536   Canterbury forced by Cromwell to reverse its election and choose two Crown nominees.

1543   Ferrers' Case. Commons released M.P. George Ferrers, a Plymouth burgess, from prison on the sole authority of the mace of its Serjeant-at-law.

1553   Alexander Nowell denied place in Commons because he is a representative in Convocation.

1555   Indeterminate discussion of bill to prohibit paid dependants of Crown from sitting in Commons.

1571   Thomas Clark and Anthony Bull placed in custody of the Serjeant for seeking to enter the Commons though not members.

1571   Walter Strickland's Case. Strickland introduced a bill for reform of the prayer book. For this invasion of her prerogative the Queen forbade him his place in the Commons. After an outcry, the Queen relented and Strickland took his place.

1572 Lord Cromwell's Case. Members of House of Lords protected against arrest.

1576 8 February: Peter Wentworth, M.P. for Tregony, speaks out in favour of liberty of parliament, 9 February: Committed to Tower, 12 March: Queen remits sentence.

1576 February: Edward Smalley's Case. Confirms that servants of M.P.s are also privileged against arrest.

1581 House of Commons established its right to determine whether elected M.P.s are duly qualified.

1584 Finnies Case. Viscount Bindon unsuccessfully claims privilege against arrest for his servant Finnies.

1585 Parry's Case. Dr William Parry sequestered and executed for conspiracy against the Queen.

1586 The Commons decided in favour of the first disputed election in the case of Norfolk. Thereafter a standing committee to decide disputed elections was appointed at the opening of each parliament.

1587 Peter Wentworth put questions regarding the importance of parliament in the constitution which were adjudged unconstitutional. He and other members were arrested and put in the Tower.

1589 House of Commons decided to issue writs of *supersedeas* when an M.P. had a writ of *nisi prius* brought against him. Sir Edward Hoby moved that the proceedings of the House of Commons be secret.

1593 Case of Thomas Fitzherbert. He had been arrested for debt before his return as an M.P. had been received by the Sheriff. He claimed immunity from arrest as an M.P. but the point was established that the privilege did not extend to those who were not technically Members despite their election.

1601 Goodwin's Case. The House of Commons had to argue its case to settle disputed elections.

Major Legislation, 1485–1601

The legislation of the Tudor Parliaments was designed to maintain law and order, defend the nation and conserve the existing economic and social fabric of the realm. These were traditional areas of parliamentary involvement although rapid economic developments made for intensified central government activity and more legislation. The responsibility for enforcing much of this legislation lay with the county Justices of the Peace. Royal proclamations also played an important part in enforcing the legislative message. In addition, the Crown and its ministers brought about the break with Rome in concert with parliament and, after 1529, 'acts of parliament habitually dealt with the spiritual jurisdiction exercised by the King as supreme head' (Elton, *The Tudor Constitution*, p. 231).

Listed below are the major pieces of legislation on the Tudor Statute Book. The reference in italics is to the statutes of the realm. The year stated in this reference is the regnal year which did not coincide with the calendar year.[1]

1485

Act regarding title of King Henry VII. *1 Henry VII, c.1(a)*.

Act orders that Gascony and Guinne wines must be imported in English ships with majority of crew English-born. *1 Henry VII, c.8*.

1487

Act giving the Court of Star Chamber authority to punish divers misdemeanours. *3 Henry VII, c.1*.

Act against taking of bail by Justices. *3 Henry VII, c.3*.

Act against usury £100 penalty for each transaction. Cases to be tried by Chancery or Justices of the Peace to avoid sympathetic treatment by urban magistrates. *3 Henry VII, c.5*.

Act forbidding exports of unfinished and undyed cloth above value of £2. Designed to protect the English cloth-finishing industry. *3 Henry VII, c. 11*.

---

[1] Detail of the regnal years is to be found in C.R. Cheney, *Handbook of Dates for Students of English History*, London, Royal Historical Society, 1961.

1488

Act extends 1 Henry VII, c. 8 to include Toulouse woad; orders that masters and mariners of ships should be English-born; forbids English traders to use foreign ships when English ships are available. *4 Henry VII, c.10.*

Act for Justices of the Peace, for the due execution of their commissions. Justices required to encourage criticism of themselves. *4 Henry VII, c.12.*

Act limiting benefit of clergy. *4 Henry VII, c.13.* Those convicted of felony (theft and manslaughter) might claim benefit of clogy on a first offence if they could read.

Act against engrossing on Isle of Wight. Emphasised military effects of the depopulation caused by consolidation of holdings. *4 Henry VII, c.16.*

1489

Act regarding tillage, against depopulation. All occupants of 20 acres or more of land which has been tilled for the past three years must maintain it under tillage or surrender half the profits to the lord of the manor. *4 Henry VII, c.19.*

1495

Act that no person going with the King to the wars shall be attaint of treason. *11 Henry VII, c.1.*

Act regulating usury. Forbids practice of loans made on security of land on condition that part of land revenues goes to lender. *11 Henry VII, c.8.*

Act regulating wages. Fixed maximum rates of pay. Allowed lower rates of pay where customary. Very harsh. *11 Henry VII, c.22.*

1504

Act against making of unlawful ordinances by craft guilds. Henceforth the Chancellor, Chief Justices or Assize Justices to inspect and approve guild bye-laws. Designed to prevent companies fixing prices of commodities. *19 Henry VII, c.7.*

Statute of Liveries. Statute reinforcing existing legislation against the keeping of retainers. *19 Henry VII, c.14.*

1510

Act regarding apparel. *1 Henry VIII, c.14.*

Act for a subsidy to be granted to the King (Tonnage and Poundage). *1 Henry VIII, c.20.*

1512

Act regarding woollen cloth. Orders wages to be paid in money and not in kind or victuals.

Orders maintenance of standards in pulling of woollen yarn. *3 Henry VIII, c.6.*

1515

Act regarding artificers and labourers, fixing hours of labour. Winter: Daylight hours; mid March to mid September: 5 a.m.-7 or 8 p.m. Half an hour breakfast; one-and-a-half hours for dinner and rest. Act fixed labourers' wages at 3d a day (winter) and 4d a day (summer, spring) with additional overtime during harvest. Fixed artisans' pay at 6d a day (summer, spring), 5d a day (winter). *6 Henry VIII, c.3.*

Act orders reconversion of pasture land to arable use and rebuilding of decayed houses. *6 Henry VIII, c.5.*

Act concerning the King's General Surveyors. Justifies and authorises the activities of the 2 General Surveyors. *6 Henry VIII, c.24.*

Act orders conversion of land back to arable use in villages where most of the land use was traditionally tillage. Population ordered to return. *7 Henry VIII, c.1.*

1523

Act to protect Norwich worsted finishing industry. Forbids worsteds woven in Norfolk or Suffolk to be finished and dyed anywhere except Norwich. *14 & 15 Henry VIII c.3.*

(Private) Act of Attainder of Edward, Duke of Buckingham. *14 & 15 Henry VIII, c.20.*

1530

Act of general pardon. *21 Henry VIII, c.1.*

Act concerning sanctuary. *21 Henry VIII, c.2.*

Act to regulate burial and probate fees. *21 Henry VIII, c.5.*

Act to regulate mortuaries. *21 Henry VIII, c.6.*

Act limiting clerical pluralism and engagement in trade. *21 Henry VIII,* c.13.

Act fixing fee for apprenticeship at 2s 6d maximum. *22 Henry VIII, c.4.*

An Act concerning the pardon granted to the King's spiritual subjects of the province of Canterbury for the Praemunire. Known as Act for the Pardon of the Clergy. Clergy forced to submit to modified royal supremacy. *22 Henry VIII, c.15.*

1531

Act regarding benefit of clergy. *23 Henry VIII, c.1.* Act abolishing benefit of clergy for those charged with murder or robbery.

Act reiterating Navigation Acts of Henry VII. *23 Henry VIII, c.7*

An Act that the appeals in such cases as have been used to be pursued to the See of Rome shall not be from henceforth had nor used but within this realm. Known as Act of Appeals. *24 Henry VIII, c.12.*

An Act concerning conditional restraint of payment of annates to the See of Rome. Known as Act in Restraint of Annates. To come into force in 1532. *23 Henry VIII, c.20.*

1534

Act forbidding export of victuals except to supply Calais or ships at sea. *25 Henry VIII, c.2*.

Act regarding tillage, forbidding any individual from holding more than 2,000 sheep or having more than two farms except in the parish where he lived. *25 Henry VIII, c.13*.

Heresy Act. Confirmed legislation against Lollardy (and thereby many of the new Lutheran heresies) but withdrew penalties against those who attacked the Papacy. *25 Henry VIII, c.14*.

Act restricting manufacture of cloth in Worcestershire to Worcester and four other towns. *25 Henry VIII c.18*.

Act for the Submission of the Clergy to the King's Majesty. Enactment of 1532 Submission of the Clergy. Convocation must obtain Crown approval for all measures. Crown is ultimate source of appeal in all ecclesiastical disputes. *25 Henry VIII, c.19*.

An Act restraining the payment of annates. Known as the Act in Restraint of Annates, this made former Act (*23 Henry VIII, c.20*) permanent. King to appoint bishops and abbots. *25 Henry VIII, c.20*.

An Act for the exoneration of exactions paid to the See of Rome. Known as Act of Dispensations. Archbishop of Canterbury not the Pope the authority for future dispensations from the canon law. Fixed scale of fees. Abolition of Peter's Pence and other papal taxes. *25 Henry VIII, c.21*.

Act of Succession. Succession to lie with heirs of Henry and Anne Boleyn. Treason to dispute succession. Oath to be administered. *25 Henry VIII, c.22*.

An Act concerning the King's Highness to be Supreme Head of the Church of England and to have authority to reform and redress all errors, heresies and abuses the same. Known as Act of Supremacy. Henry declared Supreme Head on Earth of the Church of England. To visit clergy, supervise preachers, try heretics, make doctrinal pronouncements. *26 Henry VIII, c.1*.

Act of Succession. *26 Henry VIII, c.2*.

Act concerning First Fruits and Tenths. Taxes, formerly paid to Pope, to pass to Crown. *26 Henry VIII, c.3*.

Treason Act. Treason to include verbal attacks on monarch. *26 Henry VIII, c.13*.

1535/6

An Act concerning the forging of the King's sign manual, signet and privy seal. Makes forgery of royal signature and lesser seals treasonable offences in addition to the already treasonable offence of forging the great seal. *27 Henry VIII, c.2*.

Statute of Uses. *27 Henry VIII, c.10*.

Act appointing an Ecclesiastical Commission of 32 persons for the making of ecclesiastical laws. *27 Henry VIII, c.15*.

Act reiterates 1489 statute of depopulation. King to receive half profits of lands not yet reconverted under that Act. *27 Henry VIII, c.22.*

Beggars Act established parish as poor relief unit. First statute which accepted state's responsibility for poor relief. *27 Henry VIII, c.25.*

An Act of Union with Wales imposes English system of administration and representation on Wales. Henceforth, Wales has J.P.s, Lieutenants and M.P.s. *27 Henry VIII, c.26.*

Act establishing Court of Augmentations. *27 Henry VIII, c.27.*

Act for Dissolution of the Lesser Monasteries. All houses with annual income of less than £200 to surrender to King. Those who have received grants of monastic land must maintain under tillage such land as has been tilled for the past 20 years. *27 Henry VIII, c.28.*

Act for maintenance of standards in making of woollen cloth.

Act exempting universities and colleges from payment of first fruits and tenths. *27 Henry VIII, c.42.*

1536

Act regarding abjuration and benefit of clergy. *28 Henry VIII, c.1.*

Act forbidding Masters to bind apprentices not to set up in competition without licence from Master Wardens or Fellowships. This forced guilds to tolerate establishment of new independent shops. *28 Henry VIII, c.5.*

Act regarding succession. *28 Henry VIII, c.7.*

An Act extinguishing the authority of the bishop of Rome (the Pope). *28 Henry VIII, c.10.*

1539/40

Act that proclamations made by the King shall be obeyed. *31 Henry VIII, c.8.*

Act authorising new bishoprics. *31 Henry VIII, c.9.*

Act for the placing of the Lords in Parliament. Determines precedence and places King's Secretary above all bishops and peers without high state office and only below the great officeholders of state and household. *31 Henry VIII, c.10.*

An Act for the dissolution of abbeys. Known as Act for the Dissolution of the Greater Monasteries. *31 Henry VIII, c.13.*

An Act for religion, abolishing diversity in opinions. Known as Act of Six Articles. Reactionary. Reimposes Catholic orthodoxy. *31 Henry VIII, c.14.*

Statute of Wills. *32 Henry VIII, c.1.*

Navigation Act with comprehensive terms directed against use of foreign shipping for English import trade. *32 Henry VIII, c.14.*

Act of succession. *32 Henry VIII, c.25.*

Act of Leases. *32 Henry VIII, c.28.*

Act establishing Court of First Fruits and Tenths. *32 Henry VIII, c.45.*

1542

Act for religion. *34 & 35 Henry VIII, c.1.*

Act giving monopoly of coverlet manufacture in Yorkshire to City of York. Guild of coverlet makers empowered to seek out offenders. *34 & 35 Henry VIII, c.10.*

Act for certain ordinances in the King's Majesty's dominion and principality of Wales. Setting up 4 Courts of Great Sessions under permanent judges to exercise common-law jurisdiction in the 12 Welsh shires. *34 & 35 Henry VIII, c.26.*

1543

Act for succession of Crown. *35 Henry VIII, c.1.*

Act for the Advancement of True Religion. Forbade labourers and all women below rank of gentlewoman from reading Scriptures. *35 Henry VIII, c.5.*

1545

Chantries Act empowers King to dissolve chantries but it is not implemented. *37 Henry VIII, c.4.*

Act sanctioning usury. Interest rate of 10 per cent permitted. *37 Henry VIII, c.9.*

1547

Act for the sacrament, against Revilers and for Receiving in Both Kinds. Persons who ridicule the mass are to be punished. Communion in both bread and wine extended to laity. *1 Edward VI, c.1.*

Act for the Election of Bishops. *1 Edward VI, c.2.*

Vagabonds Act (also known as Sturdy Beggars Act). A sturdy beggar might be made a slave for 2 years and, should he run away, be made a slave for life (repealed clause in 1549). Cottages to be erected for the impotent poor. *1 Edward VI, c.3* (repealed, 1550).

Act for the repeal of certain statutes concerning treasons etc. Known as 1st Treasons Act of Edward VI. *1 Edward VI, c.12.*

An Act whereby certain chantries, colleges, free chapels and the possessions of the same be given to the King's Majesty. Known as The Chantry Act or Chantries Act. All chantries, collegiate churches, hospitals, guilds, fraternities etc. dissolved. Craft Guilds made to surrender religious possessions. University colleges excepted. *1 Edward VI, c.14.*

1548/9

An Act for the uniformity of service and administration of the sacraments throughout the realm. Known as First Act of Uniformity. Enforces Cranmer's Prayer Book as only legal service book. Penalties to be enforced against those encouraging or using other forms and attacking the new Book. *2 & 3 Edward VI, c.1.*

Act forbidding labourers to combine to improve pay and conditions. *2 & 3 Edward VI, c.15.*

Act taking away divers laws against the marriage of priests. *2 & 3 Edward VI, c.21.*

Act ordering fasting from meat on Fridays and Saturdays. Aims to encourage eating of fish and, thereby, increase the size of the fishing fleet and the number of men employed thereby. *2 & 3 Edward VI, c.19.*

1549/50

Act for abolition of divers books and images. All images, including roods, to be destroyed. *3 & 4 Edward VI, c.10.*

Act for ordering ecclesiastical ministers, consecrating bishops etc. *3 & 4 Edward VI, c.12.*

1551/52

An Act for the uniformity of common prayer and administration of the sacraments. Known as Second Act of Uniformity. Orders use of revised Prayer Book from November 1552. *5 & 6 Edward VI, c.1.*

Act ordering the gathering of parish alms. The local householders were to assemble and select two collectors to gather parish alms. Anyone who refused to give alms was to be reported to the bishop. *5 & 6 Edward VI, c.2.*

Act for the keeping of Holy Days and fast days. *5 & 6 Edward VI, c.3.*

Act against enclosures. Appoints permanent commission to seek out offenders. *5 & 6 Edward VI, c.5.*

Act regulating production of cloth. Specifications laid down for 22 types of cloth, stipulating proper weights. Searcher employed to enforce the acts. Only applied in rural areas. *5 & 6 Edward VI, c.6.*

Act to bring down the price of wool. It was aimed at the middlemen who were frequently blamed for the high price of wool. Henceforward wool purchase was restricted to merchants of the staple and manufacturers. *5 & 6 Edward VI, c.7.*

Act restricting weaving to those who have served seven years' apprenticeship. Act regulating apprenticeship. Masters to keep 1:3 journeyman apprentice ratio. Masters prevented from hiring journeymen by week or for short periods. Designed to prevent exploitation of apprentices as cheap labour and to provide some security of employment while ensuring high standards. *5 & 6 Edward VI, c.8.*

Second Treason Act of Edward VI. Added offences against the royal succession and religious orthodoxy but otherwise returned to position of *26 Henry VIII, c.13* (1534). *5 & 6 Edward VI, c.11.*

Act for marriage of priests and legitimation of their children. *5 & 6 Edward VI, c.12.*

Act against usury. Repeals 1545 Act and reiterates centuries-old sanctions. *5 & 6 Edward VI, c.20.*

Act protecting hat and coverlet industry of Norwich. *5 & 6 Edward VI, c.24.*

Act for keepers of alehouses to be bound by recognisances. All alehouse keepers required to have licence from Justices of the Peace. The J.P.s to take recognisance from the licensee. *5 & 6 Edward VI, c.25.*

1553/4

Act repealing certain treasons (*1 Mary 1, st.I, c.1*). Repeals Henrician and Edwardian acts and returns to the *status quo* of *25 Edward III, st.5, c.2.*

Act of Repeal revokes major Edwardian legislation. *1 Mary, I, st.I.*

Brawling Act. Makes it an offence physically to abuse the sacrament. *1 Mary, st.2, c.3.*

1554

Act regarding cloth making, designed to deal with decay of corporate towns which included among other remedies a clause relaxing the apprenticeship rules. An earlier restriction reserving weaving to those who have served full apprenticeship now made applicable to countryside alone in response to appeal from urban clothiers. *1 Mary, c.7.*

1554/5

An Act repealing all statutes. . .made against the see apostolic of Rome since the 20th year of King Henry VIII, and also of the establishment of all spiritual and ecclesiastical possessions and hereditaments conveyed to the laity. Known as second Act of Repeal. Revokes anti-papal measures passed since 1529. *1 & 2 Philip & Mary, c.8.*

Act forbidding export of victuals, grain or wood. Grain can only be exported when there is a glut and prices are lower than 6s 8d a quarter. *1 & 2 Philip and Mary, c.5.*

Act remedying decay of corporate towns. *1 & 2 Philip & Mary, c.7.*

Second Treason Act of Mary. Protected Philip with treason penalties. *1 & 2 Philip and Mary, c.10.*

Weavers' Act restricts still further the number of apprentices and looms permitted a rural manufacturer. *2 & 3 Philip & Mary,* c.11.

Act confirming legislation of 1489 and makes it apply to all houses with 20 acres of land. *2 & 3 Philip & Mary, c.2.*

1557

Act regarding woollen cloths. Orders that cloth manufacture should be restricted to certain corporate and market towns which had had an industry for ten years. Certain exemptions. It extends control of cloth specification of *5 & 6 Edward VI, c.6* to some towns. *4 & 5 Philip & Mary, c.5.*

1559

Act of Supremacy. Queen is 'supreme governor' of Church of England. Empowered to visit church by royal commission and exercise the supremacy by commission. Marian Acts of repeal themselves repealed.

Revocation of Heresy Acts. Papal supremacy abolished. Oath of Supremacy to be administered, backed by heavy penalties including those for high treason. *1 Elizabeth I, c.1.*

An Act for the uniformity of common prayer and divine service in the church, and the administration of the sacraments. Known as the Elizabethan Act of Uniformity. Enforced Edwardian Prayer Book and worship as in 1549. *1 Elizabeth I, c.2.*

Act regarding Queen's title to the throne. *1 Elizabeth I, c.3.*

Act (*1 Elizabeth I, c.9.*) excepting parts of Essex from *4 & 5 Philip and Mary, c.5.*

Act repealing protective legislation against foreign shipping. A response to Emperor Charles V's retaliatory ban on English shipping in return for Henry's protective tariffs of 1540. *1 Elizabeth I, c.13.*

1563

Act orders administration of Oath of Supremacy to all graduates, schoolmasters and M.P.s. *5 Elizabeth I, c.1.*

Act regarding tillage, against depopulation. Confirms statutes of Henry VII and Henry VIII. All land which had been under tillage for four years since 1528 must remain under tillage. No land currently tilled must be converted to pasture. *5 Elizabeth I, c.2.*

Alms Act. If an individual refuses to obey the bishop's exhortation to give alms, he can be bound over for £10 to appear before the J.P.s. The J.P.s may imprison the person if he still refuses to pay. A move towards a compulsory poor rate. Backs ecclesiastical persuasion with secular penalties. *5 Elizabeth I, c.3.*

Statute of Artificers. Many clauses treating regulation of industry and agriculture. *5 Elizabeth I, c.4.*

(1) Applied guild apprenticeship system nationwide. Seven-year apprenticeship compulsory in all urban crafts. Established property qualifications for apprenticeship which effectively barred entry to sons of labouring poor. Regulated number of apprentices per master and journeyman thus preventing excessive use of cheap labour.

(2) Fixed maximum but not minimum wage rates. J.P.s to meet to assess and settle standard wage rate in line with prices annually at Easter. Rates to be approved by Privy Council and applied in the next year.

Act for maintenance of the navy. Orders use of English shipping in coastal trade and to import French woad and wines. Raises price limit for wheat under which grain can be exported to 10s a quarter. Wednesday ordered as additional fish day to encourage fishing industry. *5 Elizabeth I, c.5.*

1566

Act limiting Benefit of Clergy. Abolished for rapists, burglars and cutpurses working in gangs. *8 Elizabeth I, c.4.*

Act for exportation, orders wrought and dressed cloths to be exported in ratio of one to every nine unfinished cloths. *8 Elizabeth I, c.6.*

1571

Second Treasons Act of Elizabeth. Includes denial of Supremacy and accusing the Queen of heresy. *13 Elizabeth I, c.1.*

Act against Papal Bulls. Obtaining a papal bull is a treasonable offence. *13 Elizabeth I, c.2.*

Act against fugitives over the sea. To deal with seminary priests. Those who have gone abroad without passport to return within six months or lose their possessions. *13 Elizabeth I, c.3.*

Act sanctioning usury. Repeal of 1552 legislation. Interest rate of 10 per cent maximum. Penalties for excess interest charges. *13 Elizabeth I, c.8.*

Subscription Act orders allegiance to 39 Articles of Religion by all ordinands. *13 Elizabeth I, c.12.*

Act regarding tillage, permits export of grain when price of wheat in country of export is moderate. Local authorities will determine when conditions permit. *13 Elizabeth I, c.13.*

1572

Vagabonds Act, known as Poor Relief Act. Severe penalties for vagrant poor. J.P.s to make a register of all the local poor and to raise a rate to house the impotent and aged. *14 Elizabeth I, c.5.*

1575/6

Act (*1 Elizabeth I, c.16*) exempts parts of Gloucestershire, Wiltshire and Somersetshire from *4 & 5 Philip & Mary, c.5.*

1576

Act for Relief of Poor. Cities and towns to provide wool etc. to supply work for the able-bodied poor at the direction of J.P.s. Houses of correction to be built and those who refuse to work to be incarcerated in them. *18 Elizabeth I. c.3.*

Act pertaining to Benefit of Clergy. Felons claiming the 'book' to serve twelve months' imprisonment should the secular judge so decide. *18 Elizabeth I, c.7.*

1580/1

Act to Retain the Queen's Subjects in their due Obedience. Death penalty for those teaching the Papal Supremacy. Fines and imprisonment for those hearing Mass. £20 a month fines for those who refuse to attend church (recusants). *23 Elizabeth I, c.1.*

Act against seditious words and rumours uttered against the Queen's excellent majesty. Death penalty for a second offence. *23 Elizabeth I, c.2.*

1584/5

Act for safety of the Queen, provision to be made for the surety of the Queen's most royal person. *27 Elizabeth I, c.1.*

An Act against Jesuits, seminary priests and such other like disobedient persons. *27 Elizabeth I, c.2.*

Act repeals *5 Elizabeth I, c.5*; Wednesday no longer a fish day. *27 Elizabeth I.*

1592/3

An Act to retain the Queen's Subjects in Obedience. Aimed at Puritans. *35 Elizabeth I, c.1.*

An Act against popish recusants. Aimed at Catholic subjects. *35 Elizabeth I, c.2.*

Act reducing penalties for breaking fish days. Centrally sets price limit of corn at 20s per quarter; when price falls below this export is permitted. Repeals that part of *5 Elizabeth I, c.3* (1563) which prevented conversion of tilled land to pasture. *35 Elizabeth I, c.7.*

1597/8

Act ordering repair of 'houses of husbandry' which had fallen into disrepair in last seven years. Half those which had decayed in the previous seven years also to be repaired. *39 Elizabeth I, c.1.*

Act for Relief of the Poor. Remained on statute book until 1834. Made 4 overseers of the poor, chosen every Easter by the J.P.s, in charge of poor relief. The overseers were to bind children as apprentices, provide the adult but able poor with work, to relieve the aged and infirm. They were empowered to build hospitals for the latter. A compulsory rate on inhabitants was to fund their work and the assessment was to be made at parish level. *39 Elizabeth I, c.3.*

Act for Punishment of Rogues. J.P.s authorised to establish houses of correction for rogues and vagabonds. Rogues would either be whipped and returned to native parish or placed in a house of correction. *39 Elizabeth I, c.4.*

Act clarifying terms of Statute of Artificers. J.P.s to fix wage rate for all labourers, weavers, spinsters and workmen and workwomen. *39 Elizabeth I, c.12.*

Act regarding cloth, for regulation of cloth manufacture north of the Trent. Reiterates terms of *5 & 6 Edward VI, c.6.* Specifically forbids use of the 'tenter' frame for stretching cloths after fulling. An outcry. *39 Elizabeth I, c.20.*

1601

Act for Relief of Poor. A codification of the 1598 poor relief legislation. *43 Elizabeth I, c.2.*

Local Government

The shires, like the church, were administered by the Crown via a system of local government officers and courts. The Tudors possessed no permanent, expert and salaried bureaucracy. They relied instead upon the interest of the local elite (broadly speaking the gentry rather than the overmighty nobility who might be perceived as a challenge to strong royal government) in stable, peaceable government and paternalistic protection of the people to run the country. In theory the system of Assizes complemented and monitored the work of the Justices of the Peace. In some areas the Crown was represented by a Council (e.g. the Council of the North) and J.P.s and Assize Judges worked with that institution.

Special Problems of the Borders

Unsettled border regions. Threat of foreign invasion from Ireland and Scotland. Dangerous independence of the Marcher lords who defended kingdom against such invasion. For example: Dacre, Percy and Neville families in the Northern Borders; Courtenays in Devon and the West; palatine jurisdictions in Cheshire and Lancashire. There is some suggestion that Henry VII proposed a council for the Midlands. Certainly his mother, Margaret Beaufort, exercised regional jurisdiction from Collyweston, Stamford between 1499 and 1505.

The North before 1530

Richard, Duke of Gloucester, and his private Council administered the north for his brother Edward IV.

1484 Richard III appointed Earl of Lincoln Lieutenant and gave him a council to administer the region with formal status as a court of law.

1485 Henry VII relied on Percy family until Northumberland's murder in 1489.

1487–c.1509 Intermittent Council

1509–22 Lapse of central control in North.

1522 Wolsey aware of need for buffer against Scots.

1525 Duke of Richmond made Lieutenant and given a Council, staffed by lawyers and civil servants, to administer royal lands in North and exercise wide civil and criminal jurisdiction. Ineffectual in face of local opposition

Wales and the Marches before 1536

1471 King Edward IV made his heir Prince of Wales and Lord of the Marches (Cheshire, Shropshire, Worcestershire, Gloucestershire, Herefordshire) and appointed Council with responsibilities therein.

1483 Council of Wales and Marches ceased to exist.

1493 Prince Arthur Tudor made Earl of March and given similar powers; Council based at Ludlow; Bishop William Smith (from 1490, formally President, 1501–12) made President.

1501 Council continued by commission.

1525 Wolsey reinforced the Council's powers: Princess Mary made figurehead; Council given considerable powers to maintain order, hear suits and receive petitions under Presidency of John Veysey, Bishop of Exeter.

1530s Henry VIII's attempt to combat power of nobility in remote and lawless regions.

The Council of the North

In 1530 the Council was reformed; Cuthbert Tunstall, Bishop of Durham, became President and his powers confined to Yorkshire. Tunstall was weak as President and was replaced in 1533 by the even more disastrous Henry Percy, 6th Earl of Northumberland. The Henrician government embarked on a policy of territorial aggrandisement and broke the Percy monopoly on power. Some continuity was provided by the continuance of John Uvedale, Richmond's Secretary, as Secretary to the Council until 1560.

1530–3 Cuthbert Tunstall, Bishop of Durham, President of the King's Council in the North.

1533–6 Henry Algernon Percy, 6th Earl of Northumberland (b.1502, d.1537). 1536: Debt-ridden, he surrendered lands to King in return for £1,000 annuity. Resigned late 1536.

1536–7 Thomas Howard, 3rd Earl of Norfolk. As lieutenant supervised defeat of Pilgrims of Grace and was the chief royal agent in the area, although not President, until Cuthbert Tunstall resumed office.

1537–8 Cuthbert Tunstall resumed control.

1538–40 Robert Holgate, Bishop of Llandaff. Was moderate Protestant Archbishop of York from 1544 until he was deprived of office in 1554.

1550–60 Francis Talbot, 5th Earl of Shrewsbury. A conservative in religion who was put in office by Earl of Warwick who was Warden of the Marches and anxious to minimise the powers of the Council. Sir Thomas Gargrave rescued the Council from Talbot's inept rule. Talbot lived in Sheffield and not at York.

1561–3 Henry Manners, 3rd Earl of Rutland, revived residence at King's Manor, York and looked set to revive the fortunes of the Council but died in 1563.

1564 Brief Presidency of Ambrose, Earl of Warwick. Resigned because he could not face the thought of the northern winter.

1564–8 Thomas Young, Archbishop of York. A lazy and ineffectual President who left the North dangerously devoid of royal control on the eve of the Northern Rebellion.

1568–72 Thomas Radcliffe, 3rd Earl of Sussex. Had long experience of assertion of central control as Lord Deputy of Ireland, 1557–64. Destroyed power of rebel earls. 1570–2: Absentee President.

1572–95 Henry Hastings, 3rd Earl of Huntingdon. He had no lands in the North but over his long Presidency developed great insight into its affairs. Was praised by the Queen for his 'vigilant and watchful care' and staged energetic campaign against Catholic recusancy.

1596–9 Matthew Hutton, Bishop of Durham, made Archbishop of York and *de facto* President of the Council. Cecil forced him (an ally of Essex) to retire.

1599–1603 Thomas Cecil, 2nd Lord Burghley. The energetic, anti-recusant elder brother of Robert Cecil.

The Council in the Marches

Precedent: From 1499 to 1505 an unofficial Council of the Midlands was presided over by Margaret Beaufort at Collyweston, near Stamford, Lincs.

After 1536 the Council controlled Wales and six English border shires (Monmouthshire, until 1604; Herefordshire; Worcestershire; Shropshire; Cheshire, until 1569; Gloucestershire, Bristol excluded in 1562. After 1542 the Justice of Cheshire (from 1578 known as the Chief Justice) was normally a member of the Council and *de facto* Vice-President. The chief official was from at least 1525 the Secretary, who normally combined in his person the offices of clerk and clerk of the signet.

1534 Rowland Lee made Bishop of Coventry and Lichfield and President of the Council in the Marches.

1536 Thomas Cromwell imposed by statute English administration on Wales, which henceforth had J.P.s, Lords Lieutenant and M.P.s as did English shires. Council in the Marches given jurisdiction over Wales and Marches, including prerogative power. It advised on the appointment of

J.P.s, Sheriffs and Lords Lieutenant; supervised local government; organised the defence of the coastline; enforced economic legislation emanating from Westminster; acted as 'starre chamber and chauncerie corte for Wales' handling criminal and civil business and supporting the Crown's religious policies.

1534–43 Energetic and strong presidency of Bishop Rowland Lee, who frequently toured the Marches and Wales.

1543–8 Presidency of Richard Sampson, also Bishop of Coventry and Lichfield, lawyer, civil servant and faithful servant of Henry VIII.

1548–50 John Dudley, Earl of Warwick, never seems to have met his Council and surrendered his office to a supporter, William Herbert, when he became immersed in national affairs.

1550–3 William Herbert (b.1501–d.1570, made 1st Earl of Pembroke, 1551), became Lord President.

1553–5 Nicholas Heath, restored Marian Bishop of Worcester.

1555–8 William Herbert's second term of office – ended when Queen criticised him for inadequate administration.

1558–9 Gilbert Bourne, Bishop of Bath and Wells. Deprived by Elizabeth.

1559 John Williams, Lord Williams of Thame. (Treasurer of Court of Augmentations, 1544–54). Supporter of Mary who was given control of Princess Elizabeth, 1554. Arrived at Ludlow, June 1559; d. October 1559.

1560–86 Sir Henry Sidney (b.1529–d.1586). Long beneficial administration. Bitter factional divisions in the Council after 1575. Sidney was frequently absent and a series of Vice-Presidents were appointed to run the Council until 1580.

1586–1602 Henry Herbert, 2nd Earl of Pembroke. Son of William. Married daughter of predecessor. Popular because Welsh speaking. He was energetic and reform-minded but he antagonized the lawyers on the Council to such an extent that he was unable to effect the overhaul of the inefficient and corrupt council as he had wished.

The Council of the West
Set up in wake of Henry VIII's suppression of Exeter Conspiracy in 1537 when power of the Courtenays, Marquesses of Exeter, seemed threatening, to control Cornwall, Devon, Dorset and Somerset. Shortlived and ill documented. Had ceased to exist by 1547.

- **Originated in concern for national security.**

The Shires

The central government depended upon local officials to implement its policies as expressed in statute and proclamation and, therefore, upon a partnership between the centre and the local worthies. The student of local government at regional, county and parish level is faced with a bewildering array of offices and institutions. There are the ancient offices of sheriff, coroner, escheator and customer (all possessed of continuing if decreasing significance) existing alongside new offices (such as those of the new regional councils or the lords and deputy lieutenants) or old offices which were changing in their functions and increasing in their importance (such as Justices of the Peace). Then one has to reconcile the parallel jurisdictions of the ecclesiastical and the lay parish and their associated officials. Comforting is the view that this was an era of experimentation in local government, a period when the Crown was seeking to negotiate local co-operation in the government of the realm whilst also attempting to monitor the success of this co-operation in achieving its own ends and to prevent sedition, rebellion and invasion.

Parish Officers: the Ecclesiastical Parish

Churchwardens
– Unlike the constables, watchmen and surveyors of highways, church wardens were lay ecclesiastical officers.
– Appointed in different ways according to the custom of the parish: by the minister, or by the parish assembled in the vestry meeting, or by the minister and vestry together.
– Guardians and keepers of the fabric and furniture of the church (excluding the chancel which was the parson's responsibility), and representatives of the parishioners.
– Empowered to levy church rate to care for upkeep of church.

Parish Clerk
– Originally an official in minor holy orders but this changed at the reformation when he had to be at least 20 years old, literate, 'sufficient for his office' and of good reputation.
– Usually selected by incumbent but sometimes, by custom, by parish.

- Has freehold in office.
- Duties associated with organising church for worship.

Sexton
- Chosen by incumbent or, where custom dictates, by minister and parishioners.
- Paid by churchwardens.
- Cleans church, opens pews, provides candles, digs graves, helps keep peace in the church and churchyard.

- **Parallel existence of ecclesiastical and lay parish.**

Parish Officers: the Lay Parish

Constables
- Origins in the ancient offices of tithingman, headborough or borsholder current in the time of Alfred the Great
- Chosen by the jury of the Court Leet or by 2 Justices.
- Petty constables charged with keeping the peace within the parish or township.
- Serve summonses and warrants of the J.P.s.

Watchmen
- Deputies or assistants of the constables who guard the peace at night.

Surveyors of Highways
- Worked under supervision of J.P.s.

Overseers of the Poor
- Worked under supervision of J.P.s.

The Shire Officers

Sheriff
Under the early Tudors the sheriff was the principal royal official in most counties. The duties of the office were largely legal – he supervised the prisons, empanelled juries, implemented sentences – but he also, before Elizabeth's reign, collected taxes and subsidies, put down sedition and rebellion and arrested 'heretics'. The office was already in decline by the late fifteenth century, it was expensive and onerous and possessed little real power but it continued to be sought after because of the status it conferred.

- **Practical powers in decline under Tudors but sought after because status-conferring.**

Coroner
- Late twelfth century office. Before that coroners charged with keeping the pleas of the Crown.
- Chiefly but not exclusively judicial duties, primarily concerned with inquiring into suspicious deaths and, where there is reason to suppose unnatural death, setting up an inquest.
- Chosen for life by the freeholders of the county at a court summoned by the sheriff for that purpose.
- Had to possess lands worth £20 per annum.

Escheator
- Protects feudal rights of Crown in the shires.

Customer
- Collector of customary taxes in the shires.

High Constable
- Charged with keeping peace within the administrative district of the hundred (a subdivision of a shire).

Lord Lieutenant
Lieutenants had been appointed by Henry VIII and Edward VI for defensive purposes and by the reign of Elizabeth the lieutenant was the most important local Crown officer. It was, however, a military office and there were *ad hoc* rather than permanent and continuous appointments. It was not until the 1580s, when the Spanish threat seemed to demand a more organised local defence system, that lords lieutenant appointments were for life. Innovatory development.

Duties:
- keeping up-to-date muster roll of able-bodied men able and prepared to fight when required
- stock-keeping of arms
- maintenance of stock of arms and ammunition
- marshalling defence as and when need arose.

Tenure: chief aristocrats of region, they sometimes acted as Lords Lieutenant for a group of counties; after 1580 appointments were often for life.

Deputy Lieutenants – served for 1 shire only; more than 1 per shire; did most of the real work of the office.

- **Innovatory development**
- **Military role and significance.**

Justices of the Peace

Most of the work of implementing statutes and royal proclamations in the localities fell to the Justices of the Peace. The office of the Justice was ancient (dating back to the twelfth century) and had become an established part of local government by the 1320s. The Justices supervised the work of the surveyors and overseers of the poor.

Royal Commissions of the Peace – Appointed between 30 and 60 local men, not necessarily with any legal training, to serve as Justices for very modest remuneration. Selection made on basis of advice offered by judges acquainted with the shires via the Assize circuit and Lord Chancellor. To serve was a coveted honour among the gentry of Tudor England. Most J.P.s inactive. Work done by Quorum.

Quorum – An inner circle of trusted Justices, including those with legal training, nominated to the quorum. Member of quorum essential when important session takes place.

Custos Rotulorum – Member of quorum appointed to keep the records (rolls) of the Justices.

Clerk of the Peace – Appointed as permanent official to give advice on procedure etc.

Quarter Sessions – Quarterly meeting of the Justices.

Criminal Jurisdiction of Justices of the Peace
- Powers of arrest, search, imprisonment.
- Full sentencing powers, including the death penalty by hanging.
- Punishment most commonly whipping, placing in the stocks, and fines.

Administrative Jurisdiction of Justices of the Peace
- Even more important role of J.P.s hampered by inadequacy of parish officials (e.g. constables and overseers).
- Routine work undertaken at Quarter Sessions but also at more frequent and informal petty sessions.
- Role of implementing reformed poor law.

- **Not a Tudor innovation but exploited to the full by the Tudors as the instrument for the implementation of royal policy throughout the realm**
- **Harnessed local interests in the service of central government.**

Assizes

Some crimes beyond the jurisdiction of the Justices had to be referred to the Assizes.

From the twelfth century onwards, paid judges were sent out to groups of counties to hear cases of both a civil and a criminal nature. From the end of the thirteenth century sessions or courts of this kind were held three times a year in each county. But it was not until the reign of Edward III that circuits were established for grand assizes composed of judges drawn from the Common Pleas, King's, Bench and Exchequer courts. The Tudors built upon this system which provided the main and ultimate source of justice at county level and monitored the work of the J.P.s. There were 6 circuits:

- *Home:* Essex, Herts, Kent, Surrey, Sussex
- *Oxford:* Gloucestershire, Herefordshire, Oxfordshire, Salop, Staffordshire, Worcestershire
- *Western:* Berks, Cornwall, Devon, Dorset, Hampshire, Somerset, Wiltshire
- *Norfolk:* Bedfordshire, Buckinghamshire, Cambridgeshire, Huntingdonshire
- *Midland:* Derbyshire, Leicestershire, Linconshire, Nottinghamshire, Northamptonshire, Rutland, Warwickshire
- *Northern:* Cumberland, Durham, Lancashire, Northumberland, Westmorland, Yorkshire

Twice a year the judges began a circuit which covered 50 principal towns in England. Each session lasted a few days. Cases were referred to the Assizes from the Quarter Sessions. Mainly criminal cases were brought before the Justices of Assize (felonies were being taken out of the hands of the J.P.s) although civil cases were also heard. Cases of theft, murder and treason had to be heard by the Assizes.

Clerks of the Assize
Permanent officials who organised circuit and record keeping.

- **Brought accessible common law to localities**
- **Brought centrally trained lawyers to localities**
- **Not especially harsh – few hangings**
- **Provided government with only direct knowledge of state of the country as a whole. Prior to the circuit the Justices received instructions (a charge) from the government in Star Chamber and after the circuit they prepared a report for the government.**
- **Provided mechanism for monitoring work of J.P.s**
- **Dialogue between central and local interests provided for by attendance of local Commission of Peace (i.e. the J.P.s) at Assize**
- **Expense account allowed to Assize Justices after 1573 in theory makes them less open to bribery but in practice lavish 'hospitality' poured on Judges by local commission, sheriff etc.**

The Central and Church Courts

In the Tudor period many different types of law pertained – common law, statute law, law of equity, civil law, canon law, manorial custom. These laws were administered in a plethora of courts which often had parallel and rival jurisdictions. Common Law Courts, Privy Council and Prerogative Courts, Admiralty Courts, Ecclesiastical Courts, Parliament itself, at the centre. Regional Councils, Quarter Sessions, Assizes, Hundred Courts, Manorial Courts, Borough Courts, and a whole variety of ecclesiastical courts in the counties and dioceses. The precise boundaries between the jurisdiction of, for example, the Justices of the Peace and the Assizes were blurred so that, with certain exceptions, the same types of case might appear before either. The ecclesiastical and the common law courts each claimed jurisdiction in some of the same areas. Today we tend to view this situation with something like alarm and to assume that the triumph of the common law over the rest was a foregone conclusion and the existence of other courts and legal systems an inconvenient and somehow unimportant anomaly. This was far from the case. The government of England and Wales was not yet completely centralised and unified, and it was not only the King's or common law which ran. The Tudor period not only saw the full flowering of the Prerogative Courts and the Civil and Canon Law Courts at the centre as the monarch and his/her ministers sought to centralise both administration and order but also extremely important Manorial Courts (leet and baron) and Hundred Courts which oversaw and controlled life in the localities.

- **Different types of law**
- **Parallel and rival jurisdictions**
- **Triumph of common law not inevitable**
- **Other types of law important too**
- **Centralising tendency but not fully realised as yet.**

Common Law and Equity Courts

The Common Law Courts had developed out of the Royal Council. The common law was the King's law which, because it belonged to the whole community of the realm, was common. The King or the council was not, however, the ultimate appeal court where common law cases were concerned: this was parliament. The common law procedures grew up in the twelfth century and by the fifteenth century the common law courts were rigidly set in their ways. New courts of law, the chancery and the council, developed in the fifteenth and sixteenth centuries to complement the common law courts. Procedures designed to provide a more efficient administration of the law developed in a rather haphazard fashion out of the petitions which were frequently addressed to the monarch and which passed through the hands of the Lord Chancellor and the council. This equitable jurisdiction developed apace and, once the court of Chancery kept records after 1530, became established. Equity law was practised in every new court which developed after 1400 – the equity side of the exchequer; the courts of star chamber, requests and the Duchy of Lancaster; the revenue courts set up under Thomas Cromwell; the regional councils and the palatinate courts of Durham, Lancaster and Chester. The law which was administered by these courts was essentially the common law; until the development of substantive equity law in the seventeenth century, it was the procedure which differed. Equity proceedings were in English.

Court of King's Bench
Chief Justices of the King's Bench

1485   William Huse

1495   John Finieux

1526   John FitzJames

1539   Edward Montagu

1545   Richard Lyster

1552   Roger Cholmley

1553   Thomas Bromley

1555   William Portman

1557   Edward Saunders

1559   Robert Catlin

1574   Christopher Wray

1592   John Popham

For centuries cases were heard by the King in person advised by his council or *curia*. In the twelfth century the King's Bench emerged as a separate court. In 1178 King Henry II appointed five judges to hear cases in the King's Bench and in 1268 the Chief Justice was made president of the court. Initially the court heard only cases touching the rights of Crown and subjects but it developed into an appeal court which retried cases where an incorrect verdict was suspected. In the sixteenth century its civil jurisdiction was significant. During the Tudor period it encroached on the work of the Court of Common Pleas, claiming jurisdiction over trespass cases which were technically criminal in nature. Its genuinely criminal jurisdiction was normally exercised in the Assize Courts by commissions of oyer and terminer.

Court of Common Pleas

Chief Justices of Common Pleas

1485   Thomas Bryan

1500   Thomas Wood

1502   Thomas Frowyk

1506   Robert Read

1519   John Ernle

1521   Robert Brudenell

1531   Robert Norwich

1535   John Baldwin

1545   Edward Montagu

1553   Richard Morgan

1554   Robert Brooke

1558   Anthony Browne

1559   James Dyer

1582   Edmund Anderson

In 1272 a Chief Justice was first appointed for this ancient court which heard civil suits between subjects. The court was established at Westminster. It had jurisdiction over all civil actions and heard appeals from local courts. Appeal from the Court of Common Pleas was to the King's Bench. It was the busiest Tudor central court and the slowest. During the reigns of the Tudors the Court of King's Bench encroached upon its jurisdiction.

Court of Exchequer

Lord Treasurers
(By this time a largely honorary position awarded to prominent courtiers.)

1484   John Tuchet, Lord Audley

1486   John Dynham, Lord Dynham

1501   Thomas Howard, Earl of Surrey, first Duke of Norfolk

1522   Thomas Howard, Earl of Surrey, 2nd Duke of Norfolk

1547   Edward Seymour, 1st Duke of Somerset and Protector

1550   William Paulet, 1st Earl of Wiltshire, 1550, and 1st Marquis of Winchester, 1551

1572   William Cecil, 1st Lord Burghley (d. 4 Aug. 1598)

1599   Sir Thomas Sackville, 1st Lord Buckhurst, 1st Earl of Dorset 1604

Chancellors and Under-Treasurers
1559   Sir Walter Mildmay

1589   John Fortescue

1603   Sir George Home, 1st Earl of Dunbar, 1605

Chief Barons of the Court of Exchequer
1485   Humphrey Starkey

1486   William Hody

1522   John FitzJames

1526   Richard Broke

1529   Richard Lyster

1545   Roger Cholmley

1552   Henry Bradshaw

1553   David Brook

1558   Clement Heigham

1559   Edward Saunders

1577   Robert Bell

1577   John Jeffrey

1578   Roger Marwood

1593   William Periam

The Court of Exchequer was originally the Crown's finance office, involved with the collection of revenue, where accounting was done in squares. (The name derives from the Latin *scaccorium* for chess board. Revenue collection involved disputes and Exchequer then took on the guise of a common law court dealing with financial litigation using Latin pleadings The Court, *Exchequer of Pleas*, gradually became separated from the revenue office and became an independent court of law in 1579 presided over by the Lord Treasurer (or Chancellor of the Exchequer) and a number of judges known as barons. The court also heard cases of appeal and petition (equity).

Court of Chancery
Masters of the Rolls

1485 Robert Morton, later Bishop of Worcester

1486 David William

1492 John Blythe, later Bishop of Salisbury

1494 William Warham, later Archbishop of Canterbury

1502 William Barnes, later Bishop of London

1504 Christopher Bainbridge, later Archbishop of York

1508 John Yonge, later Dean of York

1516 Cuthbert Tunstall, later Bishop of London and Durham

1522 John Clerke, later Bishop of Bath and Wells

1523 Thomas Hannibal

1527 John Taylor, Archdeacon of Derby and Buckingham

1534 Thomas Cromwell

1536 Christopher Hales

1541 Sir Robert Southwell

1550 John Beaumont

1552 Sir Robert Bowes

1553 Sir Nicholas Hare

1557 Sir William Cordell

1581 Sir Gilbert Gerrard

1594 Sir Thomas Egerton

Initially each individual action in the royal courts was begun by a writ issued by the Chancellor, the King's private secretary. Out of this function grew the Court of Chancery as a court of equity (i.e. of appeal and petition) designed to remedy deficiencies in the common law. The Chancellor presided in person over suits where the common law had failed to reach a verdict or was unable to act. It had the advantage of being more flexible than the common law courts and of being able to put all witnesses on oath. As the Tudor period progressed it lost much of this flexibility and effectiveness through bureaucratisation. When the Chancellor was not present the Master of the Rolls was president.

The Court of Chancery grew out of the Chancellor's issue of writs to commence actions in the royal courts.

Prerogative Courts

Privy Council

Trial by jury was recognised as obligatory in cases involving life or property but in other matters the monarch's Privy Council exercised the Crown's prerogative to try a wide variety of cases. It might at times assume the jurisdiction normally exercised by other courts – for instance in the late fourteenth century it examined and punished heretics, business which would normally have come before the church courts.

Star Chamber

During the fifteenth century the Privy Council when engaged in judicial business began to assemble in the Star Chamber in the Palace of Westminster. In 1487 an act of Parliament authorised this Star Chamber to 'punish divers misdemeanours'. The Court of Star Chamber became more important under Wolsey. In 1540 it was given its own clerk, who kept a minute book separately from that of the Privy Council, and the court was now distinct from the Privy Council. It was, however, composed of the Privy Councillors and the two Chief Justices of King's Bench and Common Pleas.

Court of Requests

The Court of Requests was a court in which the impecunious could plead their rights – especially in respect of trade and landholding – before a court appointed by the Crown in anticipation of speedy and efficient redress. Under the Yorkist monarchs and Henry VII, Privy Councillors were delegated to hear the poor men's requests but under Henry VIII it developed as a separate court, staffed by civil lawyers known as Masters of Requests. Its jurisdiction paralleled that of the Court of Common Pleas, which regarded it with the utmost suspicion and rivalry, seeking at every turn to undermine the stature of the Requests.

Court of High Commission

The royal supremacy meant that the Crown had the right and duty to declare on doctrinal and theological matters, to determine issues of discipline and ceremonial, and to administer the church. The Crown delegated some aspects of this supreme headship (and governorship under Elizabeth) to others. Thomas Cromwell became the King's vicegerent (Vicar-General) in spiritual matters. Special Commissions were given jurisdiction by the King over other areas of church affairs. Out of these commissions grew the Court of High Commission.

A statute of 1559 established an ecclesiastical commission to deal with 'errors, heresies, crimes, abuses, offences, contempts and enormities, spiritual and ecclesiastical', chiefly emanating from Roman Catholicism. The Commission, which sat more or less continuously, was not made into a formal court until about 1580. Archbishop Whitgift used it as an instrument of repression of extreme Protestantism during the latter part of Elizabeth's reign.

Civil Law Courts

Court of Admiralty

In the middle ages local courts in the chief ports, for example in Bristol and the Cinque Ports, dealt with disputes involving trade and navigation. Admiralty law grew up to meet the needs of merchants and, because so many of the merchants were foreigners, was based upon Roman or civil law rather than common law. By 1357 a Central Court of Judges with a criminal jurisdiction, dealing chiefly with piracy was in existence. New courts developed dealing with civil maritime cases. These Courts sat at Doctors' Commons and shared their personnel with the ecclesiastical courts, which also administered civil law. In the early fifteenth century all the central maritime courts were amalgamated under a Lord High Admiral. In 1536 the former criminal jurisdiction exercised by the Court of Admiralty was transferred to the common law courts. Throughout the Tudor period its civil jurisdiction over important commercial cases, whether they involved overseas traders or not, expanded. Simultaneously the common law courts began to claim jurisdiction over those cases which would formerly have been heard by local commercial courts. This battle between the common lawyers and other members of the legal profession lasted into the next century.

Church Courts

(These are also known as Courts Christian or, more commonly, Ecclesiastical Courts)

From the thirteenth century onwards English bishops held regular and frequent visitations of their dioceses. The purpose of visitation was to collect information about the state of the diocese (regarding its spiritual and moral as well as its administrative and financial health) and to set into motion the process of correction. This periodic inspection detected whether or not the church's laws (canons) were being implemented and observed at local level. A machinery for the visitation and correction of the secular (parochial clergy and others who did not belong to a rule) as well as the regular clergy (that is those who belonged to a rule or order) was properly established in the later fifteenth century. This system was taken over and further developed by the 'reformed' church of the sixteenth century. As more and more studies of the sixteenth century assume a basic knowledge of this system, an outline account of visitation and the manner in which it relates to the other ecclesiastical courts and to the secular courts is offered here.

Visitation
Primary visitation of diocese during first year of episcopate.

Triennial visitations of diocese thereafter.

Inhibition of all other ecclesiastical jurisdiction during the course of the visitation.

Articles of Inquiry – Canon 119 of 1604 made printed articles of inquiry, to guide the responses of churchwardens or questmen, compulsory but they were already widely in use.

General Monition was sent to all the rural deaneries in the diocese summoning to each visitation centre (there was usually one centre for each three or four deaneries) 'all parsons and vicars to exhibit letters of orders, certificates of subscriptions and dispensations, all preachers, lecturers, curates, readers, schoolmasters and ushers to exhibit licences, all impropriators and farmers of tithes to exhibit endowments and pay pensions and procurations, all churchmen and sidesmen to take their oaths and make presentments, executors to bring in the wills of their testators, all criminals and delinquents to answer articles . . .'

Presentments would include, for example, a note if the church was in disrepair, if the schoolmaster had no licence, if the vicar was an absentee or refused to wear the surplice or kept an alehouse in the vicarage, if there were **recusants**, if unmarried people cohabited, if a layman or woman held heretical opinions.

Records of presentments were made and citations were prepared calling those whose offences were considered serious to appear before the visitor for correction. Sometimes those cited failed to appear and a second citation was issued. The penalty for failure to appear in response to this second call was minor **excommunication** or suspension. Those who did appear to answer for their conduct might be summarily punished or dismissed or referred to the Consistory Court of the diocese for summary correction through mere office procedure.

Visitation Injunctions – Bishop defined the particular areas of his concern regarding the state of the diocese. He ordered conformity where necessary. In these Injunctions there might be reference to recently published canons of the church (laws) or orders from the Crown or archbishops.

To make matters even more complicated, each archdeacon also held his own visitations but, unless you are engaged in a project within this area, this should not bother you.

If you are very interested in finding out more, read Dorothy M. Owen, *The Records of the Established Church in England*, British Records Association, Archives and the User, no 1, 1970, which gives a good, brief account.

The visitation system underpinned the work of the superior ecclesiastical courts within each diocese. Presentments at visitation were often the basis for mere office cases in the Visitation Court immediately or later in the Consistory Court.

Consistory Court

The Consistory Court of the Bishop exercised several types of jurisdiction. Much business was heard at the Consistory Court itself (often within the cathedral building) but it might also be heard elsewhere (even in an inn) and by deputies and commissioners. Much of the historian's knowledge of popular attitudes and behaviour (deferential, sexual, and moral as well as religious) rests upon information revealed in the work of the Visitation and Consistory Courts. A number of books discuss such evidence but an especially good treatment is Martin Ingram, *Church Courts, Sex and Marriage in England, 1570–1640*, Cambridge, 1987.

Office Jurisdiction

Mere Office
The procedure was normally heard in open court by the judge (who was,

except in serious cases, normally not the bishop but his vicar-general or chancellor or a deputy). It was not a jury trial. Before 1660 the accused could use the procedure of compurgation or purgation to prove his innocence. Under this system several of the accused's neighbours, of accepted good reputation, were required to swear his or her innocence on oath. The number of compurgators required varied according to the gravity of the offence from three to about nine. If the accused was found guilty, the punishment was normally penance, which involved a solemn public confession in church on one or more days. On occasion, even after the reformation, the penitent was required to wear a white shift and hold a wand. Sometimes this punishment was commuted for a fine. This penance had to be certificated to the court.

Plenary Jurisdiction

This was exercised either in connection with office (correction) cases promoted by a third party or with the ecclesiastical equivalent of civil suits between party and party (instance suits). It was quite frequently used to try ordinary office cases where the evidence was difficult to interpret as it offered fewer opportunities for lawyers to claim a non-suit. Defendant and plaintiff appointed proctors (the civil law equivalent of a barrister). The accused answered articles or tabled questions. Witnesses were called both for and against and their depositions were written down. The whole procedure was more cumbersome, long drawn out and expensive than that of the Mere Office case. It was elaborate and unpopular.

Probate Jurisdiction

Disputed wills and administrations often resulted in plenary jurisdiction as above. When a will was unwitnessed or existed only as a witnessed verbal wish (noncupative wills), the matter was normally settled at a visitation unless it was queried. In that case it would result in plenary jurisdiction. When, as in most cases, the will was valid and undisputed, the named executors would exhibit it, swear an oath to its validity, and obtain **probate** by registering it in the probate act book and filing the original will with the court.

Population and Population Distribution

Data for England are back-projection figures extracted from E.A. Wrigley and R.S. Schofield, *The Population History of England, 1541–1871*, Cambridge, 1989 edition, pp. 531, 574.

Total Population

	England and Wales
1524	2.384 million
1541	2.774 million
1550	2.970 million
1569–71	3.255 million
1599–1601	4.066 million

English Urban Population [*resident in towns of over 4,000 people*]

1520	1700
6%	15%

Total of Population Living in London [*percentage*]

1520	1700
3%	10%

Urban Hierarchy

Data extracted from P. Clark and P. Slack, *English Towns in Transition*, Oxford, 1976.

1. The towns at the top of the hierarchy were the largest and richest towns, which dominated entire regions and offered a wide range of services. The category included London (population of 60,000 in 1500), which dwarfed the rest, York, Bristol, Exeter, Newcastle, Coventry and Salisbury in 1500 (with populations of 7,000 or more); and, in 1600, probably London, York, Bristol, Exeter, Newcastle, Colchester and Yarmouth (with populations of 11,000 or more in 1700).

Populations of London and Provincial Centres

There are various estimates of the population size of the capital and provincial centres. The following, then, are approximations.

	c.1520	later estimates	1603
London	60,000	120,000 (1582)	200,000
Norwich	12,000	18,000 (1579)	15,000
Bristol	10,000		12,000
York	8,000	8,000 (1548)	11,500
Exeter	8,000		9,000
Salisbury	8,000		7,000
Coventry	6,601	4,000–5,000 (1563)	7,000

2. A hundred incorporated towns with populations ranging between 1,500 and 5,000 in 1500 which acted as regional centres with hinterlands which often contained lesser market towns such as those below. These regional centres frequently had more than one market and often specialised in particular products. Typical were county towns such as Chester, Northampton, Shrewsbury, Southampton and Bury St Edmunds; the university towns of Oxford and Cambridge; several ports such as Canterbury, Hull, Portsmouth, Plymouth and Ipswich and industrial towns such as Manchester, Leeds and Birmingham. The period was a time of crisis for many such centres: Stafford, for example, was listed in 1540 as a decayed town; its fortunes revived under Elizabeth; by the seventeenth century it was in decline once more.

Population of some Regional Centres

Population of some regional centres, arranged according to their estimated size in the 1520s.

	c.1520	later estimates	1600
Oxford	5,000	5,500 (1547)	6,500
Great Yarmouth	4,000		5,000–8,000
Chester		4,000–5,000 (1563)	5,000
Worcester		4,000–5,000 (1563)	5,000
Canterbury	3,000	2,800–3,500 (1563)	5,000
Ipswich	3,000–4,000		5,500
Bury St Edmunds	3,550		4,500
Shrewsbury		2,700–3,400 (1563)	5,000
Cambridge	2,600	2,000–2,500 (1563)	6,500

3. There were between 500 and 600 small towns with low populations and population density. These included lesser market centres (Wotton-under-Edge, Gloucs.; Lutterworth, Leics.; Stony Stratford, Bucks.) and decaying ancient boroughs (Stamford, Lincs.; Winchelsea).

Population of some Market Towns

	c.1520	c.1603
Ashby de la Zouche	800	1,200
Hitchin	650	1,800
East Dereham	600	1,100

Welsh Towns

Data extracted from Joan Thirsk (ed.), *The Agrarian History of England and Wales*, Vol. IV, Cambridge, 1967.

In the 1540s, 11 per cent of the population was urban.

Carmarthen (c.2,150)

Brecon (1,500 +)

Wrexham (1,500 +)

Haverford West (1,500 +)

Caernarvon (1,000)

Cardiff (1,000)

Dolgellau (1,000)

Kidwelly (1,000)

Monmouth (1,000)

Swansea (1,000)

Tenby (1,000)

Biographical Index

This section includes a large number of short biographies of prominent men and women of the period but it is necessarily not exhaustive. I have given especial prominence to women because they have been neglected in most standard works of reference and yet are increasingly important in modern historical and cultural studies. Where good modern biographies are available I have cited them. The place of publication is London unless otherwise stated. Words in bold are detailed in Section XIV. Where dates of birth, and death are not available, fl. (floreat) has been used to indicate the date, or range of dates, during which the individual is known to have been alive.

J.P. Justice of the Peace; K.B. Knight of the Bath; K.G. Knight of the Garter; P.C. Privy Councillor; R. Rector; S.J. Society of Jesus.

Alençon (Duke of), Francis 1554–84: youngest son of Catherine de Medici and youngest brother of Charles IX of France; negotiations for his marriage with Elizabeth I took place between 1572–6 and 1578–84, when he died. In 1574 he became Duke of Anjou in the stead of his brother, who took the Crown of Poland. He is, however, normally referred to as Alençon to distinguish him from this brother. In October 1578 he became Protector of the Netherlands by a treaty with the States General. Elizabeth seemed serious about the match but by 1579 she no longer wanted it. Nevertheless in the early 1580s the courtship was revived as a diplomatic ploy to retain a French alliance.

Allen (Cardinal) William (1532–94): Oxford-educated, uncompromisingly Catholic priest whose promising career was cut short by Elizabeth's accession. 1561: Exiled in Louvain; 1562: returned to Lancashire and concentrated on bringing lapsed Catholics back to the faith; 1565: forced to seek safety in household of Duke of Norfolk but fled to Netherlands later that year, never to return; 1568: founded English College at Douai to train missionary priests and educate sons of English Catholics; 1578: English College left Douai for Rheims; intrigued v. Elizabeth; 1589: took large part in revision of Vulgate; 1582: involved in production of Douai Bible (1609) but d. before its completion.

André (of Toulouse), Bernard (fl. 1509): Royal poet and historiographer and tutor to Prince Arthur Tudor, eldest son of Henry VII.

Anger Jane: Famous for participation in a gender debate organised by the printer Thomas Orwin. 1589: *Jane Anger; her protection for women to defend them against the scandalous reports of a late surfeiting lover, and all other like Venerians that claime so to be overcloyed with women's kindness.* The name is assumed to have been a pseudonym.

Anjou (Duke of), Henri 1551–89: second son of Catherine de Medici and younger brother of Charles IX of France. Marriage with Elizabeth proposed in 1570. Courtship served to keep France friendly during crisis of Ridolfi plot. He is not to be confused with his younger brother, Francis Duke of Alençon and Anjou (q.v.).

Anne of Cleves (Queen) (1515–57): 4th wife of Henry VIII. Daughter of John, Duke of Cleves. Thomas Cromwell arranged this m. to form a strategic alliance against the Emperor Charles V and Francis I of France. King averse to match. Cromwell arrested and executed in June 1540 and m. to Anne annulled on 9 July. She was pensioned off in Lewes and given title of King's 'sister'!

Arundel Mary (fl. 1540s): Daughter of a Cornish knight; sometime before 1542 she m. Robert Ratcliffe, Earl of Sussex; after his death in 1542 m. Henry Fitz-Alan, Earl of Arundel, President of the Council. Translated from the Latin *The Sayings and Doings of the Emperor Severus and Select Sentences of the Seven Wise Men of Greece* which were circulated in manuscript but not published.

Ascham Roger (1515–68): Humanist educator and pioneer of English as literary language. 1538: Reader in Greek at St John's College, Cambridge; 1545: *Toxophilus*, English dialogue on archery; 1548: tutor to Princess Elizabeth; 1550–3: abroad as secretary to English ambassador to Charles V etc.; 1553: Latin Secretary to Mary I and, after 1558, to Elizabeth; 1570: *The Scholemaster*, written in late life, posthumously advocated use of gentle persuasion not force by the teacher.

Aske Robert (d. 1537): Lawyer. Leader of Pilgrimage of Grace which began at Louth in Lincolnshire in October 1536. Aske manipulated by Henry VIII to quieten the rebellion and that of Sir Francis Bigod. Imprisoned in London in May 1537. Executed in York.

Askew Anne (1521–46): Well-educated and pious daughter of a Lincolnshire gentleman; m. Thomas Kyme; 2 children; separation from husband; 1546: arrested, tortured and accused of heresy for views on sacrament as part of campaign against Queen Catherine Parr by court conservatives; 16 July 1546: burned at Smithfield.

Astley (**ASHLEY**) (Lady) Katherine (?1540–60s): Governess of Princess Elizabeth and later Woman-of-the-Bedchamber to Queen Elizabeth and sister to Lady Jane Denny. A protestant influence at court in the early days of Elizabeth's reign. She was married to the Marian exile, John Asheley, gentleman, of Norfolk who was Elizabeth's Master of the Jewel House.

Aylmer John (1521–94): Cambridge-educated tutor to Lady Jane Grey; 1553: Archd.; Marian exile; 1562: Archd. of Lincoln; 1577: Bishop of London. Published sermons and devotional works.

Babington (Sir) Anthony (1561–86): Leader of English Catholics half-heartedly involved in the Babington Plot. In 1580 on a six-month tour of France he met Thomas Morgan, agent of Mary Queen of Scots. Back in London at the Inns of Court he associated increasingly with admirers of Mary and acted as channel of communication between French embassy and Mary and assistant to the Catholic missionary priests. In late May 1586 he heard of a plot from Ballard to replace Elizabeth by Mary and tried to escape abroad. He divulged what was happening to Poley who, unbeknown to Babington, informed Walsingham. Walsingham penetrated but did not halt the communications between Mary Queen of Scots and Morgan via Babington and then foiled the plot. 18 July 1586: Mary sent letter approving murder of Elizabeth to Babington; this sounded Mary's death knell. 20 September 1586: Babington was executed at Tyburn.

Bacon Ann (1528–1610): One of the 5 daughters of Sir Anthony Cooke who were given a humanist education. Translated sermons of Fra Bernardino Ochino from Italian into English in two editions published in 1550 and 1570. Translated *Jewel's Apology* from Latin into English, 1564. It was put into print without her knowledge by Matthew Parker, Archbishop of Canterbury, who thought it would offend her modesty. She m. Sir Nicholas Bacon and became mother of Francis Bacon.

Bacon (First Baron Verulam and Viscount St Albans), Francis (1561–1626): Younger son of Sir Nicholas and Lady Ann Bacon, educated at Cambridge and Gray's Inn; 1576–9: attached to embassy in France; 1582: called to bar; 1584: M.P., Melcombe Regis; 1584: wrote *Letter of Advice to Queen Elizabeth* recommending stern anti-Catholic measures; 1586: M.P. Taunton and Bencher, Gray's Inn; 1589: M.P. Liverpool; 1593: M.P. Middlesex; 1596: Q.C.; 1597: *Essays*; 1597: M.P. Southampton; 1601: Commissioner investigating Essex Revolt and largely responsible for the Earl's conviction; M.P. St Albans; 1604: M.P. Ipswich; 1614: M.P. Cambridge University. Extremely prominent under James I who made him Lord Chancellor and raised him to the peerage in 1618. Important philosophical, literary and legal works; apart from the *Essays* these all appeared in the following century. Catherine D. Bowen, *Francis Bacon: The temper of a man*, Boston, 1963.

Bacon (Sir) Nicholas (1509–79): Educated at Cambridge and Gray's Inn; c.1557: m. Ann Co(o)ke; 1558: Lord Keeper of the Great Seal; strongly opposed claims of Mary Queen of Scots to English throne.

Bainton (Sir) Edward (fl. 1533): Protestant Vice-Chamberlain of Anne Boleyn's household who wielded considerable patronage.

Bale John (1495–1563): A student, at the same time as Cranmer, at Jesus College, Cambridge; priest who embraced Protestantism, renounced vows and took a wife. Active preacher among northern Lollards in 1530s. Known as dramatic polemicist whose splenetic attacks on Catholicism earned him nickname 'bilious' Bale. 1538: composed *God's Promises*, a cycle of Protestant mystery plays to replace the Catholic ones. Important as historian of the reform movement. He observed the similarities between English Protestantism and Lollardy and helped to establish a Protestant martyrology and a continuous and heroic evangelical history. Friend of John Foxe. A.G. Dickens, *Lollards and Protestants in the Diocese of York*, 1959; Rosemary O'Day, *The Debate on the English Reformation*, 1986.

Barlow (Bishop) William (d.1568): 1520s: heretical tracts prohibited by Wolsey in 1529; 1536: Bishop of St Asaph and St David's; 1542: founded Brecon Grammar School; 1548: Bishop of Bath and Wells; 1553: resigned see; imprisoned in Tower but escaped into German exile; 1559: Bishop of Chichester.

Barnes Robert (1495–1540): Martyr and religious writer. 1523: Prior of Austen Friars, Cambridge; 1526: arrested for opinions – recant or burn; 1528: escaped to Antwerp and came under Lutheran influence; 1531: Cromwell invited him to return to England; 1535: mission to Germany to obtain Lutheran divines' opinions on royal divorce and remarriage; 1539: negotiator for m. with Anne of Cleves; preached at Paul's Cross against Gardiner; 1540: imprisoned under bill of attainder and burned. Published religious works in both German and English.

Barrow Henry (d.1593): Educated at Cambridge and Gray's Inn. 1586: arrested by Whitgift for Brownist opinions; imprisoned in Fleet for denying authority of his judges; published account of trial; hanged at Tyburn.

Barton Elizabeth (1506–34): Nun of Kent or Holy Maid of Kent. House servant of Thomas Cobb of Aldington, Kent. Mystic and prophet, judged a genuine religious ecstatic by Dr Edward Bocking of Canterbury. Opposed Henry VIII's divorce and marriage to Anne Boleyn; Act of attainder passed against her in January 1534; hanged with Bocking and other accomplices on 20 April 1534.

Basset Mary (née Roper) (c.1520s–72): Translator, daughter of William and Margaret Roper. She m. first Stephen Clarke (d.), then James Bassett, son of Sir John Basset and Honora Grenville, Viscountess Lisle. Humanist education by Dr John Morwen; celebrated Greek and Latin scholar; noted translator; one of her translations printed in Sir Thomas More's *English Works*; restored to court favour during reign of Mary I.

Beaufort (Countess of Richmond and Derby), Margaret (1443–1509):

Queen Mother. Daughter of John Beaufort, Duke of Somerset, and descendant, through John of Gaunt, of Edward III. Married first John de la Pole in 1450 (dissolved 1453); second, Edmund Tudor, Earl of Richmond, half-brother of Henry VI, in 1455 (d. 1456); third, Henry Stafford, 2nd son of the Duke of Buckingham, in 1458. He died in 1471; lastly, Thomas, Lord Stanley, Earl of Derby, in 1472 (d.1504). Gave birth to Henry Tudor (Henry VII) when she was 13. Gave Henry VII part of his claim to throne of England and assisted him in obtaining the Crown. Important role in new reign. Declared *femme sole* in 1485; in 1485 she had in care in her household Elizabeth and Cecily of York; Edward Stafford, Duke of Buckingham; Edward Earl of Warwick; Ralph Neville, heir to Earl of Westmorland. 1488: Knight of the Garter; 1499–1505: Margaret presided over unofficial Council of the Midlands at Collyweston, a position of unprecedented power for a woman, where she was instrumental in participating in and supporting an increasingly unpopular royal regime; important patron of University of Cambridge; founder of Christ's College, Cambridge, 1505–6. Michael K. Jones and Malcolm G. Underwood, *The King's Mother, Lady Margaret Beaufort, Countess of Richmond and Derby*, Cambridge, 1992.

Becon Thomas (1512–67): Cambridge-educated clergyman. 1541 and 1543: compelled as vicar of Brenzett, Kent, to recant Protestant opinions; 1548: Rector of St Stephen Walbrook, London; Chaplain to Cranmer and Somerset and preacher at Canterbury Cathedral; 1553–4: imprisoned in Tower as seditious preacher and deprived of post as married priest; exiled in Strasbourg; 1558: restored to living; published many religious works including the famous and influential *Catechism*.

Bentham (Bishop) Thomas (1513–79): Marian exile and Elizabethan bishop. Oxford-educated theologian and linguist; 1553: removed from fellowship of Magdalen College, Oxford; 1554–7: Marian exile; November 1557: began work on Geneva Bible; c. Jan 1558: m. Maud Fawcon of Hadleigh, Suffolk; 1558: minister to Protestant congregation in Marian London; 1559: appointed Visitor in Elizabethan Royal Commission; March 1560: consecrated as Bishop of Coventry and Lichfield; 1562: preached at court; 1569: translated Books of Daniel and Ezekiel for Bishops' Bible; letter book an important source for episcopal problems in first decades of Elizabeth's reign and relations with returned exiles. R. O'Day and J. Berlatsky (eds), *The Letter Book of Thomas Bentham, Bishop of Coventry and Lichfield*, Camden Miscellany XXVII, 1979.

Bertie Catherine (née Willoughby) (1519–80): Prominent Protestant. Heiress to 11th Lord Willoughby; 1526: Charles Brandon bought her wardship to m. her to his young son, Henry, Earl of Lincoln, a child of 3; 1533: m. Charles Brandon, Duke of Suffolk; 1545: Brandon d.; 1551: both their sons d.; 1553: m. Richard Bertie, gentleman of her household; patron of Latimer and other Protestant preachers under Edward VI;

Marian exile in Weisel and Lithuania; 1559: returned to Lincolnshire and spent life raising son and daughter and acting as guardian to Lady Mary Grey. Evelyn Read, *Catherine Duchess of Suffolk*, 1962

Bilney Thomas (?1495–1531): Martyr. One of a group of Cambridge men who gathered at the White Horse – 'Little Germany' – to discuss the New Learning and religious issues. Friends with Robert Barnes, Hugh Latimer, Matthew Parker, etc.

Bocher Joan (d. 1550): Anabaptist martyr, sometimes known as the Maid of Kent. She was an associate of Anne Askew; denied the doctrine of the incarnation; imprisoned, examined by Cranmer and eventually burned at Smithfield.

Bocking (Dr) Edward (d.1534): Oxford-educated Benedictine monk of Christ Church Canterbury. He was sent to report back on Elizabeth Barton's prophecies, was accused of becoming her accomplice and was hanged as such.

Boleyn (Queen) Anne (?1501–36): Second daughter of Thomas Bullen (Boleyn), later Earl of Ormonde and Wiltshire, and a descendant of Edward I. Second wife of Henry VIII (m. 25 January 1533). Mother of Elizabeth I. Executed 19 May 1536 on charges of adultery. Her m. to Henry was the occasion for English Reformation. Debate about her sympathy with Reformation cause. M. Dowling, *Humanism in the Age of Henry VIII*, 1986; E. Ives, *Anne Boleyn*, 1987.

Boleyn (Viscount Rochford), George (d.1536): S. of Thomas and brother of Anne, Queen of England. He rose, as a consequence, to become Viscount Rochford (1530) and Warden of the Cinque Ports (1534). He fell, as a consequence. He was arraigned for incest and high treason and was executed on 17 May 1536.

Boleyn (Earl of Wiltshire and Ormonde) Thomas (1477–1539): Father of Anne and George. Diplomat and royal servant throughout early years of Henry VIII's reign; 1522: Treasurer of Household; 1525: Viscount Rochford; 1527: Joint Ambassador to France; 1529: Earl of Wiltshire and Ormonde; 1530: Lord Privy Seal and Ambassador to Charles V and also to France on matter of divorce.

Bonner (Bishop) Edmund (?1500–69): Lawyer, humanist and Catholic reformer. 1529: Chaplain to Wolsey; 1532–43: served on royal diplomatic missions especially concerning divorce; 1538: Ambassador to Paris and Bishop of Hereford; 1550: Bishop of London; accepted royal supremacy under Henry but under Edward resisted and was deprived of bishopric and imprisoned; September 1553: restored as bp; led attack on heresy in diocese (113 burnings), laying great store on sermons and catechising and reform. Deprived under Elizabeth. Died Sept. 1569 in the Marshalsea.

Borough Stephen (1525–84) 1553: Master of the only ship to survive the first English expedition to Russia; discovered Russia and named North Cape; 1556: discovered entrance to Kara Sea; wrote records of his many voyages, some of these journals reprinted by Hakluyt.

Bothwell (Earl of), James Hepburn (c. 1535–78): Son of Patrick, 3rd Earl of Bothwell, 'the Fair Earl', and Agnes, daughter of Lord Henry Sinclair. He was well-educated in the household of Patrick Hepburn, Bishop of Moray. 1556: 4th Earl of Bothwell, Warden of Scottish Marches, Lord High Admiral of Scotland; Protestant supporter of Mary of Guise, Catholic Queen Regent; 1557: commanded expedition into English borders; 1560: Bothwell went to Denmark, met, married and deserted Anna Throndsson, a Norwegian girl who later sealed his fate; 1560: met Mary Queen of Scots in Paris and was sent by her as Commissioner to Scotland; 1561: Privy Councillor; 1562: imprisoned for allegedly attempting to capture the Queen but escaped; 1564: imprisoned by the English; 1564: escaped to France, returned to Scotland and thence to France again; Mary recalled him to Scotland where he was in the ascendant; February 1565: m. Lady Jean Gordon, a Catholic; 1566: at Holyrood the night of Rizzio's murder but denied all knowledge of it; he joined Mary and Darnley at Dunbar and grew more and more influential; 9 February 1567: Bothwell blew up Darnley's house at Kirk o' Field; Bothwell acquitted in law courts and granted large tracts of land by Queen; 24 April 1567: Bothwell captured Queen (most probably with her connivance); 7 May 1567: divorced Lady Jean; 15 May 1567: m. Mary Stuart according to Protestant rites; Bothwell created Duke of Orkney and Earl of Shetland; rebellion of the Scottish lords; Queen's army melted away and Bothwell escaped via Orkney and Shetland to Denmark. Here he was imprisoned by Frederick II and went mad. R. Gore-Browne, *Lord Bothwell*, 1937.

Brandon (1st Duke of Suffolk), Charles (d. 1545): Favourite of Henry VIII; 1515: bigamously m. Mary Tudor, sister to Henry, with papal dispensation; 1520: accompanied King to Field of Cloth of Gold; 1523: commanded unsuccessful invasion of France; sought support for Henry's divorce from Catherine; 1542: Warden of Marches against Scotland; 1544: captured Boulogne as Commander of French Invasion; acted as Steward of royal household.

Bray Sir Reginald (d.1503): One of Henry VII's chief councillors; a lawyer who was originally in the service of Margaret Beaufort, managing her estates. He became Henry VII's chief administrator in respect to financial and property matters after 1485. His official position was Chancellor of the Duchy of Lancaster but his unofficial brief was general auditor of all the royal lands.

Brinklow Henry (d.1546): Franciscan. Converted to Lutheranism. Became commonwealthman during Edward VI's reign. Author, *The Complaint of Roderick Mors* (1546), an angry protest against social injustice.

His widow, Margery, m. Stephen Vaughan, Merchant Adventurer, father of Anne Locke.

Browne Robert (c.1550–c.1633) Congregationalist. Educated at Corpus Christi College, Cambridge, and ordained priest c.1573; in the late 1570s preached without licence around Cambridge against the parochial system and ordination; 1580: started, with Robert Harrison, the Brownist 'church' in Norwich; 1581: imprisoned by Bishop of Norwich for seditious preaching at Bury St Edmonds but released through Burghley's intervention; 1581: emigrated to Middleburg and published books that were prohibited in England; after a quarrel with Harrison moved to Scotland and then back to England; 1584: arrested; 1586: preacher at Northampton; 1586: excommunicated by Richard Howland, Bishop of Peterborough, submitted and became master of Stamford Grammar School; 1591–1631: Rector of Achurch, Northants; died in gaol while on charges of violent assault.

Bucer Martin (1491–1551): Major Protestant reformer and prolific author of religious works. 1523–49: leader of Reformation and preacher in Strasbourg; 1525–30: Zwinglian in Eucharistic controversy; 1531–8: sought common reformation faith in Germany and Switzerland; April 1549: contest with Charles V led him to retire to England where he was kindly received by Edward VI's court; 1549: Regius Professor of Divinity, University of Cambridge; 1550: consulted about shape of Book of Common Prayer; 1551: buried in university church; 1557: exhumed under Mary I.

Buckingham Dukes of (*See* STAFFORD)

Burghley (**BURGHLEIGH**), Lord (*See* CECIL, William)

Butts (Dr) William (d.1545): Influential Cambridge-educated evangelical. Physician to Henry VIII.

Byrd William (?1538–1623): Composer, organist and pupil of Tallis. 1563: organist of Lincoln; 1569: joint organist of Chapel Royal; 1575: granted monpoly of selling printed music and music paper; 1578–88: Catholic recusant living at Harlington, Middlesex. Prolific composer. 1575: *Cantiones . . . sacrae*; 1588: the first English madrigals; 1588:*Psalmes, Sonnets and Songs*; 1589: *Songs of Sundrie Natures* & *Liber primus Sacrarum Cantionum*; 1591: *Liber secundus*; 1607: *Gradualia*; 1611: *Psalmes, Songs*, and *Sonnets*.

Cabot John (1425–c.1500): Venetian tradesman and explorer who worked out of Bristol. Father of Sebastian. Discovered Newfoundland.

Cabot Sebastian (1474–1557): Son of a Venetian tradesman working in Bristol; 1496: with his father, John, and brothers obtained licence for voyage of discovery; 1497: discovered Nova Scotia; 1512: made map of Gascony and Guienne for Henry VIII; 1512–16: map-maker for Ferdinand of Aragon; 1519–26: pilot-major for Emperor Charles V;

1526–33: chequered career but recalled to Seville in 1533; 1544: published engraved map of world; 1547: returned to Bristol; 1548: pensioned by Edward VI; 1551: settled a dispute between Hanseatic League and London merchants; 1551: proposed formation of Company of Merchant Adventurers of London to search for North–East Passage to China; 1553 and 1556: oversaw expeditions to Russia; 1555: Mary I confirmed pension; 1557: Mary I halved his pension.

Camden William (1551–1623): Historian and antiquary. Educated at Christ's Hospital and St Paul's School and then at Oxford. 1571: excluded by Catholic fellows from All Souls, Oxford; 1571: travelled throughout England collecting archaeological materials (probably subsidised by Gabriel Goodman, Dean of Westminster); 1575–93: Usher of Westminster School; 1593: headmaster; 1578–1600: during vacations continued tours of archaeological investigation; 1586: published *Britannia*; 1589–1623: lay prebendary of Salisbury; 1597: published Greek grammar; 1597–1623: Clarenceux King-of-Arms; numerous publications in early seventeenth century; 1615: *Annales . . . regnante Elizabetha . . . ad annum 1589* (2nd part published in 1628 after his death); 1622: founded Oxford Chair of History.

Campeggio Cardinal Lorenzo (fl.1500–1534): Papal Legate and Cardinal Protector of England; 1518–1519: first mission to England; 1528–1529: second mission to England to settle the divorce issue; 1529: his legatine court at Blackfriars was adjourned and he left England; 1534: deprived of his see of Salisbury.

Campion Edmund (1540–1581): Jesuit martyr. 1580: missionary priest to England; preached and administered sacraments in Lancashire; 1581: printed *Decem Rationes* (Ten Reasons) why Roman Church was true Church and distributed it to congregation of St Mary's, Oxford; July 1581: Campion betrayed, imprisoned in Tower, racked; executed 1 December 1581.

Cartwright Thomas (1535–1603): Extreme Protestant divine and author of controversial religious works. Cambridge-educated; a precisian or Puritan in religious matters from early in Elizabeth's reign; 1565: attacked surplice; 1569: Lady Margaret Professor of Divinity; 1570: deprived of Chair for preaching against Church of England's constitution; 1571–6: went in and out of England, first to Geneva and then to the Channel Islands; 1584: Pastor of English Congregation at Antwerp; 1585: returned to England; 1586: Master of Earl of Leicester's Hospital at Warwick; 1590–2: imprisoned; 1595–8: accompanied Baron Zouche to Guernsey.

Cary (Earl of Monmouth), Robert (?1560–1639): Cousin of Elizabeth through her mother's sister Mary Boleyn Cary. His short *Memoirs* provide vivid descriptions of the Spanish Armada, the Queen herself and her death, and life on the Anglo-Scottish borders. It was he who rode to Scotland to inform James VI of Elizabeth's death.

Catherine of Aragon (Queen) (1485–1536): Youngest child of Ferdinand of Aragon and Isabella of Castile; 1501: m. Prince Arthur, heir to English throne; 1502: Arthur died, marriage unconsummated; 1509: m. Prince Henry; 24 June 1509: Henry and Catherine crowned King and Queen; 1510–18: six children of whom only 1, Mary, survived; July 1531: Henry left Catherine; Easter 1533: Archbishop of Canterbury pronounced marriage null and void and declared that marriage with Anne Boleyn was valid; 7 January 1536: died. A not inconsiderable scholar and a shrewd diplomatist. Antonia Fraser, *Six Wives of Henry VIII*, 1993.

Cavendish George (?1499–?1562): Gentleman-usher to Wolsey and author of *The Life and Death of Cardinal Wolsey* (1558), based on his first-hand knowledge of the statesman.

Cecil Mildred (1526–): Classically-educated eldest daughter of Sir Anthony Cooke. She was well-known by contemporaries for her translations from the Greek fathers, which circulated in manuscript but were never published. 1545: married William Cecil as his second wife. Mother of Robert Cecil.

Cecil (1st Earl of Salisbury and 1st Viscount Cranborne), Robert (1563–1612): Statesman and diplomat: the 'crookbacked earl'. Son of William Cecil, Lord Burghley, and Mildred his wife. 1584–7: resident in France; 1588: attached to Earl of Derby's mission to Spanish Netherlands; 1584 and 1586: M.P. for Westminster; 1588, 1593, 1597, 1601: M.P. for Hertfordshire; 1591: knighted; 1596–1608: Secretary of State; 1598: envoy to France; 1600: Commissioner for trying Essex for leaving Ireland; 1603: secured accession of James VI of Scotland to throne of England; 1603: created Baron Cecil; 1604: Viscount Cranborne; 1605: Earl of Salisbury; 1607: James I exchanged his palace of Hatfield for Theobalds and Cecil built Hatfield House.

Cecil (1st Earl of Exeter and 2nd Baron Burghley), Thomas (1542–1623): Eldest son of William Cecil. 1563: M.P. for Stamford; 1569: took up arms against Northern Rebels; 1573: served in Scotland; 1575: knighted; 1585: in army in Low Countries; 1588: served against Armada; 1598: succeeded to barony; 1599: President of Council of the North; 1601: assisted in suppressing Essex Revolt; 1605: created Earl of Exeter.

Cecil (Baron Burghley), William (1520–98): Son of a Northamptonshire squire; served in Henry VIII's household; educated at Cambridge and Gray's Inn; m. sister of Sir John Cheke; 1547–61: *custos brevium*, Court of Common Pleas; m. Mildred Cooke; 1547: M.P. for Stamford; 1549: Secretary to Somerset and imprisoned in Tower on his fall; 1550–3: Secretary of State; 1551: knighted; 1553: began building

Burghley House and Wimbledon House; in Mary I's service, 1553–8; 1555: M.P. Lincs.; 1558–72: Secretary of State; 1559: M.P. Lincs.; 1559: Chancellor of Camb. Univ.; 1560: envoy to Scotland; 1561: Master of Court of Wards; 1562: M.P. Northants; rivalry between Cecil and Leicester factions at court; 1570: organised agents to seek out conspiracies v. Elizabeth; 1571: created Baron Burghley; 1572–98: Lord High Treasurer. Until 1572: he co-ordinated Elizabeth's Privy Council, supervised the Exchequer and Court of Wards and managed parliament. After this, Walsingham assumed some of this role, especially in diplomacy.

Cecily of York   (1469–1507): 2nd surviving daughter of Edward IV and, from 1486, Henry VII's eldest sister-in-law; in household of Margaret Beaufort from September 1485; m. to Ralph Scrope but dissolved 1486; late 1487 m. Viscount Welles, halfbrother of Margaret Beaufort: 1499: d. of Welles; 1502: m. Thomas Kyme of Friskney without royal permission; banished from court and King seized estate; Margaret Beaufort intervened to achieve a settlement for Cecily in 1503. M.K. Jones and M.G. Underwood, *The King's Mother*, Cambridge, 1992.

Chancellor   Richard (d. 1556): Navigator who sailed to the Levant in 1550 and visited Archangel and Moscow in 1554 and 1555. Best known for command of Sir Hugh Willoughby's expedition to discover a northeast passage to India in 1555. Wrecked off Aberdeenshire on return from Archangel and Moscow in 1556.

Chapuys   Eustace (fl. 1529–1545): Imperial ambassador to England, 1529–1536 and 1542–1545; on his first mission plotted in Catherine of Aragon's favour. Occasionally is described, mistakenly, as Spanish ambassador.

Cheke   (Sir) John (1514–57): Classical scholar, tutor to Edward VI (1544), Provost of King's College, Cambridge (1548) and Secretary of State (1553); Marian exile; captured and brought back to England because acting as publicist for Protestants; imprisoned, recanted, d. 13 September 1557 of natural causes. His sister m. to William Cecil.

Clement   Margaret (née Gigs) (b.c.1504): Humanist. Daughter of Margaret Roper's nurse; educated with children of Sir Thomas More; m. John Clement, tutor in More's household and court physician in 1528; 5 daughters who were taught Latin and Greek; 1549: family went into exile; 1553: returned to England. Retha M. Warnicke, *Women of the English Renaissance and Reformation*, Westport, Conn., 1983.

Clifford   (Lady) Anne (1590–1676): Daughter of George Clifford, 3rd Earl of Cumberland and Margaret Russell, talented and educated dau. of the Earl of Bedford (1560–1616). Educated at court by Countess of Warwick. Tutored by the poet Samuel Daniel. 1609: m. Richard Sackville, later 3rd Earl of Dorset (d. 1624); 1630: m. Philip Herbert, 4th Earl of Pembroke (d. 1650). Important diaries and genealogies. D.J.H. Clifford, *The Diaries of Lady Anne Clifford*, Alan Sutton, 1990.

Clifford (3rd Earl of Cumberland), George (1558–1605): Eldest son of Henry, 2nd Earl, and Lady Eleanor Brandon, daughter of Charles Brandon and Mary Tudor. 1569/70: succeeded to Earldom; 1571: began education at Cambridge; 1577: m. cousin, Margaret Russell; 1590: b. of daughter; Anne; 1586–98 naval commander, taking part in the defence against the Armada (1588) and probably in the Cadiz expedition (1596) at his own expense; profligate life; died in great debt and separated from his wife.

Clitherow Margaret (1556–86): Catholic martyr. 1571: m. widower John Clitherow, a butcher; 1574: converted to Catholicism; private religious devotions; 1577–84: periods of imprisonment during which she fasted, studied and meditated; sheltered Catholic priests and invited friends to private celebrations of Mass; Mar. 1586: arrested for harbouring priests; refused to plead either innocent or guilty; torture by weights resulted in death.

Colet (Dean), John (1466–1519): Dean of St Paul's, 1504–19; founder of St Paul's School, 1509. Acquired reputation for his exposition at Oxford between 1496 and 1505 of the writings of St Paul by relating them to the purpose and context in which they were written. In 1499 he began a lifetime friendship with Erasmus.

Co(o)ke Ann (*See* BACON, Ann)

Co(o)ke (Sir) Anthony (1504–76): Tutor to Edward VI; father of Mildred Cecil, Ann Bacon and Catherine Killigrew; 1547: Knight of the Bath.; 1547–9: served on various ecclesciastical commissions; 1552: obtained church lands; 1553: imprisoned; 1554: exiled in Strasbourg; 1558: returned to England; 1559–67: M.P. Essex; active on commissions from 1559 until his death in 1576.

Co(o)ke Catherine (*See* KILLIGREW, Catherine)

Co(o)ke Mildred (*See* CECIL, Mildred)

Coverdale Miles (c. 1488–1568): Educated at Cambridge and entered Austin Friars at Cambridge in 1514. Belonged to circle of Robert Barnes at White Horse tavern. Coverdale accompanied Barnes to London to help him prepare defence against charges of heresy. 1527: Thomas Cromwell gave Coverdale money to buy theological books. 1528: Coverdale became secular priest and began to preach heresy – abandoned by Cromwell as unsafe. 1528–34: Coverdale probably in Antwerp and Hamburg with Tyndale. 1534: Jacob van Meteren, Protestant printer in Antwerp, paid Coverdale to prepare English transl. of Bible. This, printed in Cologne, was imported into England. It was based upon German and Latin sources and made use of Tyndale's transls; 1539: came to England to work on Great Bible at Cromwell's request, 1540: after Cromwell's fall wandered abroad; 1548: resident at Windsor in Cranmer's company; 1551: Bishop of Exeter; 1553: deprived because of m.; 1553: invited to Denmark – preached to English refugees at Wesel and then returned to Bergzabern; 1558: in Geneva; 1559: returned to England, not as bp, but participated in consecration of Archbp Matthew Parker; 1563: refused See of Llandaff; 1566: resigned living of St Magnus near London Bridge because he refused to conform.

Cox (Bishop) Richard (1500–81): Educated at Cambridge. Headmaster of Eton; 1544–50: Tutor to Prince Edward; 1547–53: Dean of Christ Church, Oxford; 1547–52: Vice-Chancellor of Oxford; 1548–50: Commissioner to revise the liturgy; 1549: Dean of Westminster; 1553: imprisoned under Mary; 1554–8: Exiled, chiefly in Frankfurt (Knox/Cox controversy); 1559: Bishop of Norwich; 1559–80: Bishop of Ely; struggled against royal attempts to deplete financial resources of See of Ely. Felicity Heal, *Of Prelates and Princes*, Cambridge, 1980.

Crane Elizabeth (fl.1580s): Harbourer of Marprelate press. A wealthy widow who allowed Marprelate press to use two of her houses between April and November 1588. She was arrested but refused to plead guilty and was released.

Cranmer (Archbishop) Thomas (1489–1556): Educated Cambridge. 1529: Treatise defending royal divorce; 1530: part of Earl of Wiltshire's embassy to Charles V; 1533: returned to England as Archbishop of Canterbury, pronounced royal divorce, declared Henry's m. to Anne Boleyn lawful; defended royal supremacy; 1536: declared m. with Anne Boleyn null and void, promulgated ten articles of doctrine; 1539: unsuccessfully opposed six articles, supported divorce from Anne of Cleves; 1540: did not defend Cromwell; 1541: informed on Catherine Howard to Henry; 1542: defended Great Bible v. Gardiner and was cleared of charges of heresy by Henry; 1547: member of council during Edward VI's minority; 1548: chaired production of first Edwardian prayer book; 1550: proposals for reform of canon law, *Reformatio Legum Ecclesiasticarum*; 1552: instrumental in revisions of prayer book; 1552: promulgated 42 articles of religion; 1553: signed Edward's will barring Mary from succession; 1553: impr. as supporter of Queen Jane and heretic; 1554: released to answer charges; 1555: refused to recognise papal jurisdiction; condemned as heretic by Cardinal Pole:, 1556: recanted all but rejection of transubstantiation; burnt at stake repudiating recantation, 21 March 1556. Jasper Ridley, *Thomas Cranmer*, Oxford, 1962.

Cromwell (Earl of Essex), Thomas (?1485–1540): 1503: present at Battle of Garigliano; spent period in Florence and then as clerk in Antwerp; c.1510–3: second visit to Italy and audience with Pope Julius II; possibly a clerk to a Venetian merchant; c.1513: lawyer; 1523: M.P.; 1524: member of Gray's Inn; 1525: Commissioner appointed by Wolsey to inquire into smaller monasteries; later 1520s: secretary to Wolsey; c.1529: instrumental in persuading Henry VIII to make himself head of church; 1531: member of Privy Council; 1532: Master of Court of Wards and Master of Jewel House; 1533: Chancellor of Exchequer; 1534: King's Secretary and Master of the Rolls, pushed suit of treason against Bp John Fisher; 1535: Vicar-General, organised general visitation of church and compilation of *valor ecclesiasticus*; 1536: moving spirit in dissolution of smaller religious houses, attended Anne Boleyn to Tower, made Lord Privy Seal and Baron Cromwell of Oakham; 1537: Knight of the Garter and Dean of Wells; 1539: overseer of printing of Bible in English, Lord Great Chamberlain, negotiated Henry's m. with Anne of Cleves; 1540: created Earl of Essex; 1540: executed for treason. Assigned pivotal role by historians in reorganisation of the central administration during the 1530s, amounting in the opinion of some to a revolution in government. Lively debate concerning his Protestantism. See 'King or Minister?' in Section XV below. A.G. Dickens, *Thomas Cromwell and the English Reformation*, 1959.

Crowley Robert (c.1518–88): Educated at Magdalen College, Oxford. A commonwealthman during the reign of Edward VI. Author of a commonwealth tract, *The Way to Wealth* (1550) and of a collection of cautionary tales in verse, *The Voice of the Last Trumpet* (1550).

Cumberland Earl of (*See* CLIFFORD, George)

Dacre (Countess of Arundel) Anne (fl. 1567–90): Prominent Catholic. 1571: m. 14 year-old stepbrother Philip Fitzalan, heir to Earldom of Arundel through his mother; 1572: takes shelter in house of Earl of Arundel and his daughter Jane (Fitzalan) Lumley; 1580: reconciled w. Philip; 1583: a daughter; c. 1585: both received Catholic communion from William Weston; 1585: a son; Philip imprisoned in Tower until d. in 1595; educated children; assumed spiritual leadership of household; sheltered and assisted Robert Southwell, patron of English College of the Jesuits at Ghent.

Darcy (Lord) Thomas (1467–1537): Position of great power and prestige in northern counties. Opposed royal divorce and suppression of monasteries. Surrendered Pontefract Castle to the rebels on 21 October 1536 and became leader of Pilgrimage of Grace. Executed at Tower Hill on 30 June 1537.

Darnley (Earl of), Henry Stuart (1546–67): 2nd son of Matthew Stuart, Earl of Lennox and Lady Margaret Douglas, daughter of Margaret Tudor (widow of James IV of Scotland and sister of Henry VIII) by her second husband the Earl of Angus. Henry Stuart, himself born in Yorks., was next heir to the English throne after Mary of Scotland. 1565: Henry Stuart visited Mary with Elizabeth's permission and a marriage between them was encouraged by Rizzio. 29 July 1565: m. Mary Queen of Scots; highly unpopular with nobles; his unseemly behaviour alienated the Queen, who refused him access and turned to Rizzio for counsel; 9 March 1566: Darnley, implicated in the plot between both Catholics and

Protestants, admitted murderers to Holyrood and led them to Rizzio's room where he lent his dagger to commit the murder. Mary briefly reconciled with Darnley, held to him by the knowledge of her pregnancy, but she did not forgive him and denied him all political influence. He tried to leave the country but was prevented by syphilis. Mary, by now influenced by Bothwell, persuaded Darnley to go to Kirk o' Field in Edinburgh to convalesce. He was murdered there on the night of 9 February 1567.

Daubeney Giles (1451–1508): One of Henry VII's principal councillors; originally a member of Edward IV's household; 1480: Sheriff of Dorset and Somerset; 1483: rebelled against Richard III; 1485: Henry VII made him Chamberlain of the Household in Stanley's stead; 1486: made Lieutenant of Calais; 1486: as Lord Daubeney commanded troops against the Scots and the Cornish rebels.

Davies (Bishop) Richard (1501–1581): Deprived as m. priest by Mary; Marian exile in Geneva; 1560: Bishop of St Asaph; 1561: Bishop of St David's. Adviser to Burghley and Matthew Parker on Welsh ecclesiastical matters. 1567: Published Prayer Book and New Testament in Welsh. See Salesbury.

Davis (Captain) John (1543–1605): 1585: commanded expedition to find north-west passage to China financed by London merchants. Reached Greenland and Baffin Island. Several voyages including expeditions to south seas on which he discovered the Falkland Islands (1593) and the East Indies (1598). 1587: *Traverse Book* – model for future log books; 1595: *World's Hydrographical Description* – defended himself v. attacks for not discovering north-west passage and described route which later permitted Hudson to reach Hudson's Strait.

Day John (d. 1584): Most notable protestant printer, publisher and commissioner of period, who consciously used the press to further the reformation cause. Under Mary printed pamphlets from the Protestant exiles; under Elizabeth printed works by Matthew Parker, Thomas Becon, Hugh Latimer and, most famously of all, John Foxe. Day collected together the writings of Tyndale, Barnes and Frith and commissioned and printed Foxe's compilation and edition.

Dee (Dr) John (1527–1608): Noted English alchemist, astrologer, teacher of navigation and mathematician, whose activities included the antiquarian study of old manuscripts and also intelligence work in Europe in the 1580s, apparently for William Cecil, Lord Burghley. 1550s: tutor to Robert Dudley; in effect the astrologer royal to Elizabeth I; friend of Sidney and Spenser; 1570: wrote lengthy and influential preface to Henry Billingsley's English transl. of Euclid's *Elements of Geometry*; Euclid's work had been written in 300 BC and had hitherto been accessible only to scholars; Dee defended its appearance against university criticism; he also argued for the use of mathematics as a practical science to help advance

Britain's place in the world; 1583: attack on astronomical and navigational instruments and chemical apparatus etc. at his house in Mortlake; charges of atheism and conjuring up devils related to claim in Foxe's *Book of Martyrs*.

Denny (Sir) Anthony (fl.1530s and 1540s): He was educated at St Paul's and at St John's Cambridge; 1532: member of the king's Privy Chamber; 1538: one of the 2 chief gentlemen of the chamber; 1543: intervened to protect Cranmer from heresy charges; 1546: Groom of the Stool.; he controlled access to Henry VIII in his final years; allied himself with Hertford; August 1546: given control of the 'dry stamp', which allowed him to act independently of the king; barred Gardiner and other conservatives from royal presence; used the 'dry stamp' to sign royal will after Henry's death; patron of new learning and Protestant reform at court; m. to Jane Denny (q.v.).

Denny (Lady) Jane: Protestant wife of the evangelical Henrician courtier, Anthony Denny, noted for her activities in the households of Queen Anne Boleyn and Queen Catherine Parr in the 1530s and 1540s. Sister of Katherine Ashley/Astley.

Dering Edward (1540–76): Puritan divine who served as a paradigm for later generations. A Kentish gentleman who was educated at Christ's College, Cambridge early in Mary's reign, although he did not proceed to B.A. until 1560. Dedicated to the preaching of the Word and with a high Presbyterian doctrine of the ministry. February 1570: preached before Queen and alienated her by rash critique of her church; 1572: appointed reader of divinity lecture at St Paul's Cathedral and established reputation as the great Elizabethan preacher; 1572: brought before Star Chamber for sympathising with John Field – frequent attempts to silence him; 1572: collaborated with John More in the enormously influential *A Brief and Necessary Catechism* for the use of householders when catechising their families; 1572: m. Anne Locke; interesting for spiritual relationship with many prominent women of the day, including Catherine Killigrew.

Devereux Lettice (*See* DUDLEY, Lettice)

Devereux (2nd Earl of Essex), Robert (1566–1601): Eldest s. of Walter Devereux, 1st Earl, and Lettice (Dudley). Educated at Cambridge; 1587: Master of the Horse; 1588: K.G.; 1589: supporter of Don Antonio, claimant to Portuguese throne; 1590: displeased Elizabeth by m. Frances, widow of Philip Sidney; 1591–2: commanded force to assist Henry of Navarre; 1593: P.C.; 1594: campaign v. Roderigo Lopez; 1596: defeated Spanish navy at Cadiz; 1597: Master of the Ordnance, Earl Marshal; 1598: opposed Burghley's peace with Spain, Chancellor of Cambridge University; 1599: Lieutenant and Governor-General of Ireland; 1599: ordered to proceed v. Ulster but made truce with Tyrone and returned to London without permission, 25 September; 5 June 1600: charged with dereliction of duty and making treaty with enemy; released August; Feb. 1601: proclaimed traitor for plot to take control of Queen; at his trial Bacon, his former protégé, spoke for the prosecution; executed 25 Feb. 1601.

Devereux (1st Earl of Essex), Walter (?1541–76): 1569: helped put down Northern rebels; 1572: K.G. and created 1st Earl; 1573: attempted conquest of Ulster; 1575: Earl Marshal of Ireland; recalled but reappointed in 1576; reputed to have been murdered by Earl of Leicester who m. his widow, Lettice (Dudley), but no truth in this.

Dinham John Lord (d. 1501): Important member of Henry VII's council; loyal to both Edward IV and Richard III; 1486: appointed Treasurer by Henry VII; 1486–1501: remained treasurer until he was replaced by Surrey.

Doughty Thomas (fl. 1570s): Friend of Robert Dudley who accompanied Francis Drake on Voyage of Circumnavigation, 1577–80, and may have been Burghley's spy. Doughty preached mutiny to the crew of the *Pelican* and was believed by Drake and others to be using magic to destroy the expedition. Drake had him tried by jury at Port St Julian. Doughty found guilty of betraying the plan of the expedition to Burghley and spreading mutiny. He was beheaded.

Douglas (Countess of Lennox), Margaret (1515–78): Lady-in-waiting to Anne Boleyn, Anne of Cleves and Catherine Howard and Catholic claimant to throne; daughter of Queen Margaret of Scotland by her m. with Archbald Douglas, Earl of Angus, and a niece of Henry VIII; humanist education; 1531: placed in Princess Mary's household; lady-in-waiting at Queen Anne Boleyn's court; edited with Mary Howard and Mary Shelton the *Devonshire Manuscript* of poems; 1536: clandestine romance and exchange of marriage vows with Thomas Howard, brother of 3rd Duke of Norfolk (assisted by Mary Howard) revealed; Howard, suspected of plotting for crown, imprisoned in Tower and d. Oct 1537; 1540: lady-in-waiting to Anne of Cleves; 1540: clandestine liaison with Charles Howard brother of Catherine; banished from court to live with Mary Howard; 1544: m. Matthew Stuart, Earl of Lennox; mother of Charles Stuart, Earl of Lennox and Henry Stuart, Lord Darnley and thus grandmother of Arabella Stuart and James VI of Scotland, chief claimants to the succession after her death; 1565: imprisoned in Tower for arranging m. between Henry and Mary of Scotland; denounced Mary at English court in 1567 for Darnley's murder; 1572: reconciled with Mary; considered by most as best Catholic claimant to throne. R.M. Warnicke, *Women of the English Renaissance and Reformation*, Westport, Conn., 1983.

Dowland John (c.1563–c.1626): Lutenist and composer. Travelled in Italy and Germany, meeting musicians. 1588: Bachelor of Music, University of Oxford. 1597, 1600 and 1603: Published three books of *Songes or Ayres of Foure Partes* for the lute. 1605: Court lutenist to Anne of Denmark; 1625: Court lutenist to Charles I.

Dowriche   Anne (c.1545 – after 1589): Wife of Hugh Dowriche, R. of Honiton from 1587; probably the author of poem in alexandrines, *The French historie . . .*

Drake   (Sir) Francis (c.1543–96): Devonshire-born son of Edmund Drake, sailor, yeoman-farmer and Protestant preacher. 1566 and 1567: accompanied cousin John Hawkins on slaving expeditions to the New World; 1570–1, 1572, 1577–80: 3 expeditions designed to defend English Protestantism against Philip II by cutting off supply of Peruvian silver and Mexican gold from Panama and Nombre de Dios. For the third expedition Drake had the Queen's secret permission for piracy on Spanish ships. There was an additional purpose: searching for the Pacific end of the North West Passage. On the trip Drake plundered the Spanish colonies, took possession of California (which he named New Albion), and eventually returned home with immense treasure to the acclaim of the Queen and court. 1581: knighted on board *The Golden Hind*; 1585: Drake sailed as Queen's Admiral on official voyage to attack Spanish West Indies and greatly damaged the Spanish, not least by capturing over 240 guns and thus weakening the Armada. 1587: compelled Philip II to delay sailing of the Armada by 'singeing of His Catholic Majesty's Beard' by destroying at least 24 ships off Cadiz. He also contrived to cut off supplies from the Spanish fleet at Cape St Vincent and also destroyed the tunny fisheries. The capture of the *San Felipe* in the Azores served to pay the costs of the expedition twice over and Drake returned to England in triumph on 26 June 1587. 1588: Participated in defence against Armada under Lord High Admiral, Howard of Effingham, but his plan to seek out the Armada in Spanish waters was rejected. 1589: court martialled but acquitted for disobeying his commander; 1589–96: Drake in disgrace and retires to Buckland Abbey; August 1595: Drake and Hawkins sailed on expedition to defeat the Spanish. It was a miserable failure and Drake died of dysentery at Porto Bello, 28 January 1596. J.A. Williamson, *Sir Francis Drake*, 1953.

Drayton   Michael (1563–1631): Poet. Sometime page to Sir Henry Goodere of Polesworth; collaborated in dramas with Thomas Dekker and John Webster; possibly employed by Elizabeth I on diplomatic mission to Scotland; friend of Shakespeare; historical poems, sonnets and satires.

Dudley   Ambrose (c. 1528–90): 3rd son of John Dudley, Duke of Northumberland; 1549: knighted; 1553–4: supported Queen Jane his sister-in-law, but pardoned by Mary; 1560: Master of the Ordnance; 1561: succeeded John Dudley as Earl of Warwick; 1562–3: involved militarily in helping protestants of Havre; 1573: Privy Councillor; 1586: judge at trial of Mary Queen of Scots.

Dudley (Robsart), Amy(e) (1532–60): Married Robert Dudley, later Earl of Leicester, 1550; found dead at foot of staircase at Cumnor Hall, Oxfordshire. Probably breast cancer or a suicide but reputed to have been murder at command of Dudley.

Dudley Edmund (?1462–1510): Lawyer by training. 1504: Speaker of House of Commons; 1506: President of the Council. Unpopular minister, working with Richard Empson to bind nobility, through bonds and recognisances, to obedience. Resentment spilled over on Henry VII's death; the two were impeached and accused of treason on Henry VIII's accession. Executed 17 August 1510. Author, in prison, of *The Tree of the Commonwealth*. Father of John Dudley, Duke of Northumberland and grandfather of Robert Dudley, Earl of Leicester. D.M. Brodie, Edmund Dudley: minister of Henry VII', *TRHS*, 4th series, 15, 1932.

Dudley (Lord) Guil(d)ford (d.1554): 4th son of John Dudley, Duke of Northumberland; 1553: m. Lady Jane Grey, daughter of Henry Grey, Duke of Suffolk; 1554: beheaded.

Dudley (Lady) Jane (*See* GREY, Jane)

Dudley (Duke of Northumberland), John (1502–53): 1523: knighted in France; 1538: Deputy-Governor of Calais; 1542: Warden of Scottish marches; Viscount Lisle; 1542–7: Great Admiral; 1543: Knight of Garter and Privy Councillor; 1544–6: led assault on Boulogne and became Governor; 1547: joint Regent; 1547: Earl of Warwick and High Chamberlain of England; 1547: defeated Scots at Pinkie; 1549: put down Kett's rebellion at Dussindale; 1551: Earl Marshal and Duke of Northumberland; 1552: had Somerset executed; 1553: as part of agitation to place son on throne, secured letters patent from Edward VI for the 'limitation of the crown' to alter the succession and m. Guildford to Lady Jane Grey; 1553: executed for actively resisting accession of Mary Tudor; declared allegiance to Roman Church on the scaffold. Barrett L. Beer, 'The rise of John Dudley, Duke of Northumberland', *History Today*, 15, April 1965.

Dudley (Lord Lisle and Earl of Warwick), John (d.1554): Son of John Dudley, Duke of Northumberland; 1552: Master of King's Horse; 1553: supported Lady Jane Grey's claim; 1554: condemned to death but pardoned.

Dudley (Lady) Lettice (née Knollys, then Devereux) (c.1541–1634): Eldest daughter of Sir Francis Knollys. Married twice: Firstly to Walter Devereux, 1st Earl of Essex; secondly to Robert Dudley, Earl of Leicester (1578). Mother of Robert Devereux, 2nd Earl of Essex (1566–1601).

Dudley (Earl of Leicester), Robert (1532–88): 5th s. of John Dudley, Duke of Northumberland. 1550: m. Amy[e] Robsart; 1573: secret m. to Lady Sheffield; 1578: m. Lettice Knollys; 1553: M.P. Norfolk; 1553:

proclaimed his sister-in-law, Lady Jane Grey, Queen; 1554: pardoned by Queen Mary; 1559: Knight of the Garter and Privy Councillor; 1560–3: attempted, with Queen's consent, to negotiate m. with Elizabeth I; 1563: annoyed Queen and opposed by Cecil; 1569: abetted Northern Earls' rebellion; 1575: entertained Queen at Kenilworth; 1577: participated in Drake's expedition; 1581: admitted to Queen's charge of being in league with Prince of Orange; 1585: commanded expedition to assist United Provinces v. Spain; 1586: Governor of United Provinces; 1587: recalled and d. in 1588. Commonly reputed to have been poisoned. Described by Professor G.R. Elton as 'a handsome vigorous man with very little sense', Leicester made the most of his position as the Queen's favourite from the beginning of the reign. The quarrel between the Earl and William Cecil expressed itself in the Queen's Privy Council between 1568 and 1585 as 'a contest between a moderate peace policy and a Protestant war policy.' His support in the council was extremely important for the reformed Protestant cause; he was always opposed to a French marriage and determinedly, if disastrously, waged a campaign against Spain in the Netherlands. But Leicester seems to have fallen in Elizabeth's personal esteem by the late 1570s and she generally preferred Cecil's policies to his.

Duwes Giles (fl. 1490s–1509): French tutor to the children of Henry VII.

Edward IV (King) (1442–83): House of York. His eldest daughter, Elizabeth, m. Henry Tudor.

Edward V (King) (1470–83): House of York. Son of Edward IV and Queen Elizabeth Woodville. 1471: created Prince of Wales and entrusted to council of control including uncles Clarence and Gloucester; 1483: succeeded to Crown and escorted to London by Richard of Gloucester; imprisoned in Tower with Richard, Duke of York, his younger brother; deposed; supposedly murdered in the Tower by James Tyrrell.

Edward VI (King) (1537–53): Tudor. Son of Henry VIII and Queen Jane Seymour. Classical education at hands of Richard Cox, Sir John Cheke, Sir Anthony Co(o)ke and Roger Ascham; 1547: crowned King and espoused Protestant cause. Manipulated by first Edward Seymour, Duke of Somerset (maternal uncle and Protector) and second John Dudley, Duke of Northumberland; 1553: willed succession to Jane Grey (Dudley) daughter-in-law to Northumberland. W.K Jordan, *Edward VI*, 2 vols, 1970.

Egerton (Baron Ellesmere and Lord Chancellor), Thomas (1540–1617): 1592: Attorney-General; 1594–1603: Master of the Rolls; 1596 and 1603: Lord Keeper; 1597: knighted; employed by Elizabeth I on diplomatic missions; 1603–17: Lord Chancellor.

Elizabeth I (Queen) (1533–1603): Tudor. 2nd daughter of Henry VIII and daughter of Queen Anne Boleyn. 1536: parliament declares her illegitimate to secure succession for heirs of H. and Jane Seymour; 1547–9: Sir Thomas Seymour, Lord High Admiral and uncle to Edward VI, pursues her hand in m.; 1549: classical education by Roger Ascham; 1553: accompanies Queen Mary, half-sister, on triumphal route to London; refuses complicity in Wyatt's rebellion; 1554: thrown into Tower due to Stephen Gardiner's influence; 1554: released to Woodstock Palace, Oxon., and declines to conspire v. Mary; 17 November 1558: succeeded to throne; 1559: crowned by Bishop of Carlisle, declined m. with Philip II, her sister's widower; henceforth seen by Protestants as the divinely destined leader of a Protestant nation in God's plan for religious reformation; it seems that she played this part when it suited her but not ardently enough for many of her chief advisers. Need to see beyond Protestant propaganda of the reign to the real Elizabeth. Important developments: m. negotiations; church organisation: battle between radical Protestants and the 'establishment'; Spanish threat; problem of Ireland; issue of Mary Queen of Scots; conspiracies. Elizabeth d. at Richmond, 24 March 1603 – on deathbed declared succession in favour of James VI of Scotland, son of Mary Stuart. Wallace T. MacCaffrey, *Elizabeth I*, 1993.

Elizabeth of York (Queen) (1465–1503): Eldest daughter of Edward IV and Elizabeth Woodville; 1486: m. Henry Tudor (negotiations had begun while he was in exile and she is reputed to have won over Earl Stanley to his cause); 1487: coronation after suppression of Lincoln's rebellion; 1487: received her mother's forfeited lands in Duchy of Lancaster; d. 1503 after d. of Arthur, her elder son. Nancy L. Harvey, *Elizabeth of York, the Mother of Henry VIII*, New York, 1973.

Elyot (Sir) Thomas (c. 1490–1546): Author, translator, humanist and diplomat. He was the son of Sir Richard Elyot, a judge of assize on the western circuit; 1511–28: clerk of assize on western circuit; 1522: JP for Oxfordshire; 1523–30: Clerk of Privy Council; 1530: knighted; 1531: published *Boke Called the Governour*, 1531: appointed ambassador to Charles VI to obtain agreement to divorce from Catherine of Aragon; close friend of Thomas More; 1536: denies to Cromwell that he is a Catholic; 1538: published Latin-English dictionary; 1542: MP for Cambridge.

Empson (Sir) Richard (c.1450–1510): Lawyer and MP who rose to prominence late in Henry VII's reign, in association with Edmund Dudley, as royal debt collector. Arrested on Henry VII's death; trumped – treason charges resulted in his execution on 17 August 1510. Victim of Henry VIII's early attempts to court popularity.

Erasmus Desiderius (?1469–1536): Born in Rotterdam; educated by Brethren of Common Life, Deventer; 1487: Augustine monastery at Gouda; 1492: ordained as priest; studied and taught at Univ. of Paris.;

taught at Oxford (1499); 1509–14: Professor of Divinity and Greek at Univ. of Cambridge; spent last days at Basle. Began career as humanist interested in accurate recovery of classical texts and taught Latin for a living early; works such as *Adages* (1500) were student texts. On his visit to England in 1499 he was much influenced by John Colet's work on the Epistles of St Paul and henceforth turned his classical training to the transl. and interpretation of the Bible and discovery of the philosophy of Christ. Known for his close friendship with Sir Thomas More, at whose house he wrote *The Praise of Folly*. Extremely influential figure in history of education in England.

Erdeswicke Sampson (d. 1603): Historian of Staffordshire. 1553–4: student at Brasenose College, Oxford; 1593–1605: *View or Survey of Staffordshire*; friend of Sir Richard Bagot of Blithfield.

Essex (1st Earl of) (*See* CROMWELL, Thomas).

Essex (Countess of), Lettice (*See* DUDLEY, Lettice).

Essex (1st Devereux Earl of) (*See* DEVEREUX, Walter).

Essex (2nd Devereux Earl of) (*See* DEVEREUX, Robert).

Feckenham (Abbot John de (?1518–84): 1539: monk of Evesham; 1540: on dissolution of Evesham became Chaplain of Bishop Bonner; imprisoned under Edward VI; Marian Dean of St Paul's; 1556: last Abbot of Westminster, charged with restoration of convent; refused Oath of Supremacy under Elizabeth and imprisoned in various places until he d. in Wisbeach Castle, 1584.

Fenner George (d. 1618): Naval commander who accompanied Drake in the Indies voyage of 1585, against the Armada in 1588 and in the Corunna expedition of 1589. He d. of the wounds he received in this last venture.

Fenton Edward (d. 1603): A soldier and sailor who did good service suppressing Shane O'Neill's Irish rebellion in 1566. He is remembered, however, for his command of the disastrous expedition organised by the Earl of Leicester in 1582–3 to develop trade with China. A chaplain, Richard Madox, kept an interesting diary of the voyage. In 1588 Fenton commanded the 600 ton *Mary Rose* against the Armada

Ferrar (Bishop) Robert (?1504–55): Yorkshire origins. 1547: Chaplain to Protector Somerset; 1548: Bishop of St David's; 1554: deprived for being a married priest; 1555: declared heretic and burned 30 March 1555 at Carmarthen.

Field John (?1545–1588): A graduate preacher who sought a more thoroughgoing reformation of the Church of England from within, employing the Presbyterian system of church government. In the 1570s and 80s he and Thomas Wilcox were convenors of the London conference of ministers which was deliberately modelled on the *classis* of the reformed churches. They co-authored the *Admonition to Parliament* (1572). See Section V. He was very much involved in attempts to set up a Presbyterian church government in the 1580s and in the drafts of the English book of discipline presented to parliament in 1584. Important as an editor and promoter of Puritan publication and as the compiler of the 'Register' of documents pertaining to the oppression of ministers by the bishops and their officers, which is the historian's main source for the Puritan movement in the Church of England. Field had once been John Foxe's research assistant and his 'Register' was closely modelled upon Foxe's work. Patrick Collinson, 'John Field and Elizabethan Puritanism' in S.T. Bindoff *et al* (eds), *Elizabethan Government and Society: essays presented to Sir John Neale*, 1961.

Fisher (Bishop) John (1469–1535): In 1500 or 1501 became Chaplain and adviser to Lady Margaret Beaufort, mother of Henry VII. Conscientious preaching bp. Benefactor of Univ. of Cambridge on his own account and through Lady Margaret. He wanted Christ's College and St John's College, her new foundations, to become the training ground for priests and to offer a humanist and scriptural education that would improve the standards of the English clergy. He was a staunch opponent of Lutheranism but also of attempts to tax the clergy and to assert the royal supremacy. His support for Catherine of Aragon in the matter of divorce enraged Henry. On 30 April 1534 Fisher refused the Oath of Supremacy. He and Thomas More imprisoned in Tower. Executed 22 June 1535 for treason.

Fitch Ralph (c.1550–1611): A Londoner who joined John Newbury's third expedition to Cathay by way of Hormuz and India (1583); in Sept. 1584 Fitch went independently down the Ganges. Eventually he became the first Englishman to visit Burma. His travels were extensive and he did arrive at Hormuz eventually. When he returned home on 29 April 1591 he found that his family had presumed him dead and divided up his estate. He attempted to write up his travel diaries and Hakluyt used his account in the second edition of *Principal Navigations*. 1592: member of Company of Merchants of the Levant; 1596: trading in Aleppo; 1596: consul at Aleppo; 1597: consulate cancelled; returned to London.

Fitton Mary (1578–1640): Younger daughter of Sir Edward and Lady Alice Fitton. Mary was sent to court as maid of honour to Queen Elizabeth, under the chaperonage of Sir William Knollys, son of Francis Knollys, 1595. She was disgraced when she was made pregnant by the Earl of Pembroke, 1601. She left court, bore a still-born son, and went to live with her sister Anne (Fitton) Newdegate. She was twice married. She has been identified with the 'Dark Lady' of Shakespeare's sonnets.

Fitzjames (Bishop) Richard (d. 1522): Educated Merton College, Oxford; Chaplain to King Edward IV; 1483–1507: Warden of Merton

College, Oxford; 1497: Bishop of Rochester; 1499: one of the negotiators of the great intercourse; 1503: Bishop of Chichester; 1506: Bishop of London; built Fulham Palace. *See*. Richard Hunne.

Fitzroy (Duke of Richmond), Henry (1519–36): Illegitimate son of Henry VIII by mistress, Elizabeth Blount, lady-in-waiting to Catherine of Aragon. Humanist education. Favourite with King who called him 'my worldly jewel' and who with his creation of him as Duke of Richmond (1525) and Lord High Admiral, signalled that he might settle the succession on Fitzroy. 1533: Fitzroy m. Mary Howard, daughter of 3rd Duke of Norfolk and sister of Earl of Surrey, the poet. 22 July 1536: Fitzroy d. amid rumours that he had been poisoned by Anne Boleyn and her brother, Lord Rochford.

Fore(s)t John (d. 1540): Martyr, burnt for heresy in Edinburgh.

Fox (Bishop) Richard (c. 1447–1528): Accompanied Henry VII in invasion of England and on his accession made Secretary of State, Keeper of Privy Seal and Bishop of Exeter. 1491: Bishop of Bath and Wells; 1494: Bishop of Durham; 1501: Bishop of Winchester. Ecclesiastical statesman who left episcopal duties to a suffragan until retirement from Privy Seal in 1516. Rise of Wolsey (1513) spelt end to his influence at court. Humanist. Founder of Corpus Christi College, Oxford.

Foxe John (1517–87): Martyrologist. 1547: tutor to household of William Lucy, Charlecote, Warwickshire; 1548: tutor in household of Mary, Duchess of Richmond, widow of Henry Fitzroy, in whose care were the future Duke of Norfolk and Howard of Effingham. 1554: Marian exile; 1554: *Commentarii rerum in ecclesia gestarum* (A Commentary on the History of the church, and a description of the great persecutions ...) published in Strasbourg in Latin; 1555: Basle; 1559: Latin martyrology sponsored by Grindal – Foxe influenced by John Bale; 1563: enlarged and revised English version of his *Acts and Monuments of these last and perillous days*, commonly referred to as *Foxe's Book of Martyrs*. This was a call to action for the new Queen, Elizabeth, to realise God's plan for the English nation. Went into many editions, including the famous 1570 edition with woodcut illustrations. R. O'Day, *Debate on the English Reformation*, 1986.

Frith John (1503–33): Martyr. Educated at Eton and Cambridge; 1525: junior canon at Wolsey's College, Oxford; imprisoned for assisting in Tyndale's translation of New Testament; 1520: released and travelled to Marburg for six-year exile; 1531: penned *Disputacion of Purgatorye* v. More and Fisher; 1532: imprisoned in Tower for heresy; burnt at Smithfield for heresy v. purgatory and transubstantiation. Works published by John Foxe in 1573.

Frobisher (Sir) Martin (?1535–94): Prominent navigator who made his first expedition (to Guinea) in 1554 and later explored Greenland.

1588: commanded *Triumph* against Spanish Armada and was knighted; 1590: Vice-Admiral in Hawkins' expedition; 1594: d. of wound received while trying to relieve Brest.

Gardiner (Bishop) Stephen (?1497–1555): Bishop of Winchester and Lord Chancellor. 1529: King's Secretary; 1529–47: royal diplomat especially in matter of divorce; 1531: Bishop of Winchester; 10 Feb. 1535: signed declaration repudiating Pope's jurisdiction in England and in 1535 published *De Vera Obedientia*, important defence of royal supremacy; Erastian; 1539: Act of Six Articles against the Protestants was largely his work; 1540: Chancellor of Cambridge Univ.; attack on Cranmer backfired; 1547 not included in Council of Regency; imprisoned during Edward's reign; 1553: restored to bpric and made Lord Chancellor.

Gerard (Father) John (1564–1637): 1588: Jesuit missionary priest; 1594: captured and imprisoned in Tower; 1597: escaped; 1597–1606: secret mission; 1606: went abroad and spent last ten years of his life as Confessor to the English College at Rome. His autobiography is an important source. John Gerard, ed. and translated by Philip Caraman, *The Hunted Priest*, 1951.

Gilbert (Sir) Humphrey (?1539–83): Stepbrother of Walter Raleigh, educated at Eton and Oxford; 1569: served under Sir Henry Sidney in Ireland; 1570: knighted for services while in charge of Munster; 1571: M.P. Plymouth; 1578–9: attempted plantation but failed; 1583: founded first British Colony in North America at St John's, Newfoundland; lost in Southern Azores, 1583. Renowned also for his scheme for an academy for the education of royal wards. Michael Foss, *Tudor Portraits*, 1973.

Gonson (Sir) Benjamin (fl. 1550s and 1560s): 1559: Treasurer of the Navy. Daughter m. John Hawkins and Benjamin formed part of the syndicate for Hawkins' first slave-trading venture.

Goudge William (1578–1653): Educated at St Paul's, Eton and King's College, Cambridge; 1621–53: Rector of St Anne's, Blackfriars; 1622: published *Of Domesticall Duties, Eight Treatises*, an important Puritan handbook for household relations.

Greenwood John (d.1593): Educated at Cambridge. 1592: imprisoned with Henry Barrow for holding a conventicle; assisted with forming private congregation in Nicholas Lane; hanged at Tyburn with Barrow.

Greene Robert (?1560–92): Cambridge-educated professional poet and pamphleteer who lived a dissolute life and wrote about the seamier side of London society. See under 'Authors of the Tudor Period' in Section V, above. Michael Foss, *Tudor Portraits*, 1973.

Grenville (Viscountess Lisle), Honor (fl.1530s): Married first Sir John Basset; then Arthur, Viscount Lisle, illegitimate son of Edward IV. Educated her daughters Anne and Catherine Basset in French and English, in order to win them preferment; 1537: succeeded in placing one child in Queen Jane Seymour's household. R.M. Warnicke, *Women of the English Renaissance and Reformation*, 1983. *See also* Basset, Mary, above.

Grenville (Sir), Richard (?1541–91): 1559: Inner Temple; 1571, 1584: M.P. Cornwall; 1577: Sheriff, Cornwall; 1585: commanded fleet to colonise Virginia for his cousin Walter Raleigh and on return captured Spanish ship; 1586: piracy in the Azores; 1586–8: reorganised western defences; 1591: second in command of Azores Fleet; mortally wounded on *Revenge* after continuous fighting against 15 Spanish ships.

Gresham (Sir) Thomas (1519–79): Second son of Sir Richard Gresham lord mayor of London (1537) and banker to King and nobility. 1552: with Northumberland's patronage, appointed King's merchant in Antwerp; 1554: raised Spanish loan; 1558: P.C.; he was a close friend of William Cecil and recommended purification of the coinage; 1559-61: ambassador to Regent of Netherlands and served Cecil's intelligence service well; 1565: founded first English paper mills at Osterley; 1566–8: built Royal Exchange at his own expense on a site provided by the City; 1567: returned to London; 1569: raised loans from English merchants; 1570: Queen opens Royal Exchange; 1574: ceased to be royal agent; 1575: founded Gresham College. Michael Foss, *Tudor Portraits*, 1973.

Grey (Countess of Hertford), Catherine (later Seymour) (?1538–68): Daughter of Henry Grey, Duke of Suffolk, and Frances (Brandon) Grey; claim to throne through her grandmother who was Mary, daughter of Henry VII; sister of Lady Jane Grey (Dudley) and Mary Grey; 1553: m. Henry Herbert, later 2nd Earl of Pembroke; 1554: divorced Henry Herbert after her sister Jane's execution; 1554-9: maid of honour to Queen Mary; 1559–61: maid of honour to Queen Elizabeth; 1560: m. Edward Seymour, Earl of Hertford and son of the Protector Somerset, without Queen's knowledge or approval; 1561: bore Hertford a son and was imprisoned in Tower for offence against the act of 1536 which forbade those of royal blood to marry without royal assent; 1562: her marriage declared invalid by commission; 1563: bore second son to Seymour, conceived during imprisonment; 1568: d. as prisoner at Cockfield Hall.

Grey (Duchess of Suffolk), Frances (née Brandon) (1517–59): Elder daughter of Charles Brandon, Duke of Suffolk and Mary Tudor, Queen of France and Duchess of Suffolk; wife of Henry Grey and mother of Ladies Jane, Catherine and Mary Grey; until her death in 1559 treated by some as rightful heir to throne through Edward VI's willing of the succession to her and her line.

Grey (Duke of Suffolk), Henry (d. 1554): 1530: succeeded 3rd Marquis of Dorset; 1547: K.G.; 1549: Privy Councillor; 1551: created Duke of Suffolk when the male line gave out (his wife Frances was daughter of

Charles Brandon, Duke of Suffolk, and Mary, dau. of Henry VII); 1553: gave up claim to throne of his dau. Lady Jane and received Mary's pardon; 1554: joined rising v. Mary's m. to Philip of Spain; executed for treason.

Grey (Lady) Jane (1537–54): Daughter of Henry Grey, Duke of Suffolk, and Frances Brandon, elder daughter of Henry VIII's sister Mary, and, under Henry VIII's will, heir to the throne after Henry VIII's own children; 1546: placed in household of Catherine Parr; humanist classical education; 1548: Jane put into household of Edward Seymour who projected her m. to Edward VI; 1551: Jane's father made Duke of Suffolk for part in overthrow of the Seymours; 1553: m. Sir Guilford Dudley as part of Northumberland's plot to disinherit Mary in favour of Dudley family; 1553: reluctantly agreed to be proclaimed Queen; reign of c.9 days; abdicated; not executed until after Wyatt's rebellion in 1554. Alison Plowden, *Lady Jane Grey and the House of Suffolk*, 1985.

Grey Mary (later Keys) (?1540–78): daughter of Henry Grey, Duke of Suffolk and Frances (Brandon) Grey; claim to Crown through her grandmother, Mary daughter of Henry VII; sister of Lady Jane and Lady Catherine; 1565: secret m. to Thomas Keys, serjeant-porter to Elizabeth I; Keys imprisoned; 1565: placed in private custody with her stepmother Catherine Bertie, dowager Duchess of Suffolk, because she had offended against 1536 legislation which made it a treasonable offence for those of royal blood to marry without sovereign's assent; 1573: released.

Grindal (Archbishop) Edmund (?1519–83): Educated at Cambridge; Chaplain to Nicholas Ridley and to Edward VI; spent Mary's reign in exile in Strasbourg and Germany and organised work of John Foxe's martyrology; 1558: Bishop of London and commissioner for revision of liturgy; served on High Commission 1570: archbishop of York; 1576: Archbishop of Canterbury; undertook reform of Courts Christian; 1577: refused to carry out Elizabeth's order to suppress 'prophesyings'; 1577–82: suspended. Patrick Collinson, *Archbishop Grindal, 1519–1583*, Cape, 1979.

Grindal William (d.1548): Cambridge-educated tutor to Princess Elizabeth in 1544. He had been a favourite pupil of Roger Ascham.

Grocyn William (1446–1519): Famous Greek scholar and friend of Erasmus, Colet and Linacre. In 1493 gave daily Greek lectures in public in Oxford.

Grymeston Elizabeth (references between 1563 and 1603/4): A Norfolk recusant who married Christopher Grymeston. She published a counselling tract, partly in verse, for her son, *Miscellanea. Meditations. Memoratives*, in 1604. It went into several editions.

Hakluyt Richard (1552–1616): Notable cosmographer and travel writer. Educated at Westminster School and Oxford. Ordained priest and held several preferments. 1589: *The Principal Navigations*. 1599: revised and much expanded second edition detailed history of English navigation on the basis of considerable research.

Hales John (d.1571): Author and linguist without university education. 1538: groom of the King's bedchamber; 1547: J.P. Warwickshire and Middlesex; M.P. for Preston, Lancashire; 1548: Commissioner for Enquiry into Enclosures in Midlands; Somerset's right-hand man in campaign v. enclosures; attempted but failed to put 3 bills through parl. to achieve a rebuilding and a restoration of agriculture; noted for involvement with the controversial clause of the 1548 Subsidy Act to place tax on sheep and cloth. Fell out of favour with fall of Somerset. 1551: went to Germany; 1558: returned to England; 1564: imprisoned for supporting claim of Suffolk family (and Catherine Grey) to succession; Burghley secured release. Died on 28 December 1571. *See* Smith, Thomas below.

Hardwick (Bess of), Elizabeth (c.1522–7–1608): Daughter of John and Elizabeth Hardwick of Hardwick Hall, Derbs. 1542–4: m. to Robert Barley or Barlow; 1547–57: m. to William Cavendish. 6 children; 1559–64/5: m. to William St Looe; 1567–90: m. to George Talbot, sixth Earl of Shrewsbury. Devoted life to furthering interests of her Cavendish brood. Eldest son William became first Earl of Devon. 1561–2: imprisoned in Tower for involvement in m. of Catherine Grey to Edward Seymour; 1569–85: gaoler of Mary Stuart; 1578–1603: Bess spent her time trying to secure succession for her granddaughter, Arabella Stuart, daughter of the marriage (1574) between Elizabeth Cavendish and Charles Stuart, Earl of Lennox, claimant to throne; 1590–7: as dowager Countess of Shrewsbury used her own money to build Hardwick Hall, an imposing eclectic building, with state rooms probably designed with Arabella Stuart in mind. Bess was also a considerable landowner, owning glass and iron works, coal mines, quarries and forests. Open University, *Culture and Belief in Europe, 1450–1600*, Block 8, 1989.

Harington (Sir) John (1561–1612): Courtier, author and wit who invented the water closet. He was the son of that John Harington who had been imprisoned in the Tower with Elizabeth in 1554. He was Elizabeth's godson and a favourite. Educated Eton, Cambridge and Lincoln's Inn. 1596: banished from court for writing *Metamorphosis of Ajax* (with its veiled allusions to Earl of Leicester and description of the water-closet) and other satires; 1598: accompanied Essex to Ireland; 1599: was knighted by Essex and attempted to intercede for him but was dismissed from Queen's presence. Wrote description of Queen's last days.

Hastings (3rd Earl of Huntingdon), Henry (1535–95): Puritan earl. 1553: m. Catherine Dudley, daughter of Duke of Northumberland; 1560; Earl of Huntingdon; heir presumptive to Crown through his mother; 1569–70: gaoler of Mary Queen of Scots; 1570: K.G.; 1572: Lord Lieut.

of Leics and Rutl., President of Council in the North; 1588: active role v. Armada; important educational benefactor, especially to Emmanuel College, Cambridge. M. Claire Cross, *The Puritan Earl*, 1966.

Hatton (Sir) Christopher (1540–92): Courtier and Lord Chancellor. Educated at Oxford and Lincoln's Inn with Catholic upbringing and sympathies. Instrumental in bringing Mary Stuart to her trial and execution. After this he pursued a virulently anti-Catholic and anti-papal policy in sharp contrast to his earlier stance. A great favourite of the Queen. 1587: Lord Chancellor. Co-operated with Whitgift to suppress Puritans. Died deeply in debt – partly due to extravagant building programme at Holdenby, Northamptonshire (Holmby House).

Hawkins (Sir) John (1532–95): Navigator, early slave-trader (1561–2), reforming Treasurer and Comptroller of navy and naval commander against the Armada. Died at sea during Drake's expedition to West Indies. J.A. Williamson, *Sir John Hawkins, the times and the man*, Oxford, 1927 and Williamson, *Hawkins of Plymouth*, 1949.

Hawkins (Sir) Richard (?1562–1622): Son of John. 1585–6: Captain of the *Duck* in Drake's West Indies expedition; commanded *Swallow* in fight against Armada; 1593: roving commission against Spaniards resulted in his imprisonment in Seville and Madrid from 1597–1602.

Hawkins William (d. 1589): Brother of John. Partner of John in ownership of privateers. 1582: commanded West Indian expedition; 1588: fitted out ships in battle against Armada.

Henry VII (King) (1457–1509): Tudor. Son of Edmund Tudor, Earl of Richmond, and Margaret Beaufort, heir to John of Gaunt. Raised by uncle Jasper Tudor in Wales; 1471: head of House of Lancaster; refugee in Brittany; 1485: defeated and killed Richard III at Bosworth; 1486: m. Elizabeth, daughter of Edward IV, See Chronologies for further details of reign. S.B. Chrimes, *King Henry VII*, 1977.

Henry VIII (King) (1491–1547): Tudor. 2nd son of Henry VII and Elizabeth of York. See Chronologies for milestones in reign. J.J. Scarisbrick, *Henry VIII*, 1968.

Herbert (Lady) Anne (fl.1530s): Sister of Catherine Parr prized for her piety and learning.

Heron John (fl.1492–1521): One of Henry VII's principal councillors; 1492: rose from position as deputy accountant in King's Chamber to that of Treasurer of the Chamber; 1492–1521: Treasurer of the Chamber; close access to the King.

Hertford (Earl of) (*See* SEYMOUR, Edward).

Heywood John (?1497–1580): Favourite wit at court of Mary I; ballad and play writer; exiled to Malines under Elizabeth.

Heywood Thomas (d.1641): Prolific late Elizabeth and early Stuart dramatist and actor. A convinced and vociferous Protestant.

Hicks (Sir) Michael (1543–1612): Educated at Trinity College, Cambridge and Lincoln's Inn. Secretary to Sir William Cecil and Sir Robert Cecil. Brother of Baptist Hicks, 1st Viscount Camden.

Hickman Rose (fl.1550s): Daughter of Sir William Locke, evangelical mercer, and sister of Michael Lok and Henry Locke, husband of Anne Locke.

Hilliard Nicholas (1537–1619): Goldsmith, carver and limner to Elizabeth I. Engraved Great Seal, 1586. First English miniaturist. Notable miniatures of himself, Mary Queen of Scots and other worthy contemporaries.

Hoby Elizabeth (1528–1609): One of the 4 learned daughters of Sir Anthony Cooke. Twice married: first to Sir Thomas Hoby; second to Lord John Russell. 1605: translated *A Way of Reconciliation*, a treatise on transubstantiation, from French into English.

Hoby (Lady) Margaret (1571–1633): Diarist. Born Margaret Dakins; brought up in the household of the Puritan Earl of Huntingdon; married first Walter Devereux; then Thomas Sidney; then Sir Posthumous Hoby. Her Diary provides a good account of the day to day existence of a Protestant gentlewoman of means. D.M. Meads, *Diary of Lady Margaret Hoby, 1599–1605*, 1930.

Holbein Hans (1497–1543): Born in Augsburg. 1523 painted three portraits of Erasmus. 1526: came to England with introduction to Sir Thomas More. Portraits of More, Warham, More's household (design) etc. 1528–32: lived in Basle. Returned to England when many of his religious paintings in Basle were destroyed by iconoclasts. 1533: *The Ambassadors*. 1535: designed title page for Coverdale's Bible; 1536: portraits of Cranmer and Jane Seymour; 1538: portrait of Christina of Denmark for marriage negotiations; 1540: designs for *Dance of Death;* 1539: portrait of Anne of Cleves for marriage negotiations 1540: designed title page of Cranmer Bible; 1542: portaits of Sir John Russell, Norfolk and Surrey. Died of plague in London.

Holgate (Archbishop): Robert (?1481–1556): President of the North. 1534: Master of Gilbertines of Sempringham; 1536: Prior of Watton and Chaplain to Henry VIII; 1537: D.D. Cambridge; 1537: Bishop of Llandaff; collaborated on *Institutes of a Christian Man*; 1538–50: President of the Council in the North; 1545–54: Archbishop of York; deprived for m.; imprisoned but released when he submitted; important educational benefactions. A.G. Dickens, *Robert Holgate, Archbishop of York and President of the King's Council in the North*, York, 1955.

Holinshed Raphael (d. 1580?): Known to have come to London early in Elizabeth's reign and to have been employed as translator and chronicler by Reginald Wolfe. 1578: *Chronicles of England, Scotland and Ireland* published. 2nd version, 1587.

Hooker Richard (1554–1600): Oxford-educated author of *Laws of Ecclesiastical Polity*. The first four books were published on 13 March 1593 as part of concerted campaign against the Puritans exemplified by Conventicle Act (1593). Later books published in 1597 and after his death. Explained in moderate and reasoned way the doctrines of the Church of England, a far cry from the usual polemic. Michael Foss, *Tudor Portraits*, 1973.

Hooper (Bishop) John (d. 1555): 1539: went into exile in various places abroad as result of Act of Six Articles; 1549: returned to England as Chaplain to Protector Somerset, and later to Northumberland; a radical Protestant who sympathised with Zwingli rather than Luther on the Eucharist issue and strongly opposed use of vestments; 1550: refused to wear vestments on consecration as Bishop of Gloucester; imprisoned in Fleet; gave way and was consecrated, 1551; 1552: amalgamation of Sees of Gloucester and Worcester; pursued vigorous Protestant reformation in dioceses; deprived and imprisoned under Mary I; burned at stake in Gloucester, 9 February 1555.

Hooper Rachel (b.c.1547): Humanist. Daughter of Bishop John Hooper and Anne de Taerclas, a noted Latin scholar from the Netherlands. Humanist education in Latin, French, German and English. R.M. Warnicke, *Women of the English Renaissance and Reformation*, 1983.

Hopkins John (d. 1570) & Sternhold, Thomas (d. 1549): Published collection of versified psalms in 1547: went into 600 editions by mid 19th century.

Horsey (Dr) (fl. 1511–14): Bishop of London's Chancellor (*See* HUNNE, Richard).

Howard (Queen) Catherine (?1524–42): 5th wife of Henry VIII. Semi-literate daughter of Lord Edmund Howard, younger son of 2nd Duke of Norfolk. Set up by Bp Gardiner as Catholic rival to Anne of Cleves in 1539–40; m. Henry, 28 July 1540. 1541: Catherine rekindled relationship with Thomas Culpepper and Francis Dereham, her former lovers, while on royal progress to the North. 2 November 1541: Cranmer revealed all to Henry VIII. Catherine confessed eventually to adultery and was executed 13 February 1542. L.B. Smith, *A Tudor Tragedy: the life and times of Catherine Howard*, 1961.

Howard (Lord, of Effingham), Charles (1536–1624): 2nd Baron Howard of Effingham and 1st Earl of Nottingham. 1559: Ambassador to France; 1569: commanded horse v. Northern rebels; 1570: commanded squadron to watch Spanish fleet; 1573: created peer; 1583–5: Lord

Chamberlain; 1585–1615: Lord High Admiral; 1586: commissioner for trial of Mary Stuart; 1588: chief commander v. Armada; 1596: colleague of Essex on Cadiz expedition; 1601: commissioner at Essex's trial.

Howard (Earl of Surrey), Henry (?1517–47): Poet. son of Thomas, 3rd Duke of Norfolk, brother of Mary Howard, Countess of Richmond and Somerset and father of Thomas (4th Duke of Norfolk), Edward and Jane, Countess of Westmorland; educated by John Clerk; promoted as match for Princess Mary; 1532: m. Francis de Vere; 1536: Earl Marshal at trial of Queen Anne Boleyn, associated in suppression of Yorkshire Pilgrimage of Grace; 1541: K.G.; 1542: imprisoned for quarrelling; 1543: imprisoned for annoying London citizens; 1544–6: in service in France; 1547: executed on charges trumped up by Hertford. Noted for experimenting with blank verse and the so-called Shakesperian sonnet. R. Tottel's *Songes and Sonnettes*, 1557; Hester W. Chapman, *Two Tudor Portraits*, 1960.

Howard (Countess of Westmorland), Jane (Neville) (fl. 1550s–70s): Daughter of Earl of Surrey and Frances de Vere and granddaughter of Thomas, 3rd Duke of Norfolk. Humanist education as preparation for possible royal marriage with Edward VI; after Surrey's execution and Norfolk's imprisonment, she and her brothers and sisters were tutored by John Foxe in the London home of their aunt, Mary Howard, widow of Henry Fitzroy; m. Charles Neville, 6th Earl of Westmorland; 1569: implicated in rebellion of the Northern Earls but exonerated after public investigation. R.M. Warnicke, *Women of the English Renaissance and Reformation*, 1983.

Howard Mary (1519–57): Daughter of Thomas, 3rd Duke of Norfolk, and Elizabeth Stafford, daughter of 3rd Duke of Buckingham; possibly given humanist education by John Cheke alongside her brother Henry, Earl of Surrey, whom her father was grooming for m. with Princess Mary; early 1530s: joined Anne Boleyn's circle; November 1533: m. Henry Fitzroy, Duke of Richmond, illegitimate son of Henry VIII; marriage never consummated; she remained at court with Margaret Douglas and Mary Shelton as Anne's attendants; spent much effort trying to obtain adequate maintenance from Henry VIII after Fitzroy's death; her father's refusal to give her support in this turned her against both him and her brother, Surrey, so that she was willing to connive in Surrey's destruction in 1546; edited with Douglas and Shelton the *Devonshire Manuscript* of 184 poems; educated children of Earl of Surrey; patron of John Foxe and John Bale. R.M. Warnicke, *Women of the English Renaissance and Reformation*, 1983.

Howard (Lady) Mary (fl.1590s): Lady-in-waiting to Elizabeth I. Earned the ageing Queen's disapproval for insolently refusing to perform her duties and for flirting with Earl of Essex.

Howard (Earl of Surrey and 2nd Duke of Norfolk), Thomas (1443–

1524): Warrior. Son of John Howard, 1st Duke of Norfolk; 1471: fought for Edward IV at Barnet; 1478: knighted; 1483: created Earl of Surrey and K.G.; 1485: supported Richard III at Bosworth and imprisoned in Tower by Henry VII; released and estates returned to him; 1489: suppressed Northern rising; 1497: Lieutenant-general of the north, forced Scots to retreat; 1501–22: Lord Treasurer; 1510: Earl Marshal; 1513: as Lieutenant-General attained victory at Flodden; 1514: created Duke of Norfolk; 1517: put down apprentices on evil May Day; 1520: made guardian of the kingdom; 1521: presided at trial of his friend, the Duke of Buckingham. Was a consistent opponent of Wolsey. Melvin J. Tucker, *The Life of Thomas Howard, earl of Surrey and second Duke of Norfolk*, The Hague, 1964.

Howard (3rd Duke of Norfolk), (1473–1554): Warrior and opponent of Cromwell's faction. Eldest son of Thomas Howard, 2nd Duke of Norfolk; 1511; captured Andrew Barton; 1513: fought at Flodden; 1514: created Earl of Surrey; strongly opposed Wolsey (1514–24); Lord Lieutenant. of Ireland; 1521–2: led raids on French coast; 1522: as Warden General of the marches forced Scots under Albany to retreat; 1525: pacified Suffolk rebels; President of Council; turned Henry VIII v. Wolsey; 1533: Earl Marshal; 1536: sat by while niece, Anne Boleyn, was executed; suppressed Pilgrimage of Grace; 1539: led opposition to Cromwell and promoted the Six Articles; 1542: commanded army v. Scots; 1544: Lieutenant-General. of army in France; 1547–53: imprisoned and condemned to d. but saved by Henry VIII's d.; 1553: released on Mary's accession; 1554: led army v. Wyatt's rebellion.

Howard (4th Duke of Norfolk), Thomas (1536–72): Privy Councillor and conspirator. Son of Henry Howard, Earl of Surrey and grandson of Thomas, 3rd Duke of Norfolk. Brought up by Mary Howard Fitzroy and taught by John Foxe. 1553: K.B.; 1554: created Duke of Norfolk and Earl Marshal; 1559–60: Scotland; 1559: K.G.; 1562: P.C.; 1560s: endowed Magdalene College, Cambridge; 1565: public quarrel with Robert Dudley, Earl of Leicester in presence of Elizabeth; 1568: Commissioner to inquire into Scottish affairs; proposed m. with Mary of Scotland; 1569–70: imprisoned; involved in Ridolfi plot; 1572: executed for treason but denied Catholicism. Neville Williams, *Thomas Howard, Fourth Duke of Norfolk*, 1964.

Hunne Richard (d.1514): London Merchant Taylor. In 1511 Hunne refused to pay a mortuary on the death of his five-week-old child. The priest involved sued Hunne in the Consistory Court and won the case. Hunne, in retaliation, sued the priest, Thomas Dryffeld, in the Court of King's Bench under the statute of Praemunire, designed to limit the jurisdiction of the ecclesiastical courts. The church authorities then arrested Hunne and searched his house. They found prohibited books with handwritten commentary and Hunne made a qualified confession of heresy. When he would not withdraw his Praemunire Action he was sent to the Lollards' Tower at St Paul's. Two days later he was found hanged. A verdict of murder was then brought against Dr Horsey, the Bishop of London's Chancellor, but it seems more likely that the death was an accident, clumsily disguised to look like suicide. Hunne's body was later exhumed and burned for heresy on 20 December 1514. The case certainly whipped up anti-clerical feeling in London but its long term significance in the breach with Rome has been overstressed.

James III (1451–88) (King of Scotland, 1460–88): He was very unpopular in Scotland because of his blatant favouritism. In 1482 his own brother Albany joined the English army of invasion which retook Berwick. On this occasion his troops mutinied and brought the favourite, Robert Cochrane, to justice. In 1488 there was a fresh rebellion by the lowland nobility (especially the Earl of Angus) led by his eldest son (soon to be James IV) who defeated and killed him at Sauchieburn.

James IV (1473–1513) (King of Scotland, 1488–1513): He had led the army which defeated and murdered his father, James III (q.v.) Although he did penance for his father's death, James IV revoked grants made by James III and crushed the rebellion of Lennox, Lyle and Forbes in 1489; defended Eastern coast v. English piracy and improved the Scottish navy; 1495: received Perkin Warbeck and married him to Lady Katherine Gordon; 1496–7: helped Warbeck with border raids but treated with the Spanish and French who wished to end his alliance with Warbeck; 1502: signed seven-year truce with England which provided for his marriage to Princess Margaret Tudor, elder daughter of Henry VII of England; 1503: m. Margaret; important as a king who reformed Scottish legal system; against internal opposition, supported alliance with England until Henry VII's death; 1511: allied with Louis XII of France against the Holy League; 1512: signed treaty with France; 1512: sent Scottish fleet to assist Louis XII v. Henry VIII; invaded Northumberland; 1513: killed at Battle of Flodden Field.

James V (1512–42) (King of Scotland, 1513–42): Son of James IV and Margaret Tudor; educated by Gavin Dunbar, John Bellenden, David Lindsay and James Inglis; 1524: he was taken to Edinburgh by his mother and proclaimed fit to rule; 1525–1528: under control of the Earl of Angus; 1528: escaped and forced Angus to flee to England; in an alliance with clergy and commons crushed the nobility; conducted border raids until peace with England in 1534; 1537: m. Madeleine of France, daughter of Francis I; 1537: d. of Madeleine; executed Angus family conspirators; 1538: m. Mary of Guise; persecuted heretics and remained Catholic but forced church to accept reforms; 1540: forced Western Isles into submission; 1541: refused Henry VIII's request for conference; 1542: b. of daughter, Mary, later Queen of Scotland; seized lands of Crawfords, Douglasses etc.; 1542: d. just after hearing of rout at Solway. James V was also the father of at least two illegitimate children – Regent Moray and Francis 5th Earl of Bothwell.

James VI (1566–1625) (King of Scotland, 1567–1625) and King of England (1603–25): Only child of Mary of Scotland and Henry, Lord Darnley; 1567: crowned king on his mother's forced abdication; educated by George Buchanan; spent childhood and youth under the influence of various of the nobility: 1578–1582: Esmé Stuart, Earl of Lennox; 1582–1583: Protestant Nobles; 1583–1584: Earls of Argyll and Huntly; 1585–1586: Earl of Arran; 1586: concluded Treaty of Berwick with England; 1587: reconciled himself to his mother's execution in February because she had disinherited him in favour of Philip II; 1589: m. Anne of Denmark; 1596: annulled the bishops' jurisdiction; recalled Northern Earls from banishment; relations with the clergy strained during the 1590s; 1600: Gowrie conspiracy foiled; 1603: became King of England; 1604: made peace with Spain; 1604: called Hampton Court Conference to discuss liturgy; 1604: banished Catholic priests; 1605: Gunpowder Plot; 1606: harsh Recusancy Laws introduced; wished and worked for formal union of England and Scotland, etc.

Jewel (Bishop) John (1522–71): Educated at Oxford. 1555: Marian exile; 1559: Bishop of Salisbury; important defence of the Anglican Church, *Apologia Ecclesiae Anglicanae*, 1562, in which he accused Roman Church of innovation. A great preaching bp who died in harness, 23 September 1571.

Kent (*See* BARTON, Elizabeth and BOCHER, Joan).

Kett Robert (d. 1549): Tradesman and landowner of Wymondham, Norfolk. Led riot against enclosures at Norwich in early July 1549. 16,000 troops encamped on Mousehold Heath and used new Book of Common Prayer. Refused government pardon on 21 July 1549 and seized Norwich. Government troops countered and the Kett brothers, Robert and William, fled but were captured and executed. Unintentionally helped bring about fall of Protector Somerset. Michael Foss, *Tudor Portraits*, 1973.

Killgrew Catherine (fl. 1570s): One of the four learned daughters of Sir Anthony Cooke of Gidea Hall; knew Hebrew as well as Latin and Greek; she became Mrs Killigrew of Hendon and as such was a Puritan mentor of preachers such as Edward Dering. (*See* BACON, Ann; CECIL, Mildred; HOBY, Elizabeth)

Knollys Francis (?1514–96): (Pronounced Knowles.) Educated at Oxford; 1539: attended Anne of Cleves; 1542: M.P. Horsham; 1547: knighted; favourite of Edward VI and Elizabeth; 1553: exiled in Germany; 1558: Privy Councillor, Vicechamberlain of the household; 1559: M.P. Arundel; 1562, 1572, 1584, 1586, 1588, 1593: M.P. Oxfordshire; 1563: Governor, Portsmouth; 1568-9: custodian of Mary

Queen of Scots; 1572–96: Treasurer of Queen's household. Noted supporter of Puritans. Made Knight of the Garter, 1593. Father of William Knollys and Lettice Dudley.

Knox   John (?1512–72): Scottish Protestant reformer. Licensed preacher at Berwick and Newcastle during Edward VI's reign. 1552: Chaplain to Edward VI; refused See of Rochester; influenced King to add Black Rubric to 2nd Book of Common Prayer; 1554: exiled in Geneva; Knox-Cox controversy; published *The First Blast of the Trumpet Against the Monstrous Regiment of Women*, 1558, an attack on Mary Tudor. Major influence on Scottish Reformation.

Kynnersley   Lettice (née Bagot) (b. 1573, fl. 1630): Youngest daughter of Richard Bagot and Mary Dayrell; born at Blithfield, Staffs., 1573; m. Francis Kynnersley (d.1634); issue but names and dates unknown; of interest chiefly because of the light her letters to her brother Walter throw upon wider family relations in the late Tudor/early Stuart period. R. O'Day, *The Family and Family Relations in Early Modern England, France and America*, 1994.

Lambert   (alias Nicholson), John (d.1538): Martyr. Educated at Cambridge; Fellow of Queens' College, Cambridge, 1521; converted to Protestantism; ordained; when persecuted changed name to Lambert; Chaplain to English factors at Antwerp; 1532: impr. but released same year after Warham's death; 1538: burnt at stake for denying real presence.

Lancaster   (Sir) James (1554–1618): 1588: fought against Spanish Armada. 1591–94: first English expedition to East Indies. 1600: appointed Commander of first East India Company fleet. Knighted in 1603.

Lanyer   Aemilia (c.1570–1645): Possibly educated in household of Duchess of Kent. She married Alphonso Lanyer, a musician. Author of religious treatises in early seventeenth century.

Latimer   (Bishop of Worcester), Hugh (1485–1555): Martyr. Protestant preacher. Known for his biblically inspired sermons and his ringing exhortation at the stake in Oxford to his fellow martyr, Nicholas Ridley, 'Be of Good Comfort, Master Ridley, and play the man: we shall this day light such a candle by God's grace in England as, I trust, shall never be put out.' *See Sermon on the Ploughers* in Section V.

Lee   (Bishop) Rowland (d.1543?): Rewarded for services in the matter of the King's divorce from Catherine of Aragon and m. to Anne Boleyn by See of Coventry and Lichfield, to which he was consecrated on 10 January 1534. Enforced law and order in Wales as notable Lord President of the Council in the Marches of Wales; opposed policy of making Welsh J.P.s.

Leicester   (Earl of) (*See* DUDLEY, Robert).

Lever Thomas (1521–77): Important Protestant preacher during reign of Edward VI whose sermons, like those of Hugh Latimer, called for the recreation of society as a Godly commonwealth; Marian exile; returned as minister of St John's, Bablake, Coventry c.1559; 1560–77: Archd. of Coventry; uneasy relationship with Bishop Bentham because of Lever's desire for speedy further reformation. Important proposals for further reformation of the ministry.

Lily William (?1468–1522): Graduate of Oxford who studied classical languages and culture in Italy. 1512–22 High Master of St Paul's School, London. Contributed Latin *syntax* with English rules to Colet's *Aeditio* which was printed in 1527. Later St Paul's Grammar always known as *Lily's Latin Grammar. See* Section V.

Linacre Thomas (?1460–1524): Classical scholar and physician. Studied at Florence with children of Lorenzo the Magnificent. Intimate friend of Grocyn, Colet and Erasmus and of Aldus Manutius, the greatest contemporary Italian printer. It was he who taught Thomas More Greek and he was a noted Latin grammarian but his chief interest was in medicine. 1509: became Henry VIII's doctor and built up practice of prominent men, including Wolsey, Warham and Fox.

Lisle (Viscount) (*See* DUDLEY, John).

Locke Anne (née Vaughan) (b.c. 1532, fl.1590s): Representative perhaps of the women who played such an important part in the history of early English Protestantism. Described as 'soul-mate' of John Knox. Daughter of Stephen Vaughan, diplomat and Merchant Adventurer, and one of the silkwomen of Anne Boleyn and step-daughter of Margery Vaughan, previously Margery Brinklow, a staunch Protestant. Married: Henry Locke, Protestant Mercer with Antwerp interests and neighbour of her father in Cheapside (d.1571); Anne m. the Puritan preacher Edward Dering. Dering d. (1576); then c. 1582 m. Richard Prowse, Exeter draper and M.P. in 1584. 1556: John Knox sought to persuade her and her family into exile. 8 May 1557: Anne Locke went to Geneva with her two infant children. Translated some of Calvin's sermons. 1559: returned to husband in Cheapside. 1583: John Field dedicated edition of Knox's work on the temptations of Christ to Mrs Prowse. 1590: Anne Prowse published writings including translation of Jean Taffin's *Of the markes of the children of God* from the French. See Patrick Collinson, *Godly People*, 1983.

Lok Michael (fl. 1550–1615): Son of Sir William Locke, friend of Henry VIII, sometime Sheriff of London, and brother of Henry Locke, husband of Anne Locke, and Rose (Locke) Hickman. He was a traveller, friend of Martin Frobisher and adventurer in the Cathay and Levant Companies. 1577: Governor of Cathay Company; 1592–4: Consul for Levant Co. at Aleppo; 1613: translated part of Peter Martyr's *Historie of the West Indies*.

Lopez Roderigo (d.1594) 1586: Portuguese-Jewish Physician-in-Chief to Elizabeth I. Crypto-Jew. First House Surgeon at St Bartholemew's Hospital. Tried by Earl of Essex for complicity in Spanish plot to murder Don Antonio, pretender to the Portuguese Throne, and Elizabeth I. 7 June 1594: Lopez was hanged at Tyburn. He is thought to have been the model for Shakespeare's Shylock.

Lovell (Sir) Thomas (1453–1524): A chief advisor and prominent member of the council of Henry VII; joined the 1483 rebellion in favour of Henry; 1485: appointed Chancellor of the Exchequer; 1485: Treasurer of the Household; 1485: Speaker of the House of Commons.

Lumley (Lady) Jane, (Fitzalan) (c.1540–78): Eldest daughter of Earl of Arundel; humanist education; translated from the Greek; m. Lord Lumley, Cambridge classmate of her brother. Manuscripts survive in Arundel-Lumley collection. Gave home to Anne Dacre, Countess of Arundel. R.M. Warnicke, *Women of the English Renaissance and Reformation, 1983.*

Lyly John (?1554–1606): Oxford-educated professional dramatist who wrote light plays to be performed by children of the Chapel Royal and St Paul's and was selected by bishops to counter-attack Martin Mar-prelate. Best known for *Euphues, The Anatomy of Wit* (1579).

Marlowe Christopher (1564–93): Educated at Cambridge. In the early 1580s he acted as government spy on recusants overseas. Member of Sir Walter Raleigh's 'Little Academy' discussion group; accused of atheism before Privy Council. Works include: *Dido, Queen of Carthage; Tamburlaine the Great; The Jew of Malta; Edward II; Dr Faustus.* Died in tavern brawl under somewhat suspicious circumstances.

Mar-Prelate Martin (*See* PENRY, John).

Mary Stuart (Mary, Queen of Scots) (1542–87): 3rd but only surviving child of James V and Mary of Guise; Queen in 1542; 1548–61: raised in France as Catholic; 1558: m. Francis II; 1560: d. of Francis; 1561: returned to Scotland. For remainder of life see Chronologies.

Mary Tudor (Queen of France) (1496–1533): Younger daughter of Henry VII and Elizabeth of York. 1508–14: contracted to marry Charles of Castile (later Emperor Charles V); 1514: m. Louis XII of France; 1515: m. Charles Brandon, Duke of Suffolk, to H's annoyance; 1516: gave birth to son; 1520: visited Field of Cloth of Gold; 1532: refused to accompany H. and Anne Boleyn to meet Francis I; one of her daughters, Frances Brandon, was the mother of Lady Jane Grey. W.C. Richardson, *Mary Tudor, The White Queen,* 1970.

Mary I (Queen) (1516–58): Tudor. 3rd but only surviving child of Henry VIII and Catherine of Aragon; humanist classical education; 1525: made Princess of Wales at Ludlow; 1533: declared illegitimate and placed in care of Lady Shelton at Hatfield; 1536: reconciled to H. on Anne's death and in 1537 was chief mourner at Jane Seymour's funeral; 1544: declared capable of inheriting crown after H's legitimate heirs. For remaining events see Chronologies. David Loades, *Mary Tudor*, 1989.

Mayne Cuthbert (1544–77): 1576: Missionary priest in Cornwall; 1st seminary priest to be executed in England.

Mendoza Bernardino de (fl. 1580s): Spanish ambassador. Expelled after Throckmorton Plot for complicity.

Mildmay (Sir) Anthony (d.1617): S. of Sir Walter Mildmay. Educated at Cambridge and Gray's Inn in the 1570s; 1596: knighted; 1596–7: ambassador to Henry IV of France. m. Grace Mildmay in 1567.

Mildmay (Lady) Grace (c.1552–1620): Daughter and co-heiress of Sir Henry Sherrington. 1567: m. Anthony Mildmay, son of Sir Walter; wrote autobiography and works of devotion and medicine for manuscript circulation; had large-scale medical practice. L. Pollock, *Of Faith and Physic*, 1993.

Mildmay (Sir) Walter (?1520–89): Educated at Christ's College, Cambridge and Gray's Inn in 1540s; 1545: Surveyor-General of Court of Augmentations; 1547: knighted and made Revenue Commissioner; 1550: Auditor of Mint accounts; 1560: directed issue of new coinage; 1566: Chancellor of Exchequer and Auditor of Duchy of Lancaster; 1586: Commissioner at trial of Mary of Scotland; 1585: founded Puritan Emmanuel College, Cambridge; benefactor of Christ's Hospital, London, Christ's College, Cambridge etc. MP for various boroughs and counties, 1545–88. Father of Anthony Mildmay. Stanford E. Lehmberg, *Sir Walter Mildmay and Tudor Government*, Austin, 1964.

More (Sir) Thomas (1478–1535): Son of Sir John More, judge of the Common Pleas and King's Bench in the early 1520s. Educated London, household of Archbishop John Morton, Oxford, New and Lincoln's Inns in the 1490s; 1497: intimate of Grocyn, Colet and Erasmus; contemplated priesthood but gave this idea up in favour of public service and law; 1504: MP; 1509: Bencher of Lincoln's Inn; 1511 and 1516: Reader at Lincoln's Inn; 1510: Under Sheriff of London; 1515: envoy to Flanders on trading mission; 1516: completed Latin *Utopia* (see Section V); 1515: JP for Hants; 1518: came to Henry VIII's notice as opponent of Crown in Star Chamber; 1520: present at Field of Cloth of Gold; 1521: knighted; 1521: Under Treasurer of England; 1521: accompanied Wolsey to Calais and Bruges; 1523: Speaker of House of Commons; 1525: High Steward of Cambridge Univ; 1524–32: High Steward of Oxford Univ.; 1525: Chancellor of Duchy of Lancaster; 1527: part of Wolsey's entourage at Amiens; 1528: *Dialogue* (English attack on Tyndale); 1528: JP for Hants.; 1529: Lord Chancellor; 1532: resigned over his opposition to Henry's relaxation of heresy laws; 1533: in retirement engaged in religious controversy with Tyndale and Frith; 1534: refused to compromise on supremacy of Pope and validity of m. with Catherine of Aragon although swore oath to new succession; committed to Tower; 6 July 1535: executed for high treason; head exhibited on London Bridge. Important writer and patron of the arts as well as statesman. English works published in collected form in 1557. Collection of Latin works published 1563. Canonised by Roman church, 1935. Alistair Fox, *Thomas More. History and Providence*, 1982; J.A. Guy, *The Public Career of Sir Thomas More*, 1980.

Morgan   Thomas (1543–1606): 1569: secretary to Gilbert Talbot, Earl of Shrewsbury, to serve Mary of Scotland's interests; 1572: dismissed service for conspiracy; 1573: secretary to James Beaton, Mary's ambassador in Paris; 1583: imprisoned in Bastille after Elizabeth's intervention; 1586: helped organise Babington Plot using Gilbert Gifford as intermediary with Mary and advised Mary to send Babington letter of approval; released 1590 and travelled abroad.

Morgan   (Bishop) William (c.1541–1604): Cambridge-educated translator of Bible into Welsh. This independent translation was supported by Whitgift and published in 1588. 1595: Bishop of Llandaff; 1601: Bishop of St Asaph.

Morton   (Cardinal Archbishop) John (?1420–1500): Cardinal and Archbishop of Canterbury. Lancastrian during Wars of Roses but after Battle of Tewkesbury, 1571, allied himself with the Yorkist cause. Allied with Tudor cause after Edward IV's death. 1486: Henry VII made him Chancellor and Archbishop of Canterbury. 1493: Cardinal. Ecclesiastical reformer. Taxed nobility by means of 'benevolences' – unpopularity of 'Morton's fork'. Responsible for much important building on Archbp's estates.

Nashe   Thomas (1567–1601): University-educated professional writer whose rumbustious, rollicking style is famous. He was enlisted, along with John Lyly, to spearhead a pamphlet counter-attack to Martin Marprelate. *See* Lyly, John, Section V. *See also* Penry, John below.

Newdegate   Anne (née Fitton) (1574–1618): Elder daughter of Sir Edward and Lady Alice Fitton of Gawsworth, Cheshire. She m. Sir John Newdegate of Arbury, Warwickshire, 1587. For the first nine years of her married life she lived with her parents. Chiefly interesting because of her revealing correspondence with her parents and Sir William Knollys (who professed to her his love for her sister Mary Fitton).

Norfolk   (1st Duke of), (Sir) John Howard (?1430–1485):. For Thomas, Earl of Surrey and 2nd Duke of Norfolk (1443–1524), Thomas, (3rd Duke of Norfolk) (1473–1554), and Thomas (4th Duke of Norfolk) (1536–1572), *See* HOWARD. Further detail provided in Section XIII.

Norris (Norreys) (Sir) John (?1547–97): Military commander who was made Lord-President of Munster in 1584.

Northumberland (Duke of; Regent of England) (See DUDLEY, John).

Norton Thomas (1532–84): A lawyer and poet who as MP opposed the Catholics and in the early 1580s examined many recusants under torture.

Nowell (Dean), Alexander (c.1507–1602): Educated at Oxford; 1551: Headmaster of Westminster School and Prebendary of Abbey; noted as preacher under Edward VI; Marian exile; 1560: Dean of St Paul's; produced three catechisms, including the 'Large Catechism' (approved by Convocation in 1563 and published in 1572) and the short catechism included in the 1549 Prayer Book.

Paget Charles (d.1612): Catholic son of William, 1st Baron Paget of Beaudesert. Educated at Cambridge; 1572: secretary to James Beaton, Mary Stuart's ambassador to Paris; English spy; 1583: visited England but accused of conspiracy; 1584: English ambassador demands extradition; 1587: attainted; 1588: in service of King of Spain but acted as Cecil's agent; advocated James VI's claims and gave up Spanish employment in 1599. Pardoned by James I.

Paget (3rd Baron Paget), Thomas (d.1590): Educated at Cambridge; fled to continent after discovery of Throckmorton's Plot; received pension from Spain.

Paget (1st Baron Paget of Beaudesert), William (1505–63): Educated at St Paul's School and Cambridge. One of Henry VIII's principal Privy Councillors 1541–7; 1547: M.P. Staffs. K.G.; Somerset supporter who played large part in plot to set aside Henry VIII's will and proposed a protectorate in the Council; 1551: arrested for conspiracy v. Warwick's life; 1552: degraded from K.G.; 1553: member of Jane's P.C. but put name to proclamation of Mary I; P.C.; 1556: Lord Privy Seal; resigned offices in 1558.

Parker (Arcbishop) Matthew (1504–75): Educated at Cambridge; 1527: ordained priest; associated with the Cambridge reformers but moderate; 1535: Chaplain to Anne Boleyn; 1544: Master of Corpus Christi College, Cambridge; 1552: Dean of Lincoln; 1554: supported Queen Jane and was deprived of offices by Queen Mary; lived in hiding; 1559: reluctantly accepted See of Canterbury from Elizabeth; 1563–8: involved in transl. of Bishops' Bible. A noted moderate who used his patronage to check the spread of Puritanism. No courtier. V.J.K. Brook, *A Life of Archbishop Parker*, Oxford, 1962.

Parkhurst (Bishop) John (?1512–75): Oxford-educated scholar who converted to Protestantism; Marian exile; 1560: Bishop of Norwich; his letter book is an important source for the affairs of the diocese of

Norwich. R.A. Houlbrooke (ed.), *The Letter-book of John Parkhurst*, Norfolk Record Society, Vol. XLIII, 1974–5.

Parr (Queen) Catherine (1512–48): Four-times married daughter of Sir Thomas Parr of Kendal. When she married Henry VIII in 1543 she was just about to marry Thomas Seymour, brother of Jane; began a classical humanist education when Queen; 1544: assumed regency while H. was in France; her life was threatened because of her Protestant leanings and explicitly Lutheran writings; commissioned translation of Erasmus's *Paraphrases* into English to encourage lay Bible reading; c. April 1547: secretly m. Thomas Seymour and later received royal assent; gave birth to daughter Aug. 1548. M. Dowling, *Humanism in the Age of Henry VIII*, Croom Helm, 1986.

Parry William (d. 1585): Well-to-do Catholic who acted as spy for Burghley on English Catholics abroad in late 1570s. From 1582 secretly began to side with Catholic cause but continued to play a double-game. In 1584 he confessed his plotting to Elizabeth and was pardoned but it was not long before he conspired again, this time with Edmund Neville, to kill the Queen. Confessed and was hanged at Westminster, 2 March 1585.

Parsons Robert (1546–1610): Jesuit priest. 18 April 1580: he and Campion and seven other Jesuits set out from Rome for England. He toured Northampton, Derby, Worcester and Gloucester, preaching and saying the Mass in house churches. 1581: persecution of the Catholic printing press and capture of Campion led Parsons to flee to France, where he founded the English School at Eu and, then, St Omer. The years that followed were spent intriguing against Elizabeth in Rome, where he was briefly Rector of the English College in 1588, and in Spain where he managed English seminaries from 1588 onwards. 1596: returned as Rector of English College in Rome; faced with Archpriest controversy; d. Rome, 15 April 1610.

Penry John (1563–93): Pamphleteer who, between 1587 and 1590, published through the secret press of Robert Waldegrave a series of pamphlets attacking, especially, the bps Further tracts, known as the Mar-Prelate Tracts (because their author used the penname, Martin-Mar-Prelate), were produced through the efforts of Penry, John Udall and Job Throckmorton but no-one knows for certain who Martin was. Penry denied that he was Mar-Prelate. He was executed for treason on another charge on 29 May 1593.

Perkins William (1558–1602) (*See* Section V).

Philip II (King of Spain and Consort of Queen Mary I) (1527–98): 1554: m. Mary at Winchester Cathedral; K.G. and advised Mary to pardon Elizabeth; 1555: left England for Spain; 1557: returned to England to encourage support for Spain in Low Countries; 1558: overtures to m. Elizabeth but m. Isabella, daughter of King of France; 1588: sent Armada v. England.

Pole (Earl of Suffolk), (Sir) Edmund de la, (?1472–1513): Pretender to the English throne; he was the son of John de la Pole, 2nd Duke of Suffolk, who died in 1491 and Elizabeth Plantagenet, sister of Edward IV. He was therefore a descendant of Edward III. Like his father, Edmund initially supported Henry VII after Bosworth and led a company against the Blackheath rebels in 1496; but he became disaffected and escaped to Flanders in 1499; returned to favour at court; 1501: went to Court of Emperor Maximilian who had promised assistance to Yorkist claimants to the throne; 1504: imprisoned by Duke of Gueldres; 1506: was handed over to Henry VII; imprisoned in Tower of London; 1509: executed on Henry VIII's accession.

Pole (Earl of Lincoln), John de la (?1464–1487): Eldest son of John de la Pole, 2nd Duke of Suffolk, and Elizabeth Plantagenet, sister of Edward IV; he was, therefore, in the line of succession from Edward III; 1567: created Earl of Lincoln; a supporter of Richard III; 1483: President of the Council of the North; 1486: made lord lieutenant of Ireland; 1486: heir-presumptive to the throne; after Henry VII's accession he still conspired; supported Lambert Simnel; 1487: slaughtered at Battle of Stoke.

Pole Richard de la (d.1525): Pretender to the throne of England; son of John de la Pole, 2nd Duke of Suffolk, and Elizabeth Plantagenet, sister to Edward IV, and, therefore, descendant of Edward III; 1501: he escaped abroad with his brother, Edmund; 1509: exempted from Henry VIII's general pardon; 1512: recognised as King of England by Louis XII of France; 1514: left France when England and France made peace; -1519: lived at Metz; 1523: plotted with Scots to invade England; 1525: was killed supporting Francis I of France at the Battle of Pavia.

Pole (Countess of Salisbury), Margaret (1473–1541): Daughter of George, Duke of Clarence, brother of Edward IV, and Isabel Neville; sister of Edward, Earl of Warwick; c.1491: m. Sir Richard Pole (d.1505), gent. of Bucks; 3 sons, Henry Courtenay, Lord Montague (executed 1538), Geoffrey, and Reginald, later Cardinal Pole; 1513: Henry VIII creates her Countess of Salisbury and returns family estates of Salisbury to atone for execution of Edward, Earl of Warwick; governess to Princess Mary; 1533: dismissed when she refused to hand royal jewels to Anne Boleyn; 1536: returned to court; 1536: publication by her son Reginald of *De Unitate Ecclesiastica* seals her fate; May 1539: Act of Attainder passed; 1541: executed at Tower on news of Sir John Neville's Yorkshire rebellion.

Pole (Cardinal and Archbishop) Reginald (1500–58): Cardinal and Archbishop of Canterbury. Yorkist claimant to throne through George,

Duke of Clarence, his grandfather. Opposed divorce from Catherine of Aragon; 1536: published *De Unitate Ecclesiae* which made reconciliation with King impossible; Pole's mother and brother executed in retaliation; Pole in prolonged exile; 1536: Cardinal; prospective m. with Mary Tudor; 1554: returned to England as Archbishop of Canterbury; d. 1558.

Ponet (Bishop) John (1516–56): Humanist and friend of Ascham, Cheke and Cecil at Cambridge. 1547: Chaplain to Cranmer; 1549: tract defending clerical m.; 1550: Bishop of Rochester; 1551–3: Bishop of Winchester; 1553: deprived as married priest; participated in Wyatt's rebellion and went into exile; 1556: died Strasbourg. Contribution to political thought considerable: *Short Treatise of Politike Power*, 1556. *See* Section V.

Poynings (Sir) Edward (1459–21): Supporter of Henry VII in 1485; 1493: Governor of Calais; 1494: Lord Deputy in Ireland to Prince Henry, the Governor; he assembled a parliament which passed laws restricting Irish independence, including Poyning's Law (no act of Irish parl. valid unless previously submitted to English P.C.); 1495: drove Perkin Warbeck into exile in Scotland; 1496: recalled and made Warden of **Cinq Ports** and Comptroller of Royal Household; K.G.; 1513: negotiated league of partition v. France.

Prowse Anne (*See* LOCKE, Anne).

Raleigh (Sir) Walter (?1552–1618): Educated at Oxford. Military and naval commander and author. 1581: favourite of Elizabeth; 1585–6: organised plantation of Virginia; 1588: influence at court reduced by quarrel with Earl of Essex and (1592) his affair with and m. to Elizabeth Throckmorton, Elizabeth's lady-in-waiting; 1595: expedition to Manoa; 1596: brilliant performance v. Cadiz; 1597: distinguished part in expedition to Azores. S. Coote, *A Play of Passion*, 1993.

Rizzio (RICCIO) David (?1533–66): Italian-born French secretary to Queen Mary Stuart; became powerful; seized in her presence and murdered by Darnley and Morton.

Rich Penelope (c. 1562/3–1607): Daughter of Walter Devereux, 1st Earl of Essex and sister of Robert, 2nd Earl; 1581: m. Lord Robert Rich, later Earl of Warwick. 1591: Sir Philip Sidney published *Astrophel & Stella* in praise of her; 1601: she lived in open adultery with Lord Mountjoy; 1605: divorced by Lord Rich; m. Mountjoy, now become Earl of Devonshire.

Rich (Sir) Richard (?1496–1567): 1529: M.P. Colchester; 1533: Solicitor General; 1536: M.P. for Essex and elected Speaker of Commons; 1536: engaged in suppression of monasteries; 1540: deserted Cromwell; 1547: created Baron Rich; 1548: Lord Chancellor; 1549: saw bill of attainder v. Seymour through parl.; employed by Warwick in proceedings v. Gardiner and Bonner; 1551: resigned Great Seal; 1553: first declared for Jane and then for Mary; 1553–8: persecuted Protestants; 1564: founded Felsted Grammar School.

Richard III (King of England) (1452–85): York; Younger brother of Edward IV. Predeceased by infant male offspring. Defeated and slain by Henry Tudor at Bosworth Field, 1485.

Richmond (Duke of) (*See* FITZROY, Henry; TUDOR, Edmund).

Ridley (Bishop) Nicholas (?1503–55): Martyr. Outstanding Latin and Greek scholar, educated at Cambridge; 1537: Chaplain to Cranmer; gradual move towards Protestantism; 1548: declared he did not believe in transubstantiation but still believed in spiritual presence; 1547: Bishop of Rochester; 1547–53: engaged in carrying out reformation; 1549: Bishop of London; in Vestiarian Controversy stuck out v. John Hooper arguing that vestments were required by law to be worn by a bp at his consecration. 16 July 1553: Ridley denounced Mary I in sermon at Paul's Cross; deprived of see; 1554: public disputation at Oxford by Cranmer, Ridley and Latimer; declared heretic and excommunicated; refused to recant and continued to write Protestant treatises; burned at stake in Oxford, 16 October 1555; agonising death. Jasper Ridley, *Nicholas Ridley: a biography*, 1957.

Ridolfi Roberto di (1531–1612): Italian Catholic banker in Marian London. Remained influential in Elizabeth's reign and from 1567 was secret papal agent. 1568: plotted to marry Duke of Norfolk to Mary of Scotland, to secure her eventual succession to the English throne and the restoration of Catholicism. Cecil and Walsingham uncovered some of his activities but released him in 1570. Ridolfi continued to plot but was abroad when the scheme was uncovered and Norfolk and others arrested. He retired to Florence.

Robsart Amy (*See* DUDLEY, Amy).

Rogers John (c.1500–55): First Protestant martyr of Mary's reign. Orthodox Catholic priest who, as Chaplain to Merchant Adventurers at Antwerp, came under influence of William Tyndale. He took responsibility for compiling a translated version of the Bible (known as the Matthew Bible), including Tyndale's New Testament and incomplete Old Testament, adding work from Coverdale and a preface, commentary, calendar and almanack by himself. This was drawn upon as main source of Great Bible, 1539. c.1551: Divinity lecturer at St Paul's; 1554: imprisoned in Fleet for opposition to Mary I; Protestant confession of faith; burned at Smithfield, 1555.

Roper Margaret (née More) (c.1504–44): Humanist and translator. Renowned daughter of Sir Thomas More and Jane Colt, who was given a humanist education (incl. Latin, Greek, rhetoric, philosophy, logic, mathematics and astronomy) in a household which included two sisters and a brother, a stepsister, a ward and the daughter of her nurse. Fêted by Erasmus and Pole as Latin scholar, poet and translator 1523: m. William Roper, 1st child born; 1524: published translation of Erasmus' treatise on the Paternosters; 5 further children. *See* Basset, Mary. R.M. Warnicke, *Women of the English Renaissance and Reformation*, 1983.

Russell (2nd Earl of Bedford), Francis (?1527–85): Lord President of Wales. Cambridge-educated son of John Russell, 1st Earl of Bedford. 1553: supported Jane Grey; 1553–5: imprisoned; 1555: escaped to continent; 1558: P.C.; 1564: Warden of East Marches and K.G.; 1576: Lord President of Wales.

Russell (1st Earl of Bedford), John (1486–1555): Lord Admiral; Lord Privy Seal. 1520: at Field of Cloth of Gold; 1522: accompanied Thomas Howard, Earl of Surrey to France; 1527: ambassador to Pope Clement; 1536: active in suppressing Pilgrimage of Grace; 1537: Comptroller of King's Household; 1538: P.C.; 1539: created Baron Russell and made K.G.; 1540: Lord Admiral; 1542, 1547 and 1553: Lord Privy Seal; 1549: helped suppress Western Rebellion; 1550: Earl of Bedford; 1553: began by supporting Jane Grey but joined Queen Mary; 1554: ambassador to Spain to conclude m. treaty with Philip. Diane Willen, *John Russell, First Earl of Bedford. One of the King's Men*, Royal Historical Society, 1981.

Russell (Countess of Cumberland), Margaret (later Clifford) (1560–1616): Talented and well-educated daughter of Francis Russell, 2nd Earl of Bedford. Unhappily m. to George Clifford, 3rd Earl of Cumberland (1558–1608) in 1577, from whom she eventually separated, Mother of Anne Clifford (1590–1676).

Sadler (Sadleir) (Sir) Ralph (1507–87): statesman and diplomat. Specialised in Anglo-Scottish relations. In 1547 was part of the Council of Regents appointed by Henry VIII for minority of Edward VI. Spent Mary Tudor's reign in retirement but during Elizabeth's reign was one of Cecil's right-hand men. 1568: Chancellor of Duchy of Lancaster; 1572 and 1584: Warder of Mary of Scotland; 1586: On the commission that condemned Mary to death. On his d., 30 March 1587, was said to be richest commoner in England. A.J. Slavin, *Politics and Profit: a study of Sir Ralph Sadler, 1507–47*, Cambridge, 1966.

Salesbury William (c.1517–c.1600): Oxford-educated translator of New Testament into Welsh (1567). 1547: English-Welsh dictionary.

Salisbury Countess of (*See* POLE, Margaret).

Saunders Elizabeth (fl.1580s): A Catholic nun who toured Berkshire and Hampshire in the 1580s and was imprisoned in Winchester Bridewell. Eventually escaped and went abroad.

Seymour (Duke of Somerset), Edward (c.1506–52): University-educated brother of Queen Jane Seymour. In royal service in 1520s and

1530s; 1537: P.C. and created Earl of Hertford; 1541: K.G.; 1542: Lord
High Admiral; 1543: Lord Great Chamberlain; 1547: decisive victory
over Scots at Musselburgh; with Paget concealed d. of Henry VIII until
Edward VI brought to London; 31 January 1547/8: made Protector;
1549: attainder of brother Thomas Seymour lost him much of his popularity; 1549: rebellions v. his religious reforms; 1549: imprisoned in
Tower; 1550: deposed as Protector; Feb. 1550: pardoned and gradually
restored to some influence; Oct. 1551: arrested on charge of conspiracy to
murder Warwick; beheaded on Tower Hill. There is a portrait by
Holbein.

Seymour (Earl of Hertford), Edward (?1539–1621): Son of Edward
Seymour, Duke of Somerset, and his second wife; educated alongside
Edward VI; 1547: knighted at coronation of Ed. VI.; 1552: succeeded to
Dukedom but title and estates forfeited; 1559: created Baron Beauchamp
and Earl of Hertford; 1560: unwisely contracted secret marriage with
Lady Catherine Grey without Queen's permission – awakened memories
of the Greys' claims to the throne and fear of linking these with Seymour
ambitions; 1561: imprisoned in Tower for this offence; 1571: released;
1572: member of Gray's Inn; Sept. 1591: Queen's progress to Hertford's
Hampshire home marks his return to favour; 1602, 1608: Lord-Lieut. of
Somerset and Wiltshire; 1605: ambassador extraordinary to Brussels;
1612–19: High Steward of revenues to Queen Anne, Consort of James I.

Seymour (Queen) Jane (?1509–37): Eldest child of Sir John Seymour
and Margaret (née Wentworth), descendant of Edward I. Lady-in-waiting to Catherine of Aragon and, then, Anne Boleyn; m. Henry VIII as
3rd wife, 30 May 1536. No sympathy with Reformation. Reconciled
Henry VIII with daughter Mary; pleaded with Henry for monasteries
during Pilgrimage of Grace. Mother of Edward VI. Died shortly after his
birth by after effects of caesarean section, 24 October 1537.

Seymour Jane (fl.1540s and 1550s): Daughter of Edward Seymour,
Duke of Somerset. Named after her aunt, Queen Jane Seymour, and
given advanced humanist education by Nicholas Denisot to prepare
her for royal marriage with cousin Edward VI; 1550: Jane, Anne and
Margaret Seymour published their Latin distichs on death of Margaret
of Navarre – the first original Latin work by a female to be published
in the sixteenth century; Jane and Margaret were ladies-in-waiting
upon Queen Mary. Thomas Becon dedicated *The Governance of Virtue* to
her. R.M. Warnicke, *Women of the English Renaissance and Reformation*,
1983.

Seymour Thomas (?1508–49): Younger brother of Edward Seymour
and Jane. Diplomatic and military missions in 1530s and 1540s. 1547:
P.C., K.G., created Baron Seymour of Sudeley and Lord High Admiral;
c.April 1547: secret m. to Catherine Parr; formed project to m. Jane Grey
to Edward VI; suit for hand of Elizabeth after Catherine's death (Sept.

1548) landed him in Tower; executed for treason. G.W. Bernard, *The Tudor Nobility*, 1992.

Shakespeare William (1564–1616): Grammar-school educated actor, poet and playwright; raised in Stratford on Avon but made career in London. *See* Section V.

Shrewsbury (Countess of) (*See* HARDWICK, Bess of).

Sidney (Sir) Henry (1529–86): Lord Deputy of Ireland and President of Wales.

Sidney (Countess of Pembroke), Mary (1561–1621): Sister of Sir Philip Sidney; knew French, Italian and Latin; edited Philip Sidney's *Arcadia*; translated a number of works in manuscript; published an elegy for Philip Sidney, 'The Doleful Lay of Clorinda', 1595.

Sidney (Sir) Philip (1554–86): Poet, statesman and soldier. Son of Sir Henry Sidney and brother of Mary. Educated Shrewsbury School and Christ Church Oxford. Founder member of *Areopagus*, a literary club to which Spenser and others belonged; loved Lady Penelope Rich (Devereux) and dedicated sonnets to her but married Frances, daughter of Francis Walsingham; 1585: joint Master of Ordnance; anti-Catholic policies; 1585: Governor of Flushing; d. of wound during battle to relieve Zutphen. His works were all published posthumously. Michael Foss, *Tudor Portraits*, 1973.

Simnel Lambert (?1475–1525): Son of Thomas Simnel of Oxford. Impostor who was presented by the Oxford priest, Richard Symonds, first as Richard Duke of York and then as the Earl of Warwick, nephew of Edward IV, in attempt to win Crown from Henry VII. Crowned King Edward VI in Dublin 1487. Plots against Henry VII with Margaret of Burgundy, sister of Edward IV, Earl of Lincoln and Lord Lovell. Henry VII paraded real Earl of Warwick in London. 4 June 1487: Lambert Simnel's troops met those of Henry VII and fought Battle of Stoke (near Newark), last battle of Wars of Roses. Simnel made a scullion and later a falconer and still alive in 1525, when he attended the funeral of Thomas Lovell.

Skelton John (c.1460–1529): Highly regarded poet during his day. He was a distinguished classicist, although not a humanist, known for translation from the Latin. He moved from early, quite elaborate and sophisticated verse ('The Bowge of Court', 1498) to bawdy, rough and caustic works deliberately resisting modern cultivated styles (e.g. 'Colin Clout', 'Speak Parrot' and 'Why Come Ye Not to Court', all written in the 1520s as attacks on Wolsey and abuses in the church, and 'The Tunning of Elinor Rumming', 1517). 1489: entered Holy Orders; Court Poet to Henry VII; tutor to Prince Henry (VIII).

Smith (Sir) Thomas (1513–77): Elizabeth's 1st ambassador to France.

Prominent humanist. Professor of Greek at Cambridge. Author of *De Republica Anglorum* (1583) describing the government and constitution. He is thought to have been the author of the important but anonymous *Discourse of the Commonweal* (long attributed to John Hales), which was apparently written in late 1549 but not published until 1581. This, the most important of the so-called commonwealth tracts, propounded the political and economic beliefs of the commonwealth group.

Speed John (c.1552–1629): Cartographer and historian. A London tailor who made maps of several English counties and wrote *History of Great Britaine* in 1611.

Somerset (Duke of) (*See* SEYMOUR, Edward).

Southwell (Lady) Anne (1574–1636): Poet and letter writer. Her works exist in manuscript. She m. twice: first, Sir Thomas Southwell; then Sir Henry Sibthorpe.

Southwell Robert (1561–95): Poet and martyr. 1586: Jesuit missionary priest in London, Sussex and the North; 1589: Chaplain to Countess of Arundel; 1592: Arrested, imprisoned and harshly tortured by Topcliffe; February 1595: tried for treason; 21 February 1595: hanged at Tyburn.

Spenser Edmund (1552–99): Patriotic Protestant poet of tremendous influence. Invented Spenserian stanza. Educated at Merchant Taylor's School, London and Cambridge; 1578: entered household of Earl of Leicester and joined Sir Philip Sidney's circle, the *Areopagus*; 1580: secretary to Lord Grey de Wilton, Lord Deputy of Ireland; 1589: completed the sophisticated, serious and pictorially vivid allegory, *The Faerie Queene*; 1598: recalled to London.

Stafford (3rd Duke of Buckingham), Edward (1478–1521): Courtier. Eldest son of Henry, 2nd Duke of Buckingham (executed 1483) and Katherine Woodville; 1485: royal ward in care of Lady Margaret Beaufort, his great-aunt; 1509: P.C.; 1520: at Gravelines with Henry VIII; 1521: executed on trumped up charges.

Stafford (2nd Duke of Buckingham), Henry (1454–83): Supporter of Richard III. Grandson of Humphrey Stafford, 1st Duke; 1483: supporter of Richard III and Chamberlain at his coronation; 1483: turned coat; captured and executed at Salisbury. C. Rawcliffe, *The Staffords*, 1978.

Stafford (1st Baron Stafford), Henry (Lord) (1501–63): Courtier and servant of the Crown. 1532: K.B.; 1547: M.P. Stafford; loyal conservative servant of all the Tudors from Henry VIII to Elizabeth. A.H. Anderson, 'Henry, Lord Stafford (1501–1563) in local and central government', *E.H.R.*, 78, 1963.

Standish (Bishop) Henry (d.1535): Bishop of London, FitzJames, tried to prevent Dr Horsey from being tried in a secular court over the Hunne case on the grounds than no cleric could be summoned before a secular court. Crown appointed Standish to plead its case in public debate at Blackfriars on 10 March 1515. Standish did so successfully but was summoned before Convocation to explain his action. At a further public debate Standish again defended the secular view. Then at another meeting at Baynard's Castle Henry VIII compromised by dropping charges against both Horsey and Standish. Standish was rewarded with the See of St Asaph and remained in favour with the King.

Stanley (Sir) William (d.1495): This brother of Thomas, Earl of Derby, was made Justiciar of North Wales and granted Derbyshire estates by Richard III but, after banishment by Richard for supposed treachery, deserted to support Henry Tudor decisively at Bosworth Field. 1485: K.G. and Lord Chamberlain; 1485: beheaded as supporter of Warbeck. Barry Coward, *The Stanleys Lords Stanley and Earls of Derby, 1385–1672*, Chetham Society, 1983.

Stowe John (?1525–1605): Chronicler, member of Society of Antiquaries. 1580: *The Chronicles of England* (later editions known as *The Annales of England*); 1598: *The Survey of London*.

Stuart (Lady) Arabella (1575–1615): Daughter of Elizabeth Cavendish and Charles Stuart, Earl of Lennox, younger brother of Darnley and claimant to English throne. Secretly m. William Seymour also in line to throne; d. in Tower.

Stuart Henry (*See* DARNLEY, Earl of).

Stuart Mary (*See* MARY STUART, Queen of Scots).

Stucley (Sir) Thomas (c.1520–78): Adventurer. Early career in households of Duke of Suffolk and Earl of Somerset at home and abroad; imprisoned by Northumberland; engaged in buccaneering against French ships in late 1550s; 1560s: tried to found colony in Florida in Queen's name but used it as a cover for piracy; 1569: imprisoned for high treason at Dublin Castle for joining Shane O'Neill in Ireland. Released. Specialised in fiasco conspiracies v. Elizabeth until his death in Morocco in 1578 at the Battle of Alcazar.

Suffolk Charles (Duke of) (*See* BRANDON, Charles).

Suffolk Henry (Duke of) (*See* GREY, Henry).

Suffolk Catherine (Duchess of) (*See* BERTIE, Catherine).

Tallis Thomas (?1510–85): Noted musician and organist who was an early composer of settings for the Anglican liturgy and excelled in religious compositions for voices. 1576: with William Byrd allocated royal monopoly of printed music for 21 years.

Throckmorton (Abbess) Elizabeth (d.1547): Last Abbess of Denny, convent of Order of Minoresses in Cambridge. After Dissolution returned to her home in Coughton, Warwickshire, with two or three nuns and continued to follow the rule privately. R.M. Warnicke, *Women of the English Renaissance and Reformation*, 1983.

Throckmorton Francis (1554–84): Well-born Catholic conspirator. Agent for the plan of the Duc de Guise to invade Scotland and England simultaneously, remove Elizabeth with the help of the English Catholics, and replace her with Mary of Scotland. Walsingham uncovered and foiled the plot in 1583, with the aid of a spy named Fagot. After twice being placed on the rack, Throckmorton confessed and was executed at Tyburn.

Thynne Joan (1558–1612): Ran estate at Longleat during her husband John Thynne's absences at court; acted to take possession (by physical action) of Caus Castle from Lady Stafford; 1604: on husband's death went to live at Caus Castle. An entrepreneur in lead-mining.

Topcliffe Richard (1532–1604): 1572: M.P. for Beverley; 1586–1604: M.P. for Old Sarum; 1573: entered Burghley's service. In this capacity tortured and otherwise tormented English Catholics.

Tudor (Prince) Arthur (1486–1502): 1st son of Henry VII and Elizabeth; 1489: K.B.; 1501: m. Catherine of Aragon.

Tudor (Earl of Richmond), Edmund (?1430–56): Eldest son of Owen Tudor and Katherine of Valois, widow of Henry V, and father of Henry VII. Married Margaret Beaufort, descendant of Edward III through John of Gaunt.

Tudor (Earl of Pembroke and Duke of Bedford), Jasper (?1431–95): Second son of Owen Tudor who brought up his nephew Henry Tudor, later Henry VII. 1485: created Duke of Bedford; 1492: Earl Marshal; helped put down insurrections of Simnel and Lovell and Stafford; 1492: commander in France.

Tunstall (Bishop) Cuthbert (1474–1559): Oxford, Cambridge and Padua-educated humanist, bp and statesman who during the Henrician revolution remained a Catholic by doctrine but supported the royal supremacy. 1516: Master of the Rolls; 1522–30: Bishop of London; 1523: Keeper of Privy Seal; 1530–53 (deprived): Bishop of Durham; 1537: President of Council of North; 1550: wrote *De Veritate Corporis et Sanguinis . . . in Eucharista* when in prison for inciting rebellion; 1553: restored as Bishop of Durham by Mary; 1559: refused Oath of Supremacy to Elizabeth and was deprived.

Tusser Thomas (c. 1524–80): Educated at St Paul's, Eton and Cambridge; musician at court in household of William Paget; introduced culture of barley at Cattiwade, Suffolk; 1557: *Hundreth Good Pointes of Husbandrie* – went into two larger editions in 1570 and 1573.

Tyndale William (d. 1536): Oxford-educated translation of Bible into English. 1524–5: translated New Testament at Cologne and Worms; 1525: imported copies into England; 1526: Wolsey's denunciation; exile; won Henry VIII's approval for *The Obedience of a Christen Man* (1528); 1531: engaged in bitter controversy with Thomas More; 1535: imprisoned by imperial officers at Vilvorde; 1536: strangled and burnt at stake. Of great importance in development of English Bible, vernacular style, and as a model for English Protestant preachers.

Udall John (?1560–92): Cambridge-educated friend of John Penry; 1588: published anonymously anti-episcopal *The State of the Church and A Demonstration*; 1588: deprived of benefice; 1590: impr. for complicity in **Marprelate**; 1591: sentenced to death; 1592: pardoned but d.; 1593: posthumous publication of Hebrew grammar and dictionary.

Udall Nicholas (c.1505–56): Headmaster of Eton, 1534–41. Author of first known English comedy, *Ralph Roister Doister*. Impr. for sexual misdemeanour. Master of Chapel Royal under Mary I and Headmaster of Westminster School.

Vergil Polydore (?1470–?1555): Italian papal official who gained royal patronage. 1502: came to England as sub-collector for Peter's Pence; 1505: commissioned by Henry VII to write history of kingdom; 1508: Archdeacon of Wells.

Vernon (Countess of Southampton), Elizabeth (c.1580-post 1655): Maid of Honour of Elizabeth I; secretly m. Henry Wriothesley, 3rd Earl of Southampton.

Walsingham (Sir) Francis (1532–90): Secretary of State involved in foreign affairs, 1568–90. Staunch and uncompromising Protestant; wanted Protestant foreign policy of alliance with Huguenot French against Spain; fought for removal of Mary of Scotland. Unravelled Ridolfi Plot, 1568 and Throckmorton Plot, 1583. Organised large and effective secret service. Conyers Read, *Mr Secretary Walsingham*, 3 vols, 1925; Michael Foss, *Tudor Portraits*, 1973.

Warbeck Perkin (c.1474–99): Impostor. Son of Tournai customs official. Posed as Earl of Warwick (illegitimate son of Richard III) and as Richard, Duke of York (son of Edward IV) as Yorkist pretender in opposition to Henry VII. Welcomed and acknowledged as Richard IV by Emperor Maximilian in 1493, and given refuge by James IV of Scotland in 1495. Threat of war drove Warbeck into Cornwall but his following there disappeared in the face of the King's troops. Henry VII treated him clemently on his capture but Warbeck's involvement in a further conspiracy in 1499 resulted in his decapitation.

Warham (Archbishop) William (?1450–1532): 1494: Master of the Rolls; 1496: negotiated m. between Catherine of Aragon and Arthur

Tudor; 1502: Bishop of London; 1504: Archbishop of Canterbury and Lord Chancellor; 1509: crowned Henry VIII. After 1515 Warham's public role muted, when Wolsey in the ascendant. Disliked Henry's divorce and break with Rome but proved poor defender of the Church, despite declaration in February 1532 that he would repeal all the statutes passed against the church since the beginning of that parliament. Intended to resist Henry's threat of writ of Praemunire. Died on 23 August 1532.

Warwick (Earl of) (*See* DUDLEY, John and DUDLEY, Ambrose).

Wentworth Peter (c.1524–96): MP noted for his championship of Parliament's right to discuss matters normally considered to belong to the Crown prerogative (i.e. the succession and religious questions), and for his consequent imprisonment.

Weston William (?1550–1615): Oxford, Paris and Douai-educated Superior of Jesuit Mission in England in 1584; 1586–1603: imprisoned in various places including Wisbech Castle where he quarrelled with secular priests; 1603: allowed to go abroad. William Weston, ed. and translated by Philip Caraman, *The Autobiography of an Elizabethan*, 1951.

Wheathill Anne (fl.1584): 1584: author of a book of prayers, *A Handfull, of holesome (though homelie) hearbs* . . .

Whitgift (Archbishop) John (c.1530–1604): Educated at St Anthony's School, London, and Cambridge. Academic career at Cambridge included Mastership of Pembroke Hall and Trinity College and Regius Professorship of Divinity; 1571: Dean of Lincoln; 1577: Bishop of Worcester; 1577–80: Vice-President of Marches of Wales; 1583–1604: Archbishop of Canterbury; 1586: P.C.; favourite of Elizabeth who pursued policy of enforcing religious uniformity; 1595: drew up **Lambeth Articles**. V.J.K. Brook, *Whitgift and the English Church*, 1957.

Whittingham (Dean) William (?1524–79): Educated at Oxford. Extreme Protestant. Marian Exile. 1554: Knoxian in Frankfurt dispute with Cox. 1555: moved to Geneva; 1559: succeeded Knox as minister; 1557: published translation of New Testament; 1560, largely responsible for Geneva Bible; 1560: returned to England in service of Ambrose and Robert Dudley; 1562: Chaplain to Ambrose Dudley, Earl of Warwick, in war against France; 1563: Dean of Durham; 1566, Parker's Advertisements forced Whittingham to abandon the Genevan practices he had introduced to Durham Cathedral.

Wilkinson Jane (fl. 1530s): Silkwoman of Anne Boleyn who worked with William Latymer to import scriptural works for the Queen.

Willoughby Catherine (*See* BERTIE, Catherine).

Willoughby (Sir) Hugh (d.1554): Soldier and navigator who died searching for a trade route to China via the North-East passage. Knighted at Battle of Stoke, 1487.

Wolsey (Cardinal Archbishop of York and Ecclesiastical Statesman), Thomas (c.1473–1530): 1507: Chaplain to Henry VII, Dean of Lincoln; 1512: Bishop of Hereford; 1513: Bishop of Tournai; 1514: Bishop of Lincoln resigned to become Archbishop of York in same year, 1515: Cardinal and Lord Chancellor; 1518: Papal Legate; various sees held in plurality with York. 1515–29: effectively King's Chief Minister. Built Hampton Court Palace. Conducted a foreign policy designed to bring glory to Henry VIII and to oppose the rise of France but there is some evidence between 1514 and 1522 of a peace policy, designed by Henry and Wolsey, culminating in Peace of London, 1518, signed by 24 nations. Domestic policy continued emphasis of Henry VII on order and defence of dynasty against threats, making use of the Court of Star Chamber. Used parliament little, and taxed highly to finance the foreign policy. Policy against enclosures. Founded Cardinal College (later Christ Church), Oxford. Lost King's favour when he failed to secure annulment of Henry's m. to Catherine of Aragon, 1527–9. Fall of Wolsey, August to November 1529. 3 November 1529: Henry saves Wolsey from arraignment by Parliament and returns him to See of York. Wolsey negotiates with Pope. Government ordered his return to London. Wolsey d. at Leicester en route.

Wyatt (Sir) Thomas (c.1503–42): Poet, diplomat, lover of Anne Boleyn. Son of Sir Henry Wyatt, courtier; Cambridge-educated squire to Henry VIII; 1529: High Marshal of Calais; lover of Anne Boleyn before her m.; 1533: P.C.; 1536: imprisoned in Tower when Anne's infidelities uncovered; 1537: knighted; 1537–9: ambassador to Charles V; 1541: imprisoned in Tower on Cromwell's fall but released; 1542: M.P. for Kent; there is a portrait after Holbein in the National Portrait Gallery; introduced Petrarchian sonnet form into England from Italy.

Wyatt (Sir) Thomas (c.1521–54): Rebel. Son of Sir Thomas Wyatt the poet; 1554: associated with Edward Courtenay, Earl of Devonshire, in conspiracy to prevent m. of Mary I to Philip II of Spain; marched on Blackheath, entered Southwark but was deserted by followers in London; executed on Tower Hill for treason. David Loades, *Two Tudor Conspiracies*, 1965.

Genealogical Tables

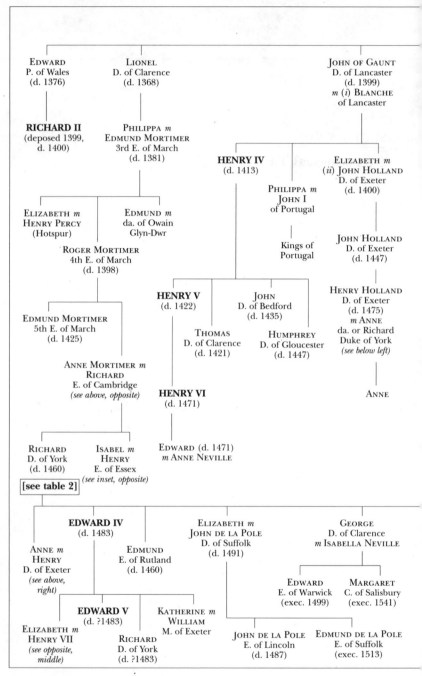

1. The Descendants of Edward III

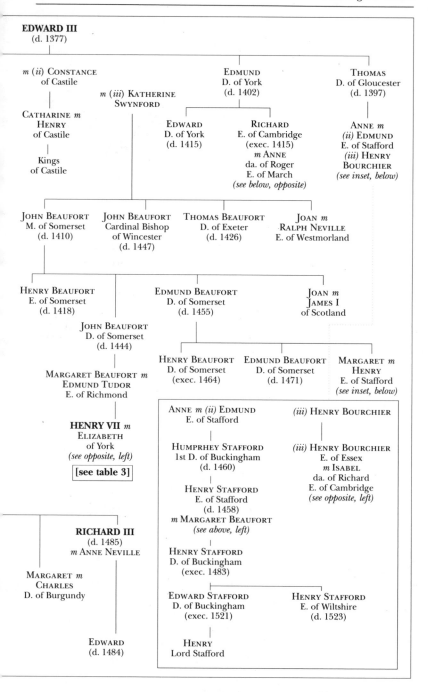

EDWARD III
(d. 1377)

m (ii) CONSTANCE
of Castile

m (iii) KATHERINE
SWYNFORD

CATHARINE *m*
HENRY
of Castile

Kings
of Castile

EDMUND
D. of York
(d. 1402)

EDWARD
D. of York
(d. 1415)

RICHARD
E. of Cambridge
(exec. 1415)
m ANNE
da. of Roger
E. of March
(see below, opposite)

THOMAS
D. of Gloucester
(d. 1397)

ANNE *m*
(ii) EDMUND
E. of Stafford
(iii) HENRY
BOURCHIER
(see inset, below)

JOHN BEAUFORT
M. of Somerset
(d. 1410)

JOHN BEAUFORT
Cardinal Bishop
of Wincester
(d. 1447)

THOMAS BEAUFORT
D. of Exeter
(d. 1426)

JOAN *m*
RALPH NEVILLE
E. of Westmorland

HENRY BEAUFORT
E. of Somerset
(d. 1418)

JOHN BEAUFORT
D. of Somerset
(d. 1444)

MARGARET BEAUFORT *m*
EDMUND TUDOR
E. of Richmond

EDMUND BEAUFORT
D. of Somerset
(d. 1455)

HENRY BEAUFORT
D. of Somerset
(exec. 1464)

EDMUND BEAUFORT
D. of Somerset
(d. 1471)

JOAN *m*
JAMES I
of Scotland

MARGARET *m*
HENRY
E. of Stafford
(see inset, below)

HENRY VII *m*
ELIZABETH
of York
(see opposite, left)

[see table 3]

ANNE *m (ii)* EDMUND
E. of Stafford

HUMPRHEY STAFFORD
1st D. of Buckingham
(d. 1460)

HENRY STAFFORD
E. of Stafford
(d. 1458)
m MARGARET BEAUFORT
(see above, left)

HENRY STAFFORD
D. of Buckingham
(exec. 1483)

(iii) HENRY BOURCHIER

(iii) HENRY BOURCHIER
E. of Essex
m ISABEL
da. of Richard
E. of Cambridge
(see opposite, left)

RICHARD III
(d. 1485)
m ANNE NEVILLE

MARGARET *m*
CHARLES
D. of Burgundy

EDWARD
(d. 1484)

EDWARD STAFFORD
D. of Buckingham
(exec. 1521)

HENRY
Lord Stafford

HENRY STAFFORD
E. of Wiltshire
(d. 1523)

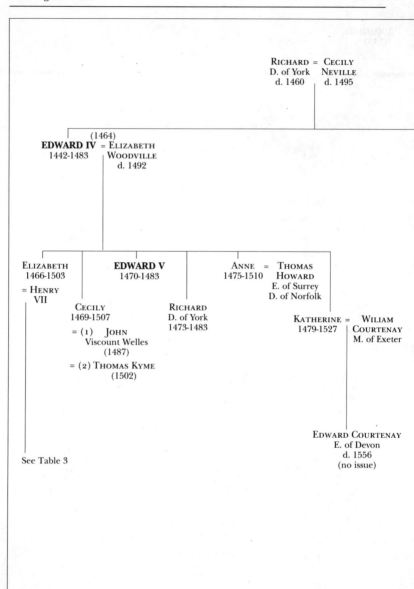

2. Descent of Edward IV and his siblings

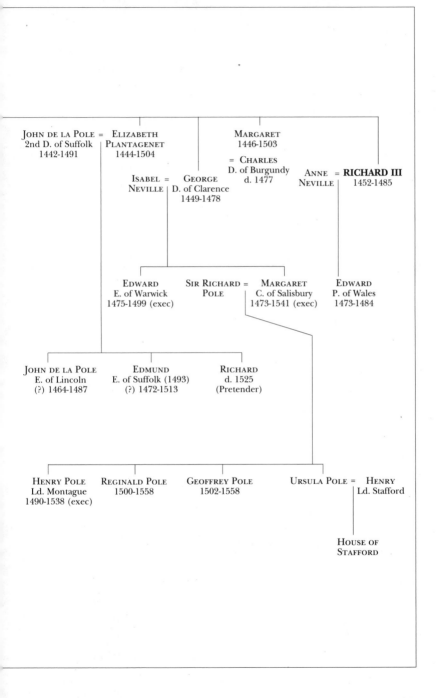

JOHN DE LA POLE = ELIZABETH
2nd D. of Suffolk | PLANTAGENET
1442-1491 | 1444-1504

MARGARET
1446-1503

= CHARLES
D. of Burgundy
ISABEL = GEORGE   d. 1477
NEVILLE | D. of Clarence
1449-1478

ANNE = **RICHARD III**
NEVILLE | 1452-1485

EDWARD
E. of Warwick
1475-1499 (exec)

SIR RICHARD = MARGARET
POLE | C. of Salisbury
1473-1541 (exec)

EDWARD
P. of Wales
1473-1484

JOHN DE LA POLE
E. of Lincoln
(?) 1464-1487

EDMUND
E. of Suffolk (1493)
(?) 1472-1513

RICHARD
d. 1525
(Pretender)

HENRY POLE
Ld. Montague
1490-1538 (exec)

REGINALD POLE
1500-1558

GEOFFREY POLE
1502-1558

URSULA POLE = HENRY
| Ld. Stafford

HOUSE OF
STAFFORD

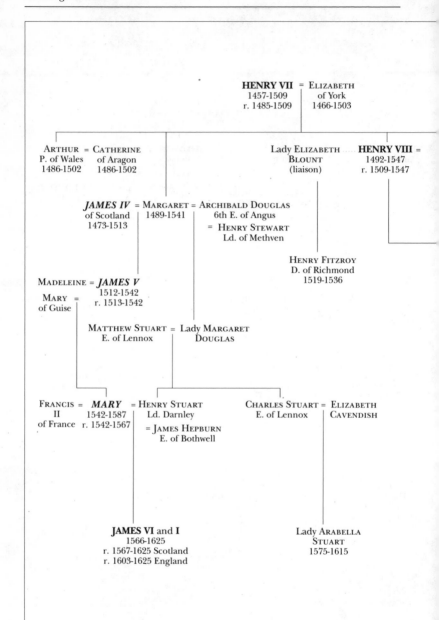

3. Descent of Henry VII and Elizabeth of York

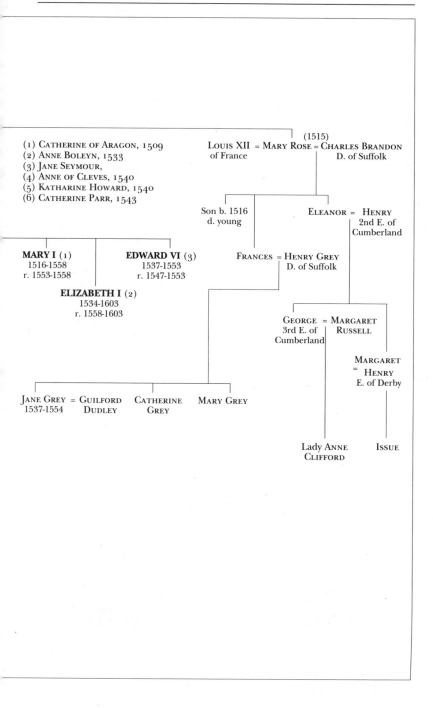

(1) CATHERINE OF ARAGON, 1509
(2) ANNE BOLEYN, 1533
(3) JANE SEYMOUR,
(4) ANNE OF CLEVES, 1540
(5) KATHARINE HOWARD, 1540
(6) CATHERINE PARR, 1543

(1515)
LOUIS XII = MARY ROSE = CHARLES BRANDON
of France   D. of Suffolk

Son b. 1516
d. young

ELEANOR = HENRY
2nd E. of
Cumberland

MARY I (1)
1516-1558
r. 1553-1558

EDWARD VI (3)
1537-1553
r. 1547-1553

FRANCES = HENRY GREY
D. of Suffolk

ELIZABETH I (2)
1534-1603
r. 1558-1603

GEORGE = MARGARET
3rd E. of | RUSSELL
Cumberland

MARGARET
= HENRY
E. of Derby

JANE GREY = GUILFORD
1537-1554   DUDLEY

CATHERINE
GREY

MARY GREY

Lady ANNE
CLIFFORD

ISSUE

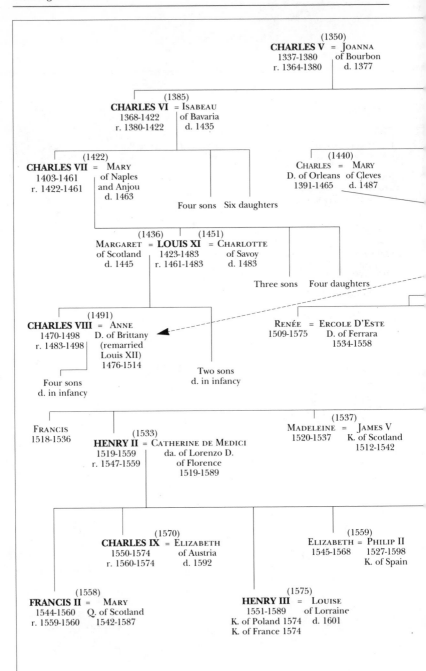

(1350)
CHARLES V = JOANNA
1337-1380   of Bourbon
r. 1364-1380   d. 1377

(1385)
CHARLES VI = ISABEAU
1368-1422   of Bavaria
r. 1380-1422   d. 1435

(1422)
CHARLES VII = MARY
1403-1461   of Naples
r. 1422-1461   and Anjou
            d. 1463

(1440)
CHARLES = MARY
D. of Orleans of Cleves
1391-1465   d. 1487

Four sons   Six daughters

(1436)   (1451)
MARGARET = **LOUIS XI** = CHARLOTTE
of Scotland   1423-1483   of Savoy
d. 1445   r. 1461-1483   d. 1483

Three sons   Four daughters

(1491)
CHARLES VIII = ANNE
1470-1498   D. of Brittany
r. 1483-1498   (remarried
            Louis XII)
            1476-1514

RENÉE = ERCOLE D'ESTE
1509-1575   D. of Ferrara
            1534-1558

Four sons
d. in infancy

Two sons
d. in infancy

FRANCIS
1518-1536

(1533)
HENRY II = CATHERINE DE MEDICI
1519-1559   da. of Lorenzo D.
r. 1547-1559   of Florence
            1519-1589

(1537)
MADELEINE = JAMES V
1520-1537   K. of Scotland
            1512-1542

(1570)
CHARLES IX = ELIZABETH
1550-1574   of Austria
r. 1560-1574   d. 1592

(1559)
ELIZABETH = PHILIP II
1545-1568   1527-1598
            K. of Spain

(1558)
FRANCIS II = MARY
1544-1560   Q. of Scotland
r. 1559-1560   1542-1587

(1575)
HENRY III = LOUISE
1551-1589   of Lorraine
K. of Poland 1574   d. 1601
K. of France 1574

4. The Valois Dynasty (France)

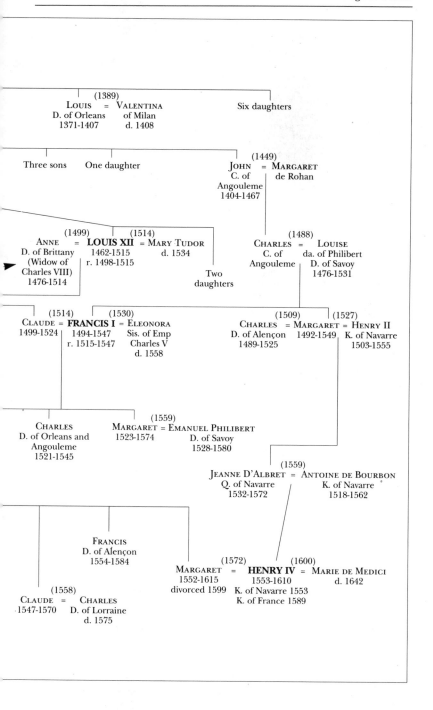

(1389)
LOUIS = VALENTINA   Six daughters
D. of Orleans   of Milan
1371-1407   d. 1408

Three sons   One daughter   (1449)
                          JOHN = MARGARET
                          C. of   de Rohan
                          Angouleme
                          1404-1467

(1499)   (1514)   (1488)
ANNE = **LOUIS XII** = MARY TUDOR   CHARLES = LOUISE
D. of Brittany 1462-1515   d. 1534   C. of   da. of Philibert
(Widow of   r. 1498-1515   Angouleme   D. of Savoy
Charles VIII)   1476-1531
1476-1514   Two
                    daughters

(1514)   (1530)   (1509)   (1527)
CLAUDE = **FRANCIS I** = ELEONORA   CHARLES = MARGARET = HENRY II
1499-1524 1494-1547 Sis. of Emp   D. of Alençon 1492-1549 K. of Navarre
        r. 1515-1547 Charles V   1489-1525   1503-1555
                d. 1558

CHARLES   (1559)
D. of Orleans and MARGARET = EMANUEL PHILIBERT
Angouleme   1523-1574   D. of Savoy
1521-1545   1528-1580

                    (1559)
                JEANNE D'ALBRET = ANTOINE DE BOURBON
                Q. of Navarre   K. of Navarre
                1532-1572   1518-1562

            FRANCIS
            D. of Alençon
            1554-1584   (1572)   (1600)
                    MARGARET = **HENRY IV** = MARIE DE MEDICI
                    1552-1615 1553-1610   d. 1642
(1558)   divorced 1599 K. of Navarre 1553
CLAUDE = CHARLES   K. of France 1589
1547-1570 D. of Lorraine
      d. 1575

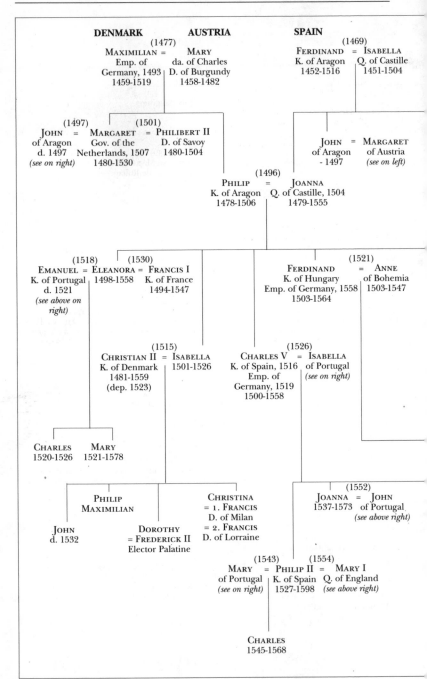

5. The intermarriage of the major European powers

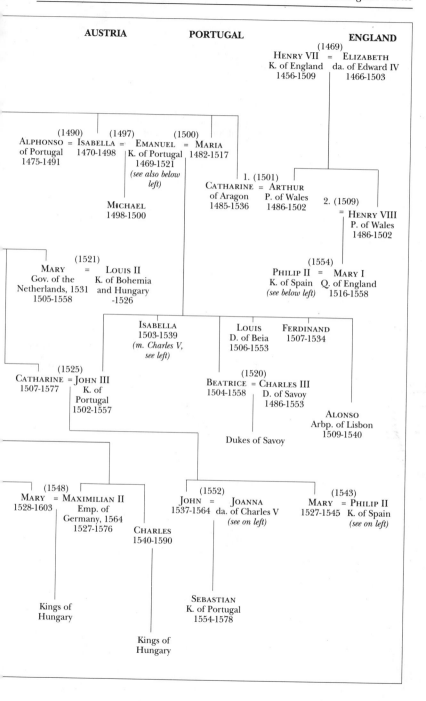

AUSTRIA **PORTUGAL** **ENGLAND**

(1469)
HENRY VII = ELIZABETH
K. of England da. of Edward IV
1456-1509 1466-1503

(1490) (1497) (1500)
ALPHONSO = ISABELLA = EMANUEL = MARIA
of Portugal 1470-1498 K. of Portugal 1482-1517
1475-1491 1469-1521
(see also below left)

1. (1501)
CATHARINE = ARTHUR
of Aragon P. of Wales 2. (1509)
1485-1536 1486-1502
= HENRY VIII
P. of Wales
1486-1502

MICHAEL
1498-1500

(1521)
MARY = LOUIS II
Gov. of the K. of Bohemia
Netherlands, 1531 and Hungary
1505-1558 -1526

(1554)
PHILIP II = MARY I
K. of Spain Q. of England
(see below left) 1516-1558

ISABELLA
1503-1539
*(m. Charles V,
see left)*

LOUIS FERDINAND
D. of Beia 1507-1534
1506-1553

(1525)
CATHARINE = JOHN III
1507-1577 K. of
Portugal
1502-1557

(1520)
BEATRICE = CHARLES III
1504-1558 D. of Savoy
1486-1553

ALONSO
Arbp. of Lisbon
1509-1540

Dukes of Savoy

(1548)
MARY = MAXIMILIAN II
1528-1603 Emp. of
Germany, 1564
1527-1576

(1552)
JOHN = JOANNA
1537-1564 da. of Charles V
(see on left)

(1543)
MARY = PHILIP II
1527-1545 K. of Spain
(see on left)

CHARLES
1540-1590

Kings of
Hungary

SEBASTIAN
K. of Portugal
1554-1578

Kings of
Hungary

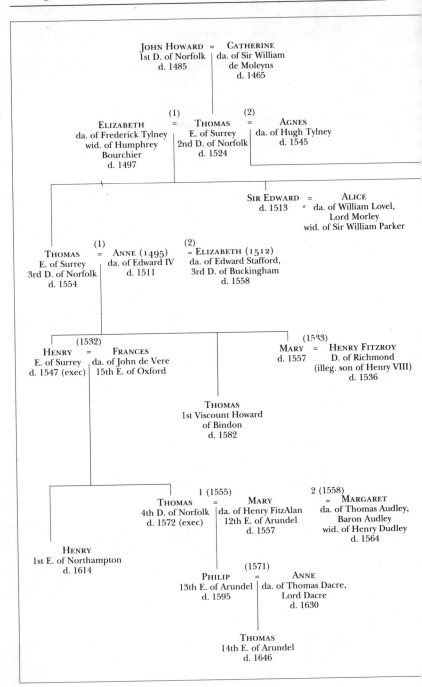

6. The Howards

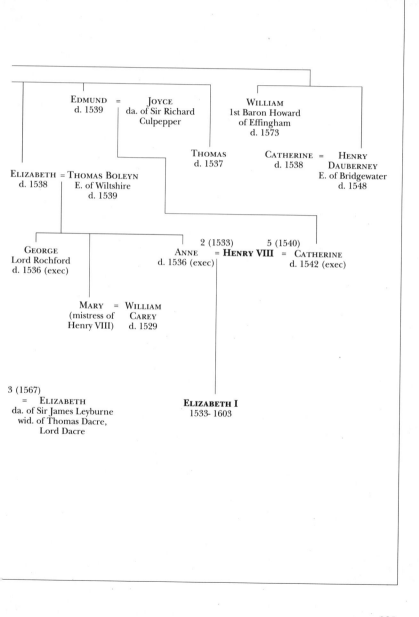

EDMUND
d. 1539

= JOYCE
da. of Sir Richard
Culpepper

WILLIAM
1st Baron Howard
of Effingham
d. 1573

THOMAS
d. 1537

CATHERINE
d. 1538

= HENRY
DAUBERNEY
E. of Bridgewater
d. 1548

ELIZABETH
d. 1538

= THOMAS BOLEYN
E. of Wiltshire
d. 1539

GEORGE
Lord Rochford
d. 1536 (exec)

2 (1533)   5 (1540)
ANNE   = **HENRY VIII** = CATHERINE
d. 1536 (exec)   d. 1542 (exec)

MARY
(mistress of
Henry VIII)

= WILLIAM
CAREY
d. 1529

3 (1567)
=   ELIZABETH
da. of Sir James Leyburne
wid. of Thomas Dacre,
Lord Dacre

ELIZABETH I
1533- 1603

Tudor Titles: Who was Who

One of the most confusing aspects of English history books is the habit of referring to key individuals by their title only. For example, one reads of the Earl of Essex in 1540 and 1599 or the Duke of Suffolk in 1550 and 1552 or the Bishop of London in 1530 and in 1570, yet it was not the same Earl of Essex or the same Duke of Suffolk or the same Bishop of London. The listing below cites the titles to which reference is most frequently made and gives the name and identity of the holder of this title with dates. The dates are those of holding the title. I have added further detail where it will help identification and avoid confusion.

Bedford	1549–55 Lord John Russell created 1st Earl of
	1555–85 Francis Russell, son of 1st Earl
	1585–1627 Edward Russell
Burghley	1570–98 Sir William Cecil, created Lord Burghley of Burghley
	1598–1623 Thomas Cecil
Canterbury, Archbishop of	1454–86 Thomas Bourchier
	1486–1500 John Morton
	1501 Thomas Langton
	1501–3 Henry Deane
	1504–32 William Warham
	1533–53 (deprived) Thomas Cranmer
	1559–75 Matthew Parker
	1576–83 Edmund Grindal
	1583–1604 John Whitgift
	1604–10 Richard Bancroft
Chancellor, Lord	1485 Thomas Rotherham, Archbp of York
	1485–7 John Alcock, Bp of Winchester and Ely
	1487–1500 John Morton, Archbp of Canterbury
	1515–29 Thomas Wolsey, Archbp of York etc.
	1529–32 Sir Thomas More
	1533–44 Sir Thomas Audley (created 1st Lord Audley in 1538). He had been Keeper since 1532
	1544–7 Lord Thomas Wriothesely, created 1st Earl of Southampton in 1547
	1547–51 Lord Richard Rich

	1552–3	Thomas Goodrich, Bp of Ely. He had been Keeper in 1551–2
	1553–5	Stephen Gardiner, Bp of Winchester
	1556–8	Nicholas Heath, Archbp of York
	1579–87	Sir Thomas Bromley
	1587–91	Sir Christopher Hatton

Chief Justice of the King's Bench

1485–95	William Huse
1495–1526	John Finieux
1526–39	John FitzJames
1539–45	Edward Montagu
1545–52	Richard Lyster
1552–3	Roger Cholmley
1553–5	Thomas Bromley
1555–7	William Portman
1557–9	Edward Saunders
1559–74	Robert Catlin
1574–92	Christopher Wray
1592–1607	John Popham

Chief Justice of the Common Pleas

1485–1500	Thomas Bryan
1500–02	Thomas Wood
1502–06	Thomas Frowyk
1506–19	Robert Read
1519–21	John Ernle
1521–31	Robert Brudenell
1531–5	Robert Norwich
1535–45	John Baldwin
1545–53	Edward Montagu
1553–4	Richard Morgan
1554–8	Robert Brooke
1558–9	Anthony Browne
1559–82	James Dyer
1582–1605	Edmund Anderson

Coventry and Lichfield, Bishop of

1459–1490	John Hales
1493–96	William Smith
1496–1502	John Arundel
1503–31	Geoffrey Blythe
1534–43	Rowland Lee
1543–54	Richard Sampson
1554–9 (deprived)	Ralph Baynes
1560–79	Thomas Bentham
1580–1609	William Overton

Desmond

1529–41	James Fitzmaurice FitzGerald, 12th Earl of
1541–58	James Fitzjohn FitzGerald, 13th Earl of
1558–83	(recognised 1560) Gerald FitzJames FitzGerald,

son of 13th Earl, inherited as 15th Earl of

1600–01   James FitzGerald, never succeeded his father as Earl but was known as 'Queen's Earl of Desmond' and the 'Tower Earl' becuase of lengthy imprisonment (16 years) in Tower following the 14th Earl's rebellion

1598–1601   (d. 1607) John Fitzthomas FitzGerald, assumed title of Sugan Earl of, but was not accepted as Earl

Dorset

1485–1501   Thomas Grey, restored Marquis of

1501–30   Thomas Grey, third son of 1st Marquis, 2nd Marquis of

1530–51   Henry Grey, 3rd Marquis of (Father of Lady Jane and made Duke of Suffolk, 1551)

Durham, Bishop of

1485–94   John Shirwood

1494–1501   Richard Fox

1502–05   William Sever

1507–08   Christopher Bainbridge

1509–23   Thomas Ruthall

1523–9   Thomas Wolsey *in commendam*

1530–59 (restored)   Cuthbert Tunstall

1561–76   James Pilkington

1577–87   Richard Barnes

1589–95   Matthew Hutton

1595–1606   Tobias Matthew

Essex

1493–1540   Henry Bourchier, 2nd Bourchier Earl of Essex

1540–40 (executed)   Thomas Cromwell, Lord Cromwell of Wimbledon

1543–forfeited 1553   Baron William Parr of Kendal (brother of Queen Catharine and connected with Earldom of Essex through brief marriage to Anne Bourchier, d. of Henry, Earl of Essex). Parr was also Marquis of Northampton 1547–53 (forfeited), 1559–71 d. but was not restored to Earldom of Essex in 1559

1572–6   Walter Devereux, 2nd Viscount Hereford

1576–1601   Robert Devereux

Hertford

1537–47   Sir Edward Seymour, Viscount Beauchamp of Hache, created Earl of *see* Somerset

1559–1621   Edward Seymour, restored Earl of (1560: secretly married Lady Catherine Grey, daughter of Duke of Suffolk and sister of Lady Jane; 1561: imprisoned in Tower for treasonable act; 1571: released.)

Huntingdon

1529–45   George Hastings, Baron Hastings, Earl of

1545–61   Francis Hastings, Baron Hastings

	1561–95 Henry Hastings. In line of descent to throne. President of North. Married to Catherine Dudley, daughter of Northumberland in 1553. 'The Puritan Earl'

**Keeper, Lord
(of the
Great Seal)**

1500–02   Henry Deane, Archbp of Canterbury

1502–04   William Warham, Archbp of Canterbury (became Lord Chancellor in 1504)

1532–3   Sir Thomas Audley (was Lord Chancellor, 1533–44)

1547   William Paulet, 1st Lord St John

1551–2   Thomas Goodrich, Bp of Ely. Was Lord Chancellor, 1552–3

1558–79   Sir Nicholas Bacon. Lord Keeper

1592–6   Sir John Puckering. Lord Keeper.

1596–1603   Sir Thomas Egerton. Lord Keeper. Created 1st Lord Ellesmere in 1601

Kildare

1478–1513   Gerald FitzMaurice FitzGerald, son of Thomas the 7th Earl, inherited as 8th Earl of Kildare, known as 'the Great Earl'

1513–34   Gerald FitzGerald, son of 8th Earl, inherited as 9th Earl

1534–7 (executed)   Thomas FitzGerald, son of 9th Earl, inherited as 10th Earl of Kildare

1554–85   Gerald FitzGerald, son of 9th Earl, inherited as 11th Earl of Kildare

Lincoln

1467–87   John De La Pole, Earl of (Eldest son of John, 1st Duke of Suffolk and Elizabeth, sister of Edward IV). Supported Lambert Simnel and was killed at Battle of Stoke

1525–34   Henry Brandon, son of Charles, Duke of Suffolk

1572–85   Lord Edward Fiennes de Clinton made Earl of

**Lincoln,
Bishop of**

1480–94   John Russell

1496–1514   William Smith

1514   Thomas Wolsey

1514–21   William Atwater

1521–47   John Longland

1547–51   Henry Holbeach or Rands

1552–4 (deprived)   John Taylor

1554–6   John White

1557–9 (deprived)   Thomas Watson

1560–71   Nicholas Bullingham

1571–84   Thomas Cooper

1584–95   William Wickham

1595–1608   William Chaderton

Lisle

1533   Arthur Plantagenet, Viscount

1542   John Dudley, Baron Somerai, Basset and Teyes and Viscount Lisle

1562–80   Ambrose Dudley, Lord Lisle and Earl of Warwick

London,
Bishop of

1450–89   Thomas Kempe

1489–96   Richard Hill

1496–1501   Thomas Savage

1502–03   William Warham

1504–05   William Barons

1506–22   Richard FitzJames

1522–30   Cuthbert Tunstall

1530–9   John Stokesley

1540–9 (deprived)   Edmund Bonner

1550–3 (deprived)   Nicholas Ridley

1553–9   Edmund Bonner. (Dates refer to restoration and deprivation of office.)

1559–70   Edmund Grindal

1570–7   Edwin Sandys

1577–94   John Aylmer

1594–6   Richard Fletcher

1597–1604   Richard Bancroft

Norfolk

1483–5   John Howard, 1st Howard Duke of Norfolk. Slain on Bosworth Field where he supported Richard III

1514–24   Thomas Howard, 2nd Howard Duke of

1524–54   Thomas Howard, 3rd Howard Duke of (he forfeited the title, 1547, but was restored August 1553)

1554–72 (executed)   Thomas Howard, 4th Howard Duke of

Northampton

1547–53 (attainted)   Baron Parr of Kendal, Earl of Essex, created Marquis of (Brother of Queen Catharine)

1559–71   William Parr restored. Extinct by 1571

1604   Henry Howard made 1st Earl of

Northumberland 1470–89   Sir Henry Percy, son of 3rd Earl, inherited as 4th Earl. Killed near Thirsk during Yorkshire Rebellion

1489–1527   Sir Henry Algernon Percy inherited as 5th Earl

1527–37   Sir Henry Algernon Percy, son of 5th Earl, inherited as 6th Earl. This was the Harry Percy who had been Anne Boleyn's youthful lover

1551–3 (executed)   John Dudley, Earl of Warwick, made Duke of

1557–71 (executed 1572)   Sir Thomas Percy, grandson of the 5th Earl who had been attainted, restored to Earldom as 7th Earl

1572–85   Sir Henry Percy, brother of 7th Earl, inherited as 8th Earl

1585–1632   Sir Henry Percy, son of 8th Earl, inherited as 9th Earl. Known as 'Wizard Earl' because of scientific experiments

Nottingham
1483–92   William de Berkeley created Earl of
1525–36   Henry Fitzroy, Duke of Richmond and Somerset, created Earl of. This was Henry VIII's illegitimate son
1596–1624   Lord Charles Howard of Effingham created 1st Earl of

Ormond(e)
1477–1515   Thomas Butler, 7th Earl of Ormond
1492   Thomas Bullen (Boleyn) created Baron Ormond
1515–28   (relinquished) Sir Piers Butler (inherited as 8th Earl of Ormond. When Henry forced him to relinquish title to Boleyn, he created Butler Earl of Ossory in compensation
1529–38   Sir Thomas Boleyn, created Earl of Wiltshire and Ormond
1538 restored–1539 d.   Sir Piers Butler, 8th Earl
1541–6   James Butler, Viscount Thurles, restored as 9th Earl of Ormond, died in London from poisoning
1546–1614   Thomas Butler, son of James, inherited as 10th Earl. Known as 'Black Earl'. Brought up a Protestant at Henry VIII's court

Oxford
1485–1513   John de Vere, restored as 13th Earl of
1514–26   John de Vere, nephew of 13th Earl, inherited as 14th Earl of
1526–40   John de Vere, second cousin of 14th Earl, inherited as 15th Earl of
1540–62   John de Vere, son and heir of 15th Earl, inherited as 16th Earl of
1562–1604   Edward de Vere inherited as 17th Earl of

Pembroke
1532–6   Anne Boleyn, Marchioness of (created 1 September 1532)

Pembroke
1551–70   William Herbert, grandson of William Herbert, Earl of Pembroke of the First Creation, was created 1st Earl of Pembroke of Second Creation
1570–1601   Henry Herbert, Lord Herbert, inherited as 2nd Earl of. He married Catherine Grey in 1553 but divorced her in 1554 after Jane Grey's execution. He married Mary Sidney in 1577, after Catherine's death in 1568

Rochford
1495   Thomas Bullen (Boleyn) Baron Ormond (grandfather to Anne Boleyn) created Baron Rochford of Rochford
1525–30   Thomas Boleyn, son of the above, created Viscount Rochford

1530–36 (executed)   George Boleyn, son of Thomas Boleyn Earl of Wiltshire and Ormonde and brother of Anne Boleyn, created Viscount Rochford

Salisbury   1513–41 (executed)   Margaret Plantagenet, daughter of George, Duke of Clarence, brother of Edward IV, married by Henry VII to Sir Richard Pole (d. 1505) of Bucks. and given lands in atonement for d. of her brother Edward, Earl of Warwick; created Countess of, and made governess of Princess Mary. Mother of Reginald and Henry Pole (*see* section XI) 1539: Act of Attainder, 1541: executed

Shrewsbury   1473–?   George Talbot, son of John, 3rd Earl, inherited as 4th Earl of

1538–60   Francis Talbot, 2nd son of 4th Earl, inherited as 5th Earl of

1560–90   George Talbot, son of 5th Earl, inherited as 6th Earl of. In 1568 he married Elizabeth known as 'Bess of Hardwick'

1590–1616   Gilbert Talbot, 2nd son of 6th Earl, inherited as 7th Earl of. He married Mary Cavendish, daughter of Bess of Hardwick

Somerset   1500   Edmund Tudor, infant 3rd son of Henry VII (died 1500)

1525–36   Henry Fitzroy created Duke of Somerset. Illegitimate son of Henry VIII

1547–52 (executed)   Edward Seymour, Earl of Hertford, created Duke of

Southampton   1537–42   William FitzWilliam, Lord High Admiral, created Earl of

1547–50   Sir Thomas Wriothesley, Knight of the Garter and Lord Chancellor, created first Wriothesley Earl of Southampton

1550–81   Henry, son of Thomas 1st Earl, inherited as 2nd Earl of

1581–1624   Henry, son of 2nd Earl, inherited as 3rd Earl when aged only 8. This was Shakespeare's patron and friend

Strange (of Knockyn)   1559   Henry Stanley, Lord Strange
1590   Ferdinando Stanley

Suffolk   1455–92   John de la Pole, restored to be 2nd De La Pole Duke of Suffolk. Supported Richard III at Bosworth but swore fealty to Henry VII

1492–3   Edmund de la Pole, Duke of. He surrendered the dukedom February 1493

1493–1513   (executed) Edmund de la Pole created Earl of

1514–45   Charles Brandon, Duke of. He married first Mary Tudor; then Catherine Willoughby (Bertie)

1545–c.51   Henry, son of Charles, Duke of Suffolk while student at Cambridge.

1551   Charles, son of Charles, briefly Duke of

1551–4 (executed)   Henry Grey, Marquis of Dorset. He was Lady Jane Grey's father

Surrey
1483–1514   Thomas Howard, restored as Earl of Surrey in 1489. He became 2nd Howard Duke of Norfolk

1514–24   Thomas Howard, eldest son of Thomas, 2nd Duke of Norfolk, Earl of Surrey. He became 3rd Howard Duke of Norfolk

1524–47 (executed)   Henry Howard son of Thomas 3rd Duke of Norfolk, called Earl of Surrey by courtesy

1553–4   Thomas Howard restored to title

1554–72 (executed)   Thomas Howard, his grandson, made Earl of

1572?   Philip Howard, eldest son of Thomas, 4th Duke of Norfolk, attended Cambridge in 1570s with courtesy title of Earl of. Became Earl of Arundel when he married Mary Fitzalan, the heir

1604–46   Thomas Howard, son of Philip restored to Earldom of Surrey in 1604

Sussex
1529–42   Sir Robert Radcliffe, son of John, 1st Baron Fitzwalter, created 1st Earl of Sussex. Name is occasionally given as Ratcliffe.

1542–57   Sir Henry Radcliffe, son of 1st Earl, inherited as 2nd Earl of

1557–83   Sir Thomas, eldest son of 2nd Earl, inherited as 3rd Earl of

1583–93   Sir Henry Radcliffe, son of 2nd Earl, inherited from brother as 4th Earl of

1593–1629   Robert Radcliffe, son of 4th Earl, inherited as 5th Earl of

Tyrone
1542–59   Con Bacach O'Neill, created 1st Earl of (also given as Con Bacagh O'Neill)

1559–60   Shane O'Neill, son of Con, recognised by Elizabeth on accession but revoked in 1560

1560–2   Brien O'Neill, grandson of Con

1585–1614 (forfeited title)   Hugh O'Neill, grandson of Con, admitted Earl in 1585

Confusion is added to this tale by the existence of Sir Turlough Luineach O'Neill (c.1530–1595) who was Lord of Tyrone and a contender for Shane O'Neill's position

Warwick
1475–99 (executed) Edward son of George, Duke of Clarence, and Earl of Warwick
1547–51 John Dudley, Viscount Lisle, a descendant of Richard Beauchamp, Earl of Warwick, 1401–39. He was later Duke of Northumberland
1551–4 Lord John Dudley. Eldest son of John Dudley, Duke of Northumberland. He was styled Earl of Warwick during Northumberland's lifetime

Willoughby
1580 Peregrine Bertie made Baron Willoughby of Eresby

Winchester, Bishop of
1447–86 William Wayneflete
187–92 Peter Courtenay
1493–1501 Thomas Langton
1501–28 Richard Fox
1529–30 Thomas Wolsey
1531–51 (deprived) Stephen Gardiner
1551–3 (deprived) John Ponet
1553–5 Stephen Gardiner, restored in 1553
1556–9 (deprived) John White
1561–80 Robert Horne
1580–4 John Watson
1584–94 Thomas Cooper
1595 William Wickham
1596 William Day
1597–1616 Thomas Bilson

Worcester, Bishop of
1476–86 John Alcock
1486–97 Robert Morton
1497–8 Giovanni de' Gigli
1498–1521 Silvestro de' Gigli
1523–33 Geronimo de' Ghinucci
1535–9 (resigned) Hugh Latimer
1539–43 John Bell
1543–51 Nicholas Heath
1552–4 (deprived) John Hooper
1554–5 (restored in 1554) Nicholas Heath
1555–9 (deprived) Richard Pates
1559–71 Edwin Sandys
1571–6 Nicholas Bullingham
1577–83 John Whitgift
1584–91 Edmund Freke
1593–5 Richard Fletcher
1596–7 Thomas Bilson
1597–1610 Gervase Babington

York, Archbishop of
1480–1500 Thomas Rotherham
1501–07 Thomas Savage

1508–14   Christopher Bainbridge
1514–30   Thomas Wolsey
1531–44   Edward Lee
1545–54 (deprived)   Robert Holgate
1555–9 (deprived)   Nicholas Heath
1561–8   Thomas Young
1570–6   Edmund Grindal
1577–88   Edwin Sandys
1589–94   John Piers
1595–1606   Matthew Hutton

Glossary

Accession Day Tilts   By the 1570s the Queen's accession day, 17 November, had become a national holiday marked by elaborate tournaments under the control of Sir Henry Lee. These court tournaments revived the cult of chivalry in the interests of Protestant patriotism.

Adiaphora   Greek for 'things indifferent'. In Germany a group of Protestants argued that certain Catholic practices (such as confirmation, extreme unction, the Mass without belief in transubstantiation, and veneration of saints) might be conceded in the interests of peace without compromising essential Protestant doctrine. In England there was some argument of this kind surrounding the use of vestments and rituals such as the cross in baptism, kneeling at the name of Jesus, and the use of the ring in marriage.

Advowson   Right to appoint one in holy orders to an ecclesiastical benefice. Treated under English civil law as a piece of property which can be transferred by sale or grant. *See* 'hac vice presentations' and 'benefice'

Affective Family   Used by late twentieth-century historians to describe the family knit together by sentiment which is thought by some (notably Lawrence Stone) to have emerged for the first time in the early modern period.

Affines (Affinity)   At this time meant relations (or relationship) by marriage. *See* 'Consanguinity'.

All Saints' Day (All Hallows)   1 November. An important feast of the pre-reformation church.

All Soul's Day   2 November. An important feast of the pre-reformation church.

Amicable Grant   Wolsey's attempt to raise money for the French war in 1525. Without parliamentary sanction Wolsey levied one third of clergy goods and one sixth of laymen's goods. After massive demonstrations in Suffolk, Wolsey was persuaded to withdraw the tax.

Anabaptist   Umbrella term to cover sects which denied the truth of infant baptism.

Annunciation (Lady Day)   25 March. Used as the starting point of the year in England from the twelfth century down to 1752, although 1 January was accounted New Year's Day, following the Roman tradition. It occurs as a Red Letter Day in the Book of Common Prayer. *See* 'Holy Days'.

Anti-clericalism   Opposition to the clergy as a body. Some debate about its importance.

Aragonese Faction   Sometimes used by historians to describe those at Henry VIII's court who supported Catherine of Aragon in the divorce proceedings and opposed Cromwellian religious reforms. There is some doubt whether such a 'faction' existed.

Arches, Court of   Court of appeal for the Province of Canterbury. Its equivalent for the Province of York was Chancery. Court of Arches was physically located in the church of St Mary le Bow (St Mary of the Arches, *de arcibus*), London.

Archpriest Controversy   In 1599, 31 roman Catholic secular priests, led by William Bishop (c.1553–1624), appealed to Rome to cancel the appointment of George Blackwell (c.1545–1613) as Archpriest and superior of the English mission on the grounds that the pro-Jesuit policy was harming the Roman Catholic cause in England. The group was known as the Appellant Priests. This initial appeal was unsuccessful but further appeals in 1601 and 1602, with the backing of the French ambassador, resulted in Blackwell's reprimand and in January 1603 a renunciation of the policy of seeking to replace Elizabeth.

Aristocracy   Used in several senses. By some historians used to describe titled members of society with their families (that is, the nobility) and by others to include both the peerage and the gentry, whether titled or no.

Armada(s)   A fleet of warships. Most frequently used to describe fleet sent by Philip II of Spain against England in 1588.

Ascension Day   Thursday following 'Rogation Sunday' and 'Rogation Days' (q.v.). It was one of the chief feasts of the year and kept on the 5th Thursday after Easter.

Ash Wednesday   First day in Lent. This was the day when, traditionally, the whole congregation assembled for general penance. The Book of Common Prayer of 1549 prescribed a communion service for this day.

Assumption of the Blessed Virgin Mary   15 August. This important feast-day of the Catholic church was removed from the Book of Common Prayer of 1549 and not restored in those of 1552 and 1559.

Attainder   An act of parliament was passed to stage an execution without trial. The title and possessions of the attainted passed to the Crown. This was the method favoured by the Tudors for ridding themselves of opponents.

Audience, Court of The Provinces of Canterbury and York each had a court of audience at which serious cases (often involving clergy) were heard in the presence of the Archbishop. Similar courts were held in each diocese, when they were commonly special sessions of the Consistory Court presided over by the bishop.

Augmentations, Court of This was a government department created in 1536 to administer the new Crown revenues from the dissolved monasteries. In 1547 it was amalgamated with the Court of General Surveyors and both were absorbed by the Exchequer in 1554.

Baptism Christian initiatory rite. Spiritual regeneration signalled by water and the sign of the cross. Debate concerning the nature of baptism both among the reformers themselves and between the Protestants and the Catholics. Book of Common Prayer accepted baptism as a sacrament and clung to Catholic doctrine that baptism was necessary for salvation. Roman Catholics restated their doctrine at Council of Trent and emphasised fact that baptism was not only a sign of grace but actually conferred grace upon the baptised.

Bedlam *See* 'Bridewell'.

Benefice An ecclesiastical office with prescribed duties attached, in reward for which certain revenues were given (known as temporalities). For examples, a vicarage was a benefice and so was a prebend. The vicar discharged a cure (care) of souls in exchange for which he received the small tithes from his parishioners. A prebendary's duties were associated with the cathedral, and in exchange for their performance he drew revenues from a given portion of land.

Benefit of Clergy Clergy charged with felonies exempted from secular trial. Applied to all those who were tonsured (i.e. in minor as well as major orders) as well as to nuns. Extended to all those who could read a Latin passage at a time when it was assumed that only the clergy would have this skill. Not completely abolished in England until 1827 but benefit of clergy removed at the reformation for many categories of offence.

Benevolence So-called free gifts made by the wealthy to the Crown. Richard III made them illegal but both Henry VII and Henry VIII used them.

Bible *See* p. 95–8.

Bishops' Book Popular name for *The Institution of a Christian Man*, 1537. This statement of the doctrine of Henry VIII's church was drawn up by a committee of bishops but, although published, never received royal approval. *See* 'King's Book'.

Black rubric In September 1552 John Knox complained, in a sermon before Edward VI, against the directive in the new Prayer Book for communicants to adopt a kneeling position. Cranmer refused to alter the wording. The Council then inserted the 'Black Rubric' into the Prayer Book (apparently on its own authority). This Rubric denied any intention to adore the elements of bread and wine or to imply that they were the body and blood of Christ. (*See* 'Elevation of the host', q.v.).

Blois, Treaty of   Treaty of 1572 between England and France. The English hoped thereby to isolate Spain and to prevent France invading Flanders.

Bond of Association, 1584   *See* pp. 26–7, 63.

Border Wardens   Officials appointed to wardenries of the East, West and Middle Marches on the border with Scotland for purposes of supervision and defence.

Bosworth, Battle of   22 August 1485, Richard III was surrounded at Bosworth Field, Leicestershire, after his rash advance to support his vanguard. He was defeated and died. Victory of Henry Tudor. Sir William Stanley's troops deserted to Henry's side.

Bridewell   Workhouses. Houses of correction. Name derives from Henry VIII's Palace of Bridewell at Blackfriars, London, which in 1553 was given by Edward VI to the City of London as a workhouse for vagrants and troublesome apprentices. This also ran the Bethlehem hospital for the insane, commonly known as 'Bedlam' (q.v.), and was linked to the St Thomas's and St Bartholemew's Hospitals and to Christ's Hospital for destitute children. This scheme was widely copied by magistrates elsewhere but the local Bridewells frequently lost their 'workhouse' aspect and turned into prisons for the poor.

Bruges, Treaty of   Secret treaty (1521) between Emperor Charles V and Henry VIII providing for a joint invasion of France before March 1523. Did not materialise. English staged campaign (autumn 1523), and with minimal help from Charles got nowhere.

Buggery   In 1534 parliament passed the first legislation against buggery in all its forms, homosexual and heterosexual, and named the offence punishable by the death penalty.

Bull   From the Latin word *bulla* meaning seal. Denotes a written order or mandate from the Pope. It would be sealed by the papal signet on wax or kept in a seal-box.

Calais   This small port was captured by the English in 1347. Sole surviving possession of the Hundred Years War, this town and its small pale became important for trading and strategic reasons. It was garrisoned but the English neglected its defences. The town sent M.P.s to parliament until the French captured the port in 1558.

Calendar, Gregorian Bull of Pope Gregory XIII on 24 February 1582 introduced a reformed calendar which cut ten days out of 1582 (5–14 October inclusive) to compensate for earlier divergences between the calendar and the solar year, and introduced a leap year every fourth year. Year began officially on 1 January. Catholic states adopted the new style in the sixteenth century but Protestant states did not do so, in general, until the eighteenth. Known as 'new style'. *See* 'Calendar, Julian'.

Calendar, Julian Unreformed Roman calendar retained in Protestant countries beyond the Tudor period. Known as 'old style'. No leap years. *See* 'Calendar, Gregorian'.

Calvinism The theology of John Calvin (1509–64), French reformer and theologian, who shaped the reformation in Geneva. This was formulated in his *Institutes* (final edition published in Latin, 1559). He accepted various tenets of Lutheranism (Scripture as the only rule of faith; the denial of free-will after the Fall; justification by faith alone without works) but added the doctrines of predestination, the certainty of salvation and the impossibility of losing grace. On the question of the Lord's Supper, Calvin stood some way between Luther's belief in the Real Presence and Zwingli's view of the breaking of bread and drinking of wine as mere symbolism. Calvin was also concerned to reform the worship of Christians. Its nature was determined in the Scriptures and to his mind rejection of the Commandment not to worship images was a grave affront to God's majesty. He, and the churches who followed his teaching, reaffirmed the centrality of spiritual worship and drew strict boundaries between the spiritual and material which on occasion led to civil disobedience in a war against the idols (iconoclasm). It represented a determined move away from a worship in which ritual and sacraments produced predictable and specific effects. This approach sharply distinguished the Calvinists from the Lutheran churches which retained much of what Archbishop Laud was later to describe as 'the beauty of holiness' and clung to the centrality of the doctrine of justification by faith alone as a protection against material instrumentality in religion.

The Second Helvetic Confession of 1566, which summed up Calvinistic theology, was accepted by many Protestant countries but not by England. Many of the 'precise' Christians of Elizabethan England wished for a further reformation of the English church to bring it in line with the Calvinist continental churches.

Cambridge Group for the History of Population and Social Structure Founded by T.P.R. Laslett and E.A. Wrigley to apply French demographic research techniques to English sources. Began with simple work on parish registers but progressed to sophisticated family reconstitution, analysis of time series and aggregative back-projection.

Canon law Ecclesiastical law pertaining to faith, morals and discipline.

It had been built up gradually from papal and conciliar legislation. Some canons were universally binding; others only had local application.

Capitalism In a capitalist economic system the means of production are privately owned by a few 'capitalists' and labour is separated from the means of production and socialised. Maximum profit is the purpose of economic activity. Acquisitiveness is regulated by the market place and is otherwise untrammelled unless it infringes the law. Capitalists pursue those modes of economic behaviour which appear most systematic, rational and appropriate to achieve maximum profit. Under early capitalism, entrepreneurs sought to establish the principles of acquisitiveness, competition and rational economic behaviour; home industry remained prevalent and technology was primitive – the few factories there were yielded low output. The suggestion that Calvinism caused, or was at least conducive to, the growth of capitalism in the sixteenth century, first posited by Max Weber, was adapted to the English Puritan case by R.H. Tawney, *Religion and the Rise of Capitalism* (1926). But their thesis has come under considerable attack. Historians now argue that neither Protestantism nor even Calvinism was a necessary condition for the emergence and development of rational capitalism but the link is, nevertheless, still stressed by non-specialists.

Cateau-Cambrésis, Treaties of In 1559 both England and Spain signed separate treaties with France, ending hostilities. The French retained Calais (q.v.) for 8 years but renounced territorial ambitions in Italy.

Catechisms A popular manual of Christian doctrine adopting a dialogue form of question and answer for use orally. An ancient form although the term seems to have originated in the sixteenth century. The reformation saw a flood of catechisms, Protestant and Catholic.

The prayer book catechism was from 1549 to 1662 printed directly before the confirmation rite and the parish priest was ordered to instruct the young of the parish on Sundays and Holy Days. The catechism contains an explanation of the covenant entered into on baptism, the Apostles' Creed, the Ten Commandments and the Lord's Prayer. Alexander Nowell, Dean of St Paul's under Elizabeth, appears to have been responsible for much of the catechism. (*See* 'Thomas Becon' and 'Alexander Nowell' in Section XI.)

Celibacy (of clergy) Vow of perfect chastity required of all admitted to major orders in the Catholic church from the eleventh century onwards. Abolished in church of England in reign of Henry VIII. Revived by Mary I. Elizabeth known to favour celibacy of clergy.

Chalice Cup used to administer the consecrated wine at the Eucharist.

Chamber, Royal *See* Section VI.

Chancery, Court of   *See* Section IX.

Chantries   Used to describe the little chapels in which the Masses for the dead were said and the endowments of the same chapels. Became very numerous in the fourteenth and fifteenth centuries. The Chantries Act (1547) dissolved chantries and diverted endowments elsewhere. Debate about the deleterious effect of this dissolution upon educational provision.

Chaseabout Raid   James Stuart, Earl of Moray's failed rebellion against Mary Stuart after her attempted Catholic coup in summer 1565. Name derived from indecisive character of the action. They chased about Scotland without ever meeting. Moray took refuge in England.

Chivalry   Describes originally the medieval knightly class which owed military service to feudal overlord or King. Came to be identified with the aristocracy and lost its military function. Chivalry often transferred to describe the distinctive customs, codes of morality (emphasising courage, loyalty, skill, various Christian virtues, and the defence of womankind), and ritual and display which became associated with it.

Church Ales   These were fund-raising events, originating in the middle ages, traditionally involving the sale of beer.

Cinque Ports (Five Ports)   A group of ports in south-east England (originally Hastings, Sandwich, Romney, Dover and Hythe although others such as Winchelsea and Rye were later added) which from the thirteenth century onwards furnished most of the English Navy and received various privileges in return, including jurisdiction over the coast from Seaford in East Sussex to Birchington in Kent. Their Lord Warden was therefore a powerful dignitary.

Classis, classes   One of the hierarchy of courts within the Presbyterian system of church government. It consisted of the ministers and respresentative elders of the churches within a given area. For some time it was argued that a Presbyterian system of classes operated within Elizabethan Puritanism – the Conference of ministers focussed on Dedham in Suffolk being frequently cited as an example of a classis in operation – but an effective challenge was made to this argument by Patrick Collinson who questioned its relationship with other classes (and, therefore, its position in a national hierarchy of presbyeterian government) and its rejection of episcopacy as an acceptable form of church government.

Coinage   Pound Sterling = 240 pennies or pence (d); 20 shillings (s)
Shilling Sterling = 12 pennies or pence (d)
Groat = 4 pennies or pence (d)
Penny
Half-penny
Farthing = quarter penny

Mark Sterling = 160 pennies or pence (d); 13s 4d
Half Mark Sterling = 80 pennies or pence (d); 6s 8d; one third of a pound. Known as the Noble or double florin
Mite = one twenty-fourth of a penny. Used for accounting purposes only and no coin of this denomination minted.

Collegiate churches These were churches governed by a corporation or college of secular clergy (q.v.). Many were suppressed at the Reformation although a few survived; for example, St George's Chapel, Windsor.

Colloquy used by Erasmus to describe a 'conversation' or dialogue. Used to describe a meeting or conference (the modern form is colloquium).

Commission A formal charge to perform a given function and a delegation of the necessary powers to fulfil this charge. This was a common instrument of both civil and ecclesiastical government during the Tudor period. See, for example, the Ecclesiastical High Commission (*see* Section IX).

Common Prayer, Book of Official prayer book of church of England. Contains order of service for morning and evening prayer, eucharist, baptism, matrimony, burial, confirmation and other rites, the psalter and (from 1552) the ordinal.
1549 First Prayer Book of Edward VI (enforced by Act of Uniformity)
1550 Ordinal
1552 Second Prayer Book of Edward VI. Recast Holy Communion Service; included introductions to morning and evening prayer; ordered the use of surplice instead of vestments in the ornaments rubric; removed references to 'mass' and 'altar'; included, without parliamentary authority, so-called 'black rubric' or declaration on kneeling during the communion.
1553 Mary I repealed Prayer Books and restored old services.
1559 Elizabethan Book of Common Prayer. Omits the black rubric.

Commons, House of Lower house of parliament at Westminster. In 1485 it had 296 members representing 37 counties and 111 boroughs. The number of constituencies grew so that by 1603 there were 406 members representing 90 county seats and 370 borough seats. See Section VII for dates of sessions.

Commonwealth Term used to convey the interests of the entire community of England – the *res publica*.

Commonwealthmen A term used by some historians and others to describe a group of lay and clerical Protestants during the reign of Edward VI who agitated for reform of the state involving the curbing of corruption in the interests of the entire commonwealth. The precise composition (and, indeed, the very existence) of this group has been contested. See entries for Brinklow, Crowley, Hales, Latimer, Lever and Smith in Section XI

Communion (1) Fellowship between Christians. (2) Group or denomination of Christians sharing a common creed (q.v.). (3) The sacrament of the Eucharist

Communion in One Kind Catholic practice at the Eucharist of offering the consecrated bread but not the wine to laypeople. Only the priest took the Communion in 'both kinds'. It was, however, common for the laity to partake in wine at the absolution of sin.

Communion in Both Kinds Protestant practice of offering both consecrated bread and wine to all communicants, lay and spiritual.

Conciliar Adjectival form of council.

Conciliar Government Government by council; as, for example, the Privy Council and its offshoots, Star Chamber, Court of Requests and Court of High Commission.

Conciliar theory maintained that supreme authority in the Catholic church lay with a General Council and not the Pope. The conciliar movement or 'conciliarism' reached its apogee in the fifteenth century.

Consanguinity Relationship by blood. *See* 'Affines (Affinity)'

Consistory In the church of England this described the Diocesan Bishop's court. In the Roman Catholic Church it was also the assembly of cardinals called together by, and meeting in the presence of, the Pope.

Constables *See* Section VIII.

Consubstantiation This is an interpretation of the Eucharist, espoused by the Lutherans, which sees the consecrated bread and wine as coexistent with but not transformed into the body and blood of Christ. *See* Transubstantiation'.

Convocation Each province had its own representative assembly of clergy, known as Convocation. Since the thirteenth century they had each been composed of an Upper House (of bishops) and a Lower House (of clergy). Originally these were called to grant clerical taxation to the Crown but they came to deliberate on and make laws or canons for the church. The act of parliament which embodied the Submission of the Clergy (1534) considerably curtailed Convocation's legislative powers. After the reformation it was accepted that Convocation would be dissolved at the same time as parliament.

Cope A liturgical vestment resembling a long cloak.

Cornish Rising Thomas Flamank, a Bodmin lawyer, and James, Lord Audley led a rebellion in 1497 against the levying of taxes for Scottish wars. A force of thousands moved east, killing a tax commissioner at Taunton, but was defeated by Giles, Lord Daubeney at the Battle of Blackheath on 13 June 1497.

Corpus Christi   Latin meaning 'body of Christ'. Name of an important religious festival on the Thursday after Trinity Sunday (in June) honouring the Eucharist. It assumed a prominent part in the culture of sixteenth-century towns prior to the Reformation. Frequently the occasion of a fair, as at Coventry.

Council, General   Assembly of Bishops of the whole Catholic church, convened by the Pope.

Council, Great   Until the death of Henry VII it was relatively common for the King to hold meetings of the Great Council. This has sometimes been seen as indicative of the weakening of the independent power of the nobility. *See* Section VI.

Council, Local   Also known as synods. Persisted in Church of England after Reformation.

Council of the North   *See* Section VIII.

Council in the Marches of Wales   *See* Section XIII.

Council of the West   *See* Section XIII.

Counter-Reformation   Term commonly employed to describe movement within Roman Catholic Church to halt spread of Protestantism and win back converts. More fashionable to use term Catholic Reformation, which does not see the cause of Catholic reform purely in terms of reaction to Protestant activity.

Courts, Inns of   *See* 'Inns of Court'.

Court, The   Both temporal and spiritual rulers had courts. Sixteenth-century rulers, in general, carried on the medieval peripatetic tradition of moving their entourage around with them from castle to castle and palace to palace. The monarchs displayed their power and influence to other potentates by means of outward show at court. Sometimes the monarch would take his court abroad to impress a fellow ruler, as Henry VIII effectively did at the Field of the Cloth of Gold (q.v.) in 1520. Sovereigns also maintained their control at home by patronage (or withholding of patronage) at court.

The royal household formed the basis of the court. Subjects angled for a place on the permanent establishment of this household – such a place (as, for example, Groom of the Chamber) brought with it free board and lodging and the potential for influence. But certain great men and women were also accorded 'bouge of court' (the right to food, drink, lodging, and fuel in the royal households not only for themselves but a specified personal retinue). In the 1540s the members of the Privy

Council were accorded 'bouge of court' as were Gentlemen of the Privy Chamber. Others had to apply to the monarch for permission to attend the court and thus influence events. When the monarch withheld permission this was considered a mark of disfavour.

Court life was not always a matter of receiving and entertaining foreign ambassadors and their retinues or listening to the counsel of advisers. Highly organised entertainment was provided – including sports such as tennis, hunting, jousting and masques – and within a carefully controlled etiquette cultural activities were encouraged. 'Courtship' between the men and women of the court was in itself a highly-charged form of entertainment. Monarchs sought to keep it within the bounds of the chivalric code and through it to exercise their own patronage. Elizabeth, for example, felt that she had rights over the marriage of her maids of honour.

Creed From the Latin *credo* meaning I believe. A summary and declaration of main articles of Christian faith. The three creeds (Apostles', Nicene and Athanasian) had their origins in the early church.

De Heretico Comburendo An Act passed by parliament in 1401 as first step in suppression of Lollardy (2 Henry IV, c.15). Persons suspected of holding heretical opinions to be arrested and tried by canon law. If found guilty, the ecclesiastical judge was to hand the heretic over to the secular courts for the death sentence. Death was by burning at the stake. *De Heretico Comburendo* (sometimes *De Haeretico Comburendo*) was repealed under Henry VIII, restored by Mary I and finally repealed by Elizabeth I.

Delegates, Court of Created in 1534 as final court of appeal from archbishops' courts. Previously such appeals had gone to Rome (25 Henry VIII, c.19). Commission appointed for each separate case.

Diocese Territorial unit of administration under the ordinary jurisdiction of a bishop. Normally divided into parishes which are grouped into rural deaneries and archdeaconries.

Dissolution Term commonly used to describe dissolution of the monasteries by the acts of 1536 and 1539.

Divorce After the Reformation England was the only Protestant country with no form of legalised divorce. Elsewhere it was available to those who could prove adultery (especially by a wife), desertion or extreme cruelty. A commission to revise the canon law (originating in 1534) proposed a similar system but this never reached the statute book. There were, however, judicial separations and some seem to have interpreted this condition as conferring a right to remarry, although the church never conceded this. A full divorce might, however, be legalised by a private act of parliament. This meant that a full divorce was only available to those rich and influential enough to secure such an act.

Dominicans   An order of preaching friars founded in 1215.

Dower   *See* 'Jointure'.

Dowry   The portion which the bride brought to the marriage, in exchange for which she became entitled to support from her husband's property for the remainder of her life in the form of a dower of a third of his estate. *See* 'Jointure'.

Dry Stamp   At the close of Henry VIII's reign, when he was ill, and during the minority of Edward VI, documents were stamped with the royal signature which was then inked in by authorised clerks. In the possession of first Somerset, and then Northumberland, it was the key to authority and power. Elizabeth I made sure that no-one else had access to it.

Earl Marshal   This was one of the great offices of state. The Earl Marshal presided over the College of Arms and the High Court of Chivalry (making grants of arms and titles and judging disputes) and might deputise for the monarch in command of the armies or in emergency summoning of parliament. In the fifteenth century (until 1485) it was a hereditary office of the Dukes of Norfolk. The sixteenth-century Dukes of Norfolk were granted the office for life only. When the fourth Duke was executed in 1572 the office was granted to the Earl of Shrewsbury and, on his death, it lapsed until Essex was appointed Earl Marshal in 1597. Essex seems to have intended to exploit the powers of the office.

Easter Day (Pascha)   A variable feast calculated to be the Sunday after full moon on or next after 21 March. Should you wish to calculate when Easter occurred in any particular year (and any feast dependent upon the date of Easter) consult C.R. Cheney, *Handbook of Dates for Students of English History*, 1961.

Ecclesiastical   Of or relating to the church. Not the same as religious.

Elevation of the Host   The 'host' was the consecrated bread which Catholics believed to be the sacrament or the body of Christ. By the fifteenth century it was common to elevate the host for adoration during the Eucharist. The acceptance of 'communion of the eyes' (which permitted the sick who could not swallow it, yet to gaze upon it and receive grace) reinforced this emphasis on 'viewing' the host. The host was regarded not only as a passive object to be worshipped, but also as an active object which worked wonders. There was much controversy within Catholicism concerning such teachings; the Protestants declared them anathema.

Empire, Holy Roman   Claim to universal empire based on succession to Roman Empire and especially active under Charles V of the House of Hapsburg. Austria, parts of southern Germany, the Netherlands,

Franche-Comte and Spain, Naples, Sicily, Sardinia and the Balearics and the Spanish possessions in the Americas were all part of Charles V's inheritance between 1516 and 1519 as eldest son of Philip of Burgundy and Joanna of Castile. In 1519 Charles was elected Holy Roman Emperor in preference to Francis I of France. The remainder of the period saw a struggle for Hapsburg succession in central Europe and immense Hapsburg-Valois rivalry in which England was embroiled. For a good discussion see H.G. Koenigsberger, George L. Mosse and G.Q. Bowler, *Europe in the Sixteenth Century*, Longman, 1989.

Emperors 1440–93 Frederick III of Hapsburg
1493–1519 Maximilian I (m. to Mary of Burgundy united the inheritance of Austria and Burgundy)
1519–56 Charles V. As the eldest son of Philip of Burgundy and Joanna of Castile, inherited Spain and her possessions along with Austrian and Burgundian possessions. He abdicated in 1556 and died in 1558.
1556–64 Ferdinand I (brother of Charles V)
1564–76 Maximilian II (son of Ferdinand and preferred by German electors to Philip II of Spain, Charles V's son)
1576–1612 Rudolf II

Enclosure Enclosure of land to extinguish common grazing rights over it for sheep pasture by private individuals. Mostly affected the Midlands. Controversial topic in sixteenth-century England when the pressure of population upon ever-shrinking commons became an issue.

Engrossment Amalgamation of two or more farms into one, allowing all but one farmhouse to decay and leading to depopulation. Often spoken of in same breath as enclosure (q.v.) but did not inevitably accompany it.

Entail Legal arrangement whereby land etc. is settled on a number of persons in succession so that it cannot be treated as the absolute possession of any of them for purposes of sale etc.

Erastian Policies subordinating the church to the state.

Escheator From 1377/8 escheators (royal officials) were responsible for a single county or a group of counties to the Exchequer of Audit for their investigation of the Crown's feudal rights, including wardship (q.v.).

Eucharist (from the Greek for Thanksgiving.) Also known as Communion, the Sacrament, the Lord's Supper.
    The central rite of Christian worship based upon the Last Supper when Jesus 'took bread, gave thanks and brake it, and gave it unto them, saying, This do in remembrance of me'. 'Likewise after supper he took the cup' and, saying that the wine was his blood shed for many, bade the disciples to drink from the cup. The precise meaning of this ritual gave rise to enormous controversy during the Tudor period: some argue that

in it lay the fundamental difference between Catholic and Protestant. (*See* 'Consubstantiation', 'Elevation of the host', 'Mass', 'Sacrament', 'Transubstantiation', q.v.) Before the Reformation the Catholic laity received the bread only; the Protestant reformers introduced communion in both kinds (bread and wine) for the laity, thus removing a symbol of the separation between the clergy and the laity.

Evil May Day   Xenophobic riots led by apprentices against foreigners and their property during the traditional May Day celebrations in 1517. Some of the rioters were subsequently executed. The most serious civil unrest in Tudor London.

Excommunication   Literally 'out of communion'; offenders against the canon law were punished by either greater or lesser excommunication. Greater excommunication involved complete isolation from the community of Christians as well as being prevented from sharing in the bread of the Eucharist. No Christian might trade with or commune with one suffering this penalty. Absolution from excommunication could be obtained by performing a set penance (traditionally wearing a white shirt and carrying a wand and confessing to one's sins in public – at church – in front of the congregation on a specific number of days) and presenting a certificate to this effect to the church court. The problems were those of over use, enforcement of the sanction, and the growing tendency for such penalties to be commuted into money payments.

Exercises   Exercises of preaching or lectures by combination were 'a device for regular provision of preaching, typically in a market town and weekly, on market day, or once a month'. These sermons were provided by a rota of ministers who voluntarily combined to offer this service. Sometimes the sermon would be followed by a conference of the ministers and a meal. While broadly speaking 'Puritan', these combination lectures or exercises were part of the tradition and life of the church in England.

Family, Extended   Used in several senses but most usually by historians (as opposed to historical demographers) to mean the *entire* family, co-resident or not, including grandparents, parents, uncles, aunts, adult offspring and children. Not to be confused with the Extended Family Household (*See* 'Household, Extended Family').

Family, Stem   Term which describes a downwards extended family co-residing. *See* 'Household, Stem Family'.

Feoffees   Trustees.

Field of Cloth of Gold   Elaborately staged meeting between 'courts of Henry VIII and Francis I of France in June 1520 near Calais. Expensive chivalric display.

First Fruits and Tenths   Beneficed clergy were obliged to pay (to the Crown after the Reformation) the first year's revenue from their benefice as specified in the *Valor Ecclesiasticus* or King's Books and, thereafter, a tenth of this income annually. What this really meant for the clergy has been hotly debated by historians. How realistic were the assessments contained in the *Valor Ecclesiasticus*?

Flodden, Battle of Battle on 7 September 1513 between James IV of Scotland and Henry VIII of England. Major English triumph. James IV killed and succeeded by infant James V, whose mother, Margaret Tudor (sister to Henry VIII), was now Regent.

Forty-Two Articles Defined the Eucharist in 1553 in a Zwinglian sense (the bread and wine are symbols of Christ's body and blood) and argued that justification before God was by faith alone, works playing no part in salvation and purgatory being a fiction.

Freewillers A small Protestant sect in south-east England, under the leadership of Henry Harte, during Edward VI's reign. The sect clung to a belief in the importance of freewill in the acquisition of salvation. It supported religious toleration. It was opposed by other Protestant groups, who espoused predestination. The group was persecuted under Mary I and disappeared without trace.

Gavelkind In Kent (and some other areas) free lands were divided equally among all the deceased's sons by the customary rule of gavelkind. But, in the same county, some copyholds of inheritance were divided amongst all the children, male *and* female and some only to the youngest son or child by ultimogeniture (q.v.). Even in cases where gavelkind prevailed, it seems to have been common for some of the beneficiaries to 'sell' their land to one of their number to prevent breaking up the estate into impossibly small units. *See* 'Partible Inheritance' and 'Wills, Statute of'.

Grand Tour Practice of sending a young gentleman to complete his education by travelling in Europe, learning modern languages and studying Italian art, and meeting major figures. It came into its own in the reign of Elizabeth and was well established by 1600.

Great Rebuilding Between c.1570 and c.1640 many of the aristocracy (gentry and nobility) built new and often magnificent houses.

Habit The distinctive dress which distinguished the cleric from the lay person and which was compulsory. There were continuing attempts throughout the century to enforce the rule that clergymen must not dress as laymen.

Hac Vice Presentations Ecclesiastical patrons were often unwilling to alienate advowsons (q.v.) entirely but would grant (for a sum of money) the right to present to an ecclesiastical benefice to a third party. In this way many people of relatively small means acquired patronage for their relatives and friends.

Hanaper Ancient name for the financial department of the Chancery into which fees were paid for letters patent and writs.

Henry, Louis Mid twentieth-century French demographer who developed technique of family reconstitution involving record linkage between baptismal, marriage and burial registers. Enormous influence on English historical demography.

Heresy Traditionally bishops, popes, general councils, universities and inquisitorial offices had defined orthodox belief and, therefore, heresy (departure from orthodox belief). There had always been contests about ultimate authority in this process (between, for example, popes and general councils) but new problems arose when Henry VIII severed the allegiance of his church from Rome. The orthodox doctrine of the church of England became a real issue and one upon which monarchs and lay and ecclesiastical subjects did not always agree. Moreover, opinion shifted from day to day it seemed: what was orthodoxy today was heresy tomorrow. See, for example, the difference between the Ten Articles (q.v.) of 1536 and the Act of Six Articles (q.v.) of 1539.

Holy Days The Catholic church designated a very large number of holy days. On such days the laity and the clergy were forbidden to work and obliged to attend mass. While the Church of England abolished many of these, there were still a large number of holy days, including all Sundays and all those days for which the Book of Common Prayer provides a proper collect, epistle and gospel reading in its calendar. They included the feasts of Circumcision (1 Jan.), Epiphany (6 Jan.), Ascension Day (5th Thursday after Easter), Corpus Christi, Saints Peter and Paul (29 June), Assumption of the Blessed Virgin Mary (15 Aug.), All Saints (1 Nov.) and Christmas Day. Many holy days had a civic, agricultural and/or economic significance.

Household, Extended Family Part of Peter Laslett's household typology. Describes those households containing a conjugal unit and children plus other relatives and any servants.

Household, Multiple Family Part of Peter Laslett's household typology. Describes households containing more than one conjugal (*see* 'Household, Simple Family') unit connected by kinship or marriage plus any servants. Includes Stem Family (*See* 'Family, Stem') but also households in which conjugal units of brothers and sisters co-reside.

Household, Simple Family Part of Laslett's household typology. Describes the type of household of which the conjugal relationship was the structural principle. It might include a married couple, or a married couple with children, or a widowed person with children and any servants.

Household, Stem Family (*la famille souche*) Part of mid-nineteenth-century Frenchman Frédéric Le Play's typology of households. Describes a household in which a downwards extended family of two married couples and their children co-reside. For example: husband and wife, their eldest son and his wife, their grandchildren. Any unmarried adult children might also co-reside.

Household   Term used by contemporaries to describe the co-residential domestic unit. This comprised a nuclear family of father, mother and dependent children and servants. Closer inspection frequently reveals that the 'nuclear family' which formed the core of this unit was much more fluid in form than the historical demographers suggest.

Humanism   Intellectual movement characterised in our period by a preoccupation with recovery of the ancient world of Greece and Rome, its texts and its values. This recovery led to a growing vision of active involvement in civic affairs as one of the most worthwhile of human activities and education for such a vocation as a priority. Christian humanists (such as Erasmus) used this knowledge to further understanding of the Scriptures.

Husbandry   Farming.

Iconoclasm   Destruction of images and other church furnishings and decorations considered to detract from Protestant teaching that salvation is not assisted by works or the intercession of the saints and that God alone must be worshipped. *See* 'Calvinism'.

Iconography   Pictorial or symbolical representation of ideas.

Index, The (*index librorum prohibitorum*)   Paul IV in 1557 exhibited a list of books which Catholics were expressly forbidden to read or possess. The practice was continued by future popes.

Inflation (Price Rise)   There has been much debate surrounding the extent and causes of the phenomenon of inflation. Prices of foods rose by seven times between the early sixteenth and the mid seventeenth century and some industrial products saw a three-fold rise. Population pressure and a much increased supply of money certainly contributed to inflation but do not provide a convincing total explanation. The inflow of Spanish silver cannot explain a price rise in England which predates it or explain the discrepancy between the rise in food and industrial prices. Population pressure is more convincing as an underlying but not sole cause. Harvest failure, changes in output for other reasons and the debasement of the coinage in the 1540s all played their part.

Injunctions   Royal: a series of royal proclamations on ecclesiastical affairs (1536; 1538; 1547; 1554; 1559).

Episcopal or Visitation: a bishop issued a number of injunctions indicating what should be done in his diocese.

Inns of Chancery   A number of the Inns associated with the barristers at common law in London possessed no licensing powers. They seem to have been used largely as preparatory schools for the Inns of Court (q.v.). A youth would register and live at an Inn of Chancery while serving as a clerk in one of the offices of the common law courts. Later he might move to an Inn of Court while training for the bar. Members of the Inns of Court learned their own trade by teaching in the Inns of Chancery. They were in decline by the seventeenth century and certainly did not constitute an essential preparation for the Inns of Court.

Inns of Court   During the fourteenth century a dozen or so Inns grew up associated with the barristers (apprentices) at common law. Four of these – known as Inns of Court – had the power to licence pleaders at the bar (barristers) from about 1454–5. They were Gray's Inn, Lincoln's Inn, Inner Temple, Middle Temple. The licensing system gave rise to the development of an educational system within the Inns to prepare apprentices for a legal career. This education was an apprenticeship at law rather than academic training *per se*. But the Inns formed other extremely important social functions in the Tudor period. They were used as finishing schools for elite youths who had no intention of practising law. A residential period at one of the Inns of Court (especially the fashionable Gray's Inn) was a shared experience and source of connection for many M.P.s and J.P.s.

Jesuits   Religious order founded by the Spaniard Ignatius Loyola (1491–1556) in 1534 specifically to quash heresy. Pope Paul III recognised the order in 1540 and henceforth its activities were directed by the Papacy. Characterised by a piety expressed through rigorous spiritual exercises designed to train and discipline the human will. It was a missionary order which became involved in education at all levels. Active in England. Conflict between Catholic secular priests and laity and the Jesuits. *See* 'Archpriest Controversy'.

Jointure   A settlement, on marriage, of lands or income to be held jointly by wife and husband and then, on the husband's death, by the widow. This was an alternative to the widow's rights, under common law, to a dower (q.v.) third of her deceased husband's estate.

Justices of Assize   *See* Section VIII.

Justices of the Peace   *See* Section VIII.

Justification by Faith Alone (*Solofideism*)   Characteristic Lutheran teaching that the Christian is saved by faith in Christ alone and not by works of any kind.

Kett's Rebellion   *See* Section III.

King's Bench, Court of   *See* Section IX.

King's Book, 1543 Popular title for *The Necessary Doctrine and Erudition of a Christian Man* 1543, which was a revision of the Bishops' Book of 1537. Henry VIII commissioned the Bishops of Salisbury (Salcot), Worcester (Heath) and Westminster (Thirlby) under Cranmer's supervision to revise the 1537 book which had been Protestant in tone and substance. The King's Book defended transubstantiation (q.v.) and salvation by works.

Knights of the Garter Membership of this order of chivalry was restricted to the monarch and 25 knights and some foreign potentates. Places in the order were in practice controlled by the monarch and Henry VIII tried to raise its status.

Knockdoe At the Battle of Knockdoe in Galway in 1504 the Earl of Kildare (*see* Section XIII) defeated Macwilliam of Clanricarde. It was a milestone in Kildare's rise to supremacy under Henry VII's reign. Reputed to have been the first occasion on which guns were used in an Irish battle.

Lammas 1 August. It was customary to consecrate bread made from the first ripe corn of the harvest at mass on this day; the name derives from 'loaf' and 'mass'. The day had more than religious significance. In Coventry, for example, the so-called Lammas pastures were re-opened to common use on 1 August (until 2 February, Candlemas, the end of Winter). *See* 'Holy Days' (q.v).

Lambeth Articles Issued in 1595 by John Whitgift (*see* Section IX) as a Calvinist restatement of doctrine of the Church of England.

Law Terms These were variable in length because they depended upon the dating of Easter and other church feasts. Broadly speaking they were as follows: Michaelmas (c. 6 October–25 November); Hilary (20 January to 22 February); Easter (Wednesday following 2nd Sunday after Easter to Feast of Ascension nearly 4 weeks later); Trinity (Morrow of Trinity for 3 weeks – laid down for 1541 by 32 Henry VIII, c.21).

Leases, Act of (32 Henry VIII, c.28) Forbade reversionary leases of more than 21 years or three lives.

Leases, Act of Ecclesiastical (13 Elizabeth I, c.10; 14 Elizabeth I, c.14; 18 Elizabeth I, c.11) These acts limited ecclesiastical and collegiate leases to those for 21 years or three lives.

Leases, Beneficial The property was leased at a relatively low annual rental in exchange for a heavier entry fine than would otherwise be the case. Gradual replacement by leasing at commercial rents and relinquishment of entry fines.

Leases, long-term for years or lives A comparatively heavy entry-fine was charged by the landholder for a lease of property either for a term of years or for a term of lives. In the latter case the lease would hold good until the death of all those specified in the will as 'lives'. Act of Leases (32 Henry VIII, c.28) disallowed reversionary leases for more than 21 years or 3 lives and acts during Elizabeth's reign placed similar restrictions on ecclesiastical landlords. By the end of Elizabeth's reign it seems that leases for 21 years were most common, with those for three lives running second.

Legate, Papal (*Legatus a Latere*) A papal official whose commands could only be rejected via successful appeal to the Pope himself. Cardinal Wolsey was unusual in receiving the office for life.

Lent A forty day period of fast preceding Easter and beginning with a communal act of penance on Ash Wednesday (q.v.). One meal a day, which might include fish but not meat, and a light collation at night were allowed. The observance of Lent was ordered in the Book of Common Prayer. The behaviour of the people during Lent continued to be regulated by the secular as well as the religious authorities.

Limning Miniature painting. In the 1520s Henry VIII initiated the practice of commissioning miniature portraits of members of the royal family and, later, of prospective members. In the 1570s, however, the business was opened up and nobles, gentry and merchants commissioned miniatures from Nicholas Hilliard. Miniatures were used as 'tokens' to underline family and/or patronage relations.

Little Germany Sardonic nickname accorded the White Horse Inn in St Edward's Parish, Cambridge, where associated young Cambridge scholars to discuss the new German doctrines in the early 1520s. *See* 'Robert Barnes' and 'Thomas Bilney' in Section XI.

Liturgy Used to decribe the prescribed public services of the church. Also used to refer to the mass.

Livery A badge derived from the coat of arms used to mark the goods and servants of the armigerous classes. Wearing the insignia or livery of the lord indicated that a 'servant' acted under his protection and authority and was thus under obligation to do him service. Armies in the sixteenth century were customarily made up of bands of men wearing the livery of a lord and under just such an obligation. The system had its advantages and disadvantages for the central government – it reduced costs but it also reduced reliability.

Lollardy Early Tudor heresy was largely inspired by Wycliffite and Lollard survival, particularly in the Chilterns, London, Essex and Kent. Lollard beliefs included a tendency to Biblical fundamentalism, an insistence upon the importance of preaching and the vernacular bible, anticlericalism and condemnation of ritual aspects of worship. There was, however, no national organisation and no precise Lollard creed. During the later years of Henry VIII their traditional Lollard beliefs tended to merge with imported Lutheran ideas. By far the best general discussion of Lollardy and its relation to Protestantism remains A.G. Dickens, *The English Reformation*, 1989.

Maids of Honour   Six young ladies who were not official staff of the Privy Chamber under Elizabeth but performed functions within the chamber. Elizabeth saw herself as controlling their 'marriages' but, in fact, her control was far from unchallenged by the young ladies themselves. Lady Catherine Grey, in line of succession, secretly married the Earl of Hertford; Bess Throckmorton secretly married Walter Raleigh; Lady Mary Howard insolently refused to hold open the Queen's cape and flirted with the Earl of Essex; Mary Fitton was made pregnant by the Earl of Pembroke. The position was one of indirect political influence and patronage.

Marian Exile   During the reign of Mary considerable numbers of Protestant clergy and others who were closely associated with the Protestant regimes of Edward VI's reign fled to the Continent. Congregations of English were established in many cities in Germany and Switzerland, notably Frankfurt, Geneva, Zurich, Strasbourg and Basel. After the accession of Elizabeth connections made during the Exile both with other English exiles and their foreign hosts proved influential in the shaping of the Elizabethan Church of England.

Market(s)   There were 800 or so market towns in England and Wales, with hinterlands of variable size. In general market towns clustered most thickly in the South-West, Hertfordshire, the Midlands, Kent and Suffolk. About 300 of the markets were specialising in particular produce to some extent by the end of the century. The markets were carefully regulated by the charter (which fixed the days of the market) and by the town which employed a number of market officers such as sweepers, bellmen, inspectors (lookers, conners and testers) and toll gatherers. The tolls were used to keep the market in good repair and for charitable purposes. See Joan Thirsk (ed.), *The Agrarian History of England and Wales, Volume IV, 1500–1640*, Cambridge, 1967 for an excellent account of marketing.

Martin Mar-prelate   *See* Section XI.

Marriage   The Catholic church viewed marriage as a sacrament. Free and mutual consent formed the essential basis of this union which was designed for the procreation and education of children. A simple contract (not necessarily within the ecclesiastical context or rules) constituted a valid marriage. There were impediments to *ecclesiastical* marriage, some of which might render it invalid. The church, however, while recommending parental consent to a match, did not regard such approval as essential. This position led to considerable friction between parents (who thought that they had the right to decide whom their children married) and the church. During the sixteenth century clandestine marriages (which took place secretly in contravention of the church's canons) were a problem. For further discussion see R. O'Day, *The Family and Family Relationships, 1500–1900*, 1994.

Mass   A title of the Eucharist (q.v.) which was retained in the First Prayer Book of Edward VI (1549) but therafter discarded by the Church of England. This was in part because of its association with the doctrine of transubstantiation (q.v.) and the eucharistic sacrifice and in part because of its association with the doctrine of salvation by works.

Mercenaries   Foreign soldiers paid to fight for Crown. They were used to put down certain county or local rebellions where the loyalty of the militia was potentially in doubt. Expensive.

Michaelmas, Feast of St Michael the Archangel   29 September. *See also* 'Law Terms' for Michaelmas Term.

Militia   An armed force based on the county and raised by Commissions of Array. An Act for Having of Horse, Armour and Weapons, 1559, stipulated obligation of every able-bodied man, aged 16–60, to present himself at Muster (q.v.) for assessment of equipment etc.

Minor Orders   In the medieval Catholic church the orders of the church's ministry were divided into Major Orders (sub-deacon, deacon and priest, bishop) and Minor Orders (porters, lectors [readers], exorcists, accolytes). Those in Minor Orders performed largely liturgical functions and they were not ordained as those in Major Orders were. The bishop blessed the candidate and handed him the instruments he required for his office. The Minor Orders and the Subdiaconate disappeared as orders at the Reformation but there is evidence that the lectorship continued to be used and was effectively turned into an apprenticeship for those seeking holy orders. See R. O'Day, 'The Reformation of the Ministry' in R. O'Day and F. Heal (eds), *Continuity and Change: Personnel and Administration of the Church of England, 1500–1640*, Leicester, 1975.

Misprision of Treason   Charge of knowing that treason is being plotted but not revealing it.

Mitre   Shield-shaped head-dress worn by bishops at all solemn functions. It seems to have fallen into disuse in the Church of England from the Reformation to the nineteenth century.

Monopolies   A licence from the Crown by letters patent to exercise a monopoly in some area of activity, normally but not always of trade and manufacture. For instance, monopolies were allocated for the production of printed music or playing cards but they were also made for exploration and plantation of various parts of the globe. They became expecially contentious in 1601.

Mortuary An obligatory and stipulated payment to the priest on the death of a parishioner. This payment might be in kind or a money payment.

Musters Assembling soldiers either for inspection, ascertainment of numbers and equipment or other purpose. Muster Rolls are an important source for population studies.

New Year Day 1 January. Regarded as New Year's Day even when the year was calculated from 25 March!

New Year Gifts Customarily 'friends' exchanged gifts and tokens at New Year. This custom was formalised at the Tudor Court when gifts at New Year became part of the cement of the patronage system and an indicator of political fortune. The comparative value of the Crown's gifts signalled the relative importance at court of the recipients. If the monarch declined to make a gift to an individual this signified loss of political favour.

Official Reformation Often used to describe the measures by which Henry VIII broke with roman jurisdiction in contradistinction to the reformation of doctrine, worship and ministry for which some – commonly known as Protestants – worked.

Ordinal The service for the ordination of priests and deacons. Produced in 1550 after the first Edwardian prayerbook. Included in subsequent prayer books.

Ordination Ordination of bishops, priests and deacons in the Church of England was modelled upon the medieval Catholic rite. In the ceremony for the ordering of priests, the bishop placed his hands upon the head of the ordinand, who thus received the Holy Spirit and a charge to be 'a faithful dispenser of the Word of God and his Holy Sacraments'; with the gift of a Bible and the reception of the bread and wine the priest took 'authority to preach the Word of God and to minister the Holy Sacraments in this Congregation.' Ordination was to take place upon either a Sunday or a Holy Day.

There were rules governing ordination, some of which were evaded. Ordinands had to be examined by the archdeacon or the bishop's chaplains for their reputation, their age, their title, their knowledge of Scripture and their vocation.

Ornaments rubric This rubric inserted before the services for morning and evening prayer in the Prayer Book of 1552 directed that the minister should not wear vestment, alb or cope. This was altered in the Prayer Book of 1559 intending to reintroduce the practice of 1549, although a mistaken dating led to confusion.

Pale of Dublin Strip of coastal land between Dublin and Dundalk under English authority. The area was extended under Philip and Mary and Elizabeth. *See* Maps.

Papacy Bishop of Rome in direct descent from St Peter. Claimed supreme authority within western Christendom but this claim was not uncontested. The fifteenth century saw General Councils (backed by the universities) laying contradictory claims. In the sixteenth century the Papacy achieved the upper hand once again but was particularly sensitive to suggestions of the revival of conciliarism and to claims by secular threats to its authority. The Henrician Reformation can be placed fruitfully within this general context. Papal infallibility was a nineteenth-century invention.

Passion Week Week before Easter.

Parish An area under the cure of an ordained minister (who as incumbent was supported from endowed land and tithes) to whose spiritual ministrations the inhabitants had a right. It was also an important unit of civil administration. *See* Section VIII.

Parson Properly used to describe the holder of an ecclesiastical benefice who possesses all its tithes – that is a rector, whether cleric or lay. But is often used to mean any clergyman.

Partible Inheritance Divided inheritance.

Paten Dish used to carry consecrated bread at the Eucharist.

Patriarchy, Domestic Government of the family and the household by the father. Refers to the powers of the father in the Old Testament over his wife and children – to chastise, arrange the marriages of, sell or even execute without challenge. This model – in the sense of authoritarian government by the father and husband with unquestioned powers over education, marriage, careers and property – was prescribed by some sixteenth-century intellectuals as appropriate to the family of the time but historians now debate the extent to which the model was recommended and followed.

Peasant (ry) Sometimes used simply to mean those living off the land. In this sense England was clearly a peasant society in the sixteenth century. A more precise definition is sometimes implied: that the family farm, owned or leased by the family and not by individuals, is the core of the economy, which is characterised by domestic subsistence production and relatively unaffected by market forces. Alan Macfarlane's *The Origins of English Individualism*, 1978, controversially claimed that English society was not a peasant society in the latter sense because land was owned, sold, devised and willed by individuals and not families. If true, this sets English society apart from that of France, for example.

Pentecost (Whit-Sunday) 7th Sunday after Easter Day.

Pilgrimage of Grace A panicky revolt in defence of the old religion and the old economy in Lincolnshire, Yorkshire, Lancashire,

Cumberland, Westmorland, Northumberland and Durham in 1536. Leading pilgrims tried and executed following renewed unrest in early 1537. *See* Section III.

Pluralities, pluralism   The practice of holding more than one benefice (ecclesiastical office) simultaneously. In certain circumstances (for example, when the benefices concerned were far distant from one another) this could lead to gross abuse. At a time when it was difficult to recruit sufficient able clergy and when ecclesiastical benefices were frequently too poorly remunerated to support well-educated and conscientious preachers, holding livings in plurality was a practical way around the problem for both the individual ministers and the church itself. Attempts were made to curb the worst abuses. Dispensations to hold livings in plurality were issued by the Archbishops of Canterbury and York. By the canons of 1604 it was forbidden for a minister to hold benefices in plurality if they were more than 30 miles apart.

Popes   Because the occupant of the Papacy at any given time is often referred to in historical works simply as 'The Pope' without further individualisation, it is important to remember that the Papacy changed hands 19 times during the Tudor period (at a time when there were only 5 different English monarchs, 6 Holy Roman Emperors and considerable continuity in France, Spain and Portugal), and that these changes signalled others in policy and influence.

1484–92   Innocent VIII (Giambattista Cibo).

1492–1503   Alexander VI (Roderigo Borgia).

1503 (Sept.–Oct.) Pius III (Francesco Todeschini).

1503–13   Julius II (Giulio della Rovere).

1513–21   Leo X (Giovanni de' Medici).

1522–23   Adrian VI (Adrian of Utrecht).

1523–34   Clement VII (Giulio de' Medici). Hostility to imperial claims to reform Christendom and to domination of Italy. 1524: formed alliance with France v. Spain. 1527: Pope captured by Emperor Charles V, nephew of Queen Catherine of Aragon. Possibilities of papally sanctioned divorce removed. 1533: Cranmer consecrated Archbishop of Canterbury by Papal Bull. 1534: Pope threatens Henry VIII with excommunication for activating Act of Annates.

1534–49   Paul III (Alessandro Farnese).

1550–55   Julius III (Giovanni del Monte).

1555   Marcellus II (Marcello Cervini).

1556–9   Paul IV (Pietro Caraffa). Cardinal Reginald Pole quarrelled with Pope Paul IV. Pope deprived him of legacy (*see* 'Legate, Papal'); Mary refused to hand Pole over.

1559–65   Pius IV (Gian-Angelo de' Medici).

1565–72   Pius V (Michele Ghislieri). In 1570 published bull, *regnans in excelcis*, excommunicating Elizabeth I and calling on Catholics to assist in her deposition.

1572–85   Gregory XIII (Ugo Buoncompagno). Pope Gregory lends patronage to Jesuit-run English College in Rome.
1586–90   Sixtus V (Felix Peretti).
1590   Urban VIII (Giambattista Castagna).
1590–91   Gregory XIV (Niccolo Sfondrato).
1591   Innocent IX (Gian-Antonio Fachinetto).
1592–1605:   Clement VIII (Ippolito Aldobrandini). Pope appointed George Blackwell Archpriest to control Catholic clergy with exception of Jesuits.

Preamble   The first part of a last will and testament in which the testator commends his or her soul to God and sometimes reveals his or her doctrinal inclination. Historians are deeply divided on the usefulness of studies of preambles for an insight into and barometer of popular belief during the Reformation.

Praemunire   Between 1353 and 1393 a series of acts were passed to forbid the Pope and other foreigners to encroach upon the Crown's rights in ecclesiastical property and jurisdiction. Later it was altered to protect the lay courts against ecclesiastical jurisdictional claims. Appeals were made to these laws in the course of the official reformation under Henry VIII.

Prayer Book   *See* 'Common Prayer, Book of'.

Prerogative   The royal prerogative powers, which permitted the monarch to govern, were granted by the laws of the realm and defined by the common law. Some of these rights arose out of the monarch's feudal overlordship, others out of his/her personal concerns. The Crown was given a certain flexibility to act outside the law when equity demanded but not to disregard or regard itself as above the common law. The Crown could not by prerogative repeal or suspend statute. By proclamation it could make orders consistent with existing statute law.

Primogeniture   Feudal rule of inheritance by which the entire inherited landed estate, excluding only the widow's dower or jointure, passed to the eldest son or, in the absence of sons, to the daughter or daughters (as co-heiresses). The rule applied to free lands (held by knight service) and was operative only in cases of intestacy. By the Statute of Wills (1540) English men and women had freedom of testation, although there were certain restrictions. There has been much debate about the importance of this rule in English society. *See* 'Wills, Statute of'.

Privy Council   *See* Section IX.

Privy Chamber   Until the reign of Mary I the Privy Chamber was staffed by males and was the centre of court politics. During the reigns of Mary and Elizabeth, however, it was staffed by women and changed its function.

Probate   When an individual with property died and left a will the accuracy of this had to be proved and recorded in a court (hence probate) before the will could be executed and its terms followed. There were many probate courts (not all of them ecclesiastical) and complex rules governing which wills should be proved in which courts. The court in which the wills of the most prominent landowners were heard was the Prerogative Court of Canterbury which is commonly referred to as P.C.C. (*See* Section IX).

Proclamations, Act of   Empowered the King, with the consent of his council, to set forth proclamations. This was an existing and uncontested royal prerogative. Parliament met at often lengthy intervals and its statutes assumed, and sometimes specified, that the details of its programme would be left to royal proclamation. The Act (1539) attended to several uncertain aspects: the authority lying behind a proclamation; their permitted scope; how they would be enforced. The Act confirmed existing practice – for example, forbidding proclamations touching life and property. Enforcement was difficult because proclamations had no force in the courts of common law and in practice had to be pursued in the Star Chamber. Some historians think that the Act was an attempt to make proclamations enforceable in the common law courts. If so, it failed.

Proclamations   There were several different categories of proclamation: Royal, Privy Council, Lieutenants', Commissioners' and Lord Mayors' proclamations. All these might be given royal authorisation but were not the same as royal proclamations. *See* 'Proclamations, Act of'.

Proclamations, Royal   A royal proclamation was a legislative ordinance from the monarch and, in its published form, would be prefaced by the royal coat of arms; it might be made on the advice of the Privy Council; it would be signed by the monarch and issued under the Great Seal; it would be sent to officials, for example sheriffs and mayors, accompanied by a royal writ ordering public proclamation of the schedule.

The right to issue proclamations was a common law prerogative of the Crown. The proclamation was inferior to statute and common law. They touched neither life nor common law rights of property. They could create offences with penalties attached but could not create a felony or a treason. Tudor royal proclamations touched social, economic, religious and administrative matters only. *See* 'Proclamations, Act of'.

Progresses   Monarchs in the sixteenth-century led peripatetic lives. They not only moved from royal palace to royal palace but also made summer progresses through the shires. Until the Dissolution of the Monasteries it was customary for the monarch to rely upon monastic hospitality en route. Thereafter, the local notability bore the burden. Under both Edward and Mary summer progresses went into abeyance but Elizabeth revived the practice. Many houses were built expressly to entertain the Queen (for example, Longleat, Theobalds and Holdenby) and are known as prodigy houses.

Prophesyings (Exercise of Prophesying) A public conference consisting of two or three sermons on the same text, examination of the text by assembled ministers and a summary of the proceedings by a moderator, which in part grew out of Elizabethan attempts to improve the education of the parish clergy. Such large public assemblies, often the occasion for radical Protestant views and criticism of the 'but halfly-reformed' church in England, aroused the hostility of many at court. The prophesying at Southam, Warws, was the direct cause of the ban on prophesyings insisted upon by Eliabeth in 1577, which itself occasioned the suspension of Archbishop Grindal. (*See* 'Exercise' for a continuation and development of this tradition).

Prorogation (of parliament) Normal mode of terminating a session of parliament and thereby discontinuing business. However, the proroga-tions at Christmas and Easter often seem to have been regarded as adjournments which implied no termination of business.

Public Fasts In the late Elizabethan period it became reasonably common for radical Protestant ministers to call fasts, often on holy days, for further reformation. Such large assemblies were unauthorised. The canons of 1604 made it permissible for the bishop alone to call such fasts.

Purgatory Catholics believed that individual souls were judged upon death. Purgatory was a place of waiting for the sinful, who could not yet be admitted to heaven until they had discharged penance for their sins. Intercession with the Saints and the Virgin; indulgences obtained after pilgrimages and other acts of piety; masses said for the dead – all were a means of discharging sins committed upon earth which would speed the progress of an individual soul through purgatory. The Protestant reform-ers rejected the doctrine of purgatory as an expression of the doctrine of salvation by works (that is human actions) rather than by faith alone (in the saving grace of Jesus Christ).

Queen's Day (Accession Day) 17 November. *See* 'Accesson Day Tilts', (q.v.).

Rector Clerical rector was parochial clergyman who held all the tithes, great and small, of his benefice. In some benefices, however, the great tithes were held by one or more lay persons (known as impropriator/s) and only the small tithes by a clerical vicar. Also used to describe heads of Jesuit houses and some university officials.

Recusancy, Recusants A term used after about 1570 to refer to Roman Catholics who refused to attend services of the church of England in obedience to the Papal Bull excommunicating Elizabeth I. It was perceived as a serious problem especially in the North and harsh penal laws were introduced, but rather irregularly enforced. In 1581, for example, fines of £20 a month for recusancy were stipulated.

Reformed churches Refers to all those churches which subscribed to the principles of the Reformation but is used, more specifically, to distinguish the Calvinistic churches from the Lutheran. It was commonly used in this latter sense in the sixteenth century.

Reformatio Legum Ecclesiasticarum (the reform of the ecclesiastical laws) By an act of parliament of 1549 (3 & 4 Edward VI c.11) the King was authorised to set up a commission to replace the medieval canon law with a new system of order and discipline.
1551   Commission of 8 set to work on the project.
1553   *Reformatio Legum Ecclesiasticarum* presented to parliament – made redundant by Edward's death and reign of Mary.
1571   John Foxe published *Reformatio Legum Ecclesiasticarum*.
   Failure of the project to materialise meant that the church continued to flounder in an anachronistic system of law throughout the period.

religious (regular clergy) A term used to mean those clergy who lived under a rule (for example, that of St Augustine or St Benedict) in a religious house (monastery, convent etc.)

ex-religious were those clergy who withdrew from the rule and the religious house. The problem of discovering what happened to the large numbers of ex-religious in England after the dissolution of the monasteries has long exercised historians.

Rent From the early sixteenth century it became common for leases to stipulate that all or part of the rent be paid in kind (a hedge against inflation). The produce was normally used to support the household and provide feed for the landlord's stock but some was marketed. See Thirsk, *Agrarian History*, 1967 for a good discussion of the subject. *See also* 'Leases'.

Rogation Days The Monday, Tuesday and Wednesday before Ascension Day.

Rogation Sunday 5th Sunday after Easter Day.

Sanctuary Under medieval canon law a fugitive from justice or a debtor was immune from arrest in a sacred place. To some extent this right was observed but, for example, see the fate of the Stafford brothers who claimed sanctuary at Culham, Oxfordshire. (*See* Section I, 1486).

Secretary *See* Section VI

Secular Clergy All clergy who did not belong to the rule of a religious order. *See* 'religious'.

Separatist A title first applied to the followers of Robert Browne (*see*

Section XI), although it was later used to describe the Independents or Congregationalists.

Serfs Term used to describe several classes of person who were unfree in the sense that they were bound to the land on which they lived and worked and were therefore unfree to marry and move as they wished. Included domestic serfs or artisans who had no homes of their own and lived with the lord almost as slaves, and others who had holdings, homes and families. An understanding of 'serfdom', which had disappeared by the Tudor period, is helpful when we examine the development of household organisation and social hierarchy in the sixteenth century.

Servants Servants were a highly heterogeneous body of people, male and female, young and old, bound together by their relationship (temporary or permanent) of dependence upon a master or mistress. A servant was not by contemporary definition someone who scrubbed and cleaned within a domestic setting. At all but the lowest social levels, however, servants *were* used to substitute for or supplement child labour.

Shrines The Latin word from which the English is taken means a chest, and a shrine was originally a chest in which a relic was kept (reliquary). It was commonly used to mean a sacred image, especially one to which pilgrimages were made. The most important English shrines were those of St Thomas à Becket at Canterbury; Our Lady at Walsingham; St Edward the Confessor at Westminster Abbey and St Cuthbert at Durham. The Reformation rejected pilgrimages and shrines as meaningless in terms of salvation. These sites were destroyed.

Simony A word meaning the sale of spiritual things. For example, a man might offer money to persuade the bishop to ordain him or he might try to purchase an ecclesiastical benefice. The system of patronage was extremely susceptible to simony and it was probably widespread. The Canons of 1604 stipulated that all ordinands and all those receiving a benefice must swear an oath that they had not achieved their office through simony.

Six Articles, Act of Conservative religious doctrine restated and enforced by draconian penalties in 1539.

Somerset House Renaissance palace built by Lord Protector Somerset in the late 1540s. It was the first major classical building project in early modern England and its design underlined the ambitions of its owner.

Spas In the late middle ages curative springs were centres for religious cults and pilgrimages. During the reign of Elizabeth the nobility transformed the centres into secular watering places or spas offering medicinal treatment and a relaxing atmosphere. Bath was the paradigm.

Statute Act of parliament. References to statutes cite a date and a chapter number. The year is the regnal year of the session in which the statute was given royal assent. If there were 2 sessions within the same regnal year, the statutes are distinguished as belonging to statute 1 (st. 1) and statute 2 (st. 2). If a session covers two regnal years then its statutes are cited as belonging to both (e.g. 2 & 3 Edward VI). Each statute has a chapter number but the order is not strictly chronological.

St Bartholemew's Day Massacre   Massacre of the French Protestant leadership in Paris on 24 August 1572. Widely perceived to be a plot staged by Catherine de Medici but in fact a panic reaction to events. The idea of a plot seemed to confirm the existence of a Catholic League intended to wipe out Protestanism in Europe, and thus proved both emotive and influential in the shaping of future English foreign policy.

St John the Baptist, Feast Day of Nativity of   24 June. Linked with customs surrounding the summer solstice.

St Paul's Cross   Since the fourteenth century sermons had been commonplace at the Cross in St Paul's churchyard. An endowment by Bishop Thomas Kempe provided for the maintenance of the sermons. Galleries were provided for royalty and dignitaries; the throng sat on benches for which they paid a rent of 1d a sermon. The preachers were selected by the Bishop of London and his chaplains. If it rained, the sermon was transferred to the crypt of St Paul's Cathedral.

Staple Towns   Some towns were made staples by royal authority. Here a group of merchants would be given the exclusive right to purchase certain categories of goods for export. Until 1558 Calais was the chief staple and is often referred to simply as The Staple but there were other staples throughout England and Wales. The term was and is rather confusingly used also to indicate the principal markets or entrepots for certain categories of merchandise, or towns where foreign merchants were permitted to trade.

Star Chamber   *See* Section IX.

Stoke, Battle of   Battle of Stoke (1487), near Newark (not Stoke-on-Trent) at which Lambert Simnel and the Earl of Lincoln were routed. The last battle of the Wars of the Roses. It is occasionally referred to as the Battle of East Stoke.

Submission of the Clergy   *See* Section I, 1532 and Section IV, 1532.

Subsidy   A tax of a fixed amount on land or goods granted by parliament to increase the value of the tenth and fifteenth taxes to the Crown.

Suffragan Bishops   Assistants to the diocesan bishops. From the thirteenth century had held titles derived from Irish or Christian cities now occupied by Islam. In 1534 parliament substituted 34 English place names for these titles.

Sumptuary Laws   Medieval laws defining the type of dress permitted to the various social groups. Clergy, for example, were not allowed to dress as laymen. The wives of merchants must not dress as the wives of nobility or gentry. Colours, fabrics and styles were all regulated. It was part of the attempt to keep people in their foreordained social places and to make 'social climbing' obvious. This was the law but it was often contravened.

Surplice   A loose white linen liturgical tunic, with wide sleeves. In the medieval Catholic church it was the accepted garb of the lower clergy and was used by priests also except when they were celebrating mass. The Second Prayer Book of Edward VI prescribed the surplice as the only vestment to be worn by the clergy. This rubric was altered in the Prayer Book of 1559 in an attempt to revert to the wearing of vestments for the celebration of communion and probably for morning and evening prayer. The rubric now ordered a return to the situation in the second year of Edward VI's reign, whereas the first prayer book had been authorised by parliament in the third year of the reign. This mistake led the reformers to believe that the Queen did not wish them to wear the vestments, to which they so objected. (Vestiarian Controversy, q.v.)

Ten Articles, Act of   Convocation accepted these articles in 1536 as descriptive of the doctrine of the Church of England. They are, therefore, the first doctrinal declaration of the new church. Baptism, penance and Eucharist are retained as sacraments; the Eucharistic presence is called corporal and substantial but there is no mention of transubstantiation; justification (salvation) is said to be achieved by contrition and faith combined with charity; images are retained but must not be worshipped; prayers for the intercession of the saints and prayers and Masses for the dead are approved.

Tenth and Fifteenth   This was the standard parliamentary tax on landed property. Those towns represented in parliament paid a tenth; the rest paid a fifteenth.

Thirty-Nine Articles   (First version, 1563; full set, 1571.) Attempt by Convocation to define the doctrine of the Church of England in relation to the religious controversies of the day, especially clarifying the position on purported medieval corruptions of Catholic teaching. Not a creed (q.v.). Were a slightly modified version of the Forty-Two articles agreed in 1553. Were approved by Convocation and subscription to them was required of the clergy.

Tillage   Ploughing the land.

Tithe   A tenth part of the produce of land (praedial); of the fruits of labour (personal) and those arising partly out of the ground and partly from work (mixed) offered to the clerical incumbent of a parish benefice. If the incumbent was a rector he would receive the great tithes (wheat, oats etc.) and the small (chickens, goats, lambs etc.) but when the parish was appropriated the great tithes fell to the lay impropriator and only the small to the clerical vicar. Some tithes were compounded (i.e. a fixed annual payment was made in lieu of tithe). Others had apparently fallen into disuse. Suits for recovery of tithe filled the ecclesiastical courts of this and the succeeding century and exacerbated poor relations between clergy and laity as well as between lay impropriators and laymen.

Transubstantiation Doctrine that after consecration the bread and wine of the communion service cease to be bread and wine except in appearance and become the real body and blood of Christ. Firmly held by Catholic Christians.

Treason On the accession of Henry VIII treason was narrowly defined by a fourteenth-century statute which made it treason to plot the death of the sovereign, his Queen-consort or the heir apparent; to violate the Queen or the wife of the heir apparent; to wage war in the realm; or to kill the Lord Chancellor or the judges performing their offices. In practice treason was interpreted much more loosely than this and criticism of the actions and person of the monarch were effectively suppressed thereby. After 1534, however, parliament progressively revised the law relating to treason, broadening it to include, for example, forgery of any of the royal seals. Once a person, great or small, was indicted for treason, legal counsel was denied.

Ultimogeniture Also known as Borough English. Right whereby youngest son or child inherits entire estate. This was apparently relatively uncommon but occurred in some copyholds of descent, especially in Kent and certain boroughs.

Uses *See* 'Wills, Statute of'.

Valor Ecclesiasticus Official and comprehensive valuation of ecclesiastical and monastic revenues made in 1535. Popularly known as the King's Books. This valuation followed on the 1534 Act of Annates (26 Henry VIII, c.3) whereby the Crown appropriated the first fruits of every benefice (living) and a tenth of the annual income of every benefice.

Vestiarian Controversies Disputes concerning proper clerical dress during the reigns of Edward VI and Elizabeth. The matter was discussed prior to the publication of the First Prayer Book of Edward VI (1549); controversy flared in 1550 when John Hooper declined to wear vestments during his consecration as Bishop of Gloucester and some sort of compromise was reached although Hooper finally agreed to wear the surplice and rochet on important occasions; the surplice and rochet were the only vestments allowed in the second Prayer Book of 1552; there was a renewal of trouble with the restoration of vestments (including a cope for the Holy Communion) in 1559 and Matthew Parker's insistence that the law be obeyed in 1566; 37 London clergy who refused obedience were deprived and there was unrest; the bishops themselves were divided and so no consistent policy was pursued.

Vicar   From the Latin word for 'a substitute'. Popular name for clergyman who serves a parish of which the great tithes have been appropriated. This arrangement dated back to the middle ages when churches were often appropriated to monasteries, which received the tithe income and appointed a secular priest or 'vicar' to serve the cure on their behalf. On the dissolution of the monasteries the King granted the rectorial tithes to others (often laymen) who were known as impropriators or rectors but the endowment of a vicarage remained intact.

Vicar-General   A bishop's substitute in exercise of his jurisdiction. Position frequently held by Chancellor of Diocese.

Vicegerent (in spirituals)   Office of deputy in religious matters created by Henry VIII and bestowed upon Thomas Cromwell in 1535. Involved a delegation of the King's prerogative as head of the church and Cromwell may have held courts similar to those held by Wolsey as Papal Legate (q.v.). The vicegerency disappeared after Cromwell's fall and temporary ecclesiastical commissions exercised delegated powers.

Visitation   From the late fifteenth century the college of heralds undertook visitations throughout the realm checking the claims to arms of county families and establishing the descent of these claims. *See* Section IX for ecclesiastical visitations.

Wardship   When a child from a family in England or Wales whose land was held by knight-service was orphaned as a minor, he or she became a royal ward. Until the child came of age the Crown as guardian had rights over the marriage and education of the ward and administered the estates. A peculiarly English institution.

Wards, Court of   *See* Section VI.

Westminster   Until 1529 the medieval Palace of Westminster was the chief London residence of the monarch as well as the centre for the legal and administrative business of government. A series of fires left it in poor repair and the monarch began to use Whitehall (q.v.) as his residence. Westminster was still used for important state ceremonies and the legal and new administrative courts, and in mid century became the permanent home for the House of Commons (in the dissolved college of St Stephen) and the House of Lords (in the Painted Chamber).

Whitehall   Formerly York Place, the London home of Cardinal Wolsey, Archbishop of York. In 1529 acquired by Henry VIII as a replacement residence for the medieval palace of Westminster (q.v.).

Wills, Statute of   Chiefly important because it permitted testators freely to will much or all of their land depending on how they held it. In general landowners wished to provide for all of their children and not simply the heir at law. Until the Statute of Uses of 1536 (which abolished the 'use', whereby landowners appointed trustees or feoffees to hold and administer portions of their estate after their death for a third party who was not the legal heir, according to instructions stipulated in a will) there had been ways around the ban on testation of freehold land away from the male heir. There was an outcry following the Statute of Uses and the Statute of Wills (1540) responded by making it legal to will freehold land. Those holding land by knight-service must first deduct the dower or jointure rights of the widow, then they might (should they so wish) will away up to two thirds of the freehold estate, the remaining third being reserved to the heir at common law. There was free testation of lands held by socage tenure. It was already possible to will away lands and property held by leasehold because these were accounted 'moveable property'.

Women's Legal and Property Rights

Under the common law:

Single women (spinsters and widows) of full age might inherit and administer land, make a will, sign a contract, own chattels, sue and be sued, make feoffments (trusts), seal bonds etc. without any guardian or proxy.

A married woman had no such rights. During her marriage or *couverture*, her husband gained title to the rents and profits of her land but he may not sell or lease the land which belongs to her; she was not allowed to make a will except with his express permission. She had the right to common law dower of at least one third of her late husband's freehold estate for her life; the dower was sometimes increased or made specific by protective jointure; she had no such right with respect to copyhold land except (where it existed) by local custom of freebench. By the mid sixteenth century the man could sell, give away or devize any of his freehold estate excepting the widow's and heir's portions. The remainder of his estate was completely untrammelled.

Under equity law:

Married women did have a legal identity and could sue and be sued in the equity courts. Married women who had property of their own did defend it in the equity courts. Many of these women before marriage had made marriage contracts or settlements which were invalid in the eyes of the common law but were acknowledged as permissible under equity law. Such settlements might, for example, arrange for a wife to receive an income of her own during the marriage, allow her to administer her own properties, and protect the inheritance of children from former marriages.

Under ecclesiastical law:

Married as well as single women had a legal identity. On marriage a woman with property would enter a common bond to protect this property in her own interest and that of any children from former marriages. She might also take out bonds to provide sums of money for her personal use during her husband's lifetime. A widow was commonly the executrix of her husband's will and as such applied in the courts for probate of the will. In cases of intestacy the widow was automatically granted administration. Under probate jurisdiction a widow defended her marriage settlement by listing property reserved for herself and/or her children under these bonds as expenses to be deducted from the estate before bequests were paid. If there were difficulties involving the payment of these bonds, as a widow she might sue for satisfaction under the common law.

Worship The manner in which God was worshipped reflected the theology of the various sixteenth-century Christian churches.

Catholicism was a religion of ritualism and sacramentalism. The seven sacraments of the church were means of acquiring grace or salvation and the priest alone administered these sacraments. There were a whole series of channels which God had instituted to communicate and apply the power of the original salvation (Christ's death upon the cross and resurrection) to man – the church, the priesthood and the sacramental system, the intercession of saints and so forth. The layout of Catholic churches, the apparel of the personnel, the form of the service, all reflected this theology. The church gave prominence to the administration of the sacraments. Among them pride of place was given to the Lord's supper but near the entry to the church, symbol of Christian initiation, stood the font, at which babies were baptised. The confessional marked the place where each Christian confessed his or her sins, and was given a penance to perform. The altar, whereon the Eucharist was administered and from which the priest pronounced absolution, was centrally placed at the East End of the church. Upon it were arranged the cross and candles, ornate chalice (cup for the wine) and pyx (plate for the bread), and the missal (Mass service book). The idea that this sanctuary (sacred place) was the preserve of the priesthood, a holy and set apart place, was emphasised by the grandeur, the symbolism of the furnishings, by the candles and the sanctuary lamp, and most of all by the physical separation between it and the congregation by the rood screen (bearing statues of Christ on the cross, the Virgin and St John). Within the sanctuary only the priest mounted the steps to the altar to celebrate the Mass. He was served by an acolyte. The priest showed the elements of bread (the host) to the congregation who adored the Mass. The laity were permitted to partake only of the bread, not the wine. The stations of the cross and the stained glass of the windows reminded the laity of the supreme sacrifice Christ had made for them. Statues of the saints around the church encouraged worshippers to pray to the saints and the Virgin Mary for intercession with Christ for salvation. In chantry chapels priests said Masses to intercede for the dead.

Luther sharply rejected this idea of the church as a priestly-sacramental way to salvation, which he believed was the result of a one-to-one relationship between the individual and God and the faith in Christ's power to save which ensued. The instrumentality of ritual was denied. Luther did, however, retain in his doctrine of consubstantiation a belief in the real presence of Christ at the communion of bread and wine. Lutheran churches retained many Catholic religious practices which were not regarded specifically as abuses. Latin Masses continued to be said on Holy Days (q.v.) and a considerable number of these were kept. The form of the communion was not significantly altered. Preachers heard parisioners' confession before communion although no penances were imposed. There were unresolved disputes about whether the host (bread) should continue to be elevated for adoration (q.v.); whether the cross should be used in prayer; whether the formula of exorcism should be used at baptism and so on. Church interiors were not greatly changed. High altars, crucifixes, organs, stained glass windows, even special Mass vestments remained. The pulpit, however, now stood prominently – the Word of God in the Scriptures was the sole rule of faith.

In those churches influenced by the theology of Calvin the changes in the furnishing of the church building, the form of the services and the paraphernalia of worship were more profound. For the most part the old churches, once used for Catholic worship, were adapted for Protestant worship but they were stripped of all statuary and embellishment because of the view that these reinforced belief in the instrumentality of ritual and image, and owing to the idea that any practice not specifically recommended in Scripture was superfluous and probably superstitious. Stained glass windows, statuary, pictures, symbolic furnishings, rood screens – all disappeared. The altar became a table, around which the whole congregation gathered for communion of bread and wine. The priesthood disappeared and was replaced by a ministry, which acted to inform the laity about God's Word and not to mediate. The minister, unlike the priest in his symbolic vestments, was plainly attired. The pulpit now took pride of place.

The church of England went further than the Lutherans in curtailing Catholic practices. The liturgy became vernacular. Altars, crucifixes, statues, religious pictures, holy sepulchres, stained glass, organs, the sign of the cross, beating of the bounds (accompanied by banners, crosses and priests in vestments) all disappeared relatively quickly. The Book of Common Prayer replaced the Catholic missal on the table which replaced the altar. Wall tablets bearing the text of the Ten Commandments and other Scriptural extracts replaced the ornate reredos. The Bible was placed upon a lectern and read to the people in the vernacular. The pulpit assumed a new prominence. The priest wore surplice and stole instead of vestments. Many of the more radical English Protestants rejected the idea of priesthood as 'popish', adopting instead that of a ministry; and resisted the use of the sign of the cross, the ring in marriage and the wearing of surplice or stole. The ministry and the laity all partook of both the bread and wine during the communion. The physical separation between the priest and the congregation was also reduced as rood screens were dismantled and the communion table brought closer to the nave. The placing of the pulpit and the lectern in the body of the church reinforced this change. *See* 'Vestiarian Controversy'.

Bibliography

The following bibliographical essay does not pretend to be comprehensive. Instead it is divided into 'topics' for convenience of use. Attached to each is a brief summary of the nature of the topic and debates within it and a very select bibliography. Each is intended as a starting point. I have headed the bibliography with some general textbooks and general monographs which offer good coverage and should always be consulted in the first instance. Student texts, surveys and textbooks are signalled in the various sections. Annotation is offered only when the relevance of the book is not instantly obvious or when comment seems helpful. The place of publication is London unless otherwise stated.

General Books

D.C. Coleman, *The Economy of England, 1450–1750*, Oxford, 1977. Survey. Still the standard account of the economy.

Patrick Collinson, *The Religion of Protestants*, Oxford, 1982. The best review of the field.

A.G. Dickens, *The English Reformation*, 1989. A beautifully written and stimulating book, essential for an understanding of the times.

Steven K.G. Ellis, *Tudor Ireland*, Longman, 1985.

G.R. Elton, *England under the Tudors*, 1955. Unsurpassed as a general textbook for the whole period, especially as regards central government and constitutional developments.

Steven Gunn, *Early Tudor Government, 1485–1558*, Macmillan, 1994.

John Guy, *Tudor England*, Oxford, 1988. A sound and sensible survey.

Hodder & Stoughton Access to History Series. Many excellent guides to aspects of the Tudor period. Unfortunately have little in the way of bibliography.

J. Gwynfor Jones, *Early Modern Wales, c.1525–1640*, Macmillan, 1994. Useful especially for a consideration of social structure, government administration and the Reformation settlement.

H.G. Koenigsberger, G.L. Mosse and G.Q. Bowler, *Europe in the Sixteenth Century*, Longman, 1989. The second edition provides an excellent introduction to sixteenth-century Europe (including England).

Peter Laslett, *The World We Have Lost further explored*, 1983 repr. A controversial and readable book.

Roger Lockyer, *Tudor and Stuart Britain, 1471–1714*, Longman, 1985

Longman Seminar Studies in History. An extensive library of titles covering
the Tudor period. Each containing a survey of the issues, a detailed
bibliography and select sources for study.

Rosemary O'Day, *Education and Society, 1500–1800*, 1982. Offers coverage
of many social and educational developments.

Macmillan Problems in Focus Series. Some Tudor titles. Essays by established
historians with specialist knowledge especially written to introduce
students to the issues.

Macmillan Studies in Economic and Social History. Many titles covering the
Tudor period. Surveys of debates with annotated bibliographies.

David Palliser, *The Age of Elizabeth, England Under The Later Tudors, 1547–
1603*, 1983. A survey which combines a rare understanding of both
religious and socio-economic issues.

David Potter, *A History of France, 1460–1560*, Macmillan, 1994. An up to
date survey for those who need to know about contemporary developments across the channel.

Quentin Skinner, *The Foundations of Modern Political Thought*, 2 Vols,
Cambridge, 1980 repr. (Not confined to England.) Relates political
thought to the society from which it stemmed.

K. Wrightson, *English Society, 1580–1680*, 1982. Much more useful for this
whole period than the dates might suggest.

J. Youings, *Sixteenth Century England*, Harmondsworth, 1984. A readable
social history with good contemporary quotation.

King or Minister?

A debate about the balance of and employment of power within the
constitution as much as about the official reformation itself.

How far was the official reformation the creation of Henry VIII? What
role did the monarch play in policy making and government? Most
recent interpretations of the role of Henry VIII in shaping the reformation
have been reactive to A.F. Pollard's assumption that Henry was in
control after the fall of Wolsey and personally made reformation policy.
Pollard was chiefly concerned with explaining why the people of England
permitted Henry to exercise this power. While Pollard and his disciples
(for example, Bindoff) saw the Reformation as the creature of Henry's
will, they modified their voluntaristic approach. Henry designed the
Reformation but he was allowed to create it by the nation and, especially,
by parliament. Mid century, Geoffrey Elton began to present a new view
of the role of Henry in government and in the creation of the Reformation.
He questioned the assumption that Henry's reign could be divided neatly
into two: a period from 1514 to 1529 when Henry let Wolsey govern and
a period from 1529 to 1547 when Henry assumed the reins. He argued
that: (a) Wolsey had never entirely been free to do as he wished and; (b)
after Wolsey it was Thomas Cromwell who devised and controlled policy

broadly to the king's liking. He substituted a much more complex division of the reign. Cromwell established the reformed state as a limited monarchy in which parliament was an active partner and not as a despotism. Elton's views have been challenged from various standpoints. Joel Hurstfield plumped for a Tudor despotism, parliament or no. J.J. Scarisbrick returned to a modified Pollardian argument, once again exalting Henry's personal responsibility for the reformation. A.G. Dickens explored further the impact of Thomas Cromwell's own religious convictions upon the course of the official reformation.

S.T. Bindoff   *Tudor England*, 1950, 1964 repr. Survey.

A.G. Dickens   *Thomas Cromwell and the English Reformation*, 1959. Survey.

A.G. Dickens   *The English Reformation*, 1989. In depth survey.

G.R. Elton   'King or Minister?: the man behind the Henrician reformation', *History*, 39, 21–32.

G.R. Elton   *Henry VIII. An Essay in Revision*, The Historical Association, 1962, 1965 repr. Student text.

G.R. Elton   *The Tudor Revolution in Government*, 1953, 1962 repr.

A.G. Fox and J.A. Guy   *Redressing the Henrician Age: Humanism, Politics and Reform, 1986.*

Joel Hurstfield   *Freedom, Corruption and Government in Elizabethan England,* 1973.

R. O'Day, *The Debate on the English Reformation*, 1986. Student Companion to the history of the reformation in England and Wales.

A.F. Pollard, *Henry VIII*, 1905 (reprinted in 1966 by Harper Torch Books, New York).

K. Randell, *Henry VIII and the Reformation in England*, 1993. An intelligent opening up of the issues for A level students and undergraduates.

Richard Rex, *Henry VIII and the English Reformation*, Macmillan, 1993. An analytical approach.

J.J. Scarisbrick, *Henry VIII*, 1968.

The Reformation and the People

Further debate about the nature and causes of the English reformation. Geoffrey Elton, Christopher Haigh and J.J. Scarisbrick claim that the advance of Protestantism under Henry VIII and Edward VI owed almost everything to official coercion. A.G. Dickens argues that the new religion spread by conversions among the people and that it gained strength independently of the 'political' reformation. Far and away the best general account of the movement for religious reform is Dickens, *The English Reformation* (cited above), but more specialised works are also important. For instance, Dickens' own study of *Lollards and Protestants* and J.F. Davis' *Heresy and Reformation*. David Palliser has shown how continental connections prepared parts of England for Protestantism.

Penry Williams, Haigh and Scarisbrick argue that little permanent progress was achieved by the Protestants before the reign of Elizabeth. Haigh attacks the supposed force of anti-clericalism. Scarisbrick reasserts the view that England's was an official reformation and one that the English people did not want. They found the Catholic Church congenial. Detailed local studies have attempted to settle the question once and for all but have pointed instead to widespread regional variations in the response to Protestantism. Studies of, for example, the nature of the Pilgrimage of Grace are highly relevant to this debate. Local studies have also sparked interesting discussion of the use of the sources. Added to this debate about the chronology and geography of religious reformation is discussion of Henry VIII's own attitude towards Protestantism and Catholic doctrine. Patrick Collinson has pioneered studies of the nature of the religion and commitment of Protestants in England and Wales in the Elizabethan period.

M. Bowker, *The Henrician Reformation in the Diocese of Lincoln Under John Longland, 1521–47*, Cambridge, 1981.

M. Bowker, 'Lincolnshire 1536: heresy, schism or religious discontent?' in D. Baker (ed.), *Studies in Church History*, 9, Oxford, 1972, 195–212.

P. Collinson, *The Elizabethan Puritan Movement*, 1967.

P. Collinson, *The Religion of Protestants*, Oxford, 1982.

M.C. Cross, *Church and People 1450–1600*, 1976. Survey.

C.S.L. Davies, 'The pilgrimage of grace reconsidered', *Past & Present*, 41, 54–76.

J.F. Davis, *Heresy and Reformation in the South-East of England, 1520–59*, 1983.

A.G. Dickens, *Lollards and Protestants in the Diocese of York, 1509–58*, Oxford, 1959.

A.G. Dickens, 'Secular and religious motivations in the pilgrimage of grace' in G. Cumings (ed.), *Studies in Church History*, 4, 1967, Leiden, 39–64.

A.G. Dickens, 'Review of J.J. Scarisbrick, *The Reformation and the English People*,' *Journal of Ecclesiastical History*, 36, 1985, 123–6.

A. Dures, *English Catholicism, 1558–1642*, 1983. Accessible student text with good analysis and bibliography.

C. Haigh, *Reformation and Resistance in Tudor Lancashire*, Cambridge, 1975.

C. Haigh, 'The recent historiography of the English Reformation', *Historical Journal*, 1982, 25, 995–1007.

C. Haigh, 'Anti-clericalism and the English Reformation', *History*, 68, 391–407.

C. Haigh, *English Reformations: religion, politics and society under the Tudors*, Oxford, 1993.

D.M. Palliser, 'Popular reactions to the reformation, 1530–70' in F. Heal and R. O'Day (eds), *Church and Society in England: Henry VIII to James I*, 1977, 35–56. Student text.

J.J. Scarisbrick, *The Reformation and the English People*, Oxford, 1984.

W.J. Sheils, *The English Reformation, 1530–1570*, 1989. Student text. Best on institutional and doctrinal change.

L.B. Smith, 'Henry VIII and the Protestant Triumph', *American Historical Review*, 1966, 71, 1237–64.

J. Thomson, *The Early Tudor Church and Society, 1485–1529*, 1993. Survey.

P. Williams, *The Tudor Regime*, Oxford, 1979. Survey.

M.L. Zell, 'The use of religious preambles. . ..', *Bulletin of the Institute of Historical Research*, 50, 246–9.

The Church of England and the Reformation

What impact did the Reformation have upon the Church of England? What did it mean for church/state relations? Did the church as an institution maintain continuity with the medieval past or was it much changed? Did the church's function in society change?

Royal Supremacy

The royal supremacy has been much studied by historians. Claire Cross has examined the theoretical relationship between Crown and church and has sought to demonstrate relations between Crown and hierarchy within this framework. The nature of the supremacy under Henry and then under his daughter Elizabeth has been analysed by Scarisbrick, Bowker, Collinson and Elton.

Episcopacy and the Episcopate

The recruitment, role and reputation of the episcopate were as subject to change as its relationship with the Crown. Did the Crown engage in deliberate plunder of the church? Did it exploit the wealth of the church by leaving sees vacant? What were the post-reformation responsibilities of the bishops and were they left with the material resources and authority to fulfil them well?

Clergy: priests or pastors?

Did the clergy themselves change fundamentally as a result of the Reformation? The acceptance of the doctrine of the priesthood of all believers meant that the clergy had to find a new justification for their continued existence. The people did not need priests but they did need pastors. This belief became the staple of Protestant teaching on the ministerial order but this rethinking of the clergy's functions was not acceptable to many, including the Crown. Attempts to protestantise the clergy and turn them into preaching ministers were ad hoc and piecemeal, not least because the church's financial and administrative organization and its relationship with the Crown and the elite made the establishment of a clerical career structure using criteria of vocational excellence impossible.

Church Courts

Did ecclesiastical discipline, exercised through the church courts, retain its old power in society as a whole? The efficiency and authority of the ecclesiastical courts had always been very variable and limited by rival jurisdictions. In some dioceses energetic reform programmes increased the efficiency, effectiveness and business of the Courts Christian prior to the reformation but unreformed dioceses may have been in the majority. The London diocesan courts were in full decline by the 1520s. In the 1530s the jurisdiction of the bishops was challenged by the vicegerential authority of Thomas Cromwell but this was not revived under Edward or Elizabeth. The jurisdiction of the courts remained untouched and they survived in their old form. But the business of the courts revived slowly and the sanctions employed – greater and lesser excommunication – no longer frightened the laity into obedience. The creation of the High Commission overrode the diocesan structure and undermined the bishops' independent authority. The attempt to provide the church with a new code of laws in tune with its reformed character failed. The courts were asked to enforce conformity to the Elizabethan settlement at the very time when their authority was being challenged not only by those who were hauled before them during litigation but also by Protestants who did not recognise their remote discipline as appropriate to a reformed church.

M. Bowker, *The Secular Clergy in the Diocese of Lincoln, 1495–1520*, Cambridge, 1968.

M. Bowker, 'The supremacy and the episcopate: the struggle for control, 1534–1540', *Historical Journal*, 18, 1975, 227–43.

M. Bowker, 'The Henrician reformation and the parish clergy', *Bulletin of the Institute of Historical Research*, 50, 1977, 30–47.

P. Collinson, *Godly People, 1983*.

P. Collinson, *The Elizabethan Puritan Movement*, 1967.

P. Collinson, *Archbishop Grindal, 1519–83. The Struggle for a Reformed Church*, 1979.

M.C. Cross, *The Royal Supremacy in the Elizabethan Church*, 1969. Student text. Useful documents as well as text.

H. Davies, *Worship and Theology in England from Cranmer to Hooker, 1534–1603*, 1970. Monographic Survey.

G.R. Elton, *The Tudor Constitution*, 1960.

F. Heal, *Of Prelates and Princes. A Study of the Economic and Social Position of the Tudor Episcopate*, Cambridge, 1980.

F. Heal and R. O'Day (eds), *Church and Society in England, Henry VIII to James I*, 1977. Student text.

P. Heath, *The English Parish Clergy on the Eve of the Reformation*, 1969.

R.A. Houlbrooke, *Church Courts and the People during the English Reformation, 1520–70*, Oxford, 1979.

M. Ingram, *Church Courts, Sex and Marriage in England, 1570–1640*, Cambridge, 1987.

R. O'Day, *The English Clergy. The Emergence and Consolidation of a Profession, 1558–1642*, Leicester, 1979.

R. O'Day, and F. Heal (eds), *Continuity and Change. Personnel and Administration of the Church in England, 1500–1642*, Leicester, 1976.

J.J. Scarisbrick, *Henry VIII*, 1968.

R.M. Wunderli, *London Church Courts and Society on the Eve of the Reformation*, Camb. Mass., 1981.

The Mid Tudor Crisis

The debate here is: was there a crisis during the reigns of Edward VI and Mary I and if so of what did it consist?

Since the Second World War, historians have accorded this period, previously regarded as a rather uninteresting interlude set between the reigns of Henry VIII and his daughter Elizabeth, considerable attention. Some have suggested that it was one of crisis. But what is a crisis? There were certainly problems but did they really threaten the state with collapse? A sensible approach to the question seems to be to identify the problems – political, socio-economic, religious and diplomatic – and assess their gravity. Studies focus on the potential constitutional crisis caused by the accession of a minor, nine-year old Edward VI; on England's weak international position; the severity of economic and associated social problems; the causes of and responses to religious change; the relationship between religious thought and socio-economic policy.

M.L. Bush, *The Government Policy of Protector Somerset*, 1975.

G.R. Elton, 'Reform and the "Commonwealth-men" of Edward VI's reign' in P. Clark *et al* (eds), *The English Commonwealth, 1547–1640*, Leicester, 1979.

J. Guy, *Tudor England*, Oxford, 1988. Survey.

W.R.D. Jones, *The Tudor Commonwealth, 1529–1559*, 1970.

J. Loach and J. Tittler (eds), *The Mid-Tudor Polity, c.1540–1560*, 1980. Student text.

D.M. Loades, *The Reign of Mary Tudor*, 1991.

D.M. Loades, *The Mid-Tudor Crisis, 1545–1565*, 1992. The debate conveniently presented in a nutshell to students.

D.C. Coleman, *The Economy of England, 1450–1750*, Oxford, 1977. Survey.

A. Fletcher, *Tudor Rebellions*, 1968. Excellent treatment of the issues for students.

R. O'Day, *Economy and Community*, 1975. Student text.

R. O'Day, 'Hugh Latimer. Prophet of the Kingdom', *Historical Research*, 65, 1992, 259–76.

J. Youings, *Sixteenth Century England*, 1984. Survey.

Religion and Foreign Affairs

England's foreign policy was so dominated by her religious turmoil that it seems appropriate to couple the two together in a bibliography. However, other issues were also of great importance. For example, Henry VII was anxious to protect his country from invasion and his throne from usurpation and this anxiety permeated English foreign policy during the reign of his granddaughter, Elizabeth, also; Henry VIII and Wolsey used foreign policy as a way to enhance their respective reputations; late in his reign Henry VIII again looked for glory abroad; the expansion and protection of overseas trade was also an issue throughout the period.

S. Doran, *England and Europe, 1485–1603*, 1986. Useful opening up of the issues for students. Good bibliography.

S. Ellis, *Tudor Ireland*, 1985.

R. Lockyer, *Henry VII*, 1968 Highly recommended as student introduction to a period, and problems, now rather unfashionable but nonetheless crucial.

K. Randell, *Henry VIII and the Government of England*, 1991. Student text. Excellent discussion of the issues involved.

J. Warren, *Elizabeth I: Religion and Foreign Affairs*, 1993. A first rate student introduction to the subject.

R.B. Wernham, *After the Armada: Elizabethan England and the Struggle for Western Europe*, Oxford, 1984.

Parliament

Early and Mid Tudor parliaments

The reigns of the first four Tudors constitute one of the most important phases in the development of parliament as an integral part of the English constitution. Not only the Reformation Parliament (1529–36) was important. During the first half of the century parliament developed as an institution with its own bureaucracy, archives, place of assembly and increasingly standardised rules and procedures. The judges pronounced that for a new bill to become law, the assent of the House of Commons was essential. During the Reformation Parliament the King-in-Parliament became sovereign and, as a result, the areas of royal prerogative upon which parliament might not trespass diminished considerably. Yet there were also strong elements of continuity. For example, the House of Lords remained the most influential chamber.

G.R. Elton, *The Tudor Revolution in Government*, Cambridge, 1953.

G.R. Elton, *The Tudor Constitution*, Cambridge, 2nd edn, 1982.

G.R. Elton, *Studies in Tudor and Stuart Politics and Government*, 2 vols, Cambridge, 1974.

A. Fox and J. Guy, *Reassessing the Henrician Age: Humanism, Politics and Reform, 1500–50*, Oxford, 1986. Survey.

M.A.R. Graves, *The House of Lords in the Parliaments of Edward VI and Mary*, Cambridge, 1981.

M.A.R. Graves, *Early Tudor Parliaments, 1485–1558*, 1990. Student text. Good treatment of the issues with bibliography.

S.E. Lehmberg, *The Reformation Parliament, 1529–36*, Cambridge, 1970.

S.E. Lehmberg, *The Later Parliaments of Henry VIII, 1536–47*, Cambridge, 1977.

J. Loach, *Parliament and the Crown in the Reign of Mary Tudor*, Oxford, 1986.

Elizabethan Parliaments

Until the 1970s and 1980s the prevailing orthodoxy regarding the significance of Elizabeth's Parliaments was that they provided an essential apprenticeship for the assertiveness of their Stuart successors. A.F. Pollard and J.E. Neale noted a shift in the balance of power: the House of Lords was in decline and the Commons in ascendancy. In Elizabeth's reign there was not only a critical element in the Commons but also an organised opposition with its own programme. This work prepared the way for W. Notestein's important study of the manner in which the House of Commons seized the parliamentary initiative from the Early Stuart monarchs. Revisionist studies have, from the standpoint of a study of Parliament as a developing institution, challenged this thesis. Parliament spent much of its time discussing humdrum business and not challenging the Crown's programme. There was no organised opposition. There were such links of patronage between Lords and Commons as to render relatively meaningless a claim that the Commons was in the ascendant. The House of Lords, moreover, provided the focus for resistance to the Elizabethan settlement.

S.T. Bindoff, 'The making of the statute of artificers' in S.T. Bindoff, *et al* (eds), *Elizabethan Government and Society: essays presented to Sir John Neale*, 1961.

D.M. Dean, 'Enacting Clauses and Legislative Initiative, 1584–1601', *Bulletin of the Institute of Historical Research*, 57, 1984, 140–8.

G.R. Elton, *Studies in Tudor and Stuart Politics and Government*, 2 vols, Cambridge, 1974; Vol. IV, published 1992.

G.R. Elton, 'Parliament in the sixteenth century: Functions and Fortunes', *Historical Journal*, 22, 1979, 255–78.

G.R. Elton, 'Enacting Clauses and Legislative Initiative, 1559–71', *Bulletin of the Institute of Historical Research*, 53, 1980, 183–91.

M.A.R. Graves and R.H. Silcock, *Revolution, Reaction and the Triumph of Conservatism. English History, 1558–1700*, 1984.

M.A.R. Graves, 'The Management of the Elizabethan House of Commons: the Council's "Men-of-Business"', *Parliamentary History*, **2**, 1983, 11–38.

M.A.R.Graves, *Elizabethan Parliaments, 1559–1601*, 1987. Enlightening student text with good bibliography.

P.W. Hasler, *The House of Commons, 1558–1603*, 3 vols, *The History of Parliament*, 1981.

N.L. Jones, *Faith by Statute. Parliament and the Settlement of Religion, 1559*, 1982.

J.E. Neale, *The Elizabethan House of Commons*, 1949.

J.E. Neale, *Elizabeth I and her Parliaments*, 2 vols, 1953 and 1957.

W. Notestein, *The Winning of the Initiative by the House of Commons*, 1924.

A.F. Pollard, *The Evolution of Parliament*, 1964, 2nd edn.

The Economy

The process of social and economic change is now seen by historians as a long one and we look now for continuities as well as dramatic changes in our analysis of the period before industrialisation. Nonetheless, some features of the Tudor period are regarded as of especial significance in the process of change and historians are continually revising their interpretations.

For a general student introduction to the issues see:

B. Coward, *Social Change and Continuity in Early Modern England*, 1988. Enlightening student text with excellent bibliography and documents. Useful also for study of the 'Educational Revolution', 'the People' and 'Culture' (see below).

N. Heard, *Tudor Economy and Society*, 1992. Extremely useful opening up of the issues and debates. Sadly little in the way of bibliography.

E. Kerridge, *Trade and Banking in Early Modern England*, 1988, provides a very useful introduction to difficult subject matter.

The Fourteenth Century Crisis

It is thought that there was a demographic, social, commercial and industrial crisis which began in the mid fourteenth and lasted until the mid sixteenth century. This, it is argued, ended with a period of recession in the middle of the Tudor period. It was followed by a period of expansion which lasted until the mid seventeenth century. Other scholars stress continuity rather than change and write of a long sixteenth century stretching from c.1450 or 1500 to as late as 1650.

General Interpretations of the Crisis

R. Brenner, 'Agrarian Class Structure and Economic Development in Pre-industrial Europe', *Past & Present*, 70, 1976. Posits a crisis caused by the collapse of landlord-tenant relationships. It is class struggle which is the principal determinant of social change. Rent strikes and popular discontent, culminating in the Peasants' Revolt of 1381, resulted when elites raised their rents etc. during a time of rising prices. The position of the elites worsened when the peasants abandoned their small holdings. In the fifteenth century the landlords could no longer extract labour services from tenants and had instead to rely on reduced rents for their income. It was, according to this account, the gentry and yeomen who turned to commercialised farming in the early sixteenth century who reaped the benefit from this situation. They employed wage labour to farm their small estates more efficiently. This marked the move from feudal to capitalist production.

See also T.H. Aston and C.H.E. Philpin (eds), *The Brenner Debate. Agrarian Class Structure and Economic Development in Pre-Industrial Europe*, Cambridge, 1985. Reprints Brenner's original article and several pertinent essays by noted specialists.

J. Hatcher, *Plague, Population and the English Economy, 1348–1530*, 1977. An excellent student introduction to the controversy. Hatcher suggests a 'Malthusian crisis' – in the thirteenth century the English population rose to about 6 million. This population outstripped the production of food and deaths from starvation and malnutrition resulted. Eventually the population decreased; its recovery was checked by the bubonic plague of 1349 ('the Black Death') which killed about 2 million people; plague epidemics further reduced the population to a mere 1.5 million by the mid fifteenth century; reduced price of food, shortage of labour, surplus of land enabled gentry and yeomen to acquire more of the land and farm commercially; some of the farmers left the land to become wage labourers, attracted by higher rates of pay offered by the gentry and yeomanry.

Agrarian History

There were considerable agricultural innovations in the sixteenth century – new crops, new farming techniques – but their economic significance has been much debated. The literature pertaining to Tudor agrarian history contributes to a wider debate regarding the occurrence of an agricultural revolution prior to 1750. Many of the technical advances normally associated with the eighteenth-century 'agricultural revolution' were already being made in the sixteenth. But how widespread were such changes? What was the pace of change? Some historians urge that it was rather the commercialisation of agriculture, which forced smaller farmers off the land, that was the key change because it contributed to the breakdown of traditional society and led to class conflict and rebellion. But there is much disagreement as to the pace of commercialisation. Only farmers living close to London or other growing towns seem to have spent money on improving the yield of their arable land. Agriculture barely produced sufficient grain to keep pace with population increases.

The principal exponent of the case for an agrarian revolution was Eric Kerridge. He has been criticised by, for example, G.R. Mingay (who sees advance before the eighteenth century as gradual) and Mark Overton (who claims that Kerridge has overestimated the extent to which innovations were made) and the argument for revolution is no longer fashionable. Joan Thirsk has argued persuasively that it would be better to abandon the concept of a revolution altogether and view the history of agricultural development as a continuum displaying periods of more or less rapid change which might vary from agricultural region to agricultural region. Historians, however, disagree on how best to identify discrete regions and some awareness of the debate in this context is necessary.

L.A. Clarkson, *The Pre-industrial Economy in England, 1500–1750*, 1971. Survey.

D.C. Coleman, *The Economy of England, 1450–1750*, Oxford, 1977. Survey.

B.A. Holderness, *Pre-Industrial England. Economy and Society, 1500–1750*, 1976. Survey.

E. Kerridge, *The Agricultural Revolution*, 1967.

J.D. Marshsll, 'Why Study Regions?', *Journal of Regional and Local Studies*, 5, 1985, and 1986.

G.E. Mingay, 'Review of E. Kerridge, *The Agricultural Revolution*', *Agricultural History Review*, 17, 1969.

R.B. Outhwaite, 'Progress and backwardness in English agriculture, 1500–1650', *Economic History Review*, 2nd Ser., 39, 1986.

Joan Thirsk (ed.), *The Agrarian History of England and Wales*, Vols IV and V, Cambridge, 1967, 1984 and 85.

Joan Thirsk, *The Rural Economy of England. Collected Essays*, 1985.

Joan Thirsk, *England's Agricultural Regions and Agrarian History, 1500–1750*, 1987. Outstanding explanatory text for students, with bibliography.

There are so many relevant local studies of high quality that I have elected to list none here. I refer the reader to the excellent list in Thirsk, *England's Agricultural Regions*, 1987.

The Place of Industry in the Economy

Some historians have argued that there was an industrial revolution in Tudor and Stuart England. Certainly there is evidence of industrial activity. It seems probable that the large and poorly paid labour force looked to producing industrial goods to supplement their income from the land.

Industry was organised either within the traditional craft workshops or by putting-out. There were a few instances of centralised production where the equipment necessary made small-scale production impracticable (mining, glassmaking etc.) but the national, as opposed to local, importance of such enterprises is now doubtful. Some Marxist historians, such as L. Medick, have argued forcefully that there was a period of proto-industrialisation which led directly to the industrialisation of the eighteenth and nineteenth century. According to this theory the development of cottage industry in the rural cloth industry (beginning as early as the thirteenth century) led to the spread of capitalism. It fostered the use of larger, more advanced machinery. Within the cottage, all members of the family were dependent for their livelihood upon the work of cloth production and formed, therefore, a sort of industrial proletariat. This was important for the future but over all such industry did little to absorb surplus agricultural labour.

L.A. Clarkson, *The Pre-industrial Economy in England, 1500–1750*, 1971. Survey.

L.A. Clarkson, *Proto-Industrialization: The First Phase of Industrialization?*, 1985. Student text. A thorough-going exploration of the concept of protoindustrialization as a contribution to the debate about the origins of the industrial revolution of the eighteenth century.

D.C. Coleman, *The Economy of England, 1450–1750*, Oxford, 1977. Survey.

P. Kriedte, H. Medick and J. Schlumbohn, *Industrialization Before Industrialization*, Cambridge, 1981.

J. Thirsk, 'Industries in the Countryside' in F.J. Fisher (ed.), *Essays in the Economic and Social History of Tudor and Stuart England*, Cambridge, 1961.

Inflation and the Price Rise

Contemporaries were aware of the price rise and sought to explain it. Historians have also proffered various explanations both monetary and real or physical. Was it due to the debasement of the currency and the subsequent importation of Spanish silver? (Some understanding of the quantity theory of money is necessary but the chronology of inflation is also at issue.) This thesis has proved difficult to either prove or disprove. Or was it due to the pressure of population upon the available food supply? Or was it explained by a combination of both real and monetary factors? The worst period of inflation seems to have been before 1560 although poor harvests in the late 1580s and 1590s again put pressure on prices.

P. Bowden, 'Agricultural Prices, Farm Profits and Rents' in Joan Thirsk (ed.) *The Agrarian History of England and Wales, IV, 1500–1640*, Cambridge, 1967, 595–695.

Y.S. Brenner, 'The Inflation of Prices in Early Sixteenth Century England', *Economic History Review*, 2nd ser., 14, 1961, 225–39.

Y.S. Brenner, 'The Inflation of Prices in England, 1551–1650', *Economic History Review*, 2nd ser., 15, 1962, 266–84.

P. Clark, 'Crisis Contained? The Condition of English Towns in the 1590s' in P. Clark (ed.), *The European Crisis of the 1590s*, 1985.

R.B. Outhwaite, *Inflation in Tudor and Stuart England*, 1969. A good historiographical account for students.

R.B. Outhwaite, 'Dearth, the English Crown and the "Crisis of the 1590s" in P. Clark (ed), *The European Crisis of the 1590s*, 1985.

R.B. Outhwaite, *Dearth, Public Policy and Social Disturbance in England, 1550–1800*, 1991. Up to date and accessible student guide to the debates and the literature.

R. Smith, *Population History of England, 1000–1540*, Manchester, 1992. The most up to date survey.

E. Carus Wilson, *Essays in Economic History*, Vol II, 1962. In this are reprinted two of the seminal articles by E.H. Phelps Brown and S.V. Hopkins on wages and prices.

Overseas Trade and Exploration

Historians debate both the relative importance of the overseas trade to the total economy and the precise extent and nature of overseas trade. The period is seen as falling into two phases: down to 1550, the overseas trade is dominated by the export of woollen cloth to the Low Countries; from 1500 onwards, attempts are made to open up world markets and to extend trade within Europe. Many historians describe the age as one of mercantilism (in which the intervention of the state in the economy is overt and important). The government is seen by some as issuing trade and plantation charters and monopolies from the 1550s onwards to assert state control of overseas trade, and as adopting an aggressive foreign policy in order to win new markets. Others have seen the fourteenth century crisis (q.v.) as the beginning of the development of a world economic system in which capitalistic long distance trade was established. There was an urgent need both for foodstuffs and for bullion to pay for warfare and government; as a result there was aggressive overseas exploration and colonisation and opening of long distance trade routes.

R. Brenner, *Merchants and Revolution: commercial change, political conflict and London's overseas traders, 1550–1653*, Cambridge, 1993.

D.C. Coleman, *The English Economy, 1450–1750*, Oxford, 1977. Survey.

R. Davis, *English Overseas Trade*, 1500–1700, 1973. Student text. Remains a good historiographical survey of interpretations.

I. Wallerstein, *The Modern-World System*, 1974.

The Educational Revolution and the Emergence of the Learned Professions.

In 1964 Lawrence Stone published a seminal article, 'The Educational Revolution', in which he charted a revolution in both elementary and higher education. The upper and middle classes in society encouraged the spread of schooling and opened up its benefits to the classes below them. They had faith that education, controlled by an elite, would bring about the betterment of society.

The popularity of such a view was enhanced by the conviction among Protestants that all should be able to read the Word of God whatever their social station and by the spread of literacy throughout the social hierarchy. The elite themselves flocked to the universities and Inns of

Court in ever increasing numbers so that more young people partook in higher education in the early seventeenth century than at any time afterwards until the late nineteenth century. Other scholars challenged the precise details of Stone's account but agreed with his basic thesis. (*See* Curtis, Kearney, Knafla, McConica, Morgan, O'Day, Prest, Simon.) There have been, however, some who challenged the thesis itself (*See* Cressy, Russell) And there have been others who have concentrated on curriculum developments (*See* Curtis, O'Day, Prest). The causes and consequences of developments in education have given rise to much debate. For instance, Brooks, O'Day and Prest have charted the growth of professions and opened up discussion about the nature of professions and the relationship between professions and society.

Jonathan Barry & Christopher Brooks (eds), *The Middling Sort of People: Culture, Society and Politics in England, 1550–1800*, Macmillan, 1994. Some of the essays are relevant. See especially that by Christopher Brooks.

C.W. Brooks, 'The Common Lawyers in England, c.1558–1642' in W. Prest (ed.), *Lawyers in Early Modern Europe and America*, 1981.

D. Cressy, *Literacy and the Social Order*, 1980.

J.H. Hexter, 'The Education of the Aristocracy in the Renaissance' in J.H. Hexter, *Reappraisals in History*, 1963.

M.H. Curtis, *Oxford and Cambridge in Transition*, Oxford, 1959.

H. Kearney, *Scholars and Gentlemen. Universities and Society*, 1970.

L. Knafla, 'The Law Studies of an Elizabethan Student', *History of Law Quarterly*, 1969.

J. McConica (ed.), *The History of the University of Oxford, Vol. III, The Collegiate University*, Oxford, 1986.

R. O'Day, *Education and Society, 1500–1800*, 1982. General monograph for students and scholars.

R. O'Day, *The English Clergy, The Emergence and Consolidation of a Profession, 1558–1642*, 1979.

W. Prest, *The Inns of Court*, 1972.

W. Prest (ed.), *The Professions in Early Modern England*, 1987. Contains important contributions from O'Day, Prest, Pelling, Cressy, Hainsworth and Roy.

E. Russell, 'The Influx of Commoners into the University of Oxford before 1581: an optical illusion', *English Historical Review*, 92, 1977.

Q. Skinner, *Foundations of Modern Political Thought*, 2 vols, Cambridge, 1978. Accessible and stimulating on the relationship between the education of the elite and thinking about the state.

J. Simon, *Education and Society in Tudor England*, Cambridge, 1967. General and accessible monograph.

M. Spufford, 'The Schooling of the Peasantry in Cambridgeshire, 1575–1700', *Agricultural History Review*, Supplement, 1970.

L. Stone, 'The Educational Revolution in England, 1560–1640', *Past & Present*, 1964.

L. Stone (ed.), *The University in Society*, Vol. I, Princeton, 1974. Contains important articles by V. Morgan, J. McConica and Stone himself.

The People

Standard of Living and Social Configuration

As in so many other contexts, historians tend to discuss these issues with reference to a 'long sixteenth century' which begins around 1450 or 1500 or even 1560 and ends in 1650. Obviously great care has to be exercised to discern which part of this time-span is being referred to at any point in the literature.

If we are to tackle any of the issues listed in this bibliography we require a good understanding of the Tudor social hierarchy and the standard of living and communal and domestic organisation of each social group. Yet it is notoriously difficult to describe the social order in the first place let alone to ascertain how elites, middling sort and lower orders lived their lives. There is a literature too voluminous to list here; the works below represent some but only some of the best books and articles.

In general terms the aristocracy probably benefited most from the economic developments of the Tudor period with gentry, yeomen, some prosperous husbandmen also profiting but to a lesser extent if they rented land. Merchants and craftsmen suffered mixed fortunes: they received higher prices for their products and paid lower wages to their employees but they had to pay more for their raw materials and faced sluggish home markets and uncertain foreign ones. However, the number of individuals who were entirely dependent upon manufacture or trade for a livelihood was relatively low. The lower orders did relatively much worse. Their standard of living was the victim of high prices and rents, low wages and lack of land. They were also relatively much more insecure than the higher orders of society. However, recent studies have emphasised that there was considerable heterogeneity among the lower orders as among the middle and upper sorts and each stratum requires separate analysis. The growth of towns, with their special societies and problems, has been emphasised by some historians, adding to the complexity of any analysis of Tudor society and the standard of living of its people.

Jonathan, Barry (ed.), *The Tudor and Stuart Town . . .*, 1990.
G.R. Batho, 'Landlords in England', in J. Thirsk (ed.), *The Agrarian History of England and Wales, IV, 1500–1640*, Cambridge, 1967.
A.L. Beier, *Masterless Men: the vagrancy problem in Britain 1560–1640*, 1985.
P. Clark and P. Slack (eds), *English Towns in Transition, 1500–1700*, Oxford, 1976. Student text.
P. Clark and P. Slack (eds), *Crisis and Order in English Towns 1500–1700*, 1972.

Barry Coward, *Social Change and Continuity in Early Modern England, 1500–1750*, 1988. Student text. An insightful survey of this highly complex subject.

D. Cressy, 'Describing the Social Order of Elizabethan and Early Stuart England', *Literature and History*, 3, 1976.

Paul Griffiths (ed), *The Experience of Authority in Early Modern England*, Macmillan, 1994. A number of essays dealing with aspects of authority. These vary in quality. Some are particularly relevant to this topic; others relate more closely to the culture of the period.

Felicity Heal and Clive Holmes, *The Gentry in England and Wales, 1500–1700*, Macmillan, 1994. Up-to-the minute synthesis of recent work on a key social group.

D. Hey, *An English Rural Community. Myddle under the Tudors and Stuarts*, Leicester, 1974.

A. Kussmaul, *Servants in Husbandry in Early Modern England*, Cambridge, 1981.

R.B. Outhwaite, *Dearth, Public Policy and Social Disturbance in England, 1550–1800* Macmillan, 1991.

P. Slack, *Poverty and Policy in Tudor and Stuart England*, 1987.

M. Spufford, *Contrasting Communities: English Villagers in the Sixteenth and Seventeenth Centuries*, Cambridge, 1979 edition.

L. Stone, *The Crisis of the Aristocracy, 1558–1641*, Oxford, 1965.

L. Stone, 'Social Mobility in England 1500–1700', *Past & Present*, 33, 1966.

L. Stone and J.C.F. Stone, *An Open Elite? England 1540–1880*, Oxford, 1984.

J. Thirsk, *Economic Policy and Projects: The Development of a Consumer Society in Early Modern England*, Oxford, 1978.

K. Wrightson and D. Levine, *Poverty and Piety in an English Village: Terling 1525–1700*, 1979.

Population

See also 'Inflation and the Price Rise' and 'Standard of Living and Social Configuration' (above); 'Domestic Organisation, Household and Family' (below). There has been debate concerning the precise size of the population, population mobility, population distribution and the impact of population growth upon economy and society. These issues are treated in most of the general texts at the beginning of this bibliography.

E.A. Wrigley and R.S. Schofield, *The Population History of England, 1541†1871, A Reconstruction*, Cambridge, 1989 (paperback edition with new introduction).

Domestic Organisation, Household and Family

Historical demographers have been to the forefront of those who have described the residential patterns of the population. They have established that most of the population (below the elites) lived in small **households** comprising the simple nuclear family plus live-in **servants**. Historians have demonstrated the way in which this household was the primary socio-economic and religious unit in Tudor society and in so doing have demonstrated that the simple nuclear family was not so simple after all. The incidence of complex nuclear family households has been underlined. Some historians have also studied the relationship between the co-residential domestic unit and the wider family. The family and household roles of husbands, wives, widows, widowers, children, siblings, aunts and uncles, grandparents and servants have also received considerable attention. The controversy surrounding the suggestion that family life in the early Tudor period (and the middle ages) was emotionally cold and that **affective family** life only gradually evolved has led to a much more convincing appreciation of the variety of family experience. (Words in bold, above, are explained in Section XIV.)

P. Aries, *Centuries of Childhood*, 1962. Accessible and controversial general monograph.

Lloyd Bonfield *et al*, *The World We Have Gained*, Oxford, 1986.

M. Chaytor, 'Household and kinship: Ryton in the late sixteenth and early seventeenth centuries', *History Workshop*, X, 1980.

R.A. Houlbrook, *The English Family*, 1983. Student text. Especially strong on inheritance and marriage.

P. Laslett, *The World We Have Lost Further Explored*, 1983. Student text with controversial thesis.

P. Laslett and R. Wall (eds), *Household and Family in Past Time*, Cambridge, 1972.

R. O'Day, *The Family and Family Relationships, 1500–1900*, Macmillan, 1994. Student text. Emphasises lived experience and the need to study the co-residential domestic unit (or household) in relation to the wider family.

A. Macfarlane, *Marriage and Love in England, 1300–1840*, Oxford, 1986.

L. Pollock, *Forgotten Children*, Cambridge, 1983. Highly accessible general monograph.

L. Stone, *The Family, Sex and Marriage in England 1500–1800*, 1977. A controversial book which, while its central thesis has been superseded, remains important for its wealth of detail about family life.

M. Todd, 'Humanists, puritans and the spiritualized household', *Church History*, 49, 1980.

Women

Because the lives of women were very largely circumscribed by the family, many of the books in the section above treat aspects of the history of women. The following should be consulted for additional material.

P. Crawford, *Women and Religion in England, 1500–1720*, 1993.

M. Dowling, *Humanism in the Age of Henry VIII*, Beckenham, 1986. Excellent on the contribution of women.

A.L. Erickson, 'Common Law Versus Common Practice: the Use of Marriage Settlements in Early Modern England', *Economic History Review*, XLIII, 1990.

Amy Erickson, *Women and Property in Early Modern England*, Routledge, 1993. It is important to read this revisionist view of women's position in the early modern period which corrects many of the assumptions made in older specialist works and recent general texts.

A. Laurence, *Women in England, 1500–1700*, Weidenfeld & Nicholson, 1994. A synthesis of recent work on women's position in economy and society.

Open University, *The Changing Experience of Women*, 1983 Student text. Includes study of women's work and women as authority figures.

R.B. Outhwaite (ed.), *Marriage and Society: Studies in the Social History of Marriage*, 1981.

M. Prior (ed.), *Women in English Society, 1500–1800*, 1985. Accessible specialist essays.

E. Shorter, *The Making of the Modern Family*, 1976. General monograph.

Culture

See also 'Religion and the People'; 'Educational Revolution'; 'Domestic Organisation, Household and Family'; 'Women'.

Perhaps the chief debate here concerns the *nature* of culture and subcultures. Is there in every society a dominant culture, an elite culture, of which popular culture is merely an impoverished and reduced variety? Or does popular culture represent a sophisticated, complex, deep-rooted and rich rival to the elite and dominant culture? Could it be that, in some cases, the dominance of elite culture is deceptive – a feature of the higher survival rate of its expressions rather than its importance to the majority of contemporaries. Is 'popular culture' necessarily produced *by* the people or is it produced *for* the people? The study of culture involves a study of attitudes, values and norms and, some would argue, beliefs. Popular culture in the Tudor period may not have been a literate culture but our knowledge of it frequently derives from literary sources or from other elite-generated representations. Historians have to decide to what extent these sources distort our knowledge of popular culture. A manuscript play is not a performance, least of all is it the audience response to the performance. A sermon may use popular attitudes and beliefs to make its point but the points are often being made by members of an educated elite. The issues are often discussed in a broad European context.

S. Anglo   *Spectacle, Pageantry and Early Tudor Policy*, Oxford, 1969.

P. Ariés   *The Hour of Our Death*, 1981.

J. Briggs   *This Stage-Play World*, Oxford, 1983. Student text.

P. Burke   *Popular Culture in Early Modern Europe*, 1994 revised edition. The pioneering study of popular culture which remains exciting reading.

E.K. Chambers   *The Elizabethan Stage*, 4 vols, Oxford, 1923, 1974 edition. A useful source.

K. Charlton, *Education in Renaissance England*, 1965. Survey. Still the chief treatment of certain areas of education, for example the grand tour.

P. Clark, *The English Alehouse: A Social History*, 1983. Accessible in-depth study.

A.G. Dickens, *The English Reformation*, 1989. Excellent, especially on popular religious belief and mysticism.

A.G. Dickens, *The Age of Humanism*, New Jersey and London, 1972. Survey.

Jacqueline Eales and Christopher Durston (eds), *The Culture of English Puritanism, 1560–1700*, Macmillan, 1994. A volume which covers both late Tudor and Stuart England. Some interesting essays.

D. Englander, D. Norman, R. O'Day and W.R. Owens (eds), *Culture and Belief in Europe, 1450–1600, An Anthology of Sources*, Oxford, 1989. Modern annotated editions of wide variety of European (including English) texts. Texts of English mystery plays, late medieval ghost stories, Lollard trials, the writings of John Colet, William Tyndale, Hugh Latimer, Thomas More, John Dee and John White, the colloquies of Erasmus concerning women and marriage, courtship and pilgrimage, the Diary of Lady Margaret Hoby, the ecclesiastical courts, the vestiarian controversy, Scottish ballads and poetry, and the works of Philip Sidney and Edmund Spenser.

A. Fletcher and J. Stevenson (eds), *Order and Disorder in Early Modern England*, Cambridge, 1985.

A. Fox, *Politics and Literature in the Reigns of Henry VII and Henry VIII*, Oxford, 1989.

C. Gittings, *Death, Burial and the Individual in Early Modern England*, 1984.

C. Ginzburg (in translation), *The Night Battles: Witchcraft and Agrarian Cults in the Sixteenth and Seventeenth Centuries*, 1983.

Helen Hackett, *Virgin Mother, Maiden Queen: Elizabeth I and the Cult of the Virgin Mary*, Macmillan, 1994. Discusses the evidence for worship of The Virgin Queen.

Tim Harris (ed.), *Popular Culture in England, c.1500–1850*, Macmillan, 1994. A volume of essays covering a wide time span. Some of the essays are useful for this period.

M.E. James, *Family, Lineage and Civil Society: A Study of Society, Politics and Mentality in the Durham Region, 1500–1640*, Oxford, 1974.

C. Larner, *Enemies of God: The Witch-hunt in Scotland*, Oxford, 1983.

Longman York Handbooks. Provide useful and convenient guides to Shakespeare and other relevant authors and genres.

A. Macfarlane, *Witchcraft in Tudor and Stuart England*, 1970.

J.K. McConica, *English Humanists and Reformation Politics under Henry VIII and Edward VI*, Oxford, 1965.

E.W. Monter, *Ritual, Myth and Magic in Early Modern Europe*, Brighton, 1983. Accessible general monograph.

R. O'Day, 'Hugh Latimer, Prophet of the Kingdom', *Historical Research*, 1992.

Open University, *Culture and Belief in Europe, 1450–1600*, 1990. Student text. Europe includes England. Contains interdisciplinary studies of popular culture and belief (including growth of printing, sermon literature, plays as performance, interpretations of ritual etc. as well as extensive consideration of English culture).

N. Phillipson and Q. Skinner, *Political Discourse in early modern Britain*, Cambridge, 1993.

M. Roston, *Sixteenth-Century English Literature*, 1982. Excellent student text.

J. Sharpe, *Crime in Early Modern England, 1550–1750*, 1984. Student text. Enlightening study.

K.V. Thomas, *Religion and the Decline of Magic*, Harmondsworth edn, 1978. Exciting but lengthy monograph.

Maps

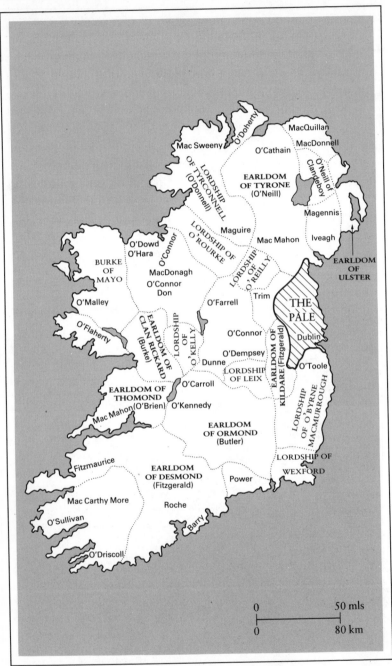

Map 1 Ireland c. 1530, showing Pale and the areas of influence

Map 2   Ireland in the early seventeenth century

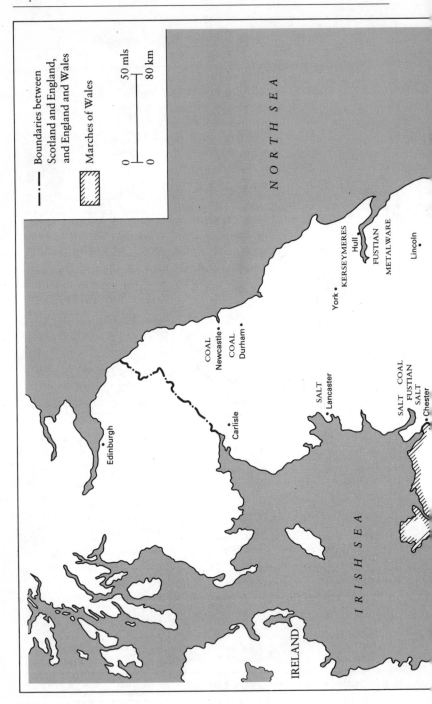

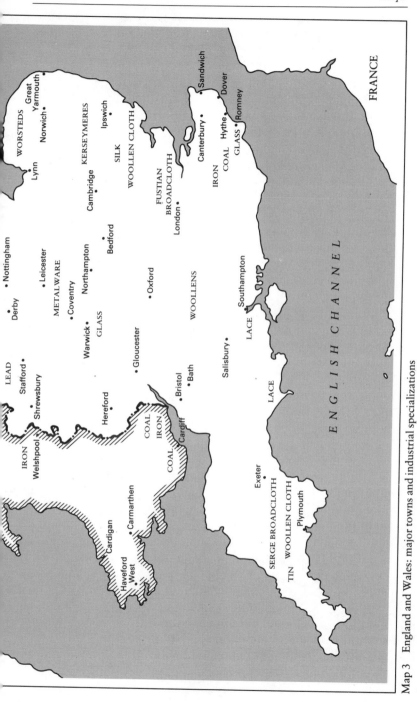

Map 3   England and Wales: major towns and industrial specializations

Index

The reader is advised to consult the alphabetical listings of authors, biographies, books, glossary and titles; the chronologies and the subject sections first and to use this index as a key to further information. In the interests of economy of space, the following categories of entry are excluded from this index: the names of persons in the Biographies Index which do not occur elsewhere in the volume (e.g. Speed, John); the titles of books which occur only in the Books or Authors listings (e.g. *De Copia*) and in the Bibliography (e.g. Prest, W. (ed.), *The Professions in Early Modern England*, 1987); the names of officeholders which occur in one list only (e.g. Mordaunt, Sir John, Speaker of House of Commons), genealogical tables and maps. Titles of people have not been included unless they help with identification; their dates, when available, have been included to facilitate identification and as a ready reference aid. Groupings of page numbers (119–20) do not imply a continuous entry.